D0928125

Alexis de Tocqueville

ON DEMOCRACY,
REVOLUTION, AND SOCIETY

THE HERITAGE OF SOCIOLOGY

A Series Edited by Morris Janowitz

Alexis de Tocqueville

ON DEMOCRACY, REVOLUTION, AND SOCIETY

Selected Writings

Edited and with an Introduction by
JOHN STONE AND
STEPHEN MENNELL

THE UNIVERSITY OF CHICAGO PRESS

CHICAGO AND LONDON

JOHN STONE is reader in sociology, Goldsmiths'
College, University of London, and an associate fellow
of St. Antony's College, Oxford University.

STEPHEN MENNELL is senior lecturer in sociology
and director of the Western European Studies Centre
at the University of Exeter.

THE UNIVERSITY OF CHICAGO PRESS, CHICAGO 60637
The University of Chicago Press, Ltd., London

Library of Congress Cataloging in Publication Data

Tocqueville, Alexis Charles Henri Maurice Clérel de,
   1805–1859.
   Alexis de Tocqueville on democracy, revolution, and
society.

   (The Heritage of sociology)
   Bibliography: p.
   Includes index.
   1. Political Science—Collected works.
2. Sociology—Collected works.   I. Stone, John,
D. Phil.   II. Mennell, Stephen.   III. Title.
JC229.T7713 1980   301.5'92'08   79–21204
ISBN 0–226–80526–3

Contents

v

Acknowledgments

We are grateful to Professor Morris Janowitz, the general editor of this series, who encouraged us in our attempt to compile this selection of Alexis de Tocqueville's sociological writings. Especially when it involved dismembering a work so closely argued and economically written as *L'Ancien Régime et la Révolution,* the task was not only difficult but engendered feelings of ambivalence. We hope, however, that a single volume containing extracts both from Tocqueville's best-known and less familiar writings will prove its value as an overall view of his thought and will encourage many more readers to study his works in their undismembered form.

The excerpts from Stuart Gilbert's translation, *The Old Régime and the French Revolution,* are copyright © 1955 by Doubleday & Company, Inc., and are reprinted by permission of Doubleday and Fontana Paperbacks (Wm. Collins and Sons, Ltd.). The extracts from Tocqueville's *Journeys to England and Ireland,* the translation by George Lawrence and K. P. Mayer (Yale, 1958; new augmented edition, New York, Arno Press, 1979), are included by permission of the editor, J. P. Mayer.

For the selections from *De la démocratie en Amérique* we have relied on Henry Reeve's classic original English translation. We have, however, compared Reeve's text with the French and, particularly where English usage has changed since his day, made minor modifications. In the same way we have made amendments to Alexander Teixeira de Mattos's translation of the *Souvenirs.* We have made no attempt to harmonize the varying styles of spelling and capitalization in the sources.

Professor Duncan Mitchell, and again Professor Janowitz, made helpful comments on the draft of our Introduction. We should finally like to thank Patricia Chandrasekera and Barbara Mennell for their help in the preparation of this book.

Oxford and Exeter, 1978   John Stone
                                                        Stephen Mennell

Introduction

Ever since their first publication, the writings of Alexis de Tocqueville have appealed to an audience far wider than any single academic discipline. Even today, his name is better known and his works deservedly more read by the general educated public than those of his contemporaries such as Auguste Comte and Herbert Spencer, who more regularly than he are counted among the major nineteenth-century "founding fathers" of sociology. It is impossible to think of Tocqueville simply as "a sociologist" in the specialized modern sense. The boundaries between the domains of the historian, the political scientist, and the sociologist were less well defined then than now, and Tocqueville would hardly have respected the frontiers had they been clear to him. His work spans all three fields.

Tocqueville in fact never uses the word sociology. His vision was of the future of democratic society, not of the future of social science. He seems never to have read Comte, whose grandiose vision of the role of the social scientist in the society of the future degenerated to near madness. Nevertheless, while Comte talked about the possibility and nature of sociology, Tocqueville actually practiced something which, we would argue, the modern sociologist can recognize as sociology. His work reflects the convulsions of social change through which he lived as clearly as does that of other nineteenth-century precursors of sociology. The sociological perspective, as the selections included in this volume have been chosen to demonstrate, was central to Tocqueville's work. But, in using that perspective, he produced a series of analyses of lasting relevance to various disciplines and to all who are interested in a broad interpretation of social and political change.

LIFE AND TIMES

Alexis Charles Henri Clerel de Tocqueville was born in Paris on 29 July, 1805, into an old, well-connected, landed family. Napoleon was then at the height of his power. The year of Tocqueville's birth was the year of one of Napoleon's greatest victories, when he crushed the armies of Austria and Russia at Austerlitz, and also of the first of his great defeats, when Nelson destroyed the French and Spanish fleets at Trafalgar. Tocqueville's father was a supporter not of the Empire but of the deposed monarchy. It was therefore not until the restoration of the Bourbons, in the person of Louis XVIII, in 1814—and more securely after Napoleon's return from Elba and final defeat at Waterloo—that the elder Tocqueville took the active part in public life natural to a man of his standing. He then served as prefect successively at Metz, Amiens, and Versailles.

Alexis, his third son, was educated—not particularly thoroughly it seems—at home and at the college in Metz. In 1826 he traveled with his second brother through Italy and Sicily.[1] The following year, at the minimum age of twenty-one, he was appointed *juge auditeur,* or magistrate, at Versailles. One of his colleagues there was Gustave de Beaumont (1802–66), who became his lifelong friend. Tocqueville's exceptional abilities were soon apparent in his performance of judicial duties. Rapid advancement in the royal service was predicted, although as Beaumont comments in his *Memoir,*[2] these predictions were based as much on Tocqueville's connections as on his abilities.

Under the restored monarchy, France was enjoying a greater measure of liberty than before. Louis XVIII had had to recognize political realities in a number of ways. The highly centralized and relatively efficient adminstrative machine inherited from the Revolution and the Empire—Tocqueville was later to argue that the centralization if not the efficiency in fact dated from the *ancien régime*—was left intact, together with most of its personnel. Napoleon's reformed legal code remained in force. Possibly most important, the returning *émigré* aristocrats had come to terms, reluctantly and resentfully, with the fact that their former lands could not be restored to them. They had passed into the hands of *nouveaux riches* who represented far too powerful a vested interest. With its lands, the old French aristocracy lost not only many of its privileges but also the social obligations which accompanied land and privilege. The crown alone reclaimed its lands. But the king now governed as a constitutional, though not a parliamentary, monarch. The king still embodied the executive power and had the initiative in proposing legislation. There was no properly formalized ministerial cabinet. On the other hand, there was a bicameral parliament which enacted legislation and voted taxes. For some years the system worked well. One reason for cooperation between king and parliament was the extremely limited franchise, which was unlikely to produce parliaments of revolutionary temper. There were something under 100,000 electors in a total population—men, women, and children—of about 26 million. This compared unfavorably with Great Britain at the time, where even before the 1832 Reform Act there were about 465,000 voters out of a total population of around 18 million.[3] Lest the wealthy taxpayers who had the vote show too great a spirit of independence, the French government through its prefects in each department took care to manipulate elections by a variety of means. Electoral corruption was scarcely confined to France; but the local magnates who in Britain did the manipulating were not themselves necessarily manipulable by the central government of the day. In France, the role of the prefects in elections was to continue long after Tocqueville's death.

The restored monarchy seemed quite established, and would probably have lasted much longer had it not been for the crass stupidity of Charles X, who succeeded his brother Louis XVIII in 1824. Charles leaned much more towards the former *émigré* "ultras." In 1830, in spite of the best efforts of the prefects, the government lost the parliamentary elections. Charles and his chief minister, Polignac, refused to accept the result and on 10

July issued the "Four Ordinances," which prohibited the publication of journals and pamphlets without government approval, restricted the franchise to the wealthiest quarter of the existing electorate, dissolved the newly elected parliament, and decreed the appointment of a more amenable one. The government seems to have been unaware that these measures would provoke resistance. But after three days of street fighting in Paris, the Duc d'Orléans, representative of the younger branch of the Bourbons, was enthroned as King Louis-Philippe.

The young Tocqueville himself gave his support to the July Monarchy without hesitation, but also without enthusiasm. While unsympathetic to the legitimist government's curbs on political liberties, he was already conscious of the potential dangers inherent in a régime imposed by revolutionary means. Tocqueville's father was one of the legitimists who resigned rather than serve as prefect under the Orléanist régime. One of Tocqueville's oldest and closest friends, Louis de Kergorlay, an army officer who in 1830 was taking part in the first stages of France's conquest of Algeria, resigned his commission and, though a young man, preferred to spend the rest of his days in retirement.

Louis-Philippe was known as "the bourgeois monarch." He dressed and behaved like a bourgeois, and he was not only France's king but also her greatest capitalist. Tocqueville regarded him with particular disdain and in his account of the collapse of the July Monarchy scathingly dismisses him as "the accident that made the illness mortal."[4] His government was a mildly reforming one. The franchise was extended to all whose annual tax payments amounted to at least 200 francs. Not that that gave the vote to an enormous number: the French electorate has been estimated at 241,000 in 1846 out of a total population of more than 35 million. Another reform was the reestablishment of elected municipal councils, though on a very restricted suffrage. The July Monarchy perhaps represented government of the people by the bourgeoisie for the bourgeoisie. Nevertheless, France seemed to be moving gradually but definitely in a democratic direction. For this reason, Tocqueville and Beaumont conceived the wish to visit the United States, to study its dem-

ocratic institutions and to discover what France had to learn
from them. In order to do so, they had to obtain leave of absence
from their duties as magistrates, and a good excuse for requesting
it was fortunately at hand. In the reforming mood of the moment,
one of the minor topics of discussion was reform of the French
prisons. It happened that the "penitentiary system" then being
tried in several of the eastern states of America had already attracted interest in Europe, and Tocqueville and Beaumont offered
to go to America to study the system and report on its potential
use in France. The offer was accepted and leave granted. But as
Beaumont wrote, "It has often been said that this mission was the
cause of Alexis de Tocqueville's expedition. It was in truth only
the pretext. His real and long premeditated object was to study
the customs and institutions of American society."[5]

Tocqueville and Beaumont landed at New York on 10 May,
1831. In the early part of their stay, they conscientiously carried
out their obligation to study the penitentiary system. That phrase,
"penitentiary system," has been weakened by familiarity and is
nowadays used simply to mean prisons. At that time, however, it
had the force of "system to induce feelings of penitence" on the
part of prisoners. The means employed was solitary confinement,
which, it was supposed, would lead the convict to reflect and
repent. The system was not in force in all prisons. It was
pioneered at a number of experimental prisons for those guilty of
serious crimes: Walnut Street and Cherry Hill in Philadelphia,
Auburn and Sing Sing in New York, and Wethersfield in Connecticut. Tocqueville and Beaumont visited all these. At Cherry
Hill Tocqueville obtained permission to speak alone with some of
the prisoners—obviously a rare concession, given the nature of
the punishment—in order to try to assess the psychological
effects of solitary confinement. In the earliest experiments, the
solitary confinement had been total, and its psychologically destructive effects had rapidly become apparent. In its modified
form, the régime allowed prisoners to work together during the
day before being locked up alone. Tocqueville recognized the
risks of solitary confinement but also saw the advantage that
minimal intercourse between prisoners helped to prevent the

prison being a school for crime. In their travels, Tocqueville and Beaumont also visited unreformed prisons which were precisely such criminal academies and where conditions presented no chance of favorable comparison with French jails.

But for the rest of their stay, Tocqueville and Beaumont were intent on studying American democracy and American society at large. Even at the most superficial level, America offered striking contrasts with France. The franchise was much more extensive. It is true that in many of the older states to vote one had not only to be white and male but to own property. But in the new states to the west of the Appalachians, where frontier conditions made all men social equals, the principle of universal (white) male suffrage had been accepted from the beginning. By the time Tocqueville and Beaumont visited America, the principle was starting to spread rapidly in the older eastern states too. The president then was Andrew Jackson, who, with his popular reputation as a hero of the frontier, represented American democracy at its most boisterous.

Tocqueville was of course anything but a superficial observer, and knew that democracy was a matter of far more than universal suffrage. He and his companion began their journey through the Union in New England, where the institutions of the township still embodied the most direct form of democracy. If the United States typified democracy, then the townships of New England revealed in microcosm the dynamics of the democratic process. It was not that he thought the township system representative of American society—clearly it was poles apart from the slave society of the South or the unruly frontier communities in the Midwest—but, rather like an anthropologist, he sought to understand the social bases of democracy by a careful scrutiny of these relatively simple settlements which were, so to speak, the "elementary forms" of democratic life.

Tocqueville and Beaumont were eager to see the newest areas of settlement as well as the oldest. Indeed in July 1831 they struck out for two weeks into the forests of Michigan, then beyond the margin of permanent white settlement. There they encountered Indians, though ones whose traditional way of life had already been much affected by contact with the whites.[6] In

December, they set out from Pittsburgh to sail down the Ohio and Mississippi rivers to New Orleans. The weather was freakishly cold, the river partially frozen, and they were shipwrecked, ending up traveling by stagecoach over appalling roads in bitter cold to Memphis. But they reached the South, where they were able to observe a social system very different both from that of New England and that of the frontier, and where the condition of the blacks made a deep impression on Tocqueville. Finally the two travelers returned to New York and embarked for Le Havre on 20 February 1832, a little over nine months after their arrival.[7]

On their return to France, Tocqueville and Beaumont set pen to paper. Most of the work on *The Penitentiary System in the United States and Its Application to France,* published in 1833,[8] seems to have fallen to Beaumont. It represents their joint thinking and appeared under both their names, but Tocqueville, somewhat guiltily, was already preoccupied with the broader canvas of *De la démocratie en Amérique.* Beaumont also subsequently wrote a novel of American manners, *Marie, or Slavery in the United States,*[9] which enjoyed considerable success after its publication in 1835. The literary endeavors of both authors were expedited by their abrupt retirement from the magistracy only two months after their return. The circumstances were accidental. Beaumont refused to appear as a prosecutor in a case in which he considered the authorities were playing a discreditable part, and was dismissed. Tocqueville thereupon immediately resigned in sympathy with his friend. Possibly, he would sooner or later have abandoned his judicial career in any case. Beaumont later commented of Tocqueville that

> though all his qualities were admirably suited to the magistracy, that was not, perhaps, the calling most suited to his abilities. Alexis de Tocqueville possessed in the highest degree the rare faculty of generalisation; and precisely because here lay his superiority, this was the constant tendency of his mind. The judge ordinarily follows the opposite tendency, derived from the habits of his profession, which stock his mind with specifics and with particular cases. Tocqueville's powers of thought were cramped by being imprisoned within the bounds of his specific duties. The irksomeness increased in proportion to the

trifling character of the case. On the other hand, his talent increased in proportion to the importance of the cause, as if the bonds which fettered his intelligence were snapped or loosened.[10]

Whatever the loss to the law, Tocqueville's new freedom enabled him to make rapid progress on *De la démocratie en Amérique,* in which his facility for discerning general principles was to make itself evident. He wrote the two volumes which constitute the first part of the work in 1832–34, and they were published in January 1835. They were an immediate and enormous success, and rapidly went through several printings.

De la démocratie en Amérique was translated and published in English in the same year. In America it was received with acclaim. As Beaumont wrote: "The Americans could not understand how a foreigner, after living among them for only a year, could with such remarkable wisdom master their institutions and manners, enter into the spirit of them, and demonstrate so clearly and logically what they themselves had until then only vaguely apprehended."[11] The book was equally well received in England, which was still feeling the reverberations of the great struggle over the 1832 Reform Act. That act, even if it only slightly extended the franchise and did not immediately break aristocratic influence in parliamentary elections, had been perceived as a blow to aristocracy and a step in the direction of democracy. The favorable reception of *Democracy in America* on both sides of the Atlantic caused Beaumont to remark that:

> Tocqueville's book, like all great intellectual works, takes its place above the narrow views of party, the accidents of the day, and the passions of the moment. For this reason, it was from the beginning, and will long continue to be, quoted as an authority by the holders of the most opposite opinions; and this explains its success both in the country where aristocracy is dominant and in that where democracy rules.[12]

In France, too, biased and superficial readers failed to observe that Tocqueville's views were much more balanced and sophisticated than their own. While conscious of the costs as well as the benefits of democracy, he was certainly no advocate of the restoration of aristocratic rule. The trend towards democracy—meaning increasing equality legally and politically, and perhaps also socially and economically—was undeniable; Tocqueville's concern was that ways be found of combining it with liberty. That many people at first only partially understood the book did not, however, prevent them from recognizing its greatness.

Tocqueville had visited England for the first time in 1833. The proximate cause of his visit may have been a desire to meet the family of Mary Mottley, whom he was to marry in 1836. But while in England he visited the House of Commons, Oxford University, and a magistrate's court. He also made the acquaintance of a number of prominent people mainly on the radical side of contemporary politics, notably Lord Radnor, Bulwer Lytton the novelist and M.P., and Nassau Senior, an important figure in the history of economics. Two years later, Tocqueville paid a second visit to England.[13] It was only a few months after the first publication of *De la démocratie en Amérique,* but now he was received as a celebrity and his circle of English friends was wider. The most famous name among them is that of John Stuart Mill. Others included Henry Reeve and the historians Hallam and Grote. Tocqueville had met Reeve in Paris, and persuaded him to translate *De la démocratie en Amérique.* Reeve, who subsequently translated the second part of that work and *L'Ancien Régime* as well, became the closest of Tocqueville's English friends. His name is not very well known today, but during his lifetime he was prominent and influential as lawyer, leader writer of the *Times,* and editor of the *Edinburgh Review.*

During his second visit to London, Tocqueville was invited to give evidence on the subject of electoral corruption to a committee of the House of Commons.[14] It is interesting to note that, just as *Democracy in America* received praise from all sides, Tocqueville's evidence was quoted in support of their cases by both sides in a debate on the subject in the House of Commons later in 1835.

England played an important part in Tocqueville's thought.[15] In *Democracy in America* it is an implicit third side in triangular comparisons with France and the United States. Later, in *L'Ancien Régime,* it is more frequently the subject of favorable comparisons with France than is America. Not that Tocqueville had a rosy view of everything British. He visited Birmingham and Manchester, leaving descriptions of these industrial towns which, though brief, put one in mind of the account which Friedrich Engels was to write a few years later.[16] In 1835 he also visited Ireland, then of course part of the United Kingdom and subject to much the same laws. Social conditions in Ireland provoked comparisons with England rather similar to those he had made between the northern and southern states in America.

Writing the second part of *Democracy in America* occupied Tocqueville during the years 1835–40. When these two volumes were published in 1840, they were received with as much enthusiasm as the first, though with possibly even less understanding. They deal not with the political institutions of democracy but with the effects of democracy on the culture, manners, and total social structure of America. To the modern reader they appear more profoundly sociological in perspective than do the earlier volumes. They carried Tocqueville to membership of the Académie Française in 1841, when he was still only in his thirties.

That the second part of *Democracy in America* was longer in composition than the first must reflect the greater difficulty and novelty of the argument. But in these years Tocqueville also took on new responsibilities. In 1836 he not only embarked on his very happy marriage with Mary Mottley but by arrangement with his two older brothers inherited the family château at Tocqueville, near Cherbourg on the Normandy peninsula. As a landed proprietor, he thenceforward greatly enjoyed caring for his estates and playing his part in the public life of his locality. In 1837 he stood for election to the Chamber of Deputies but, refusing government sponsorship, was unsuccessful. Two years later, however, when his book was not yet quite finished, he was elected to the Chamber, and represented the Valognes arrondissement continuously until 1848.

Tocqueville sat as an independent, voting with the constitutional opposition to Louis-Philippe's government. His political career did not entirely interrupt his career as an author. Almost as soon as he was elected, he was requested to prepare a report on slavery in the French colonies, which paved the way for the later abolition of slavery there. It was during 1843 that he was probably first introduced to Arthur de Gobineau, later to become notorious as the "father of racist ideology"[17] but at that time an able and promising scholar ten years Tocqueville's junior. Gobineau worked as his research assistant on a study of the effects of nineteenth century moral ideas on social behavior, being particularly useful because of his command of the German language and his knowledge of German source material. Although the two men were to disagree fundamentally on their interpretation of European society and the importance they attributed to the "racial factor" in social change, they remained good friends and maintained a correspondence until Tocqueville's death in 1859.

In 1841 and again in 1845 he travelled to Algeria to study colonialism, and in 1846 as a member of a parliamentary commission wrote a report on the subject. As a speaker he seems to have been heard with respect in the Chamber. But he did not speak very frequently, and he himself admitted that he had defects as a public speaker that derived from his very virtues as a writer—his speeches were too succinct and too tightly argued.[18]

One speech, however, which he made in the Chamber early in 1848, is celebrated. There had been no very serious disturbances in France, and the Orleanist régime seemed stable and likely to endure indefinitely. Yet on 27 January 1848, Tocqueville warned his fellow Deputies that all was not as it seemed.

> It is said that because at present there is no disturbance on the surface of society, revolution is far off.
> Gentlemen, allow me to tell you that I believe you are deceiving yourselves....
> I believe that at the present moment we are sleeping on a volcano....

This speech would have earned Tocqueville a footnote in history even if he had had no more substantial claim to fame. For the revolution happened sooner rather than later. It broke out on 22 February, less than a month after Tocqueville's speech.

Even Tocqueville could not have anticipated that the 1848 Revolution in France was to be only the first of the revolutions which in that year affected almost every state in Europe, except Britain (where Chartism was quite innocuous by comparison) and Russia. The revolutions in the Habsburg Empire and in the other states of Germany and Italy were compounded of liberalism and nationalism—historians are not entirely agreed about how much of each.[19] These states were still ruled by absolute monarchs, serfdom persisted in some parts, and political liberty was quite generally much more limited. The revolutionaries elsewhere were therefore seeking what the French had already achieved. The Germans, Italians, and Slavs wanted the national unity that France had now enjoyed for centuries. The middle classes demanded political rights and constitutional rule, which the French bourgeoisie had experienced—in however limited a form by later standards—since 1815. And the peasants demanded the abolition of feudal obligations, which in France had been irreversibly destroyed by the Revolution of 1789. The aims of the 1848 Revolution in France were therefore rather different. Indeed it involved many different groups with divergent objectives, and events unfolded in so unplanned a way that it is scarcely possible to speak of the revolution as having aims.

Like so many great historical events the Revolution of 1848 in Paris was the result of seemingly superficial and transient political events interacting—in ways unanticipated by the main protagonists in these events—with much more deeply structured social forces which most politicians had scarcely perceived. Such historical events therefore cannot be adequately described as either accidental or predetermined—a fact which fascinated Tocqueville as historian.

The resentment of which Tocqueville spoke had roots in economic distress. The mid-1840s were a time of bad harvests in Europe—of hunger in many areas, and of catastrophic famine in Ireland. In 1847 there began the first of the international economic recessions to which the growing capitalist system was to be prone for the next century. There was unemployment on a large scale in all the industrializing countries of Europe. As yet, however, France had no substantial working class in the modern sense; the workers who were to play their parts in the streets of Paris in 1848 were mainly artisans—a category which Marx usually described as "petit-bourgeoisie," although he called them "workers" when commenting on the events of 1848.[20] Their economic security was threatened not just by the general recession but also by the introduction of new industries. There were, for example, riots against the English workers then building railways in France.

Yet the Revolution of 1848 was precipitated by opposition politicians like Thiers and Odilon-Barrot who had no intention of overthrowing the régime or dynasty. As part of the normal activities of political "outs" who had decided it was their turn to be "in," they had been campaigning at a series of public banquets for universal suffrage, which was opposed by the ministry of Guizot. It was the banning of their banquet in Paris on 22 February which spread agitation to the streets. On 23 February, troops opened fire on the crowds—as so often happens, no one seemed to know who fired first—and on the following day Louis-Philippe rather abruptly threw in his hand and abdicated. Even then, there was no distinct intention of ending the monarchy. But the mob invaded the Chamber, demanding a republican government, and the Second Republic was duly proclaimed. The provisional government was an uneasy alliance of radicals like Lamartine who sought greater political liberty with socialists who wanted more fundamental reforms. They were agreed upon universal suffrage, and increased the electorate overnight from a quarter of a million to nine million. And in response to demands from the unemployed for relief, they set up "national workshops" in Paris; thousands of unemployed, including many skilled and professional workers, were put at unskilled labor on public works, and given relief out of public funds.

Tocqueville regretted the revolution. He had been no enthusiastic supporter of the fallen July Monarchy, merely regretting its fall from the constitutional point of view—any revolutionary change of régime contained a potential threat to liberty. His view, nevertheless, was that the best chance of liberty lay in establishing the Republic on a stable basis. He therefore sought election in May 1848 to the Constituent Assembly. Elected by universal suffrage, the Assembly was conservative in tone. The peasants, who made up the bulk of the electorate, were no longer the radical force they had been in 1789. Now freed from feudal overlords and the church, and owning their own land, they viewed with fear and suspicion the Parisian revolutionaries like Blanqui, Barbès, and Raspail. Tocqueville tells how, as he left for Paris, his constituents offered to come to the capital to defend the Assembly should it be threatened by the mobs. A month later, they had to fulfill their promise. One of the Assembly's first acts was to close the national workshops, which provoked the workers to spontaneous revolt and the bloodletting of the "June Days." Order was restored after units of the National Guard came to Paris from the provinces, after which the army effectively held the power.[21]

Before that, however, Tocqueville had become a member of the committee charged with drafting a constitution in little more than a month. He argued for a bicameral Assembly, but the decision went in favor of a single chamber. He also argued for the election of the president indirectly by the Assembly, rather than directly by the people. In America, the Electoral College is virtually a constitutional fiction, so the president is effectively elected directly by the voters. But Tocqueville, conscious as always of the differences between the traditions of France and America, did not wish to copy that model. In America, the tradition was of decentralization, and the powers of the federal executive were limited. In France, on the other hand, government had long been highly centralized; to make the president independent of the legislature and place all executive power in his hands would pose a threat to liberty. Tocqueville's advice was rejected.[22] The constitution accepted by the Constituent Assembly was more influenced by abstract political dogma than by Tocqueville's brand of practical reasoning. There was, in Alfred Cobban's words,

> still the old attempt to reconcile the principles of separation of powers and sovereignty of the people. All power comes from the people, but this power must be divided: the conclusion was the election of a single chamber and a unique head of government, both by universal suffrage and both directly responsible to the people, the one entrusted with total legislative authority, and the other with all executive power.[23]

The crucial decision, it soon proved, was the direct election of a president with executive power, an office without the effective checks and balances provided by the American Constitution. The presidential election took place in December 1848, and resulted in an overwhelming victory for Louis Napoleon Bonaparte, nephew of Napoleon I. From the beginnning, Tocqueville distrusted Bonaparte's intentions—this required little insight, since Bonaparte had been involved in a number of farcical minor insurrections during the Orleanist years.

Nevertheless, Tocqueville was a member of the Legislative Assembly elected in May 1849 and, after left-wing disturbances the following month, served as foreign minister in the government of Odilon-Barrot. Beaumont, who himself at this period served as French envoy in Vienna, considered that Tocqueville was much better suited to government than to opposition. Tocqueville was certainly a most effective minister, and further enhanced his European reputation. But this was to be his only term in office, and it did not last long. On 31 October, the president dismissed Odilon-Barrot's government and replaced it with a ministry of men from outside the legislature, with himself as its head. The Assembly lingered on for another two years, but with rapidly declining power. Bonaparte tried to win over Tocqueville's support, an enterprise which had no prospect of success whatsoever.

The constitution did not permit the reelection of the president to a second term of office.[24] An attempt was made to pass an amendment that would permit a second term, but it failed to receive the necessary two-thirds majority. So, on 2 December 1851, Bonaparte staged a coup d'état along the lines which have become a commonplace of the twentieth century—troops occupied strategic points in the capital and crushed resistance. The National Assembly was forcibly dissolved, though not before—with Tocqueville's prominent participation—it had recorded the strongest protest. Tocqueville and Beaumont were marched off with their fellow members and briefly imprisoned. Tocqueville wrote a long account of these events, which was smuggled to London by Mrs. Grote, wife of the historian, and published in the *Times* on 11 December. Strict press censorship was posed in France, and during 1852 manipulation of elections secured the return of a new Assembly which contained only a handful of members (literally a handful—five) who were not Bonaparte's supporters. In the autumn of 1852, the Second Empire was proclaimed, the president becoming Emperor Napoleon III. His subversion of the Republic was subsequently confirmed by a plebiscite in which 7,800,000 voted in his favor and only 250,000 against. Bonaparte's frequent appeals to the mass electorate in referendums made manifest what Tocqueville had long realized: the political forms and rituals of democracy are nothing if they have no adequate basis in social structure and culture.

Tocqueville naturally refused to take part in public life under the Second Empire. He could not even participate in local affairs, because he refused to take the required oath of loyalty. He returned instead to his writing. Already in 1850–51 he had written the *Souvenirs*—his memoirs of the period of the Second Republic and of his days as foreign minister. For political reasons they could not be published until after his death. In 1851 he conceived the idea of a study of the first French Revolution. Ostensibly an historical work, this too was far from irrelevant to the contemporary political scene that Tocqueville observed with distaste and distress. No study of the origins and course of the first Revolution and how it led to the régime of Napoleon I could fail to say a great deal, indirectly, about Napoleon III. But in order to explain what happened in 1789 and the following quarter of a century, Tocqueville had to analyze French society under the *ancien régime*, using much the same penetrating comparative method as he had employed when studying American society. The sources of his evidence were necessarily different. A historical society could not be studied by participant observation (as sociologists would now call it) and by interviewing respondents. Tocqueville turned instead to historical documents. He traveled widely to study primary sources. Other writers had already produced histories of the Revolution, but these were not to Tocqueville's purpose. To study society as it existed in provincial France before the Revolution, he spent many months in 1854 doing research in the archives of Tours. He had another reason for passing the winter in the mild climate of the Touraine—his health was already failing. In 1855 he journeyed to Germany to observe a society from which the last remnants of feudalism had not yet disappeared. Such was his thoroughness that he learned German in order to be able to study original documents. As he tells us, more than a year's work sometimes lay behind the writing of a single chapter.[25] But finally, in early 1856, he published *L'Ancien Régime et la Révolution,* the first part of what was to have been a much longer work. Once more, as happened with *Democracy in America,* the book was an enormous and immediate success. It is possibly a little less well known in the English-speaking world than the earlier book. However, if *Democracy in America* is Tocqueville's masterpiece, in the literal sense that it established him as a master, *The Old Régime* is his magnum opus, in which he surpassed himself in a work of great maturity and immense insight into social dynamics.

Tocqueville continued to work on the next volume, about the Revolution itself. In 1857 he paid his last visit to England, again for purposes of research, though no one of his celebrity could avoid public attention. The Prince Consort asked to meet him, and they seem to have impressed each other greatly. On his departure, a British naval vessel took the "champion of liberty" back to Cherbourg. But though he sketched the outlines of his study of the Revolution, he was able to finish only two chapters which dealt with Napoleon I's accession to power.[26] In 1858 it became evident that Tocqueville was suffering from advanced tuberculosis. He died at Cannes on 16 April 1859. That was almost exactly two years before Confederate guns firing on Fort Sumter signaled the beginning of the Civil War, the crisis of American democracy which Tocqueville had foreseen.

INVOLVEMENT AND DETACHMENT IN TOCQUEVILLE'S LIFE AND WORK

If Tocqueville did not achieve the same preeminence as a politician that he did as a writer, he was nevertheless a prominent figure in the French politics of his time. A sense of duty drove him to stay in public life at times when the quiet of his study would have been more congenial. The phrase "unity of theory and praxis,'' so often used to describe the connection between Karl Marx's social theories and his political activities, might be applied as rightly to Tocqueville's career. In Beaumont's judgment:

> The term thinker would be . . . inappropriate if applied to him in the ordinary sense of an abstract philosopher who takes pleasure in metaphysical speculations, who loves knowledge for its own sake, and is enthusiastically attached to ideas and theories independently of their application. Such is the real philosopher; such was not Tocqueville, whose speculations always had a practical and definite object. . . . He considered the past only as it affected the present, and foreign countries only with a view to his own. Thus his historical studies, and especially those relating to the first French revolution, were all treated in relation to the present state of France and to events of the time, which were every day becoming more serious, threatening fresh disturbances and perhaps even another revolution.[27]

Be that as it may, in his writings Tocqueville strove to handle his evidence with a high degree of scholarly detachment. His methods of research for *The Old Régime* reflect the standards of thoroughness, though not the tendency to crude empiricism, introduced into academic history by his older German contemporary Leopold von Ranke (1795–1886). This concern for truth and accuracy in the weighing of evidence was probably reinforced by Tocqueville's experience in the legal profession. Certainly it antedated his political career: in the introduction to the first part of *Democracy in America* he wrote,

> I do not know whether I have succeeded in making known what I saw in America, but I am certain that such has been my sincere desire, and that I have never knowingly moulded facts to ideas, instead of ideas to facts.
>
> Whenever a point could be established by the aid of written documents, I have had recourse to the original text. . . . I have cited my authorities in the notes, and anyone may refer to them. Whenever an opinion, a political custom, or a remark on the manners of the country was concerned, I endeavoured to consult the most enlightened men I met with. If the point in question was important or doubtful, I was not satisfied with one

testimony, but formed my opinion on the evidence of several witnesses. Here the reader must believe me upon my word.

The same passage continues:

> I could frequently have quoted names which are either known to [the reader] or deserve to be so, in proof of what I advance; but I have carefully abstained from this practice. A stranger frequently hears important truths at the fireside of his host which the latter would perhaps conceal from the ear of friendship.... I carefully noted every conversation of this nature as soon as it occurred, but these notes will never leave my writing-case; I should rather prejudice the success of my statements than add my name to the list of strangers who repay the generous hospitality they have received by subsequent chagrin and annoyance.[28]

What for Tocqueville was a matter of gentlemanly honor and delicacy has since become embodied for modern sociologists in "codes of ethics" promulgated with the authority of their professional associations.

The fact that Tocqueville's works have tended to be cited in support of their views by people of varied political persuasions is perhaps some testimony to his success in meeting his own standards. At any rate, in view of the limpid clarity of his writing, that fact is more plausibly attributed to the subtlety, balance, and detachment of Tocqueville's work than to ambiguity. Nevertheless, his political views are clearly not irrelevant to an understanding of his books. What exactly were they?

On the one hand, if the first part of *Democracy in America* is read on its own and with insufficient attention, Tocqueville may appear more wholeheartedly egalitarian than in fact he was. On the other hand, the dislike of revolutions which is evident in *The Old Régime* and the *Recollections* may lead to the opposite conclusion. Henri Peyre, for example, wrote that "Tocqueville ... evinced hostility to the thought of the century which had prepared the Revolution [and] longed for a return to the wise hierarchy and the polished wisdom of the classical age."[29] And Theodore Zeldin described Tocqueville's views on the tyranny of the majority as "the protest of an aristocrat against tendencies he did not like."[30] Yet if all three major works are studied together, it is impossible to see Tocqueville as a simple aristocratic reactionary. Tocqueville did not pose political questions in narrowly political terms. A century earlier, Montesquieu, with whom Tocqueville was often compared in his lifetime, had seen that as systems of government, monarchy, aristocracy, and democcracy were—or had been—appropriate in different societies. Tocqueville too recognized that the merits of modes of government could not be assessed in an abstract and timeless way, and he went far beyond Montesquieu in analyzing the social and historical contexts of political patterns.

Tocqueville acknowledged that there had been healthy aristocracies. But the French landed nobility had been undermined long before the Revolution by the policies of absolutist monarchs who had centralized the machinery of government and had deliberately set out to exclude the old aristocracy from the provincial administration. The aristocracy had retained and even increased its social and fiscal privileges, but the tie between privilege and duty had been cut. In Tocqueville's thought, the ties of interdependence and obligation between social groups were of central significance. He often compared the French nobility unfavorably with the nobility of England, which had flaunted its privileges less but continued throughout the nineteenth century to play a prominent part in politics and local administration. Tocqueville also wrote scathingly about the Irish aristocracy, generally absentee landlords who displayed a frozen indifference to the condition of their tenants. As for France, decimation by guillotine and forfeitures of land during the Revolution had completed the process begun by Louis XIV. An aristocracy once so shaken could never be restored.

Even Tocqueville's strong dislike of revolutions did not prevent him taking a balanced view. He acknowledged that "while one great revolution may establish liberty in a country, several revolutions in succession make orderly liberty impossible there for a long time."[31] The attempt to change entire systems of government and social organization which is implied in the very word revolution inherently posed a threat to liberty. This was the reason for Tocqueville's "hostility to the thought of the century which had prepared the Revolution."

Our Economists had a vast contempt for the past. "The nation has been governed," Letronne declared, "on wrong lines altogether; one has the impression that everything was left to chance." Starting out from this premise, they set to work, and there was no French institution, however venerable and well founded, for whose immediate suppression they did not clamour if it hampered them to even the slightest extent or did not fit in with their neatly ordered scheme of government....
      When we closely study the French Revolution we find that it was conducted in precisely the same spirit as that which gave rise to so many books expounding theories of government in the abstract. Our revolutionaries had the same fondness for broad generalisations, cut-and-dried legislative systems, and a pedantic symmetry; the same contempt for hard facts; the same taste for reshaping institutions on novel, ingenious, original lines; the same desire to reconstruct the entire system instead of trying to rectify its faulty parts.[32]

This passage makes it particularly clear that, as a political thinker, Tocqueville is to be placed in the tradition not of conservative but of liberal reformist social thought. That tradition is represented in the mid–twentieth century perhaps most notably by Karl Popper, the proponent of "piecemeal social engineering" as opposed to "historical prophecy" and revolutionary change.[33]
      Tocqueville's liberalism also led him to be cautious in his approval of democracy. He understood democracy to imply not only full political participation but also a measure of the civic and social equality which later sociologists have come to consider under the label of "citizenship."[34] His understanding of liberty, however, is rather more restricted, encompassing what Isaiah Berlin calls "negative freedom"—freedom from external political restrictions rather than the more positive concept of freedom to enjoy certain material rights.[35] In this respect Tocqueville falls clearly within the liberal range of the political spectrum; unlike Mill, who was to move more sympathetically in the direction of socialism in his mature years, he remained skeptical, if not actually fearful, about an excessive preoccupation with equality.

Perhaps the shadow of the guillotine that claimed his grandfather's life and, but for the fall of Robespierre, would have taken his father's, too, could never be finally lifted from his mind. Certainly as a practical thinker he was all too aware that, whatever the theorists of the Revolution may have hoped, equality and fraternity could conflict with liberty. Even in America, where liberty and democratic government had evolved out of initial social equality, Tocqueville noted the threat of "the tyranny of the majority." There it might manifest itself as a certain intolerance of individual deviation from the social norm. In France, during successive revolutions, the threat took an altogether more concrete form. Blanqui had already invented the phrase "the dictatorship of the proletariat," and Tocqueville was himself present on more than one occasion when legislators found themselves coerced by armed mobs. The outcome of numerous revolutions since Tocqueville's time leaves no room for doubt that he was right about the menace they often pose to free institutions and thought.

None of this, however, caused Tocqueville to oppose the *principle* of equality. He was conscious of the changing balance of power between social classes, the consequence of the spreading web of interdependence woven by the rapid changes which were creating both a capitalist class and an industrial working class. There were contrary currents, as Tocqueville indicated when he warned that "aristocracy may be engendered by industry,"[36] but the broad trend to greater equality was inevitable. He expected some of his readers to be surprised that

> firmly persuaded as I am that the democratic revolution which we are witnessing is an irresistible fact against which it would be neither desirable nor wise to struggle, I should have had occasion ... to address language of such severity to those democratic communities which this revolution has brought into being. My answer is simply that it is because I am not an adversary of democracy that I have sought to speak of democracy in all sincerity.[37]

The problem was how to ensure that as equality increased it did not override liberty.

Tocqueville's political ideal was freedom under the rule of law. The people should have as large a measure as possible of direct control over their own affairs, through thriving institutions of local government and by banding together in free associations—something very different from the decentralization found under feudalism. Strong local institutions would be a safeguard against arbitrary intervention by central authority, and against the revolutionary subversion of the state. So concentrated was the machinery of the French state that he who controlled Paris controlled France, quite possibly against the wishes of the majority of Frenchmen. Checks and balances on the executive were necessary, but the Revolution of 1789 had in no way curbed the central power.

It is a curious fact that when they envisaged all the social and administrative reforms subsequently carried out by our revolutionaries, the idea of free institutions never crossed their minds. True, they were all in favour of the free exchange of commodities and a system of *laissez faire* and *laisser passer* in commerce and industry; but political liberty in the full sense of the term was something that passed their imagination or was promptly dismissed from their thoughts if by any chance the idea of it occurred to them. To begin with, anyhow, the Economists were thoroughly hostile to deliberative assemblies, to secondary organisations vested with local powers, and, generally speaking, to all those counterpoises which have been devised by free peoples at various stages of their history to curb the domination of a central authority. "Any system of opposing forces within a government," Quesnay wrote, "is highly objectionable."[38]

Tocqueville knew his ideal could not be created by fiat. That was the direction in which reform should proceed, but France's historical experience meant that it would not be easily achieved. In America, he had observed popular respect for the law; in *The Old Régime* he was able to explain how in France arbitrary rule had encouraged widespread contempt for the law. In America and in England the tradition of local self-government was strong; in France the sale of municipal offices by the Crown had weakened the tradition. In America, people formed themselves into associations for all manner of purposes; in France the spirit of "individualism" (in Tocqueville's particular sense) and reliance on the omniscience of central government were much stronger. America had had nothing to fear from an elected chief executive, for the president's powers were balanced against those of Congress and the powers of the federal government as a whole were circumscribed by the Constitution—the government itself of course was much smaller in scale than it was to become in the twentieth century. In France, by contrast, the long-established tradition of centralized administrative power and a weak legislature made an elected president at the head of the executive a threat to liberty. These political differences could only be understood by studying their roots in the structure of society. It is true that Tocqueville's central concerns in *Democracy in America, the Recollections,* and *The Old Régime* are democracy and revolution. Yet he should not be thought of exclusively as a political sociologist, for his political interests led him to study a much wider array of social phenomena. This is particularly clear in the second part of *Democracy in America.* In explaining the difference between the first and second parts, Tocqueville used a term first employed by Adam Ferguson and then, to greater notice, by Hegel: the first part had been concerned with the political world in America, the second dealt with *civil society.*[39] In the second part he subtly explored the culture and manners of a democratic society. Modern sociologists often pay lip service to the interconnectedness of social institutions yet contrive to remain very narrowly specialized as political sociologists, industrial sociologists, sociologists of religion, and so on. Tocqueville not only saw but pursued the connections between aspects of social life which latter-day intellectual Taylorism has placed in hermetically sealed subdivisions of a discipline which, even taken as a whole, would to Tocqueville have seemed unduly limited. Apart from studying political life, he made contributions to the sociology of social stratification, race relations, slavery, colonialism, communities, voluntary associations, bureaucracy, armies, language, literature, art, religion, prisons, and crime. He even discussed the social position of women, a topic which sociologists scarcely rediscovered until late in the twentieth century. He was indeed a well-rounded sociologist.

TOCQUEVILLE AS SOCIOLOGIST

For all that, the general assumptions underlying Tocqueville's writings have to be prized out. One frequent criticism of his work is that he rarely paid much attention to formal definitions or to what modern sociologists would call "methodology" and "theory-building." He was not that kind of writer. Yet it is not difficult to discover what Tocqueville meant by his basic concepts, such as democracy and liberty, nor to discern well-thought-out theories. His sociological insight is no less profound for being left partly implicit; in fact it is enriched by the absence of excessive formalization and unnecessary abstraction.

Even Tocqueville's comparative method, for which he is most often praised, is often only half explicit, but it is highly effective.[40] He used the method consciously and continually. A particularly fine example can be seen in his argument that, in explaining the maintenance of democratic institutions in the United States, geographical circumstances are less important than laws, and laws less important than manners (see pp. 73–77, below). Here he draws comparisons first between the United States and the geographically similar but socially and politically different societies of Latin America and French Canada, and then between the eastern states of the Union and the frontier states of the West, where the laws were the same but the "manners" of democracy less well established. However, in spite of such examples, and in spite of fairly frequent references to France in *Democracy in America* and to England and Germany in *The Old Régime,* implicit comparisons are more pervasive in both books than are explicit ones. Tocqueville wrote in a letter to Louis de Kergorlay:

> Ought one to make the resemblance and differences between the two countries explicit, or write so as to enable the reader to find them out? I am not sure. In my work on America, I almost always adopted the latter course. Though I seldom mentioned France, I did not write a page without thinking of her. . . . And what I especially tried to draw out and to explain was not the whole condition of the United States but the points in which that foreign society differs from our own or resembles

us. It was always by noticing likenesses or contrasts that I succeeded in giving an interesting and accurate description of the New World. . . . I believe this perpetual silent reference to France was a principle cause of the book's success.[41]

The active part which the reader has to play in building his own comparisons out of the raw material provided by Tocqueville makes it all the more important that *Democracy in America, The Old Régime* and the *Recollections* be read in conjunction. The unelaborated comparisons in *Democracy in America* with "aristocratic societies" are much more understandable when one has read Tocqueville's analysis of such a society in *The Old Régime*. The implicit comparisons must in fact have been more comprehensible from the start to the French than to the American reader of *Democracy in America*. Similarly, Tocqueville's fear of the tyranny of the majority makes more sense in the light of France's revolutionary history.

The comparative method, as Tocqueville's friend Mill argued in his *System of Logic*,[42] is a means of discovering empirical regularities and of proceeding to theoretical generalizations. On cursory reading, Tocqueville's work may seem to be full of descriptive insights but to lack the generalizations for which many sociologists seem endlessly to strive. But Tocqueville was anything but a crude empiricist.[43] Methodological comparisons cannot be made unless one has some notion of what one wishes to observe. All observation is selective; initial expectations determine what one looks for. Observations modify theories, but modified theories then direct one's observation to new facts. For Tocqueville, journeying to America just after the July Revolution of 1830, knowledge of France and his tentative explanations of its historical experience guided his initial observation of American society. But since his comparisons were mainly left only half explicit, his general ideas too could be overlooked. Beaumont, after noting that "In his animated description of American institutions, facts are inseparably mixed with speculations," relates a telling incident.

An Englishman, author of an interesting work on the United States, was complimenting him on [the first part of *Democracy*

in America]. "What I especially admire," he said, "is that while treating so great a subject, you have so thoroughly avoided general ideas."
There could be no greater mistake; but Tocqueville was delighted. It showed him that the abstractions with which his book is filled had been so skilfully presented in a concrete form that an acute, though certainly not a profound, reader did not perceive that the particular facts were only illustrations of general principles.

But, says Beaumont, no one could make the same mistake on reading the second part of *Democracy in America,* published five years later.

In describing the intellect, feelings and manners of the Americans, it was no longer possible to conceal the presence of general ideas, and by introducing them in the form of facts [he could] render them more effective though less obvious. The book is full of reflections on reflections.[44]

Later still, *The Old Régime,* though on the surface an attempt to explain a unique historical sequence, plainly contains many insights into more general processes of social development. Should Tocqueville have stated these in a more abstract and formalized way? On the contrary, in avoiding excessive formalization in his theorizing, he seems a very modern figure, for there are many highly effective sociologists who have resisted the striving for abstraction which was fashionable in sociology in the mid–twentieth century.[45]

On this question, it is worth quoting Max Weber. Weber argued that in both sociology and history (as opposed to the natural sciences),

the most general laws, because they are most devoid of content are also the least valuable. The more comprehensive the validity—or scope—of a term, the more it leads us away from the richness of reality, since in order to include the common elements of the largest number of phenomena, it must necessarily be as abstract as possible and hence devoid of content.[46]

One example is enough to illustrate the point. Towards the end of *The Old Régime,* after showing how the general weaknesses of

French government and society came about, Tocqueville begins to discuss the circumstances which actually precipitated the Revolution. He argues that "though the reign of Louis XVI was the most prosperous period of the monarchy, this very prosperity hastened the outbreak of the Revolution." In the course of the chapter he does in fact state a proposition in fairly general though cautious terms:

> it is not always when things are going from bad to worse that revolutions break out. On the contrary, it more often happens that when a people has put up with an oppressive rule over a long period without protest suddenly finds the government relaxing the pressure, it takes up arms against it.... Patiently endured so long as it seemed beyond redress, a grievance comes to appear intolerable once the possibility of removing it crosses men's minds.... the mere fact that certain abuses have been remedied draws attention to the others and they now appear more galling; people may suffer less, but their sensibility is exacerbated.[47]

In the terminology of modern sociology, Tocqueville had seen that it is not just the state of *absolute* deprivation which has to be taken into account when explaining the outbreak of revolutions but a people's sense of *relative* deprivation. Taking his cue directly from Tocqueville, James C. Davis has shown that the generalization applies to several other revolutions before and since Tocqueville's time, and T. R. Gurr has further broadened the hypothesis to cover civil violence in general.[48] Yet the more abstract the theory is, the less useful it becomes. Tocqueville did not go so far as to say that all revolutions conformed to the pattern, still less that "relative deprivation" was a sufficient cause of them. It was one part, perhaps not a necessary part, of a sequential order. Interesting as it is to identify a "psychological factor," that does not eliminate the need to study the broader structural developments which have in any case led to that "relative deprivation" and created the social figuration within which it can wreak its effects. The attempt to discover general historical laws can also lead to a preoccupation with definitions, categories, and typologies which divert attention from the real problems of historical causality and processes of social development. C. Wright Mills defined the sociological imagination as an ability "to grasp history and biography and the relations between the two within society."[49] That Tocqueville had this ability to a superb degree stands out in the links he continually draws between individual behavior—manners, opinions, mores—and the broader structure of society. But because he did not write at length about problems of theory and method, his contribution to the understanding of processes of social development in general has been underestimated. Indeed he seems to have underestimated it himself. In a letter thanking John Stuart Mill for a copy of the *System of Logic* he said:

> I took it up and read it, or rather studied it, for I am not so familiar with these matters that I can grasp them well without giving them a great deal of thought. . . . I was particularly struck by what you said about the application of logic to the study of man. Like you, I believe that by making use of the method you outline and bearing in mind the points you make, one would give a new shape to this most important of all the sciences, and eventually put it on more solid foundations than it has had up to now. Why don't you undertake such a work? I should like you to do so both for your own sake and for ours, because you would make a success of it and we should benefit by it. One can see what you could do in this field by the way in which you treat that eternal and nagging question of human freedom, the solution of which is important not only for ethics but for politics too. The distinction you make between necessity, as you term it, and irresistibleness or fatalism is illuminating. It seems to me that there you find neutral ground on which the two opposed schools of thought—or at least the reasonable men in the two schools—could easily meet and agree.[50]

The problem of historical inevitability and human free will was one which occupied Tocqueville's thoughts. It concerned him as a matter of ethics, because a belief in the inevitability of history may lead individuals to deny all responsibility for the course of social development, a conclusion repugnant to Tocqueville. It also concerned him as a problem of historical explanation. His own writings are full of examples of long-term social trends—like the trend towards democracy and the breakup of feudalism—in which individuals seem helplessly caught up and compelled to swim with the current of history. Yet he also demonstrated the power of ideas in history: the ideas of the Enlightenment that prepared the way for the Revolution, democratic theories in the United States, the influence of abstract doctrine on the Constitution of 1848. And in the events in which he himself was involved, accidents seemed to change the course of history. Would the Republic have been declared in 1848 if an unrepresentative mob had not succeeded, by the negligence of the army, in invading the Chamber when the deputies were discussing who should be Regent for the infant successor to Louis-Philippe?

A decade after his letter to Mill, Tocqueville wrote in his *Souvenirs,* "For my part I hate those absolute systems which make all the events of history depend on great first causes linked to each other by a chain of fate and which thus, so to speak, omit men from the history of mankind."[51] In his preface to the second part of *Democracy in America* he had been very careful to deny that he saw equality as one such great first cause. Though he attributed "so many different consequences to equality," the reader was certainly not to infer that Tocqueville considered "that principle to be the sole cause of all that takes place in the present age."[52] In the *Souvenirs,* Tocqueville continued:

> I believe ... that many important historical facts can only be explained as the results of accidental circumstances, and that many others remain inexplicable. In the end chance, or rather the entanglement of secondary causes which we call chance because we do not know how to unravel them, plays a large part in all we observe taking place on the world's stage. But I firmly believe that chance accomplishes nothing that has not been prepared in advance. Antecedent facts, the nature of institutions, turns of mind, the state of manners and morals—these are the materials with which chance constructs those impromptu events which surprise and alarm us.[53]

He said this while reflecting on the February Revolution of 1848; it was "born of general causes fertilised by accidents," and it was equally superficial to attribute the episode entirely either to the former or to the latter. Tocqueville would have agreed with Marx's famous remark, made just two years later when he in turn was reflecting on Louis Bonaparte's *coup:* "Men make their own history, but they do not make it just as they please; they do not make it under circumstances chosen by themselves, but under circumstances directly encountered, given and transmitted from the past."[54] It was Marx's fate to be the father of the most absolute of systems, which some inferior hands have certainly used to "make the events of history depend on great first causes" and which, in Tocqueville's mordant phrase, has furnished them with "a few mighty reasons to extricate them from the most difficult part of their work."[55]

In fact, although he was perhaps himself only half aware of the fact, Tocqueville had pointed to a solution of the problem of "free will" versus "historical inevitability." His solution antedated both Mill's and Marx's comments on the problem. It appears in the second part of *Democracy in America,* in a chapter entitled "Characteristics of Historians in Democratic Ages" (see pp. 159–62, below) and is the more telling for being pitched in sociological rather than philosophical terms. For, although philosophers of history have always tried to frame the question in conceptual terms, the problem is actually an empirical rather than a conceptual one. Tocqueville noted that historians in aristocratic periods tend to attribute all events to the actions and intentions of particular individuals, while tending to overlook the effects of more impersonal social forces also at work. Historians in democratic societies, on the other hand, tend to minimize the influence of individuals on the course of history and to attribute all events to great impersonal social processes. Tocqueville's brilliant insight was that these differences in historiography correspond, albeit in an exaggerated way, to empirical differences in the structures of the two types of society:

I am convinced that even amongst democratic nations the genius, the vices, or the virtues of certain individuals retard or accelerate the natural current of a people's history; but the causes of this secondary and fortuitous nature are infinitely more various, more concealed, more complex, less powerful and consequently less easy to trace in periods of equality than in ages of aristocracy. . . . The historian is soon wearied by the toil; his mind loses itself in this labyrinth; and in his inability to discern or conspicuously to point out the influence of individuals, he denies their existence.[56]

What Tocqueville had perceived, in other words, was that the more dense and extensive the web of interdependence in society, the greater the control which people exercise over each other, and the more impersonal the mutual control seems. We are each dependent on so many others that the constraints on our freedom of action seem not to be imposed by any particular person. And this sense of impersonal social control and of impersonal forces in history is felt by people at large, not just by historians.

Still more important, Tocqueville realized that the more nearly equal is the balance of power between people and groups in society (and especially the balance of power between governors and governed), the more the overall course of events is uninfluenced by the actions and intentions of any particular participant.[57] The larger and more tangled the social web, the more difficult is it for any particular actor to put together an accurate picture of what is going on. To use Max Weber's word, the social process becomes more *opaque*.[58] An individual is therefore often unable to foresee clearly all the consequences of his actions. Social processes and historical events are produced by the actions of individuals, but not necessarily in accordance with their intentions, and "society" increasingly functions as if it were something separate from people, constraining and compelling them, as it were, from outside.

Tocqueville would have found this terminology strange, but the ideas themselves pervade his writings. In *The Old Régime* there are frequent references to the blindness of his contemporaries to the nature and direction of the events in which they were caught up. And his own experience in politics had made Tocqueville quite familiar with unintended consequences and with runaway social processes. In his *Souvenirs,* he wrote:

> One has to have spent a long time in politics to understand the extent to which men push each other away from their own

plans and how the destinies of the world unfold through the consequences, but often the contrary consequences, of the intentions which produce them, like a kite which flies by the opposing forces of the wind and the string.[59]

Tocqueville's understanding of the relationship between individual action and impersonal social forces points to interesting comparisons with both Marx and Durkheim.[60] When social processes are so opaque and actions so often have unforeseen consequences, it is not enough to study the motivation of individuals alone. In recognizing this, Tocqueville resembles Durkheim. But one direction in which this insight led Tocqueville was that of studying the circumstances in which whole categories of people will act together—how they become conscious of having interests in common, how a sense of class identity forms, how they take action collectively as a class. In this, Tocqueville resembles Marx. It is easy to find passages in Tocqueville which the unwary might mistake for Marx. "I am dealing here," he writes in *The Old Régime,* "with classes as a whole, to my mind the historian's proper study."[61] Indeed, class conflict is almost as much the theme of Tocqueville's work as of Marx's. Its relative absence in the United States is a theme of *Democracy in America* just as its prevalence in France is a theme of the *Recollections* and *The Old Régime.* For Tocqueville, the industrial working class did not have the unique historical destiny it had in Marx's eyes. But he was well aware of the bearing which its growth in the course of economic changes had had on the course of French revolutions (see pp. 267–73, below). And in *Democracy in America* he clearly described the effects of routine industrial labor for which Marx and modern sociologists would use the term "alienation," and asked— in an allusion to Adam Smith—"what can be expected of a man who has spent twenty years of his life in making heads for pins?" (see pp. 301–4, below). The best example, however, of Tocqueville's analysis of class interests and class consciousness is his dissection of the upper and middle classes in *The Old Régime.* He shows how, though members of these social categories were in style of life very similar to each other, differences in sources of income, in fiscal privileges, and in social status enshrined in law fragmented them into numerous separate interest groups (see pp. 199–209, below). These obstacles to a sense of broader class identity prevented action in defense of common interests, and thereby facilitated the Revolution. "If we bear in mind the number of these minute gradings and the fact that nowhere else in the world were citizens less inclined to join forces and stand by each other in emergencies, we can see how it was that a successful revolution could tear down the whole structure almost in the twinkling of an eye."[62]

The effect of the Revolution had been to destroy the legal and social foundations of these gradations without, however, creating in their place any other bases of social and political stability. Subsequent revolutions had only compounded the problem. One major effect of these changes was a shift in the nature of what has been termed "social control,"[63] and Tocqueville was well aware of the important implication of this transition. The breakdown of traditional forms of social control under the *ancien régime* was part of the process that led to the Revolution. In New England, new forms of control had been established; to take one example, American religious institutions served a totally different function from the church in France, which was intimately linked to an oppressive political establishment. There, the legitimacy of the church fluctuated with the régime, to which it was inextricably linked, while in America there was no state religion, and religious institutions were insulated from political conflicts.[64]

Another important consequence of the loosening of traditional forms of social control was the rise of "individualism," a common enough expression today but a concept the implications of which were less clear in the early years of the nineteenth century. While the growth of individualism could be a great liberating force against the dead weight of custom and tradition, it might also produce less happy results. "In a community in which ties of family, of caste, of class, and craft fraternities no longer exist," wrote Tocqueville, "People are far too much disposed to become self-seekers, practising a narrow individualism and caring nothing for the public good."[65] Here Tocqueville once again anticipates Durkheim.[66] Viewing the state of French society in the aftermath of still further turmoil—the collapse of the Second Empire in military defeat and the ensuing recriminations—Durkheim was to diagnose egoism and anomie as the problems of social atomiza- tion. Both ideas are prefigured in Tocqueville's concern with "in- dividualism" (see pp. 199–209, below). Tocqueville described the destruction of traditional corporate affiliations in the last years of the *ancien régime;* Durkheim proposed their reestablishment as a (somewhat unrealistic) solution to the problems he observed.

"Individualism" in France is the reason for its extensive dis- cussion in *Democracy in America.* The United States had the advantage of having been "born free" rather than becoming so through a democratic revolution. For, according to Tocqueville, the problem of individualism is always at its height immediately after a revolution.

> Those members of the community who were at the top of the late gradations of rank cannot immediately forget their former greatness. . . . Those on the contrary who were formerly at the foot of the social scale . . . cannot enjoy their newly acquired independence without secret uneasiness. It is, then, commonly at the outset of democratic society that citizens are most dis- posed to live apart. Democracy leads men not to draw near their fellow creatures; but democratic revolutions lead them to shun each other, and perpetuate in a state of equality the animosities which the state of inequality engendered.[67]

The propensity of Americans to join with each other in free asso- ciations for all manner of civil and political objectives, and the relative unwillingness of the French to do so, was a prime symptom of the deepest differences between French and Ameri- can societies. But though Tocqueville saw American society as socially more integrated and politically more stable, he never forgot that the Negroes and Indians were excluded from it.

If Tocqueville underestimated the extent to which industrial society would be the society of the future, he certainly did not overlook, as Marx can be argued to have done, the divisive ef- fects that race, slavery, and colonialism were to have within that society. He was, as we have seen, morally opposed to all forms of historical determinism and, while recognizing the im- portance of race relations, he did not attribute any mystical historical destiny to any specific racial group. No better illustration of this can be seen than in his reaction to Gobineau's *Essai sur l'inégalité des races humaines* (1853–55). Tocqueville not only rejected Gobineau's claim that races could be ranked hierarchically, and exposed such theories to the searchlight of historical evidence, but also warned of the selective misuse of the thesis:

> For those Americans whom you mention and who translated your book are known to me as bigoted leaders of the anti-abolitionist party. They translated the part of your book which suits their prejudices, the part which tends to prove that the Negroes belong to another, to a different and inferior race; but they suppressed the part which tends to argue that, like every other, the Anglo-Saxon race is also decaying.[68]

This intellectual rejection of racism is carried over into his specific treatment of race relations in North America, where he finds slavery not only inhuman but also contrary to the enlightened self-interest of the slave owners themselves. The persistence of slavery depends partly on the blindness and unthinking cruelty which permeates rigid caste and class systems, on the inability of people on either side of a deep social chasm to consider individuals of a different class or race as fellow members of a common humanity. In the French context, he supplies graphic illustrations of these blinkers on social perception in his references to the letters of Mme de Sévigné, in which there are jocular accounts of the brutal suppression of the Brittany tax riots of 1675, and to the conduct of Mme Duchâtelet, who without hesitation bathed naked in front of her manservants because she did not see them as fellow members of her species.[69]

As for America, Tocqueville, anticipating Myrdal's *An American Dilemma* by more than a century, points to "this society, so proud of its morality and philanthropy, [where] one meets with complete insensibility, with cold uncompassionate egotism, when the aborigines are in question."[70] But he does not blame the Americans for their attitude towards the Indians and Negroes, any more than he does the slave owners in the French colonies, for a situation which is the legacy of historical circumstance.

Is it necessary to detest these men for this? To be irritated with them? To desire to harm them? No, without a doubt, it is necessary to pity them. They are obeying a universal law of human nature: they follow an example given in every century, an example which we, ourselves, have before our eyes.[71]

For Tocqueville, racial hierarchy was simply another form of aristocracy that was destined to crumble before the onslaught of democracy and social equality. But man was not simply helpless in the face of impersonal historical forces; in a prophetic statement on Algeria he argued that the future of French rule would depend on the nature of its colonial policy. If this were unjust it would turn the country into "a fortified arena in which the two races would fight without mercy, and where one of the two would die."[72]

Thus if Tocqueville's ideal was a harmonious society, this did not blind him to existing social realities. He spoke of blacks and whites as "bound to each other without intermingling... unable entirely to separate or to combine."[73] He saw, in other words, that though society might be bound together by shared beliefs and networks of social relations, groups of men could also remain permanently interdependent through ties of conflict and exploitation.

Tocqueville is, nevertheless, certainly a precursor of present-day pluralist theories of democracy. The strength of the American political system stemmed only in part from the Constitution and its consciously sophisticated allocation of rights and responsibilities between the federal and state authorities. Tocqueville was never greatly impressed by purely constitutional contrivances; France had had more than her fair share of paper liberties. More important for American society was the tradition, which had developed in an altogether unconscious and unplanned way, of local self-government and of groups of people combining together in associations to pursue their common interests. In probing the social roots of democracy, Tocqueville had a major influence on modern political sociology.[74]

The sheer level and intensity of political activity in America impressed Tocqueville, but it was the way in which political feelings were mobilized and channeled that he felt to be particularly important. For the individual would be powerless against the forces at the command of the centralized state unless he could combine with others to represent his interests and secure his rights. Such associations would replace the countervailing power which aristocracy, so Tocqueville thought, had exercised against state tyranny in feudal times. Minority rights under majority rule could not be guaranteed by the simple formula that related each citizen to a single vote.

Political associations and other secondary institutions would arise spontaneously only if the great mass of the citizens of a democratic state were educated to use and understand their political rights. This education need not be provided just by the formal institutions of schools and universities—American education impressed Tocqueville more by its universality than by its depth. It could also be provided by the indirect effects of many other social arrangements. Tocqueville viewed the process of "political socialization" in a broad sociological sense, and understood what Robert Merton has termed the "latent functions" of institutions like the jury system or organized religion.[75] By participating in such institutions, citizens learned the rules of the democratic game, and this was the strongest bastion against the forces of tyranny, whether represented by a demagogic "democratic" dictator or by the unruly anarchy of mob violence.

The absence of these strong group affiliations intermediate between the levels of the family and the state—for example in France—was a primary cause of political instability. This is a key idea in what is nowadays embodied in one form of the "theory of mass society."[76] When a population is "atomized," its members take no regular and orderly part in politics but may from time to time erupt suddenly as a force on the political stage. A "mass society," so the argument goes, is particularly vulnerable to manipulation by demagogic leaders, and may degenerate into a totalitarian state.[77] Tocqueville anticipated the positive "fear of freedom" latent in such societies, a theme developed by Erich Fromm and other writers to explain the mass stampede towards totalitarianism in Europe during the 1930s.[78]

Thus Tocqueville acknowledged the clash of interests to be the essence of politics, but social conflict could be stabilized and moderated by a dense web of cross-cutting group affiliations. That was the significance of the strong institutions of community self-government and the innumerable associations through which Americans pursued their interests. Taken on its own, this view of politics corresponds to the classical economists' model of perfect competition between small firms. But how close is it to the realities of power in late twentieth-century industrial societies? There are distinguished writers like Robert Dahl and Talcott Parsons who consider it still basically valid. Others contend that just as the modern economy is dominated by giant corporations and the typical market structure is oligopolistic, so by an analogous and related process there have emerged large concentrations of power in the political system. Proponents of that view have included the Lynds and C. Wright Mills, and they have many successors.[79]

Closely connected with the idea of mass society is that of mass culture. Tocqueville was a pioneer in this field too. The second part of *Democracy in America,* in which he sets out to trace the effects of equality on "civil society" and on manners, represents a comprehensive study of American cultural life. Tocqueville used the word "manners" in a very broad sense. "I use the word *manners* [*moeurs*] with the meaning which the word *mores* had in antiquity; I apply it not only to manners in the proper sense ... but also to the various notions and opinions current among men, and to the mass of ideas which form their habits of mind."[80] Elsewhere, more succinctly, he defines manners as "the moral and intellectual characteristics of social men taken collectively."[81] By either definition, what Tocqueville means by manners is more or less synonymous with what modern sociologists call "culture."

That is not, of course, to say that Tocqueville lacked an interest in manners in the narrower sense. Far from it. As a student of everyday behavior, Tocqueville displays an acuteness of observation reminiscent, for the modern reader, of Erving Goffman. But unlike Goffman or ethnomethodologists like Harold Garfinkel, Tocqueville is not satisfied by the minute description of behavior, or by accounting for it ahistorically. He is always interested in how broader social and historical trends have caused patterns of everyday behavior to develop as they have. This is evident in the selections included below in pages 102–29: why attitudes to the suffering of fellow men become less harsh as society becomes more equal; why social interaction becomes less stiff and formal; why nevertheless the search for invidious status distinctions increases;[82] the effects on social relations between masters and servants, between the sexes, and within armies. Here Tocqueville's true heirs today are not Goffman and Garfinkel but writers such as David Riesman and Norbert Elias.[83]

In studying "manners" in the broader sense, Tocqueville also outlined what, to employ a term which only came into use with Karl Mannheim and his generation, must be called a sociology of knowledge of some scope and sophistication. In the brilliant and witty first chapter of the second part of *Democracy in America,* Tocqueville examines "philosophical method among the Americans" (see pp. 130–34, below). No country is less inclined to study abstract philosophy, he says, yet prevailing philosophical assumptions can be detected and accounted for. In a new and rapidly expanding society, the ideas of earlier generations have little authority; where social mobility is high, people do not adopt ideas dominant among their social class, for class consciousness scarcely exists;[84] and where social conditions are so nearly equal, there are few men whose social standing lends authority to their ideas. Therefore "each American appeals to the individual exercise of his own understanding alone." The latent American philosophy is thus Cartesian, even if Americans never read Descartes.[85]

Tocqueville went on to argue that democracy promoted an interest in applied rather than theoretical science, and to show the effects of democracy on the arts, literature, and language (see pp. 138–58, below). Perhaps here he pushed his ideas too far and overgeneralized; subsequent achievements of Americans in science, literature, and the arts may make these chapters superficially seem more dated than many other parts of his work. Yet the structure of American society has also changed since his day, so perhaps his generalizations about the connection between social structure and cultural production are not invalidated. At any rate, even if some of his conclusions are no longer true, others still strike chords, and, moreover, the reasoning by which he reaches them remains extremely instructive.

It is not difficult to find specific errors and omissions in Tocqueville's writings, many of which are undoubtedly marked by the limitations of his age. What is remarkable is the extent to which he was able to rise above such limitations and to isolate many of the critical forces operating in his day that have continued to influence the development of modern society. It is true that he tended to underplay the role of economic factors in much of his analysis[86] and that he totally ignored the catastrophic weight of war debt as a major cause of the collapse of the *ancien régime*. He also underestimated the positive contribution that central governments were to make in the development of modern welfare state societies. In his obsessive fear of the "tyranny of the majority" he often overlooked the tenacity with which privileged minorities could continue to subvert even modest moves towards greater equality and undermine liberty in formally democratic societies.

For all that, Tocqueville possessed one of the most fertile sociological imaginations of the nineteenth century. It was the political problems of his native land which drew him as a young man to visit America and England, but the comparative method which he first applied to the political systems of the three countries rapidly guided his attention to the more general social roots of democracy and revolution. Although politics remained central to his interests as a man of affairs and as a writer, his investigation of these roots led him to explore many other facets of social and cultural life, and to a mature insight into the dynamics of society which is of value to present-day scholars throughout the social sciences.

NOTES

1. His notes on this early journey have been published in tome 5, vol. 1 of the *Oeuvres Complètes*, ed. J. P. Mayer (Paris: Gallimard, 1957). Excerpts were included in Beaumont's edition of the *Oeuvres Complètes* (Paris: Michel Lévy Frères, 1860–66) and translated into English in the *Memoir, Letters and Remains of Alexis de Tocqueville* (London: Macmillan, 1861), 1:103–30.
2. *Memoir*, p. 6.
3. A. Cobban, *A History of Modern France* (Harmondsworth: Penguin, 1965),

2:78; R. T. McKenzie, *British Political Parties*, 2d ed. (London: Heinemann, 1963), p. 4.

4. *The Recollections of Alexis de Tocqueville*, trans. de Mattos (London: Henry & Co., 1896), p. 4.

5. Beaumont, *Memoir*, 1:14.

6. See Tocqueville's account of "A Fortnight in the Wilds," ibid., 1:140–207, and in *Journey to America*, ed. J. P. Mayer (London: Faber and Faber, 1959), pp. 328–76.

7. The day-by-day course of their visit has been reconstructed by G. W. Pierson in his *Tocqueville and Beaumont in America* (London: Oxford University Press, 1938). Tocqueville's American notebooks have been published under the editorship of J. P. Mayer in *Journey to America* (n. 6, above).

8. Paris: Fournier, 1833.

9. Translated by Barbara Chapman (Stanford University Press, 1958).

10. Beaumont, *Memoir*, 1:6–7 (translation slightly amended).

11. Ibid., p. 36 (translation amended).

12. Ibid.

13. Tocqueville's notes on these two visits have been published under the editorship of J. P. Mayer in *Journeys to England and Ireland* (London: Faber and Faber, 1958).

14. His evidence is reprinted in ibid., pp. 210–32.

15. See Seymour Drescher, *Tocqueville and England* (Cambridge, Mass., Harvard University Press, 1964).

16. F. Engels, *The Condition of the Working Class in England in 1844* in *Marx and Engels on Britain* (Moscow: Foreign Languages Publishing House, 1962).

17. See Michael D. Biddiss, *Father of Racist Ideology: The Social and Political Thought of Count Gobineau* (London, 1970), and idem, "Prophecy and Pragmatism: Gobineau's Confrontation with Tocqueville," *Historical Journal* 13, no. 4 (1970): 611–33.

18. See Tocqueville's self-assessment in the *Recollections*, pt. 2, chap. 3. See also Beaumont, *Memoir*, 1:50–52, and M. Lawlor, *Alexis de Tocqueville in the Chamber of Deputies* (Washington, D.C.: The Catholic University of America Press, 1959).

19. See the papers collected in Melvin Kranzberg, ed., *1848—A Turning Point?* (Lexington, Mass: D. C. Heath & Co., 1959), which also contains an excellent bibliography. See also William L. Langer's more recent *Political and Social Upheaval, 1832–1852* (New York: Harper and Row, 1969).

20. Karl Marx, *The Revolutions of 1848*, ed. David Fernbach (Harmondsworth: Penguin, 1973), pp. 129–34.

21. For Tocqueville's account of the June Days, see the *Recollections*, pt. 2, chaps. 9–10.

22. See ibid., pt. 2, chap. 11.

23. A. Cobban, *A History of Modern France*, p. 147.

24. Ironically, this momentous provision had been proposed by Beaumont and supported by Tocqueville.

25. *The Old Régime and the French Revolution* (Garden City, N.Y.: Doubleday, 1955), p. xv.

26. Beaumont published these two chapters in his edition of the *Oeuvres Complètes*, and they were translated into English in the *Memoir, Letters and Remains*,

(see excerpts in pages 242–49, below). Beaumont excluded Tocqueville's sketches on principle, but they have now been published in Mayer's edition of the *Oeuvres Complètes*, tome 2, vol. 2, and translated into English in J. Lukacs, ed., *The European Revolution and Correspondence with Gobineau* (Garden City, N.Y.: Doubleday, 1959).

27. Beaumont, *Memoir*, pp. 10–12 (translation slightly amended).

28. *Democracy in America*, trans. Henry Reeve (New York: Vintage Books, 1954), 1:lxxxii–lxxxiii.

29. Henri Peyre, "Durkheim: The Man, His Time and His Intellectual Background," in K. H. Wolff, ed., *Essays on Sociology and Philosophy by Emile Durkheim et al.* (New York: Harper and Row, 1964), p. 19.

30. T. Zeldin, *France, 1848–1945* (Oxford: The Clarendon Press, 1977), 2:394.

31. *Recollections*, p. 72 (translation amended).

32. *The Old Régime*, pp. 159, 147.

33. K. R. Popper, *The Poverty of Historicism* (London: Routledge and Kegan Paul, 1957), and idem, *The Open Society and Its Enemies* (London: Routledge and Kegan Paul, 1945).

34. See T. H. Marshall, "Citizenship and Social Class," in *Sociology at the Crossroads* (London: Heinemann, 1963); R. Bendix, *Nation-Building and Citizenship* (New York: Wiley, 1964).

35. Isaiah Berlin, "Two Concepts of Liberty," in *Four Essays on Liberty* (London: Oxford University Press, 1969), pp. 118–72.

36. See pp. 301–4, below.

37. *Democracy in America*, pt. 2, Preface.

38. See p. 224, below.

39. *Democracy in America*, pt. 2, Preface.

40. See N.J. Smelser, "Alexis de Tocqueville as Comparative Analyst," in his *Comparative Methods in the Social Sciences* (Englewood Cliffs, N. J.: Prentice-Hall, 1976).

41. Tocqueville to Louis de Kergorlay, 19 October, 1843 in *Memoir*, 1:359–60 (translation amended).

42. John Stuart Mill, *A System of Logic, Ratiocinative and Inductive* (London: Parker, 1843).

43. Or "positivist" in the misleading terminology of modern sociological controversy. See T. W. Adorno et al., *The Positivist Dispute in German Sociology* (London: Heinemann, 1976); and Anthony Giddens, ed., *Positivism and Sociology* (London: Heinemann, 1974).

44. Beaumont, *Memoir*, 1:43 (translation slightly amended). Beaumont's phrase "reflections on reflections" contains in a nutshell Alfred Schutz's idea that sociologists use "constructs of the second degree" (see another volume in this series: H. R. Wagner, ed., *Alfred Schutz on Phenomenology and Social Relations* [Chicago: University of Chicago Press, 1970]). That also serves to remind us that *Verstehen* is not some method peculiar to sociology, modern or otherwise. Tocqueville would have been impatient of the convoluted debates about *Verstehen*, but his works exemplify it on every page.

45. This issue has been discussed with reference to Tocqueville and several other writers by Arthur L. Stinchcombe in *Theoretical Methods in Social History* (New York: Academic Press, 1978). Unfortunately, this book was published too late to be taken fully into account here.

46. Max Weber, *Economy and Society* (New York: Bedminster Press, 1968), 1:80).

If Tocqueville is to be considered a historian, it is worth noting that only towards the end of his life did Weber fully reconcile himself to the label "sociologist"—he preferred to call himself a "comparative historian."

47. See p. 230, below.

48. J. C. Davis, "Toward a Theory of Revolutions," *American Sociological Review* 27, no. 1 (1962): 5–19; Ted Robert Gurr, "Psychological Factors in Civil Violence," *World Politics* 20, no. 2 (1968): 245–78.

49. C. Wright Mills, *The Sociological Imagination* (New York: Oxford University Press, 1959), p. 6.

50. Tocqueville to J. S. Mill, 27 August 1843, *Oeuvres Complètes*, tome 6, vol. 1: 344–45. (Translation by S. J. M.)

51. *Souvenirs* (Paris: Gallimard, 1942), p. 72. (Trans. by S. J. M.) This inevitably puts the modern sociologist in mind of George Homans's famous presidential address to the American Sociological Association, in which he castigated the then current school of functionalism for having precisely similar results. See G. C. Homans, "Bringing Men Back In," *American Sociological Review* 29, no. 6 (1964): 809–18.

52. *Democracy in America*, pt. 2, Preface.

53. *Souvenirs*, p. 72. (Trans. by S. J. M.)

54. Karl Marx, *The Eighteenth Brumaire of Louis Bonaparte*, in *Selected Works of Marx and Engels* (Moscow: Progress Publishers, 1968), p. 97.

55. *Democracy in America*, pt. 2, p. 103.

56. Ibid.

57. This argument has been illuminatingly developed, though apparently without any direct debt to Tocqueville, by Norbert Elias in *What is Sociology?* (New York: Columbia University Press, 1978), chaps. 3 and 6.

58. Weber, *Economy and Society*.

59. *Souvenirs*, p. 43. (Trans. by S. J. M.)

60. It may be the prominence of this problem in Durkheim's work that sensitizes us to its declaration, more *sotto voce*, in Tocqueville's. Yet it is arguable that the earlier author's handling of the issue is more successful than the later's. Durkheim struggled with it as a conceptual problem all his life without ever getting it finally straight in his mind. Tocqueville rightly saw the degree of human freedom of action as varying according to empirical social circumstances. Nor did Tocqueville reify "social facts"; compare his discussion of criminal statistics (pp. 315–19, below) with Durkheim's famous treatment of suicide rates, criticized so effectively by, among others, Jack D. Douglas in his book *The Social Meanings of Suicide* (Princeton, N.J.: Princeton University Press, 1967).

61. *The Old Régime*, p. 122.

62. Ibid., p. 77.

63. For a detailed discussion of the concept, see Morris Janowitz, "Sociological Theory and Social Control," *American Journal of Sociology* 81, no. 1 (1975): 82–108.

64. See Doris S. Goldstein, *Trial of Faith: Religion and Politics in Tocqueville's Thought* (New York: Elsevier, 1975).

65. *The Old Régime*, p. xiii. The passage continues:"Since in such communities nothing is stable, each man is haunted by a fear of sinking to a lower social level, and by a restless urge to better his condition. And since money has not only become the sole criterion of a man's social status but has also acquired an extreme

mobility . . . everybody is feverishly intent on making money, or, if already rich, in keeping his wealth intact.'' A similar idea about money as the sole criterion of social status is an important component of Merton's famous theory of deviant behavior, which is ostensibly derived chiefly from Durkheim's notion of *anomie*. (See R. K. Merton, *Social Theory and Social Structure*, enlarged ed., [New York: Free Press, 1968], pp. 185–214.)

66. Cf. S. Lukes, *Emile Durkheim* (London: Allen Lane, 1973), p. 197.

67. *Democracy in America*, pt. 2, bk. 2, chap. 3.

68. Tocqueville to Gobineau, 30 July 1856, in J. Lukacs, ed., *The European Revolution and Correspondence with Gobineau* (New York: Doubleday, 1959).

69. See below, pp. 104–5, and *The Old Régime*, bk. 2, chap. 5.

70. *Memoir*, 1:144.

71. *Oeuvres Complètes*, ed. Mayer, tome 5, vol. 1: 120–21.

72. *Oeuvres Complètes*, ed. Beaumont, tome 9, p. 443.

73. *Democracy in America*, pt. 1, chap. 18.

74. See especially S. M. Lipset, *Political Man* (New York: Doubleday, 1959).

75. Merton, *Social Theory and Social Structure*, pp. 19–84.

76. W. Kornhauser, *The Politics of Mass Society* (New York: The Free Press, 1959); Salvador Giner, *Mass Society* (London: Martin Robertson, 1976).

77. Curiously enough, Karl Marx is one of Tocqueville's fellow contributors to this tradition of thought. A famous passage in *The Eighteenth Brumaire*, a document which though so different in general political tone describes much the same events as Tocqueville's *Recollections*, deals with the political role of the French peasantry: "The smallholding peasants form a vast mass, the members of which live in similar conditions but without entering into manifold relations with each other. Their mode of production isolates them from one another instead of bringing them into mutual intercourse. The isolation is increased by France's bad means of communication and by the poverty of the peasants. . . . the great mass of the French nation is formed by simple addition of homologous magnitudes, much as potatoes in a sack form a sack of potatoes'' (pp. 171–72). They had interests in common, but their isolation prevented them organizing in their pursuit and defense. Despite this, or rather because of it, Marx argues, Louis Bonaparte was able to exploit them as a political force in the overthrow of the Republic.

78. See below, pp. 222–27; Erich Fromm, *The Fear of Freedom* (London: Kegan Paul, 1942).

79. R. A. Dahl, *Who Governs?* (New Haven: Yale University Press, 1961); Talcott Parsons, "The Distribution of Power in American Society," *World Politics* 10 (1957): 123–43; R. S. and H. M. Lynd, *Middletown* (New York: Harcourt Brace & Co., 1929); C. Wright Mills, *The Power Elite* (New York: Oxford University Press, 1956).

80. *Democracy in America*, pt. 1, chap. 17.

81. Ibid. (footnote later in the same chapter). Compare this with David Riesman's concept of "social character."

82. Here Tocqueville anticipates the argument made famous by Thorstein Veblen in *The Theory of the Leisure Class* (New York: Modern Library, 1934).

83. David Riesman et al., *The Lonely Crowd* (New Haven: Yale University Press, 1950); Norbert Elias, *The Civilising Process*, vol. 1, *The History of Manners*, (New York: Urizen, and Oxford: Basil Blackwell, 1978).

84. Here, and on several occasions when discussing social mobility, Tocqueville anticipates Sombart's famous argument in *Why Is There No Socialism in the*

46   INTRODUCTION

United States? (originally published in 1906) (London: Macmillan, 1976).

85. Over a century later, this same cultural trait—the latent liberal assumption that each individual forms his opinions by independent ratiocination—was the target of stronger critical comment by Herbert Marcuse and other members of the Frankfurt School. Marcuse contended that, on the contrary, individuals are shaped and manipulated "down to their very instincts" by mass media and other powerful social forces. (See, for example, his *One-Dimensional Man* [London: Routledge and Kegan Paul, 1964].) Other members of the school argued that American *sociology* reflected a trait of American *society:* the dominant methodology of opinion-survey research was the counterpart of "one man, one vote." In politics, they contended, that principle has much to commend it, but in sociology it is also relevant to question the empirical truth and logical validity of people's opinions, and to ask whether a particular person's position in the social structure gives his opinions more or less weight than those of others in shaping the course of events. For representative examples of this argument, see F. Pollock, "Empirical Research into Public Opinion," and T. W. Adorno, "Sociology and Empirical Research," both in P. Connerton, ed., *Critical Sociology* (Harmondsworth and New York: Penguin, 1976), pp. 225–57.

86. As Jack Lively puts it: "he wrote in parentheses what was to be the bold type of the next century's history" (*The Social and Political Thought of Alexis de Tocqueville* [Oxford: The Clarendon Press, 1962], p. 217).

1

THE SOCIAL ORIGINS
OF DEMOCRACY

THE DEMOCRATIC CHARACTER
OF ANGLO-AMERICAN SOCIETY

The social condition of the Americans is eminently democratic; this was its character at the foundation of the Colonies, and is still more strongly marked at the present day. . . . Great equality existed among the emigrants who settled on the shores of New England. (The germ of aristocracy was never planted in that part of the Union. The only influence which obtained there was that of intellect; the people were accustomed to revering certain names as symbols of knowledge and virtue. Some of their fellow-citizens acquired a power over the rest which might truly have been called aristocratic, if it had been capable of transmission from father to son.

This was the state of things to the east of the Hudson: to the south-west of that river, and in the direction of the Floridas, the case was different. In most of the States situated to the south-west of the Hudson some great English proprietors had settled, who had imported with them aristocratic principles and the English law of descent. I have explained the reasons why it was impossible ever to establish a powerful aristocracy in America; these reasons existed with less force to the south-west of the Hudson. In the South, one man, aided by slaves, could cultivate a great extent of the country: it was therefore common to see rich

From *Democracy in America*, pt. 1, chap. 3.

47

landed proprietors. But their influence was not altogether aristocratic as that term is understood in Europe, since they possessed
no privileges; and the cultivation of their estates being carried on
by slaves, they had no tenants depending on them, and consequently no patronage. Still, the great proprietors south of the
Hudson constituted a superior class, having ideas and tastes of its
own, and forming the centre of political action. This kind of aristocracy sympathized with the body of the people, whose passions
and interests it easily embraced; but it was too weak and too
short-lived to excite either love or hatred for itself. This was the
class which headed the insurrection in the South, and furnished
the best leaders of the American revolution.

At the period of which we are now speaking society was shaken
to its centre: the people, in whose name the struggle had taken
place, conceived the desire of exercising the authority which it
had acquired; its democratic tendencies were awakened; and
having thrown off the yoke of the mother-country, it aspired to
independence of every kind. The influence of individuals gradually ceased to be felt, and custom and law united together to
produce the same result.

But the law of descent was the last step to equality. I am surprised that ancient and modern jurists have not attributed to this
law a greater influence on human affairs. It is true that these laws
belong to civil affairs; but they ought nevertheless to be placed at
the head of all political institutions; for, whilst political laws are
only the symbol of a nation's condition, they exercise an incredible influence upon its social state. They have, moreover, a
sure and uniform manner of operating upon society, affecting, as
it were, generations yet unborn.

Through their means man acquires a kind of preternatural
power over the future lot of his fellow-creatures. When the legislator has regulated the law of inheritance, he may rest from his
labour. The machine once put in motion will go on for ages, and
advance, as if self-guided, towards a given point. When framed in
a particular manner, this law unites, draws together, and vests
property and power in a few hands: its tendency is clearly aristocratic. On opposite principles its action is still more rapid; it divides, distributes, and disperses both property and power.

Alarmed by the rapidity of its progress, those who despair of arresting its motion endeavour to obstruct it by difficulties and impediments; they vainly seek to counteract its effect by contrary efforts: but it gradually reduces or destroys every obstacle, until by its incessant activity the bulwarks of the influence of wealth are ground down to the fine and shifting sand which is the basis of democracy. When the law of inheritance permits, still more when it decrees, the equal division of a father's property amongst all his children, its effects are of two kinds: it is important to distinguish them from each other, although they tend to the same end.

In virtue of the law of partible inheritance, the death of every proprietor brings about a kind of revolution in property; not only do his possessions change hands, but their very nature is altered, since they are parcelled into shares, which become smaller and smaller at each division. This is the direct and, as it were, the physical effect of the law. It follows, then, that in countries where equality of inheritance is established by law, property, and especially landed property, must have a tendency to perpetual diminution. The effects, however, of such legislation would only be perceptible after a lapse of time, if the law was abandoned to its own working; for supposing the family to consist of two children, (and in a country peopled as France is, the average number is not above three,) these children, sharing amongst them the fortune of both parents, would not be poorer than their father or mother.

But the law of equal division exercises its influence not merely upon the property itself, but it affects the minds of the heirs, and brings their passions into play. These indirect consequences tend powerfully to the destruction of large fortunes, and especially of large domains.

Among nations whose law of descent is founded upon the right of primogeniture, landed estates often pass from generation to generation without undergoing division. The consequence of which is that family feeling is to a certain degree incorporated with the estate. The family represents the estate, the estate the family; whose name, together with its origin, its glory, its power, and its virtues, is thus perpetuated in an imperishable memorial of the past, and a sure pledge of the future. . . .

Most certainly it is not for us Frenchmen of the nineteenth

century, who daily witness the political and social changes which the law of partition is bringing to pass, to question its influence. It is perpetually conspicuous in our country, overthrowing the walls of our dwellings and removing the landmarks of our fields. But although it has produced great effects in France, much still remains for it to do. Our recollections, opinions, and habits, present powerful obstacles to its progress.

In the United States it has nearly completed its work of destruction, and there we can best study its results. The English laws concerning the transmission of property were abolished in almost all the States at the time of the Revolution. The law of entail was so modified as not to interrupt the free circulation of property. The first generation having passed away, estates began to be parcelled out; and the change became more and more rapid with the progress of time. At this moment, after a lapse of a little more than sixty years, the aspect of society is totally altered; the families of the great landed proprietors are almost all commingled with the general mass. In the State of New York, which formerly contained many of these, there are but two who still keep their heads above the stream; and they must shortly disappear. The sons of these opulent citizens have become merchants, lawyers, or physicians. Most of them have lapsed into obscurity. The last trace of hereditary ranks and distinctions is destroyed—the law of partition has reduced all to one level.

I do not mean that there is any deficiency of wealthy individuals in the United States; I know of no country, indeed, where the love of money has taken stronger hold on the affections of men, and where a profounder contempt is expressed for the theory of the permanent equality of property. But wealth circulates with inconceivable rapidity, and experience shows that it is rare to find two succeeding generations in the full enjoyment of it. . . .

It is not only the fortunes of men which are equal in America; even their acquirements partake in some degree of the same uniformity. I do not believe that there is a country in the world where, in proportion to the population, there are so few uninstructed, and at the same time so few learned individuals. Primary instruction is within the reach of everybody; superior instruc-

tion is scarcely to be obtained by any. This is not surprising; it is
in fact the necessary consequence of what we have advanced
above. Almost all the Americans are in easy circumstances, and
can therefore obtain the first elements of human knowledge.
In America there are comparatively few who are rich enough to
live without a profession. Every profession requires an appren-
ticeship, which limits the time of instruction to the early years of
life. At fifteen they enter upon their calling, and thus their education ends at the age when ours begins. Whatever is done afterwards, is with a view to some special and lucrative object; a
science is taken up as a matter of business, and the only branch of
it which is attended to is such as admits of an immediate practical
application.

In America most of the rich men were formerly poor; most of
those who now enjoy leisure were absorbed in business during
their youth; the consequence of which is, that when they might
have had a taste for study, they had no time for it, and when the
time is at their disposal they no longer have the inclination.

There is no class, then, in America, in which the taste for
intellectual pleasures is transmitted with hereditary fortune and
leisure, and by which the labours of the intellect are held in honour. Accordingly there is an equal want of the desire and the
power of application to these objects.

A middling standard is fixed in America for human knowledge.
All approach as near to it as they can; some as they rise, others as
they descend. Of course, an immense multitude of persons are to
be found who entertain the same number of ideas on religion,
history, science, political economy, legislation, and government.
The gifts of intellect proceed directly from God, and man cannot
prevent their unequal distribution. But in consequence of the
state of things which we have here represented, it happens, that
although the capacities of men are widely different, as the Creator
has doubtless intended they should be, they are submitted to the
same method of treatment.

In America the aristocratic element has always been feeble
from its birth; and if at the present day it has not actually been
destroyed, it is at any rate so completely disabled that we can

scarcely assign to it any degree of influence in the course of affairs.

The democratic principle, on the contrary, has gained so much strength by time, by events, and by legislation, as to have become not only predominant but all-powerful. There is no family or corporate authority, and it is rare to find even the influence of individual character enjoy any durability.

America, then, exhibits in her social state a most extraordinary phenomenon. Men are there seen on a greater equality in point of fortune and intellect, or, in other words, more equal in their strength, than in any other country of the world, or in any age of which history has preserved the remembrance . . . .

It is impossible to believe that equality will not eventually find its way into the political world as it does everywhere else. To conceive of men remaining for ever unequal upon one single point, yet equal on all others, is impossible; they must come in the end to be equal upon all.

Now I know of only two methods of establishing equality in the political world; every citizen must be put in possession of his rights, or rights must be granted to no one. For nations which arrived at the same stage of social existence as the Anglo-Americans, it is therefore very difficult to discover a medium between the sovereignty of all and the absolute power of one man: and it would be vain to deny that the social condition which I have been describing is equally liable to each of these consequences.

There is, in fact, a manly and lawful passion for equality which excites men to wish all to be powerful and honoured. This passion tends to elevate the humble to the rank of the great; but there exists also in the human heart a depraved taste for equality, which impels the weak to attempt to lower the powerful to their own level, and reduces men to prefer equality in slavery to inequality with freedom. Not that those nations whose social condition is democratic naturally despise liberty; on the contrary, they have an instinctive love of it. But liberty is not the chief and constant object of their desires; equality is their idol: they make rapid and sudden efforts to obtain liberty; and if they miss their aim, resign themselves to their disappointment; but nothing can satisfy them except equality, and rather than lose it they resolve to perish.

On the other hand, in a State where the citizens are nearly equal, it becomes difficult for them to preserve their independence against the aggressions of power. No one among them being strong enough to engage in the struggle with advantage, nothing but a general combination can protect their liberty. And such a union is not always to be found.

From the same social position, then, nations may derive one or the other of two great political results; these results are extremely different from each other, but they may both proceed from the same cause.

The Anglo-Americans are the first nation who, having faced this formidable alternative, have been happy enough to escape the dominion of absolute power. They have been allowed by their circumstances, their origin, their intelligence, and especially by their moral feeling, to establish and maintain the sovereignty of the people.

THE AMERICAN SYSTEM OF TOWNSHIPS

The local community must necessarily exist in all nations, whatever their laws and customs may be: if man makes monarchies, and establishes republics, the first association of mankind seems constituted by the hand of God. But although the existence of the local community is coeval with that of man, its liberties are not the less rarely respected and easily destroyed. A nation is always able to establish great political assemblies, because it habitually contains a certain number of individuals fitted by their talents, if not by their habits, for the direction of affairs. The township is, on the contrary, composed of coarser materials, which are less easily fashioned by the legislator. The difficulties which attend the consolidation of its independence rather augment than diminish with the increasing enlightenment of the people. A highly civilized society spurns the experiment of local independence, is disgusted

From *Democracy in America,* pt. 1, chap. 5.

at its numerous blunders, and is apt to despair of success before the experiment is completed. Again, no immunities are so ill protected from the encroachments of the central power as those of municipal bodies in general: they are unable to struggle, single-handed, against a strong or an enterprising government, and they cannot defend their cause with success unless it be identified with the customs of the nation and supported by public opinion. Thus until the independence of townships become part of the customs of a people, it is easily destroyed; and it is only after a long existence in the laws that it can enter popular beliefs. Municipal freedom is not the fruit of human device; it is rarely created; but it is, as it were, secretly and spontaneously engendered in the midst of a semi-barbarous state of society. The constant action of the laws and national habits, peculiar circumstances, and above all time, may consolidate it; but there is certainly no nation on the continent of Europe which has experienced its advantages. Nevertheless local assemblies of citizens constitute the strength of free nations. Town-meetings are to liberty what primary schools are to science; they bring it within the people's reach, they teach men how to use and how to enjoy it. A nation may establish a system of free government, but without the spirit of municipal institutions it cannot have the spirit of liberty. The transient passions and the interests of an hour, or the chance of circumstances, may have created the external forms of independence; but the despotic tendency which has been repelled will, sooner or later, inevitably reappear on the surface....

The township and the county are not organized in the same manner in every part of the Union; it is however easy to perceive that the same principles have guided the formation of both of them throughout the Union. I am inclined to believe that these principles have been carried further in New England than elsewhere, and consequently that they offer greater facilities to the observations of a stranger.

The institutions of New England form a complete and regular whole; they have received the sanction of time, they have the support of the laws, and the still stronger support of the manners of the community, over which they exercise the most prodigious influence; they consequently deserve our attention on every account.

The Township of New England is a division which stands between the *commune* and the *canton* of France. Its average population is from two to three thousand. So, on the one hand, the interests of its inhabitants are not likely to conflict, and, on the other, men capable of conducting its affairs are always to be found among its citizens.

In the township, as well as everywhere else, the people is the only source of power; but in no stage of government does the body of citizens exercise a more immediate influence. In America, the people is a master whose exigencies demand obedience to the utmost limits of possibility.

In New England the majority acts by representatives in the conduct of the public business of the State; but if such an arrangement be necessary in general affairs, in the townships, where the legislative and administrative action of the government is in more immediate contact with the subject, the system of representation is not adopted. There is no corporation; but the body of electors, after having designated its magistrates, directs them in everything that exceeds the pure and simple execution of the laws of the State. . . .

I have already observed, that the principle of the sovereignty of the people governs the whole political system of the Anglo-Americans. . . . In nations which recognize the sovereignty of the people, every individual possesses an equal share of power, and participates alike in the government of the State. Every individual is, therefore, supposed to be as well informed, as virtuous, and as strong as any of his fellow-citizens. He obeys the government, not because he is inferior to the authorities which conduct it, or that he is less capable than his neighbour of governing himself, but because he acknowledges the utility of an association with his fellow-men, and because he knows that no such association can exist without a regulating force. If he be a subject in all that concerns the mutual relations of citizens, he is free and responsible to God alone for all that concerns himself. Hence arises the maxim that every one is the best and the sole judge of his own private interest, and that society has no right to control a man's actions, unless they are prejudicial to the common interest, or unless the common interest demands his co-operation. This doctrine is universally admitted in the United States. Later I shall examine the general influence which it exercises on the ordinary actions of life: I am now speaking of the nature of municipal bodies.

The township, taken as a whole, and in relation to the government of the country, may be looked upon as an individual to whom the theory I have just alluded to is applied. Municipal independence is therefore a natural consequence of the principle of the sovereignty of the people in the United States: all the American republics recognize it more or less, but circumstances have peculiarly favoured its growth in New England.

In this part of the Union political activity originated in the townships; and it may almost be said that each of them originally formed an independent nation. When the kings of England asserted their supremacy, they were contented to assume the central power of the State. The townships of New England remained as they were before; and although they are now subject to the State, they were at first scarcely dependent upon it. It is important to remember that they have not been invested with privileges, but that they have, on the contrary, forfeited a portion of their independence to the State. The townships are only subordinate to the State in those interests which I shall term *social,* as they are common to all the citizens. They are independent in all that concerns themselves; and amongst the inhabitants of New England I believe that not a single man is to be found who would acknowledge that the State has any right to interfere in their local interests. The towns of New England buy and sell, prosecute or are indicted, augment or diminish their rates, without the slightest opposition on the part of the administrative authority of the State.

They are bound, however, to comply with the demands of the community. If the State is in need of money, a town can neither give nor withhold its concurrence. If the State projects a road, the township cannot refuse to let it cross its territory; if a police regulation is made by the State, it must be enforced by the town. A uniform system of instruction is organized all over the country, and every town is bound to establish the schools which the law ordains. In speaking of the administration of the United States, I shall have occasion to point out the means by which the townships are compelled to obey in these different cases: I here

merely show the existence of the obligation. Strict as this obligation is, the government of the State imposes it in principle only,
and in its performance the township resumes all its independent
rights. Thus, taxes are voted by the State, but they are levied and
collected by the township; the existence of a school is obligatory,
but the township builds, pays, and superintends it. In France the
State tax collector gathers the municipal taxes; in America the
town-collector receives the taxes of the State. Thus the French
Government lends its agents to the *commune;* in America, the
township is the agent of the Government. This fact alone shows
the extent of the differences which exist between the two nations.

In America, not only do municipal bodies exist, but they are
kept alive and supported, by public spirit. The township of New
England possesses two advantages which infallibly secure the
attentive interest of mankind, namely, independence and authority. Its sphere is indeed small and limited, but within that sphere
its action is unrestrained; and its independence gives to it a real
importance, which its extent and population may not always
ensure.

It is to be remembered that the affections of men generally lie
on the side of authority. Patriotism is not durable in a conquered
nation. The New Englander is attached to his township, not only
because he was born in it, but because it constitutes a social body
of which he is a member, and whose government claims and
deserves his concern. In Europe the absence of local public spirit
is a frequent subject of regret to those who are in power; everyone agrees that there is no surer guarantee of order and tranquillity, and yet nothing is more difficult to create. If the municipal
bodies were made powerful and independent, the authorities of
the nation might be disunited, and the peace of the country endangered. Yet, without power and independence, a town may
contain good subjects, but it can have no active citizens. Another
important fact is that the township of New England is so constituted as to excite the warmest of human affections, without
arousing the ambitious passions of the heart of man. The officers
of the county are not elected, and their authority is very limited.
Even the State is only a second-rate community, whose tranquil
and obscure administration offers no inducement sufficient to

draw men away from the circle of their interests into the turmoil of public affairs. The federal government confers power and honour on the men who conduct it; but these individuals can never be very numerous. The high station of the Presidency can only be reached at an advanced period of life; and the other federal functionaries are generally men who have been favoured by fortune, or distinguished in some other career. Such cannot be the permanent aim of the ambitious. But the township serves as a centre for the desire of public esteem, the want of exciting interests, and the taste for authority and popularity, in the midst of the ordinary relations of life; and the passions which commonly embroil society, change their character when they find a vent so near the domestic hearth and the family circle.

In the American States power has been disseminated with admirable skill, for the purpose of interesting the greatest possible number of persons in the common weal. Independently of the electors who are from time to time called into action, the body politic is divided into innumerable functionaries and officers, who all, in their several spheres, represent the same powerful whole in whose name they act. The local administration thus affords an unfailing source of profit and interest to a vast number of individuals.

The American system, which divides authority in the local community among so many citizens, does not scruple to multiply the functions of the town officers. For in the United States it is believed, and with truth, that patriotism is a kind of devotion which is strengthened by ritual observance. In this manner the activity of the township is continually perceptible; it is daily manifested in the fulfilment of a duty, or the exercise of a right; and a constant though gentle motion is thus kept up in society, which animates without disturbing it.

The American attaches himself to his home, as the mountaineer clings to his hills, because the characteristic features of his country are there more distinctly marked than elsewhere. The existence of the townships of New England is in general a happy one. Their government is suited to their tastes, and chosen by themselves. In the midst of the profound peace and general comfort which reign in America, the commotions of municipal discord are infrequent. The conduct of local business is easy. The political education of the people has long been complete; say rather that it was complete when the people first set foot upon the soil. In New England no tradition exists of a distinction of ranks; no portion of the community is tempted to oppress the remainder; and the abuses which may injure isolated individuals are forgotten in the general contentment which prevails. If the government is defective, (and it would no doubt be easy to point out its deficiencies), the fact that it really emanates from those it governs, and that it acts, either ill or well, casts the protecting spell of a parental pride over its faults. No term of comparison disturbs the satisfaction of the citizen: England formerly governed the mass of the colonies, but the people was always sovereign in the township, where its rule is not only an ancient, but a primitive state.

The native of New England is attached to his township because it is independent and free: his co-operation in its affairs ensures his attachment to its interest; the well-being it affords him secures his affection; and its welfare is the aim of his ambition and of his future exertions: he takes a part in every occurrence in the place; he practises the art of government in the small sphere within his reach; he accustoms himself to those forms which can alone ensure the steady progress of liberty; he imbibes their spirit; he acquires a taste for order, comprehends the union or the balance of powers, and collects clear practical notions on the nature of his duties and the extent of his rights.

POLITICAL EFFECTS OF ADMINISTRATIVE
DECENTRALIZATION IN THE UNITED STATES

Centralization has become a word of general and daily use, without any precise meaning being attached to it. Nevertheless, there exist two distinct kinds of centralization, which it is necessary to discriminate with accuracy.

Certain interests are common to all parts of a nation, such as the enactment of its general laws, and the maintenance of its

From *Democracy in America*, pt. 1, chap. 5.

foreign relations. Other interests are peculiar to certain parts of the nation; such, for instance, as the business of different townships. When the power which directs the general interests is centred in one place, or vested in the same persons, it constitutes a *central government*. In like manner the power of directing partial or local interests, when brought together into one place, constitutes what may be termed a *central administration*.

On some points these two kinds of centralization coalesce; but by classifying the objects which fall more particularly within the province of each of them, they may be easily distinguished.

It is evident that a central government acquires immense power when united to administrative centralization. Thus combined, it accustoms men to set their own will habitually and completely aside; to submit, not only for once, or upon one point, but in every respect, and at all times. Not only, therefore, does this union of power subdue them compulsorily, but it affects them in the ordinary habits of life, and influences each individual, first separately and then collectively.

These two kinds of centralization mutually assist and attract each other; but they must not be supposed to be inseparable. It is impossible to imagine a more completely central *government* than that which existed in France under Louis XIV, when the same individual was the author and the interpreter of the laws, and the representative of France at home and abroad. "L'Etat, c'est moi," he said, and he was right. Nevertheless, the *administration* was much less centralized under Louis XIV than it is at the present day.

In England the centralization of the government is carried to great perfection; the State has the compact vigour of a man, and by the sole act of its will it puts immense engines in motion, and wields or collects the efforts of its authority. Indeed, I cannot conceive that a nation can enjoy a secure or prosperous existence without a powerful centralization of government. But I am of opinion that a central administration enervates the nations in which it exists by incessantly diminishing their public spirit. If such an administration succeeds in condensing at a given moment, on a given point, all the disposable resources of a people, it impairs at least the renewal of those resources. It may insure a victory in the hour of strife, but it gradually relaxes the sinews of strength. It may contribute admirably to the transient greatness of a man, but it cannot insure the enduring prosperity of a nation. . . . Administrative decentralisation produces several different effects in America. The Americans seem to me to have outstepped the limits of sound policy, in isolating the administration of the Government; for order, even in second-rate affairs, is a matter of national importance. As the State has no administrative functionaries of its own, stationed on different points of its territory, to whom it can give a common direction, the consequence is that it rarely attempts to issue any general police regulations. The want of these regulations is severely felt, and is frequently observed by Europeans. The appearance of disorder which prevails on the surface leads him at first to imagine that society is in a state of anarchy; nor does he perceive his mistake till he has gone deeper into the subject. Certain undertakings are of importance to the whole State; but they cannot be put in execution, because there is no national administration to direct them. Abandoned to the exertions of the towns or counties, under the care of elected or temporary agents, they lead to no result, or at least to no enduring benefit.

The partisans of centralization in Europe are wont to maintain that the Government directs the affairs of each locality better than the citizens could do it for themselves: this may be true when the central power is enlightened, and when the local districts are ignorant; when it is as alert as they are slow; when it is accustomed to act, and they to obey. Indeed, it is evident that this double tendency must augment with the increase of centralization, and that the readiness of the one, and the incapacity of the others, must become more and more prominent. But I deny that such is the case when the people is as enlightened, as awake to its interests, and as accustomed to reflect on them, as the Americans are. I am persuaded, on the contrary, that in this case the collective strength of the citizens will always conduce more efficaciously to the public welfare than the authority of the Government. It is difficult to point out with certainty the means of arousing a sleeping population, and of giving it passions and knowledge which it does not possess; it is, I am well aware, an arduous task to persuade men to busy themselves about their own affairs; and it would frequently be easier to interest them in the punctilios of court etiquette than in the repairs of their common dwelling. But whenever a central administration affects to supersede the persons most interested, I am inclined to suppose that it is either misled, or wants to mislead. However enlightened and however skilful a central power may be, it cannot of itself embrace all the details of the existence of a great nation. Such vigilance exceeds the powers of man. And when it attempts to create and set in motion so many complicated mechanisms, it must content itself with a very imperfect result, or exhaust itself in fruitless efforts.

Centralization succeeds more easily, indeed, in subjecting the external actions of men to a certain uniformity, which at last commands our regard, independently of the objects to which it is applied, like those devotees who worship the statue, and forget the deity it represents. Centralization imparts without difficulty an admirable regularity to the routine of business; provides wisely for the details of police regulations; represses the smallest disorder and the most petty misdemeanours; maintains society in a *status quo* secure alike from improvement and decline; and perpetuates a drowsy precision in the conduct of affairs, which is hailed by the heads of the administration as a sign of perfect order and public tranquillity: in short, it excels more in prevention than in action. Its strength deserts it when society is to be disturbed or rapid changes made; and if once the co-operation of private citizens is necessary to the furtherance of its measures, the secret of its impotence is disclosed. Even whilst it invokes their assistance, it is on the condition that they shall act exactly as much as the Government chooses, and exactly in the manner it appoints. They are to take charge of the details, without aspiring to guide the system; they are to work in a dark and subordinate sphere, and only to judge the acts in which they have themselves cooperated, by their results. These, however, are not the conditions on which men's willing co-operation is to be obtained. They must be free to go at their own pace and be responsible for their actions. Such is human nature that the citizen would rather remain a passive spectator than march in a well-drilled column towards a goal which he knows nothing about. . . .

It is not the *administrative*, but the *political* effects of decentralisation that I most admire in America. In the United States the interests of the country are everywhere kept in view; they are an object of solicitude to the people of the whole Union, and every citizen is as warmly attached to them as if they were his own. He takes pride in the glory of his nation; he boasts of its success, to which he conceives himself to have contributed; and he rejoices in the general prosperity by which he profits. The feeling he entertains towards the State is analogous to that which unites him to his family, and it is by a kind of egotism that he interests himself in the welfare of his country.

The European generally submits to a public officer because he represents a superior force; but to an American he represents a right. In America it may be said that no one renders obedience to man, but to justice and to law. If the opinion which the citizen entertains of himself is exaggerated, it is at least salutary; he unhesitatingly has confidence in his own powers, which appear to him to be all-sufficient. When a private individual meditates an undertaking, however directly connected it may be with the welfare of society, he never thinks of soliciting the co-operation of the Government; but he publishes his plan, offers to execute it himself, courts the assistance of other individuals, and struggles manfully against all obstacles. Undoubtedly he is often less successful than the State might have been in his position; but in the end, the sum of these private undertakings far exceeds all that the Government could have done.

As the administrative authority is within the reach of the citizens, whom it in some degree represents, it excites neither their jealousy nor their hatred. As its resources are limited, everyone feels that he must not rely solely on its assistance. Thus when the administration thinks fit to interfere, it is not abandoned to itself as in Europe. The duties of the private citizens are not supposed to have lapsed because the State assists in their fulfilment; everyone is ready, on the contrary, to guide and to support it. This action of individual exertions, joined to that of the public authorities, frequently performs what the most energetic central administration would be unable to execute. It would be easy to adduce several facts in proof of what I advance, but I would rather give only one, with which I am more thoroughly acquainted. In America, the means which the authorities have at their disposal for the discovery of crimes and the arrest of criminals are few. A political police does not exist, and passports are unknown. The criminal police of the United States cannot be compared to that of France; the magistrates and public prosecutors are not numerous, and the examinations of prisoners are rapid and oral. Nevertheless in no country does crime more rarely elude punishment. The reason is that everyone conceives himself to be interested in furnishing evidence of the act committed, and in stopping the delinquent. During my stay in the United States, I witnessed the spontaneous formation of committees for the pursuit and prosecution of a man who had committed a great crime in a certain county. In Europe a criminal is an unhappy being who is struggling for his life against ministers of justice, whilst the population is merely a spectator of the conflict: in America he is looked upon as an enemy of the human race, and the whole of mankind is against him.

I believe that provincial institutions are useful to all nations, but nowhere do they appear to me to be more indispensable than amongst a democratic people. In an aristocracy, order can always be maintained in the midst of liberty; and as the rulers have a great deal to lose, order is to them a first-rate consideration. In like manner an aristocracy protects the people from the excesses of despotism, because it always possesses an organized power ready to resist a despot. But a democracy without provincial institutions has no security against these evils. How can a populace, unaccustomed to freedom in small concerns, learn to use it temperately in great affairs? What resistance can be offered to tyranny in a country where every private individual is impotent, and where the citizens are united by no common tie? Those who dread the licence of the mob, and those who fear the rule of absolute power, ought alike to desire the progressive growth of provincial liberties.

On the other hand, I am convinced that democratic nations are most exposed to fall beneath the yoke of a central administration, for several reasons, amongst which is the following.

The constant tendency of these nations is to concentrate all the strength of the Government in the hands of the only power which directly represents the people; because, beyond the people nothing is to be perceived but equal individuals thrown together in a common mass. But when the same power is already in possession of all the attributes of the Government, it can scarcely refrain from penetrating into the details of the administration, and an opportunity of doing so is sure to present itself in the end, as was the case in France. In the French Revolution there were two impulses in opposite directions, which must never be confused; the one was favourable to liberty, the other to despotism. Under the former monarchy the King was the sole author of the laws. Below the power of the Sovereign, certain vestiges of provincial institutions, half-destroyed, were still distinguishable. These provincial institutions were incoherent, ill compacted, and frequently absurd; in the hands of the aristocracy they had sometimes been converted into instruments of oppression. The Revolution declared itself the enemy of royalty and of provincial institutions at the same time. It confounded all that had preceded it—despotic power and the checks to its abuses—in indiscriminate hatred; its tendency was simultaneously to overthrow and to centralize. This double character of the French Revolution is a fact which has been adroitly handled by the friends of absolute power. Can they be accused of labouring in the cause of despotism, when they are defending that central administration which was one of the great innovations of the Revolution? In this manner popularity may be reconciled with hostility to the rights of the people, and the secret slave of tyranny may be the professed admirer of freedom.

I have visited the two nations in which the system of provincial liberty has been most perfectly established, and I have listened to the opinions of different parties in those countries. In America I met with men who secretly aspired to destroy the democratic institutions of the Union; in England I found others who attacked the aristocracy openly. But I know of no one who does not regard provincial independence as a great benefit. In both countries I have heard a thousand different causes assigned for the evils of the State; but administrative decentralisation was never mentioned amongst them. I have heard citizens attribute the power and prosperity of their country to a multitude of reasons;

but they *all* placed the advantages of local institutions in the foremost rank.

Am I to suppose that when men who are naturally so divided on religious opinions, and on political theories, agree on one point (and one of which they have daily experience), they are all in error? The only nations which deny the utility of provincial liberties are those which have fewest of them; in other words, those who are unacquainted with the institution are the only persons who pass censure upon it.

THE DISTINCTIVENESS OF THE AMERICAN FEDERAL CONSTITUTION

The United States of America do not afford either the first or the only instance of confederate States, several of which have existed in modern Europe, not to mention those of antiquity. Switzerland, the Germanic Empire, and the Republic of the United Provinces either have been or still are confederations. In studying the constitutions of these different countries, one is surprised to observe that the powers with which they invested the Federal Government are nearly identical with the privileges awarded by the American Constitution to the Government of the United States. They confer upon the central power the same rights of making peace and war, of raising money and troops, and of providing for the general exigencies and the common interests of the nation. Nevertheless the Federal Government of these different peoples has always been as remarkable for its weakness and inefficiency as that of the Union is for its vigorous and enterprising spirit. Again, the first American Confederation perished through the excessive weakness of its Government; and this weak Government was, notwithstanding, in possession of rights even more extensive than those of the Federal Government of the present day. But the more recent Constitution of the United States contains certain principles which exercise a most important influence, although they do not at once strike the observer.

From *Democracy in America,* pt. 1, chap. 8.

This Constitution, which may at first sight be confounded with the federal constitutions which preceded it, rests upon a novel theory, which may be considered as a great invention in modern political science. In all the confederations which had been formed before the American Constitution of 1789, the allied States agreed to obey the injunctions of a Federal Government;|but they reserved to themselves the right of ordaining and enforcing the execution of the laws of the Union. The American States which combined in 1789 agreed that the Federal Government should not only dictate the laws, but that it should execute its own enactments.| In both cases the right is the same, but the exercise of the right is different, and this alteration produced the most momentous consequences.

In all the confederations which had been formed before the American Union, the Federal Government demanded its supplies at the hands of the separate Governments; and if the measure it prescribed was onerous to any one of those bodies, means were found to evade its claims. If the State was powerful, it had recourse to arms; if it was weak, it connived at the resistance which the law of the Union, its sovereign, met with, and resorted to inaction under the plea of inability. Under these circumstances one of two alternatives has invariably occurred: either the most preponderant of the allied peoples has assumed the privileges of the Federal authority, and ruled all the other States in its name; or the Federal Government has been abandoned by its natural supporters, anarchy has arisen between the confederates, and the Union has lost all powers of action.

|In America, the subjects of the Union are not States, but private citizens: the national Government levies a tax, not upon the State of Massachusetts, but upon each inhabitant of Massachusetts. All former confederate governments presided over communities, but that of the Union rules individuals.|Its power is not borrowed, but self-derived. It is served by its own civil and military officers, by its own army, and its own courts of justice. It cannot be doubted that the spirit of the nation, the passions of the multitude, and the provincial prejudices of each State, tend singularly to diminish the authority of a Federal power thus constituted, and to facilitate the means of resistance to its

mandates; but the comparative weakness of a restricted sovereignty is an evil inherent in the Federal system. In America, each State has fewer opportunities of resistance, and fewer temptations to non-compliance: nor can such a design be put in execution (if indeed it be entertained) without an open violation of the laws of the Union, a direct interruption of the ordinary course of justice, and a bold declaration of revolt; in a word, without taking a decisive step which men hesitate to adopt.

In all former confederations, the privileges of the Union furnished more elements of discord than of power, since they multiplied the claims of the nation without augmenting the means of enforcing them: and in accordance with this fact it may be remarked, that the real weakness of federal governments has almost always been in exact proportion to their nominal power. Such is not the case in the American Union, in which, as in ordinary governments, the Federal Government has the means of enforcing all it is empowered to demand.

The human understanding more easily invents new things than new words, and we are thence constrained to employ a multitude of improper and inadequate expressions. When several nations form a permanent league, and establish a supreme authority, which, although it has not the same influence over the members of the community as a national government, acts upon each of the confederate States in a body, this government, which is so essentially different from all others, is called a Federal one. Another form of society is afterwards discovered, in which several peoples are fused into one and the same nation with regard to certain common interests, although they remain distinct, or at least only confederate, with regard to all their other concerns. In this case the central power acts directly upon those whom it governs, whom it rules, and whom it judges, in the same manner as, but in a more limited circle than, a national government. Here the term of Federal government is clearly no longer applicable to a state of things which must be styled an incomplete national government: a form of government has been found out which is neither exactly national nor federal; but no further progress has been made, and the new word which will one day designate this novel invention does not yet exist.

The absence of this new species of confederation has been the cause which has brought all Unions to a civil war, to subjection, or to a stagnant apathy; and the peoples which formed these leagues have been either too dull to discern, or too pusillanimous to apply, this great remedy. The American Confederation perished by the same defects.

But the confederate States of America had long formed parts of one empire before they had won their independence; they had not been used to completely governing themselves, and their national prejudices had not taken deep root in their minds. Superior to the rest of the world in political knowledge, and sharing that knowledge equally amongst themselves, they were little agitated by the passions which generally oppose the extension of federal authority in a nation, and those passions were checked by the wisdom of the chief citizens. The Americans applied the remedy with prudent firmness as soon as they were conscious of the evil; they amended their laws, and they saved their country. . . .

I have shown the advantages which the Americans derive from their Federal system; it remains for me to point out the circumstances which rendered that system practicable, as its benefits are not to be enjoyed by all nations. The incidental defects of the Federal system which originate in the laws may be corrected by the skill of the legislator, but there are further evils inherent in the system which cannot be counteracted by the peoples which adopt it. These nations must therefore find the strength necessary to support the natural imperfections of their Government.

The most prominent evil of all Federal systems is the very complex nature of the means they employ. Two sovereignties necessarily co-exist. The legislator may simplify and equalize the action of these two sovereignties, by limiting each of them to a sphere of authority accurately defined; but he cannot combine them into one, or prevent them from coming into collision at certain points. The Federal system therefore rests upon a theory which is necessarily complicated, and which demands the daily exercise of a considerable share of discretion on the part of those it governs.

A proposition must be plain to be understood by people. A false notion which is clear and precise will always meet with a greater number of adherents in the world than a true principle which is obscure or involved. Hence it arises that parties, which are like small communities in the heart of the nation, invariably adopt some principle or some name as a symbol, which very inadequately represents the end they have in view and the means which are at their disposal, but without which they could neither act nor subsist. Governments which are founded upon a single principle or a single feeling which is easily defined, are perhaps not the best, but they are unquestionably the strongest and the most durable in the world.

In examining the Constitution of the United States, which is the most perfect Federal Constitution that ever existed, one is startled, on the other hand, at the variety of information and the excellence of discretion which it presupposes in the people whom it is meant to govern. The Government of the Union depends entirely upon legal fictions; the Union is an ideal nation which only exists in the mind, and whose limits and extent can only be discerned by the understanding.

When once the general theory is comprehended, numberless difficulties remain to be solved in its application; for the sovereignty of the Union is so involved in that of the States, that it is impossible to distinguish its boundaries at the first glance. The whole structure of the Government is contrived and based on convention. It would be ill adapted to a people which has not been long accustomed to conduct its own affairs, or to one in which political awareness has not permeated to the humblest classes of society. I have never been more struck by the good sense and the practical judgment of the Americans than in the ingenious devices by which they elude the numberless difficulties resulting from their Federal Constitution. I scarcely ever met with a plain American citizen who could not distinguish, with surprising facility, the obligations created by the laws of Congress from those created by the laws of his own State; and who, after having discriminated between the matters which come under the cognizance of the Union, and those which the local legislature is competent to regulate, could not point out the exact limit of the several jurisdictions of the Federal Courts and the tribunals of the State.

The Constitution of the United States is like those exquisite productions of human industry which ensure wealth and renown to their inventors, but which are profitless in any other hands. This truth is exemplified by the condition of Mexico at the present time. The Mexicans wanted to establish a Federal system, and they took the Federal Constitution of their neighbours the Anglo-Americans as their model, and copied it with considerable accuracy. But although they had borrowed the letter of the law, they were unable to create or to introduce the spirit and the sense which gave it life. They were involved in ceaseless embarrassments between the working parts of their double Government; the sovereignty of the States and that of the Union perpetually exceeded their respective privileges, and entered into collision. To the present day Mexico is alternately the victim of anarchy and the slave of military despotism.

The second and the most fatal of all the defects I have alluded to, and that which I believe to be inherent in the Federal system, is the relative weakness of the Government of the Union. The principle upon which all confederations rest is that of a divided sovereignty. The legislator may render this partition less perceptible, he may even conceal it for a time from the public eye, but he cannot prevent it from existing; and a divided sovereignty must always be less powerful than an entire supremacy. The reader has seen in the remarks I have made on the Constitution of the United States, that the Americans have displayed singular ingenuity in combining the restriction of the power of the Union within the narrow limits of a Federal Government, with the semblance, and, to a certain extent, with the strength of a national Government. By this means the legislators of the Union have succeeded in diminishing, though not in counteracting, the natural danger of confederations. . . .

Since legislators are unable to obviate such dangerous collisions as occur between the two sovereignties which coexist in the Federal system, the first object must be, not only to dissuade the confederate States from warfare, but to encourage such institutions as may promote the maintenance of peace. Hence it results that the Federal compact cannot be lasting unless there exists in the communities which are joined together a certain number of inducements to union, which render their common dependence agreeable and the task of the Government light. The system cannot succeed without the presence of favourable circumstances added to the influence of good laws. All the peoples which have ever formed a confederation have been held together by a certain number of common interests, which served as the intellectual ties of association.

But the sentiments and the principles of man must be taken into consideration as well as his immediate interests. A certain uniformity of civilization is no less necessary to the durability of a confederation, than a uniformity of interests in the States which compose it. In Switzerland the difference which exists between the Canton of Uri and the Canton of Vaud is equal to that between the fifteenth and the nineteenth centuries; and, properly speaking, Switzerland has never possessed a Federal Government. The union between these two Cantons only subsists upon the map, and their discrepancies would soon be perceived if an attempt were made by a central authority to prescribe the same laws to the whole territory.

lOne of the circumstances which most powerfully contribute to support the Federal Government in America, is that the States have not only similar interests, a common origin, and a common tongue, but that they have also arrived at the same stage of civilization, which almost always renders a union feasible. I do not know of any European nation, however small it may be, which does not present less uniformity in its different provinces than the American people, which occupies a territory as extensive as half of Europe. The distance from the State of Maine to that of Georgia is reckoned at about one thousand miles; but the difference between the civilization of Maine and that of Georgia is slighter than the difference between the habits of Normandy and those of Brittany. Maine and Georgia, which are placed at the opposite extremities of a great empire, consequently have more real inducements to form a confederation than Normandy and Brittany, which are only separated by a bridge.

The geographical position of the country contributed to increase the facilities which the American legislators derived from the manners and customs of the inhabitants, and it is to this circumstance that the adoption and the maintenance of the Federal system is mainly attributable....

No one can be more inclined than I am myself to appreciate the advantages of the Federal system, which I hold to be one of the combinations most favourable to the prosperity and freedom of man. I envy the lot of those nations which have been enabled to adopt it; but I cannot believe that any confederate peoples could maintain a long or an equal contest with a nation of similar strength in which the Government was centralized. A people which divided its sovereignty into fractional powers, in the presence of the great military monarchies of Europe, would in my opinion, by that very act, abdicate its power, and perhaps its existence and its name. But such is the admirable position of the New World, that man has no other enemy than himself; and that in order to be happy and to be free, it suffices to seek the gifts of prosperity and the knowledge of freedom.

THE RELATIVE IMPORTANCE OF MANNERS, LAWS AND PHYSICAL CIRCUMSTANCES IN THE MAINTENANCE OF DEMOCRACY

I have remarked that the maintenance of democratic institutions in the United States is attributable to the circumstances, the laws, and the manners of that country. (I remind the reader of the general signification which I give to the word *manners,* namely, the moral and intellectual characteristics of social man taken collectively.) Most Europeans are only acquainted with the first of these three causes, and they are apt to give it a preponderating importance which it does not really possess.

It is true that the Anglo-Americans settled in the New World in a state of social equality. The low-born and the noble were not to be found amongst them; and occupational prejudices were always as entirely unknown as the prejudices of birth. Thus, as the condition of society was democratic, political democracy was established without difficulty. But this circumstance is by no

From *Democracy in America,* pt. 1, chap. 17.

means peculiar to the United States; almost all the transatlantic colonies were founded by men equal amongst themselves, or who became so by inhabiting them. In no one part of the New World have Europeans been able to create an aristocracy. Nevertheless democratic institutions prosper nowhere but in the United States. The American Union has no enemies to contend with; it stands in the wilds like an island in the ocean. But the Spaniards of South America were no less isolated by nature, yet their position has not relieved them from the burden of standing armies. They make war upon each other when they have no foreign enemies to oppose. The Anglo-American democracy is the only one which has hitherto been able to maintain itself in peace.

The territory of the Union presents a boundless field to human activity, and inexhaustible materials for industry and labour. The passion of wealth takes the place of ambition, and the warmth of faction is mitigated by a sense of prosperity. But in what portion of the globe do we meet with more fertile plains, with mightier rivers, or with more unexplored and inexhaustible riches, than in South America?

Nevertheless, South America has been unable to maintain democratic institutions. If the welfare of nations depended on their being placed in a remote position, with an unbounded space of habitable territory before them, the Spaniards of South America would have no reason to complain of their fate. And although they might enjoy less prosperity than the inhabitants of the United States, their lot might still be such as to excite the envy of some nations in Europe. There are, however, no nations upon the face of the earth more miserable than those South America.

Thus, not only are physical causes inadequate to produce results analogous to those which occur in North America, but they are unable to raise the population of South America above the level of European States, where they act in a contrary direction. Physical causes do not therefore affect the destiny of nations so much as has been supposed.

I have met men in New England who were on the point of leaving an area where they might have remained in easy circumstances, to go to seek their fortune in the wilds. Not far from that district I found a French population in Canada, which was closely crowded on a narrow territory, although the same wilds were at hand. Whilst the emigrant from the United States purchased an extensive estate with the earnings of a short term of labour, the Canadian paid as much for land as he would have done in France. Nature offers the solitudes of the New World to Europeans; but they are not always acquainted with the means of turning her gifts to account. Other peoples of America have the same physical conditions as the Anglo-Americans, but without their laws and their manners, and these peoples are wretched. The laws and manners of the Anglo-Americans are therefore that efficient cause of their greatness which is the object of my inquiry.

I am far from supposing that the American laws are preeminently good in themselves. I do not hold them to be applicable to all democratic peoples, and several of them seem to me to be dangerous, even in the United States. Nevertheless, it cannot be denied that American legislation, taken collectively, is extremely well adapted to the genius of the people and the nature of the country which it is intended to govern. The American laws are therefore good, and to them must be attributed a large portion of the success which attends democratic government in America: but I do not believe them to be the principal cause of that success. And if they seem to me to have more influence upon the social happiness of the Americans than the nature of the country, on the other hand there is reason to believe that their effect is still inferior to that produced by the manners of the people.

The Federal laws undoubtedly constitute the most important part of the legislation of the United States. Mexico, which is no less fortunately situated than the Anglo-American Union, has adopted these same laws, but is unable to accustom itself to democratic government. Some other cause is therefore at work independently of those physical circumstances and peculiar laws which enable democracy to rule in the United States.

Another still more striking proof may be adduced. Almost all the inhabitants of the territory of the Union are the descendants of a common stock; they speak the same language, they worship God in the same manner, they are affected by the same physical causes, and they obey the same laws. Whence, then, do their characteristic differences arise? Why, in the Eastern States of the

Union, does the republican Government display vigour and regularity, and proceed with mature deliberation? Whence does it derive the wisdom and the durability which mark its acts, whilst in the Western States, on the contrary, society seems to be ruled by the powers of chance? There, public business is conducted with an irregularity and a passionate and 'feverish excitement, which does not presage a long or sure future.

I am no longer comparing the Anglo-American States to foreign nations, but contrasting them with each other, and endeavouring to discover why they are so unlike. The arguments which are derived from the nature of the country and the difference of legislation, are here all set aside. Recourse must be had to some other cause; and what other cause can there be except the manners of the people?

It is in the Eastern States that the Anglo-Americans have been longest accustomed to democratic government, and that they have adopted the habits and conceived the notions most favourable to its maintenance. Democracy has gradually penetrated into their customs, their opinions, and the forms of social intercourse; it is to be found in all the details of daily life equally as in the laws. In the Eastern States the instruction and practical education of the people have been most perfected, and religion has been most thoroughly amalgamated with liberty. Now these habits, opinions, customs, and convictions are precisely the constituent elements of that which I have denominated manners.

In the Western States, on the contrary, part of the same advantages is still lacking. Many of the Americans of the West were born in the woods, and they mix the ideas and the customs of savage life with the civilization of their parents. Their parents are more intense, their religious morality less authoritative, and their convictions less secure. The inhabitants exercise no sort of control over their fellow-citizens, for they are scarcely acquainted with each other. The States of the West display, to a certain extent, the inexperience and the rude habits of a people in its infancy; for although they are composed of old elements, they have only recently been brought together.

The manners of the Americans of the United States are, then, the real cause which renders that people the only one of the American nations that is able to support a democratic Government; and it is the influence of manners which produces the different degrees of order and of prosperity that may be distinguished in the several Anglo-American democracies. Thus the effect which the geographical position of a country may have upon the duration of democratic institutions is exaggerated in Europe. Too much importance is attributed to legislation, too little to manners. These three great causes serve, no doubt, to regulate and direct the American democracy; but if they were to be classed in their proper order, I should say that the physical circumstances are less efficient than the laws, and the laws very subordinate to the manners of the people. I am convinced that the most advantageous situation and the best possible laws cannot maintain a constitution in spite of the manners of a country, whilst the latter may turn the most unfavourable positions and the worst laws to some advantage. The importance of manners is a common truth to which study and experience incessantly direct our attention. It may be regarded as a central point in the range of human observation, and the common termination of all inquiry. So seriously do I insist upon this head, that if I have hitherto failed in making the reader feel the important influence which I attribute to the practical experience, the habits, the opinions, in short, to the manners of the Americans, upon the maintenance of their institutions, I have failed in the principal object of my work.

2

THE POLITICAL STRUCTURE
OF DEMOCRACY

POLITICAL ACTIVITY IN AMERICA

It is not impossible to form an imaginary picture of the surpassing liberty which the Americans enjoy; some idea may likewise be formed of the extreme equality which subsists amongst them. But the political activity which pervades the United States must be *seen* in order to be understood. No sooner do you set foot upon the American soil than you are stunned by a kind of tumult; a confused clamour is heard on every side; and a thousand simultaneous voices demand the immediate satisfaction of their social wants. Everything is in motion around you; here, the people of one quarter of a town are met to decide upon the building of a church; there, the election of a representative is going on; a little further, the delegates of a district are travelling in a hurry to the town in order to consult upon some local improvements; or in another place the labourers of a village quit their ploughs to deliberate upon the project of a road or a public school. Meetings are called for the sole purpose of declaring their disapprobation of the line of conduct pursued by the Government, whilst in other assemblies the citizens salute the authorities of the day as the fathers of their country. Societies are formed which regard drunkenness as the principal cause of the evils under which the State labours, and which solemnly bind themselves to give a constant example of temperance.

The great political agitation of the American legislative bodies,

From *Democracy in America*, pt. 1, chap. 14.

which is the only kind of excitement that attracts the attention of foreign countries, is a mere episode or a sort of continuation of that universal movement which originates in the lowest classes of the people and extends successively to all ranks of society. It is impossible to spend more efforts in the pursuit of enjoyment.

⟨The cares of political life engross a most prominent place in the occupation of a citizen in the United States⟩ and almost the only pleasure of which an American has any idea is to take part in the Government, and to discuss the part he has taken. This feeling pervades the most trifling habits of life; even the women frequently attend public meetings, and listen to political harangues as a recreation after their household labours. Debating clubs are to a certain extent a substitute for theatrical entertainments. An American cannot converse, but he can discuss; and when he attempts to talk he falls into a dissertation. He speaks to you as if he was addressing a meeting; and if he should chance to warm in the course of the discussion, he will infallibly say 'Gentlemen,' to the person with whom he is conversing.

In some countries the inhabitants display a certain repugnance to avail themselves of the political privileges with which the law invests them; it would seem that they set too high a value upon their time to spend it on the interests of the community, and they prefer to withdraw within the exact limits of a wholesome egotism, marked out by four sunk fences and a quickset hedge. ⟨But if an American were condemned to confine his activity to his own affairs, he would be robbed of one half of his existence; he would feel an immense void in the life which he is accustomed to lead, and his wretchedness would be unbearable⟩ I am persuaded that if ever a despotic government is established in America, it will find it more difficult to surmount the habits which free institutions have engendered, than to conquer the attachment of the citizens to freedom.

This ceaseless agitation which democratic government has introduced into the political world, influences all social intercourse. I am not sure that upon the whole this is not the greatest advantage of democracy; and I am much less inclined to applaud it for what it does, than for what it causes to be done.

It is incontestable that the people frequently conducts public business very ill; but it is impossible that the lower orders should take a part in public business without extending the circle of their ideas, and without quitting the ordinary routine of their mental acquirements. The humblest individual who is called upon to co-operate in the government of society, acquires a certain degree of self-respect; and as he possesses authority, he can command the services of minds much more enlightened than his own. He is canvassed by a multitude applicants, who seek to deceive him in a thousand different ways, but who instruct him by their deceit. He takes a part in political undertakings which did not originate in his own conception, but which give him a taste for undertakings of the kind. New improvements are daily pointed out in the property which he holds in common with others, and this gives him the desire of improving that property which is more peculiarly his own. He is perhaps neither happier nor better than those who came before him, but he is better informed and more active. I have no doubt that the democratic institutions of the United States, joined to the physical constitution of the country, are the cause (not the direct, as is so often asserted, but the indirect cause) of the prodigious commercial activity of the inhabitants. It is not engendered by the laws, but the people learns how to pro-mote it by the experience derived from legislation.

When the opponents of democracy assert that a single individ-ual performs the duties which he undertakes, much better than the government of the community, it appears to me that they are perfectly right. The government of an individual, supposing an equality of instruction on either side, is more consistent, more persevering, and more accurate than that of a multitude, and it is much better qualified judiciously to discriminate the characters of the men it employs. If any deny what I advance, they have cer-tainly never seen a democratic government, or have formed their opinion upon very partial evidence. It is true that even when local circumstances and the disposition of the people allow democratic institutions to subsist, they never display a regular and methodi-cal system of government. Democratic liberty is far from ac-complishing all the projects it undertakes, with the skill of an adroit despotism. It frequently abandons them before they have borne their fruits, or risks them when the consequences may

prove dangerous; but in the end it produces more than any absolute government, and if it does fewer things well, it does a greater
number of things. Under its sway, the transactions of the public
administration are not nearly so important as what is done by
private exertion. |Democracy does not confer the most skilful kind
of government upon the people, but it produces that which the
most skilful governments are frequently unable to awaken,
namely, an all-pervading and restless activity, a superabundant
force, and an energy which is inseparable from it, and which may,
under favourable circumstances, beget the most amazing benefits. *I*
These are the true advantages of democracy.

POLITICAL ASSOCIATIONS IN THE UNITED STATES

In no country in the world has the principle of association been
more successfully used, or more unsparingly applied to a multitude of different objects, than in America. Besides the permanent associations which are established by law under the names
of townships, cities, and counties, a vast number of others are
formed and maintained by the agency of private individuals....
The most natural privilege of man, next to the right of acting for
himself, is that of combining his exertions with those of his
fellow-creatures, and of acting in common with them. I am
therefore led to conclude that the right of association is almost as
inalienable as the right of personal liberty. No legislator can attack it without impairing the very foundations of society.
Nevertheless, if freedom of association is a fruitful source of
advantages and prosperity to some nations, it may be perverted
or carried to excess by others, and a source of vigor may be
changed into one of destruction. A comparison of the different
methods which associations pursue, in those countries in which
they are managed with discretion, as well as in those where liberty degenerates into license, may perhaps be thought useful both
to governments and to parties.
The greater part of Europeans look upon an association as a

From *Democracy in America*, pt. 1, chap. 12.

weapon which is to be hastily fashioned, and immediately tried in conflict. A society is formed for discussion, but the idea of impending action prevails in the minds of those who constitute it: it is, in fact, an army; and the time given to parley serves to reckon up the strength and to inspire the troops, after which they march against the enemy. Resources which lie within the bounds of the law may suggest themselves to the persons who compose it as means, but never as the only means, of success.

Such, however, is not the manner in which the right of association is understood in the United States. In America the citizens who form the minority associate, in order, in the first place, to show their numerical strength, and so to diminish the moral authority of the majority; and, in the second place, to stimulate competition, and to discover those arguments which are most fitted to act upon the majority: for they always entertain hopes of drawing over their opponents to their own side, and of afterwards disposing of the supreme power in their name. Political associations in the United States are therefore peaceable in their intentions, and strictly legal in the means which they employ; and they assert with perfect truth, that they only aim at success by lawful expedients.

The difference which exists between the Americans and ourselves depends on several causes. In Europe there are numerous parties so diametrically opposed to the majority, that they can never hope to acquire its support, and at the same time they think that they are sufficiently strong in themselves to struggle and to defend their cause. When a party of this kind forms an association, its object is, not to conquer, but to fight. In America, the individuals who hold opinions very much opposed to those of the majority are no sort of impediment to its power; and all other parties hope to win it over to their own principles in the end. The exercise of the right of association becomes dangerous in proportion to the impossibility which excludes great parties from acquiring the majority. In a country like the United States, in which the differences of opinion are mere differences of hue, the right of association may remain unrestrained without evil consequences. The inexperience of many of the European nations in the enjoyment of liberty, leads them only to look upon freedom of association as a right of attacking the Government. The first notion which presents itself to a party, as well as to an individual, when it has acquired a consciousness of its own strength, is that of violence: the notion of persuasion arises at a later period, and is only derived from experience. The English, who are divided into parties which differ most essentially from each other, rarely abuse the right of association, because they have long been accustomed to exercise it. In France, the passion for war is so intense that there is no undertaking so mad, or so injurious to the welfare of the State, that a man does not consider himself honoured in defending it, at the risk of his life.

But perhaps the most powerful of the causes which tend to mitigate the excesses of political association in the United States is universal suffrage. In countries in which universal suffrage exists, the majority is never doubtful, because neither party can pretend to represent that portion of the community which has not voted. The associations which are formed are aware, as well as the nation at large, that they do not represent the majority. This is, indeed, a condition inseparable from their existence, for if they did represent the preponderating power, they would change the law instead of soliciting its reform. The consequence of this is that the moral influence of the Government which they attack is very much increased, and their own power is very much enfeebled.

In Europe there are few associations which do not affect to represent the majority, or which do not believe that they represent it. This belief or pretence tends greatly to increase their power, and serves admirably to legitimate their actions. For what is more excusable than violence in a righteous cause against oppression? Thus it is, in the vast labyrinth of human laws, that extreme liberty sometimes corrects the abuses of license, and that extreme democracy obviates the dangers of democratic government. In Europe, associations consider themselves in some degree the legislative and executive councils of the people, which is unable to speak for itself. In America, where they only represent a minority of the nation, they argue and they petition.

The means which the associations of Europe employ are in accordance with the end which they propose to obtain. As the principle aim of these bodies is to act, and not to debate, to fight rather than to persuade, they are naturally led to adopt a form of organization which differs from the the ordinary customs of civil bodies, and which assumes the habits and the maxims of military life. They centralize the direction of their resources as much as possible, and they entrust the power of the whole party to a very small number of leaders.

The members of these associations reply to a watchword, like soldiers on duty; they profess the doctrine of passive obedience, or rather in uniting together they at once abjure the exercise of their own judgment and free will. And the tyrannical control which these societies exercise, is often far more insupportable than the authority possessed over society by the Government which they attack. Their moral force is much diminished by these excesses. They lose the sacred quality which always characterises a struggle between oppressors and the oppressed. The man who in given cases consents to obey his fellows with servility, and who submits his actions and even his opinions to their control, can have no claim to rank as a free citizen.

The Americans have also established certain forms of government for their associations, but these are invariably borrowed from the forms of the civil administration. The independence of each individual is formally recognized. As in society at large, all the members work towards the same end, but they are not obliged to follow exactly the same track. No-one abjures the exercise of his reason and his free will; rather everyone exercises that reason and that will for the benefit of a common undertaking.

THE ROLE OF SECONDARY INSTITUTIONS

The notion of secondary powers, intermediate between the sovereign and his subjects, occurred naturally to the imagination of aristocratic nations, because such communities contained individuals or families raised above the common level, and apparently destined to command by their birth, their education, and their wealth. This same notion is naturally lacking in the minds of

From *Democracy in America*, pt. 2, bk. 4, chap. 2.

men in democratic ages for converse reasons. It can only be introduced artificially, and kept there with difficulty. On the other hand they conceive, as it were without thinking upon the subject, the notion of a sole and central power which governs the whole community by its direct influence. Moreover in politics, as well as in philosophy and in religion, the intellect of democratic nations is peculiarly open to simple and general notions. Complicated systems are repugnant to it, and its favourite conception is that of a great nation composed of citizens all resembling the same pattern, and all governed by a single power.

The very next notion to that of a sole and central power, which presents itself to the minds of men in the ages of equality, is the notion of uniformity of legislation. As every man sees that he differs but little from those about him, he cannot understand why a rule which is applicable to one man should not be equally applicable to all others. Hence the slightest privileges are repugnant to his reason; the faintest dissimilarities in the political institutions of the same people offend him, and uniformity of legislation appears to him to be the first condition of good government.

I find, on the contrary, that this same notion of a uniform rule, equally binding on all the members of the community was almost unknown to the human mind in aristocratic ages; it was either never entertained, or it was rejected.

These contrary tendencies of opinion ultimately turn on either side to such blind instincts and such ungovernable habits that they still direct the actions of men, in spite of particular exceptions. Notwithstanding the immense variety of conditions in the Middle Ages, a certain number of people existed at that period in precisely similar circumstances; but this did not prevent the laws then in force from assigning to each of them distinct duties and different rights. On the contrary, at the present time all the powers of government are exerted to impose the same customs and the same laws on populations which have as yet but few points of resemblance.

As the conditions of men become equal amongst a people, individuals seem of less importance, and society of greater dimensions; or rather, every citizen, being assimilated to all the rest, is lost in the crowd, and nothing stands conspicuous but the great and imposing image of the people at large. This naturally gives the men of democratic periods a lofty opinion of the privileges of society, and a very humble notion of the rights of individuals; they are ready to admit that the interests of the former are everything, and those of the latter nothing. They are willing to acknowledge that the power which represents the community has far more information and wisdom than any of the members of that community; and that it is the duty, as well as the right, of that power to guide as well as govern each private citizen.

If we scrutinize our contemporaries closely, and penetrate to the root of their political opinion, we shall detect some of the notions I have just pointed out, and we shall perhaps be surprised to find so much accord between men who are so often at variance.

The Americans hold that in every state the supreme power ought to emanate from the people; but when once that power is constituted, they can conceive, as it were, no limits to it, and are ready to admit that it has the right to do whatever it pleases. They have not the slightest notion of peculiar privileges granted to cities, families, or persons: their minds appear never to have foreseen that it might be possible not to apply with strict uniformity the same laws to every part, and to all the inhabitants.

These same opinions are more and more diffused in Europe. They are even spreading amongst those nations which most vehemently reject the principle of the sovereignty of the people. Such nations assign a different origin to the supreme power, but they ascribe to that power the same characteristics. Amongst them all, the idea of intermediate powers is weakened and obliterated. The idea of rights inherent in certain individuals is rapidly disappearing from the minds of men; the idea of the omnipotence and sole authority of society at large rises to fill its place. These ideas take root and spread in proportion as social conditions become more equal, and men more alike; they are engendered by equality, and in turn they hasten the progress of equality.

In France, where the revolution of which I am speaking has gone further than any other European country, these opinions have got complete hold of the public mind. If we listen attentively to the language of the various parties in France, we shall find that there is not one which has not adopted them. Most of these parties censure the conduct of the government, but they all hold that the government ought perpetually to act and interfere in everything that is done. Even those which are most at variance are nevertheless agreed upon this head. The unity, the ubiquity, the omnipotence of the supreme power, and the uniformity of its rules, constitute the principal characteristics of all the political systems which have been put forward in our age. They recur even in the wildest visions of political regeneration: the human mind pursues them in its dreams.

If these notions spontaneously arise in the minds of private individuals, they suggest themselves still more forcibly to the minds of princes. Whilst the ancient fabric of European society is altered and dissolved, sovereigns acquire new conceptions of their opportunities and their duties; they learn for the first time that the central power which they represent may and ought to administer by its own agency, and on a uniform plan, all the concerns of the whole community. This opinion, which, I will venture to say, was never conceived before our time by the monarchs of Europe, is now sinking deeply into the minds of kings, and remains there amidst all the agitation of more unsettled thoughts.

Our contemporaries are therefore much less divided than is commonly supposed; they are constantly disputing the hands in which supremacy is to be vested, but they readily agree upon the duties and the rights of that supremacy. The notion they all form of government is that of a sole, simple, providential, and creative power.

All secondary opinions in politics are unsettled; this one remains fixed, invariable, and consistent. It is adopted by statesmen and political philosophers; it is eagerly laid hold of by the multitude; those who govern and those who are governed agree to pursue it with equal ardour; it is the foremost idea in their minds, it seems innate. It originates therefore in no caprice of the human intellect, but is a necessary condition of the present state of mankind.

Freedom of the Press

There are certain nations which have peculiar reasons for cherishing the freedom of the press. For in certain countries which profess to enjoy the privileges of freedom, every individual agent of the Government may violate the laws with impunity, since those whom he oppresses cannot prosecute him before the courts of justice. In this case the freedom of the press is not merely a guarantee, but the *only* guarantee of their liberty and their security which the citizens possess. If the rulers of these nations proposed to abolish the independence of the press, the people would be justified in saying: Give us the right of prosecuting your offences before ordinary tribunals, and perhaps we may then waive our right of appeal to the tribunal of public opinion.

But in the countries in which the doctrine of the sovereignty of the people ostensibly prevails, the censorship of the press is not only dangerous, it is absurd. When the right of every citizen to cooperate in the government of society is acknowledged, every citizen must be presumed to possess the power of discriminating between the different opinions of his contemporaries, and of appreciating the different facts from which inferences may be drawn. The sovereignty of the people and the freedom of the press may therefore be looked upon as inseparable institutions; the censorship of the press and universal suffrage are two things which are irreconcileably opposed, and which cannot long be retained among the institutions of the same people. Not a single individual of the twelve millions who inhabit the territory of the United States has as yet dared to propose any restrictions to the liberty of the press. . . .

In France it is not uncommonly imagined that the virulence of the press originates in the uncertain social condition, in the political excitement, and the consequent sense of general malaise which prevail in that country; and it is therefore supposed that as soon as society has resumed a certain degree of composure, the press will abandon its present vehemence. I am inclined to think that these causes explain the extraordinary ascendency it has acquired over the nation, but that they do not exercise much

From *Democracy in America,* pt. 1, chap. 11.

influence upon the tone of its language. The periodical press appears to me to be actuated by passions and propensities independent of the circumstances in which it is placed; and the present position of America corroborates this opinion.

America is perhaps, at this moment, the country of the whole world which contains the fewest germs of revolution, but the press is no less destructive in its principles than in France, and it displays the same violence without the same reasons for indignation. In America, as in France, it constitutes a singular power, so strangely composed of mingled good and evil, that it is at the same time indispensable to the existence of freedom, and nearly incompatible with the maintenance of public order. Its power is certainly much greater in France than in the United States; though nothing is more rare in the latter country than to hear of a prosecution having been instituted against it. The reason for this is perfectly simple: the Americans having once accepted the doctrine of the sovereignty of the people, apply it with perfect consistency. They never intended to establish laws for all eternity on foundations which change from day to day. There is consequently nothing criminal in an attack upon the existing laws, provided it be not attended with a violent infraction of them. They are moreover of the opinion that Courts of Justice are unable to check the abuses of the press; and that as the subtlety of human language perpetually eludes the severity of judicial analysis, offences of this nature are apt to escape the hand which attempts to apprehend them. They hold that to act with efficacy upon the press, it would be necessary to find a tribunal not only devoted to the existing order of things, but capable of surmounting the influence of public opinion, a tribunal which should conduct its proceedings without publicity, which should pronounce its decrees without assigning its motives, and punish the intentions even more than the language of the author. Whoever had the power of creating and maintaining a tribunal of this kind would be wasting his time in prosecuting the liberty of the press, for he would be the supreme master of the whole community, and he would be as free to rid himself of the authors as of their writings. In this question, therefore, there is no middle way between servitude and extreme licence. In order to enjoy the inestimable benefits which the freedom of the press ensures, it is necessary to submit to the inevitable evils which it engenders. To expect to acquire the former, and to escape the latter, is to cherish one of those illusions which commonly mislead nations in their times of sickness, when, tired with faction and exhausted by effort, they attempt to combine hostile opinions and contrary opinions upon the same soil. . . .

The influence of the press upon America is immense. It is the power which impels the circulation of political life through all the districts of that vast territory. Its eye is constantly open to detect the secret springs of political designs, and to summon the leaders of all parties to the bar of public opinion. It rallies the interests of the community round certain principles, and it draws up the creed which factions adopt. It affords a means of intercourse between parties which hear, and which address each other, without ever having been in immediate contact. When a great number of the organs of the press adopt the same line of conduct, their influence becomes irresistible; and public opinion, when it is perpetually assailed from the same side, eventually yields to the attack. In the United States each separate journal exercises but little authority: but the power of the periodical press is only second to that of the people.

POLITICAL FUNCTIONS OF THE JURY SYSTEM

The institution of the jury, if confined to criminal causes, is always in danger; but when once it is introduced into civil proceedings, it defies the aggressions of time and man. If it had been as easy to remove the jury from the manners as from the laws of England, it would have perished under Henry VIII and Elizabeth; and the civil jury did in reality, at that period, save the liberties of the country. In whatever manner the jury is applied, it cannot fail to exercise a powerful influence upon the national character, but this influence is greatly increased when it is introduced into civil causes. The jury, and more especially the civil jury, serves to communicate the spirit of the judges to the minds of all the citi-

From *Democracy in America,* pt. 1, chap. 16.

zens. And this spirit, with the habits which attend it, is the soundest preparation for free institutions. It imbues all classes with a respect for the thing judged, and with the notion of right. If these two elements be removed, the love of independence is reduced to a mere destructive passion. It teaches men to practise equity; every man learns to judge his neighbor as he would himself be judged. And this is especially true of the jury in civil causes. For, whilst the number of persons who have reason to fear criminal prosecution is small, everyone is liable to have a civil action brought against him. The jury teaches every man not to recoil before the responsibility of his own actions, and impresses him with that manly confidence without which political virtue cannot exist. It invests each citizen with a kind of magistracy; it makes them all feel the duties which they are bound to discharge towards society, and the part which they take in Government. By obliging men to turn their attention to affairs which are not exclusively their own, it rubs off that individual egotism which is the rust of society.

The jury contributes most powerfully to form the judgment, and to increase the natural intelligence of a people; and this is, in my opinion, its greatest advantage. It may be regarded as a free public school, always open, in which every juror learns to exercise his rights, enters into daily communication with the most learned and enlightened members of the upper classes, and becomes practically acquainted with the laws of his country, which are brought within the reach of his capacity by the efforts of the bar, the advice of the judge, and even by the passions of the parties. I think that the practical intelligence and political good sense of the Americans are mainly attributable to the long use which they have made of the jury in civil causes.

I do not know whether the jury is useful to those who are in litigation, but I am certain it is highly beneficial to those who decide the litigation; and I look upon it as one of the most efficacious means for the education of the people which society can employ.

What I have said so far applies to all nations; but the remark I am now about to make is peculiar to the Americans and to democratic peoples. I have already observed that in democracies the members of the legal profession, and the magistrates, con-

stitute the only aristocratic body which can check the ir-
regularities of the people. This aristocracy is invested with no
physical power, but it exercises its conservative influence upon
the minds of men, and the most abundant source of its authority is
the institution of the civil jury. In criminal causes, when society is
armed against a single individual, the jury is apt to look upon the
judge as the passive instrument of social power, and to mistrust
his advice. Moreover, criminal causes are entirely founded upon
the evidence of facts which common sense can readily appreciate;
on this ground the judge and the jury are equal. Such, however, is
not the case in civil causes; then the judge appears as a disinterested arbiter between the conflicting passions of the parties.
The jurors look up to him with confidence, and listen to him with
respect, for in this instance their intelligence is completely under
the control of his learning. It is the judge who sums up the various
arguments with which their memory has been wearied, and who
guides them through the devious course of the proceedings; he
points their attention to the exact question of fact which they are
called upon to solve, and he puts the answer to the question of
law into their mouths. His influence upon their verdict is almost
unlimited.

If I am called upon to explain why I am but little moved by the
arguments derived from the ignorance of jurors in civil causes, I
reply, that in these proceedings, whenever the question to be
solved is not a mere question of fact, the jury has only the
semblance of a judicial body. The jury sanctions the decision of
the judge; they, by the authority of society which they represent,
and he, by that of reason and of law.

In England and in America the judges exercise an influence
upon criminal trials which the French judges have never possessed. The reason for this difference may easily be discovered;
the English and American magistrates establish their authority in
civil causes, and only transfer it afterwards to tribunals of another
kind, where that authority was not acquired. In some cases (and
they are frequently the most important ones) the American judges
have the right of deciding cases alone. On these occasions they
are, accidentally, placed in the position which French judges
habitually occupy. But they are invested with far more power

than the latter; they are still invested with the authority of the jury, and their judgment has almost as much weight as the voice of the community at large, represented by that institution. Their influence extends beyond the limits of the Courts; in the recreations of private life as well as in the turmoil of public business, abroad and in the legislative assemblies, the American judge is constantly surrounded by men who are accustomed to regard his intelligence as superior to their own. And after having exercised his abilities in deciding cases, he continues to influence the habits of thought and the characters of the individuals who took a part in his judgment.

The jury, then, which seems to restrict the rights of magistracy, does in reality consolidate its power; and in no country are the judges so powerful as there, where the people shares their privileges. It is more especially by means of the jury in civil cases that the American magistrates imbue all classes of society with the spirit of their profession. Thus the jury, which is the most energetic means of making the people rule, is also the most efficacious means of teaching it to rule well.

POLITICAL FUNCTIONS OF RELIGION

Religion in America takes no direct part in the government of society, but it must nevertheless be regarded as the foremost of the political institutions of that country; for if it does not impart a taste for freedom, it facilitates the use of free institutions. Indeed, it is in this same point of view that the inhabitants of the United States themselves look upon religious belief. I do not know whether all the Americans have a sincere faith in their religion, for who can search the human heart? But I am certain that they hold it to be indispensable to the maintenance of republican institutions. This opinion is not peculiar to a class of citizens or to a party, but belongs to the whole nation, and to every rank of society.

In the United States, if a politician attacks a sect, this may not

From *Democracy in America*, pt. 1, chap. 17.

prevent even the partisans of that very sect from supporting him; but if he attacks all the sects together, everyone abandons him, and he stands alone.

Whilst I was in America, a witness who happened to be called at the Assizes of Chester county (State of New York) declared that he did not believe in the existence of God, or in the immortality of the soul. The judge refused to admit his evidence, on the ground that the witness had destroyed beforehand all the confidence of the Court in what he was about to say. The newspapers related the fact without any further comment.

The Americans combine the notions of Christianity and of liberty so intimately in their minds that it is impossible to make them conceive the one without the other; and with them, this conviction does not spring from that barren traditionary faith which seems to vegetate in the soul rather than to live.

I have known of societies formed by the Americans to send out ministers of the Gospel into the new Western States, to found schools and churches there, lest religion die away in those remote settlements, and the rising States be less fitted to enjoy free institutions than the people from which they emanated. I met with wealthy New Englanders who abandoned the land in which they were born, in order to lay the foundations of Christianity and of freedom on the banks of the Missouri, or in the prairies of Illinois. Thus religious zeal is perpetually stimulated in the United States by the duties of patriotism. These men do not act from an exclusive consideration of the promises of a future life; eternity is only one motive of their devotion to the cause, and if you converse with these missionaries of Christian civilization, you will be surprised to find how much value they set upon the goods of this world, and that you meet with a politician where you expected to find a priest. They will tell you, that "all the American Republics are collectively involved with each other; if the Republics of the West were to fall into anarchy, or to be mastered by a despot, the republican institutions which now flourish upon the shores of the Atlantic Ocean, would be in great peril. It is therefore our interest that the new States should be religious, in order to maintain our liberties."

Such are the opinions of the Americans: and if any hold that the religious spirit which I admire is the very thing most amiss in America, and that the only element wanting to the freedom and happiness of the human race is to believe in some blind cosmogony, or to assert with Cabanis the secretion of thought by the brain, I can only reply, that those who hold this opinion have never been in America, and that they have never seen a religious or a free nation. When they return from their expedition, we shall hear what they have to say.

There are people in France who look upon republican institutions as a means towards power, wealth, and distinction. They are the *condottieri* of liberty, who fight for their own advantage, whatever be the colours they wear. It is not to these that I address myself. But there are others who look forward to the republican form of government as a tranquil and lasting state, towards which modern society is daily impelled by the ideas and manners of the time, and who sincerely desire to prepare men to be free. When these men attack religious opinions, they obey the dictates of their passions to the prejudice of their interests. Despotism may govern without faith, but liberty cannot. Religion is much more necessary in the republic which they set forth in glowing colours, than in the monarchy which they attack; and it is more needed in democratic republics than in any others. How is it possible that society should escape destruction if the moral tie is not strengthened as the political tie is relaxed? . . .

POLITICAL FUNCTIONS OF EDUCATION

Anyone who wants to judge the state of education among the Anglo-Americans must look at the one subject from two different points of view. If he only singles out the learned, he will be astonished to find how rare they are; but if he counts the ignorant, the American people will appear to be the most enlightened community in the world. The whole population . . . is situated between these two extremes.

In New England, every citizen receives the elementary notions

From *Democracy in America,* pt. 1, chap. 17.

of human knowledge; he is moreover taught the doctrines and bases of his religion, the history of his country, and the leading features of its Constitution. In the States of Connecticut and Massachusetts, it is extremely rare to find a man imperfectly acquainted with all these things, and a person wholly ignorant of them is a sort of phenomenon.

When I compare the Greek and Roman Republics with these American States, the manuscript libraries of the former and their rude population, with the innumerable journals and the enlightened people of the latter; when I remember all the attempts which are made to judge the modern republics by reference to those of antiquity and to infer what will happen in our time from what took place two thousand years ago, I am tempted to burn my books, in order to apply none but novel ideas to so novel a condition of society.

What I have said of New England must not, however, be applied indiscriminately to the whole Union. As we advance towards the West or the South, the instruction of the people diminishes. In the States which border the Gulf of Mexico, a certain number of individuals may be found, as in our own countries, who are devoid of the rudiments of instruction. But there is not a single district in the United States sunk in complete ignorance.

The reason is simple: the peoples of Europe started from the darkness of a barbarous condition, to advance towards the light of civilization. Their progress has been unequal; some of them have improved apace, whilst others have loitered in their course, and some have stopped, and are still sleeping upon the way. Such has not been the case in the United States. The Anglo-Americans arrived already civilised in that territory which their descendants occupy. They did not have to begin to learn; it was sufficient for them not to forget. Now the children of these same Americans are the people who, year by year, move into the wilds, and take with them their acquired information and their esteem for knowledge. Education has taught them the utility of instruction, and has enabled them to transmit that instruction to their offspring. In the United States society had no infancy, but was born into manhood.

The Americans never use the word 'peasant,' because they

have no idea of the peculiar class which that term denotes. The ignorance of more remote ages, the simplicity of rural life, and the rusticity of the villager have not been preserved amongst them, and they are unacquainted with either the virtues, the vices, the coarse habits, or the simple graces of an early stage of civilization. At the extreme borders of the confederate States, on the frontier between society and the wilderness, is a population of bold adventurers who pierce the solitudes of the American woods, and seek a new country there, in order to escape that poverty which awaited them in their native provinces. As soon as the pioneer arrives upon the spot which is to be his home, he fells a few trees and builds a log-house. Nothing can offer a more miserable sight than these isolated dwellings. The traveller who approaches one of them towards night-fall sees the flicker of the hearth-flame through the chinks in the walls; and at night, if the wind rises, he hears the roof of boughs shake to and fro in the midst of the great forest trees. Who would not suppose that this poor hut is the asylum of rudeness and ignorance? Yet no sort of comparison can be drawn between the pioneer and the dwelling which shelters him. Everything about him is primitive and un-formed, but he is himself the result of the labour and the experience of eighteen centuries. He wears the dress, and he speaks the language of cities; he is acquainted with the past, curious of the future, and ready for argument upon the present. He is, in short, a highly civilized being, who consents for a time to inhabit the back-woods, and who penetrates into the wilds of the New World with the Bible, an axe, and a file of newspapers.

It is difficult to imagine the incredible rapidity with which public opinion circulates through these wilds. I do not think that so much intellectual intercourse takes place in the most enlightened and populous districts of France. It cannot be doubted that, in the United States, the education of the people powerfully contributes to the support of a democratic republic. This must always be the case, I believe, where instruction which awakens the under-standing is not separated from moral education which shapes the character. But I by no means exaggerate this benefit, and I am still further from thinking, as so many people do think in Europe, that men can be instantaneously made citizens by teaching them to read and write. True information is mainly derived from experience, and if the Americans had not been gradually accustomed to governing themselves, their book-learning would not assist them much at the present day.

I have lived a great deal with the people in the United States, and I cannot express how much I admire their experience and their good sense. An American should never be allowed to speak of Europe, for he will then probably display a vast deal of presumption and very foolish pride. He will be content with those crude and vague notions which are so useful to the ignorant all over the world. But if you question him about his own country, the cloud which dimmed his intelligence will immediately disperse; his language will become as clear and as precise as his thoughts. He will inform you what his rights are, and by what means he exercises them. He will be able to point out the customs which obtain in the political world. You will find that he is well acquainted with the rules of the administration, and that he is familiar with the mechanism of the laws. The citizen of the United States does not acquire his practical science and his positive notions from books. The instruction he has acquired may have prepared him for receiving those ideas, but it did not furnish them. The American learns to know the laws by participating in the act of legislation, and he takes a lesson in the forms of government from governing. The great work of society is ever going on beneath his eyes, and, as it were, in his hands.

In the United States politics are the end and aim of education. In Europe its principal object is to fit men for private life; the interference of the citizens in public affairs is too rare an occurrence for it to be anticipated beforehand.

Casting a glance over society in the two hemispheres, these differences are evident even in superficial social behaviour. In Europe we frequently introduce the ideas and habits of private life into public affairs; as we pass from the domestic circle to the government of the State, we frequently discuss the great interests of society in the same manner in which we converse with our friends. The Americans, on the other hand, transfuse the habits of public life into their manners in private; in their country the jury is introduced into the games of schoolboys, and parliamentary forms are observed in the order of a feast.

THE TYRANNY OF THE MAJORITY

I hold it to be an impious and an execrable maxim that, politically speaking, a people has a right to do whatsoever it pleases; and yet I have asserted that all authority originates in the will of the majority. Am I then contradicting myself?

A general law—which bears the name of Justice—has been made and sanctioned, not only by a majority of this or that people, but by a majority of mankind. The rights of every people are consequently confined within the limits of what is just. A nation may be considered as a jury which is empowered to represent society at large, and to apply the great and general law of Justice. Ought such a jury, which represents society, to have more power than the society in which the laws it applies originate?

When I refuse to obey an unjust law, I do not contest the right which the majority has of commanding, but I simply appeal from the sovereignty of the people to the sovereignty of mankind. It has been asserted that a people can never entirely outstep the boundaries of justice and of reason in those affairs which are more peculiarly its own; and that consequently full power may fearlessly be given to the majority by which it is represented. But this language is that of a slave.

A majority taken collectively may be regarded as a being whose opinions and, most frequently, whose interests are opposed to those of another being, which is styled a minority. If it be admitted that a man possessing absolute power may misuse that power by wronging his adversaries, why should a majority not be liable to the same reproach? Men are not apt to change their characters by agglomeration, nor does their patience in the presence of obstacles increase with the consciousness of their strength. And for these reasons I can never willingly invest any number of my fellow-creatures with that unlimited authority which I should refuse to any one of them.

I do not think that it is possible to maintain freedom by combining several principles in the same government which are really opposed to one another. The form of government which is usually

From *Democracy in America*, pt. 1, chap. 15.

termed *mixed* has always appeared to me to be a mere chimera. Accurately speaking there is no such thing as a mixed government, (with the meaning usually given to that word) because in all communities some one principle of action may be discovered which predominates over the others. England in the last century, which has been cited as an example of this form of government, was in point of fact an essentially aristocratic state, although it comprised very powerful elements of democracy. For the laws and customs of the country were such that the aristocracy could not but be dominant in the long run, and subject the direction of public affairs to its own will. The error arose from too much attention being paid to the actual struggle going on between the nobles and the people, without considering the probable outcome of the contest, which was in reality the important point. When a community really has a mixed government, that is to say when it is equally divided between two adverse principles, it must either pass through a revolution, or fall into complete dissolution.

I am therefore of opinion that some one social power must always be made to predominate over the others; but I think that liberty is endangered when this power is checked by no obstacles which may retard it and force it to moderate its own vehemence.

Unlimited power is in itself a bad and dangerous thing; human beings are not competent to exercise it with discretion, and God alone can be omnipotent, because his wisdom and his justice are always equal to his power. But no power upon earth is so worthy of honour for itself, or of reverential obedience to the rights which it represents, that I would consent to admit its uncontrolled and all-predominant authority. When I see that the right and the means of absolute command are conferred on a people or upon a king, upon an aristocracy or a democracy, a monarchy or a republic, I recognize the germ of tyranny, and I journey onwards to a land of more hopeful institutions.

In my opinion the main evil of the present democratic institutions of the United States does not arise, as is often asserted in Europe, from their weakness, but from their overpowering strength. I am no so much alarmed at the excessive liberty which reigns in that country, as at the very inadequate securities which exist against tyranny.

When an individual or a party is wronged in the United States, to whom can he apply for redress? If to public opinion, public opinion constitutes the majority; if to the legislature it represents the majority, and implicitly obeys its injunctions; if to the executive power, it is appointed by the majority and remains a passive tool in its hands; the public troops consist of the majority under arms; the jury is the majority invested with the right of hearing of judicial cases; and in certain States even the judges are elected by the majority. However iniquitous or absurd the evil of which you complain may be, you must submit to it as well as you can.

If, on the other hand, a legislative power could be so constituted as to represent the majority without necessarily being the slave of its passions, an executive so as to retain a certain degree of uncontrolled authority, and a judiciary so as to remain independent of the two other powers, then a government would be formed which would still be democratic without incurring any risk of tyrannical abuse.

I do not say that tyrannical abuses frequently occur in America at the present day, but I maintain that no sure barrier is established against them, and that the causes which mitigate the government are to be found in the circumstances and the manners of the country more than in its laws.

3

SOCIAL RELATIONS
UNDER DEMOCRACY

THE SOFTENING OF MANNERS AS SOCIAL CONDITIONS
BECOME MORE EQUAL

It is evident that over several centuries, social conditions have tended to become more equal, and that in the course of the same period the manners of society have been softened. Are these two things merely contemporaneous, or does any secret link exist between them, so that the one cannot go on without making the other advance? Several causes may concur to render the manners of a people less rude; but, of all these causes, the most powerful appears to me to be the equality of conditions. Equality of conditions and growing civility in manners are then, in my eyes, not only contemporaneous occurrences, but correlative facts....

When all men are irrevocably ranked in an aristocratic community, according to their occupations, their property, and their birth, the members of each class, considering themselves as children of the same family, cherish a constant and active sympathy towards each other, which can never be felt in an equal degree by the citizens of a democracy. But the same feeling does not exist between classes towards each other.

Amongst an aristocratic people each caste has its own opinions, feelings, rights, manners, and modes of living. Thus the men of whom each caste is composed do not resemble the mass of their fellow citizens; they do not think or feel in the same manner, and they scarcely believe that they belong to the same human

From *Democracy in America,* pt. 2, bk. 3, chap. 1. Excerpts from Mme de Sévigné's letters trans. SJM.

race. They cannot therefore thoroughly understand what others feel, nor judge others in relation to themselves. They are sometimes eager to lend each mutual aid, but this is not contrary to what I have just said.

These aristocratic institutions, which made the beings of one and the same race so different, nevertheless bound them to each other by close political ties. Although the serf had no natural interest in the fate of nobles, he did not the less think himself obliged to devote his person to the service of that noble who happened to be his lord: and although the noble held himself to be of a different nature from that of his serfs, he nevertheless held that his duty and his honour constrained him to defend, at the risk of his own life, those who dwelt upon his domains.

It is evident that these mutual obligations did not originate in the law of nature, but in the law of society; and that the claim of social duty was more stringent than that of mere humanity. These services were not supposed to be due from man to man, but to the vassal or to the lord. Feudal institutions awakened a lively sympathy for the sufferings of certain men, but none at all for the miseries of mankind. They infused generosity rather than mildness into the manners of the time, and although they prompted men to great acts of devotion, they engendered no real sympathies; for real sympathies can only exist between those who are alike, and in aristocratic ages men acknowledge none but the members of their own caste to be like themselves.

When the chroniclers of the Middle Ages, who all belonged to the aristocracy by birth or education, relate the tragic end of a noble, their grief overflows, whereas they tell you in passing and without wincing of massacres and tortures inflicted on the common sort of people. Not that these writers felt habitual hatred or systematic disdain for the people; war between the various classes of the community was not yet declared. They were impelled by an instinct rather than by a passion; as they had formed no clear notion of a poor man's sufferings, they cared but little for his fate.

The same feelings animated the lower orders whenever the feudal tie was broken. The same ages which witnessed so many heroic acts of self-devotion on the part of vassals for their lords, were stained with atrocious barbarities, inflicted from time to time by the lower classes on the higher.

It must not be supposed that this mutual insensibility arose solely from the absence of public order and education, for traces of it are to be found in the following centuries, which became tranquil and enlightened whilst they remained aristocratic.

In 1675 the lower classes in Brittany revolted at the imposition of a new tax. These disturbances were put down with unprecedented atrocity. Observe the language in which Madame de Sévigné, a witness of these horrors, relates them to her daughter:

Les Rochers, 30 October, 1675

Dear me, how amusing your letter from Aix is. You should at least read your letters over again before sending them. You would be surprised by their charm, and that would console you for the trouble you have taken in writing at such length.

So you have kissed everyone in Provence? There would be no satisfaction in kissing everyone in Brittany unless you liked the smell of wine.... Would you like to hear the news from Rennes? They levied a tax of a hundred thousand *écus* on the townspeople, and if this sum was not raised within twenty-four hours it was to be doubled and forcibly collected by the soldiers. A whole street was evicted and expelled from the town, and it was forbidden to give them refuge on pain of death. So these wretches—old men, women who had just given birth, infants—were to be seen wandering about in tears outside the gates, not knowing where to go. The day before yesterday the rascal who had started the rioting and looting of tax records was broken on the wheel. After his death he was torn apart by horses, and the four quarters displayed at the four corners of the town. Sixty townspeople were arrested, and punishment begins tomorrow. This province is a good example to the rest, especially in showing respect to their Governors and their ladies. [To feel the point of this joke, the reader should be aware that Madame de Grignan was Gouvernante of Provence.]

Madame de Tarante went off to the woods in delightful weather yesterday. I wonder what she could have been up to—she went out by the wicket gate and came back the same way!...

In another letter she adds:

You dwell lightly on our troubles. But we are no longer so *roué*; only one this week, just to keep the wheels of justice turning. It's true that a hanging makes quite a refreshing change for me now. I have quite a different conception of justice since I came to this region. Your convicts seem to me to be like a group of gentlemen who have retired from the world to lead an easy life.

It would be a mistake to suppose that Madame de Sévigné, who wrote these lines, was a selfish or cruel person; she was passionately attached to her children, and very ready to sympathize in the sorrows of her friends. Her letters show that she treated her vassals and servants with kindness and indulgence. But Madame de Sévigné had no clear notion of suffering in any one who was not a person of quality.

In our time the harshest man writing to the most insensitive person of his acquaintance would not venture wantonly to indulge in the cruel jocularity which I have quoted; and even if his own manners allowed him to do so, the manners of society at large would forbid it. Why is this? Have we more sensibility than our forefathers? I do not know that we have; but I am sure that our insensibility is extended to a far greater range of objects.

When all the ranks of a community are nearly equal, as all men think and feel in nearly the same manner, each of them may judge in a moment the feelings of all the others: he casts a rapid glance upon himself, and that is enough. There is no wretchedness into which he cannot readily enter, and a secret instinct reveals to him its extent. It does not matter whether strangers or foes are the sufferers; imagination puts him in their place. Something personal is mingled with his pity, and makes him suffer whilst the body of his fellow-creature is tortured.

In democratic ages men rarely sacrifice themselves for one another, but they display general compassion for the members of the human race. They inflict no useless ills, and they are happy to relieve the griefs of others, when they can do so without much hurting themselves. They are not disinterested, but they are humane.

Although the Americans have in a way reduced egotism to a social and philosophical theory, they are nevertheless extremely

open to compassion. In no country is criminal justice administered with more mildness than in the United States. Whilst the
English seem disposed carefully to retain the bloody traces of the
dark ages in their penal legislation, the Americans have almost
expunged capital punishment from their codes. North America is,
I think, the only country upon earth in which the life of no one
citizen has been taken for a political offence in the course of the
last fifty years.

The circumstance which conclusively shows that this singular
mildness of the Americans arises chiefly from their social condition is the manner in which they treat their slaves. Perhaps there
is not, on the whole, a single European colony in the New World
in which the physical condition of the blacks is less severe than in
the United States; yet the slaves still endure horrid sufferings
there, and are constantly exposed to barbarous punishments. It is
easy to see that the lot of these unhappy beings inspires their
masters with little compassion, and that they look upon slavery,
not only as an institution which is profitable to them, but as an
evil which does not affect them. Thus the same man who is full of
humanity towards his fellow-creatures when they are at the same
time his equals, becomes insensible to their afflictions as soon as
that equality ceases. His mildness should therefore be attributed
to the equality of conditions, rather than to civilization and education.

How Democracy Makes Social Encounters
Among the Americans Simple and Easy

Democracy does not attach men strongly to each other, but it
places their habitual intercourse upon an easier footing.

If two Englishmen chance to meet at the Antipodes, where they
are surrounded by strangers whose language and manners are
almost unknown to them, they will first stare at each other with
much curiosity and a kind of secret uneasiness; they will then turn

From *Democracy in America*, pt. 2, bk. 3, chap. 2.

away or, if one accosts the other, they will take care only to converse with a constrained and absent air upon very unimportant subjects. Yet there is no emnity between these men; they have never seen each other before, and each believes the other to be a respectable person. Why then should they stand so cautiously apart? We must go back to England to learn the reason.

When it is birth alone, independent of wealth, which classes men in society, everyone knows exactly what his own position is upon the social scale; he does not seek to rise, he does not fear to sink. In a community thus organized, men of different castes communicate very little with each other. But if accident brings them together, they are ready to converse without hoping or fearing to lose their own position. Their intercourse is not upon a footing of equality, but it is not constrained.

When monied aristocracy succeeds to aristocracy of birth, it is no longer the same. The privileges of some are still extremely great, but the possibility of acquiring those privileges is open to all. From this it follows that those who possess them are constantly haunted by the apprehension of losing them, or of other men's sharing them; those who do not yet enjoy them, long to possess them at any cost, or, if they fail, at least to appear to possess them—which is not impossible. As the social importance of men is no longer ostensibly and permanently fixed by blood, and is infinitely varied by wealth, ranks still exist but it is not easy clearly to distinguish at a glance those who respectively belong to them. Secret hostilities then arise in the community. One set of men endeavour by innumerable artifices to penetrate or to appear to penetrate amongst those who are above them. Another set are constantly in arms against these usurpers of their rights. Or the same individual does both at once, and whilst he seeks to raise himself into a higher circle, he is always on the defensive against the intrusion of those below him.

Such is the condition of England at the present time; and I think that the peculiarity just referred to is principally due to this cause. As aristocratic pride is still extremely great amongst the English, and as the limits of aristocracy are ill-defined, everybody lives in constant dread lest advantage should be taken of his familiarity. Unable to judge at once the social position of those he meets, an Englishman prudently avoids all contact with them. Men are afraid lest some slight service rendered should draw them into an unsuitable acquaintance; they dread civilities, and they avoid the obtrusive gratitude of a stranger quite as much as his hatred.

Many people attribute these singular anti-social propensities and the reserved and taciturn bearing of the English to purely physical causes. I may admit that there is something of it in their race, but much more of it is attributable to their social condition, as is proved by the contrast of the Americans.

In America, where the privileges of birth never existed, and where riches confer no peculiar rights on their possessors, men unacquainted with each other are very ready to frequent the same places, and find neither peril nor advantage in the free interchange of their thoughts. If they meet by accident they neither seek nor avoid intercourse; their manner is therefore natural, frank, and open. It is easy to see that they hardly expect or fear anything from each other, and that they do not care to display any more than to conceal their position in the world. If their demeanour is often cold and serious, it is never haughty or constrained; and if they do not converse, it is because they are not in a humour to talk, not because they think it their interest to be silent.

In a foreign country two Americans are at once friends, simply because they are Americans. They are repulsed by no prejudice; they are attracted by their common country. For two Englishmen the same blood is not enough; they must be brought together by the same rank. The Americans remark this unsociable mood of the English as much as the French do, and they are no less astonished by it. Yet the Americans are connected with England by their origin, their religion, their language, and partially by their manners: they only differ in their social condition. It may therefore be inferred that the reserve of the English proceeds from the constitution of their country much more than from that of its inhabitants.

How Equality Divides the Americans into Numerous Small Social Circles

It may possibly be supposed that the final consequence and necessary effect of democratic institutions is to mix together all the members of the community in private as well as in public life, and to compel them all to live in common. But this would be to ascribe a very coarse and oppressive form to the equality which originates in democracy. No state of society or laws can render men so much alike, but that education, fortune, and tastes will interpose some differences between them; and, though different men may sometimes find it their interest to combine for the same purposes, they will never make it their pleasure. They will therefore always tend to evade the provisions of legislation, whatever they may be; and withdrawing to some extent from the circle within which they were to be confined, they will set up, alongside the wider political community, small private circles, united together by the similarity of their conditions, habits, and manners.

In the United States the citizens have no sort of pre-eminence over each other; they owe each other no mutual obedience or respect; they all meet for the administration of justice, for the government of the state, and in general to treat of the affairs which concern their common welfare; but I have never heard that attempts have been made to bring them all to follow the same diversions, or to amuse themselves all jumbled together in the same places of recreation.

The Americans, who mingle so readily in their political assemblies and courts of justice, are wont on the contrary to separate carefully into small distinct circles in order to taste by themselves the enjoyments of private life. Each of them is willing to acknowledge all his fellow-citizens as his equals, but he will only receive a very limited number of them amongst his friends or his guests. This appears to me to be very natural. In proportion as the circle of public society is extended, it may be anticipated that the sphere of private intercourse will be contracted. Far from supposing that the members of modern society will ultimately live in

From *Democracy in America*, pt. 2, bk. 3, chap. 13.

common, I am afraid that they may end by forming nothing but small coteries.

Amongst aristocratic nations, the different classes are like vast compounds, out of which it is impossible to get, into which it is impossible to enter. These classes have no communication with each other, but within their pale men necessarily live in daily contact; even though they would not naturally suit each other, the general conformity of a similar condition brings them nearer together.

But when neither law nor custom serves to establish frequent and habitual relations between certain men, these originate in the accidental similarity of opinions and tastes; hence private society is infinitely varied. In democracies, where the members of the community never differ much from each other, and are naturally so close that they may all at any time be jumbled in one general mass, numerous artificial and arbitrary distinctions spring up, by means of which every man hopes to keep himself aloof, lest he should be carried away in the crowd against his will.

This can never fail to be the case, for human institutions may be changed, but not man. However a community may attempt to render its members equal and alike, the personal side of individuals will always seek to rise above the common level, and to create somewhere an inequality to their own advantage.

In aristocracies men are separated from each other by lofty stationary barriers: in democracies they are divided by a number of small and almost invisible threads, which are constantly broken or moved from place to place. Thus, whatever may be the progress of equality, in democratic nations a great number of small private associations will always be formed within the general political world; but none of them will bear any resemblance in its manners to the highest class in aristocracies.

ASSOCIATIONS IN AMERICAN CIVIL LIFE.

Americans of all ages, all conditions, and all dispositions, constantly form associations. They have not only commercial and

From *Democracy in America,* pt. 2, bk. 2, chap. 5.

manufacturing companies, in which all take part, but associations of a thousand other kinds—religious, moral, serious, futile, extensive or restricted, enormous or diminutive. The Americans form associations to give entertainments, to found establishments for education, to build inns, to construct churches, to diffuse books, to send missionaries to the antipodes; and in this way they found hospitals, prisons, and schools. If it is proposed to advance some truth, or to foster some feeling by the encouragement of a great example, they form a society. Wherever, in charge of some new undertaking, you see the Government in France, or a man of rank in England, in the United States you will be sure to find an association.

I met with several kinds of associations in America of which I confess I had no previous notion, and I have often admired the extreme skill with which the inhabitants of the United States succeed in establishing a common goal for the efforts of a great many men, and in getting them voluntarily to pursue it.

I have since travelled in England, whence the Americans have taken some of their laws and many of their customs, and it seemed to me that the principle of association was by no means so constantly or so adroitly used in that country. The English often perform great things singly, whereas the Americans form associations for the smallest undertakings. It is evident that the English consider association as a powerful means of action, but the Americans seem to regard it as the only means they have of acting.

Thus the most democratic country on earth is that in which men have in our time carried to the highest perfection the art of pursuing in common the object of their common desires, and have applied this new science to the greatest number of purposes. Is this the result of accident, or is there in reality any necessary connexion between the principle of association and that of equality?

Aristocratic communities always contain, amongst a multitude of persons who by themselves are powerless, a small number of powerful and wealthy citizens, each of whom can achieve great undertakings single-handed. In aristocratic societies men do not need to combine in order to act, because they are strongly held together. Every wealthy and powerful citizen constitutes the head of a permanent and compulsory association, composed of all those who are dependent upon him, or whom he makes subservient to the execution of his designs.

Amongst democratic nations, on the contrary, all the citizens are independent and feeble; they can do hardly anything by themselves, and none of them can oblige his fellowmen to lend him their assistance. They all, therefore, fall into a state of incapacity, if they do not learn voluntarily to help each other. If men living in democratic countries had no right and no inclination to associate for *political* purposes, their independence would be in great jeopardy, though they might long preserve their wealth and their cultivation; whereas if they never acquired the habit of forming associations in *ordinary* life, civilization itself would be endangered. A people amongst which individuals lost the power of achieving great things single-handed, without acquiring the means of producing them by united exertions, would soon relapse into barbarism.

Unhappily, the same social condition which renders associations so necessary to democratic nations renders their formation more difficult amongst those nations than amongst all others. When several members of an aristocracy agree to combine, they easily succeed in doing so. As each of them brings great strength to the partnership, the number of its members may be very limited; and when the members of an association are limited in number, they may easily become mutually acquainted, understand each other, and establish fixed rules. The same opportunities do not occur amongst democratic nations, where the associated members must always be very numerous for their association to have any power.

I am aware that many of my countrymen are not in the least embarrassed by this difficulty. They contend that the more enfeebled and incompetent the citizens become, the more able and active the Government ought to be rendered, in order that society at large may execute what individuals can no longer accomplish. They believe this answers the whole difficulty, but I think they are mistaken.

A Government might take the place of some of the largest American associations; and several States of the Union have already attempted it. But what political power could ever carry on the vast multitude of lesser undertakings which the American citizens perform every day, through associations? It is easy to foresee that the time is drawing near when man will be less and less able to produce, by himself alone, the commonest necessaries of life. The task of the governing power will therefore perpetually increase, and its very efforts will extend it every day. The more it stands in the place of associations, the more will individuals, losing the notion of combining together, require its assistance: these are causes and effects which unceasingly engender each other. Will the administration of the country ultimately assume the management of all the industries which no single citizen is able to carry on? And if a time at length arrives, when, in consequence of the extreme subdivision of landed property, the soil is split into an infinite number of parcels, so that it can only be cultivated by companies of husbandmen, will it be necessary that the head of the government should leave the helm of state to follow the plough? The morals and the intelligence of a democratic people would be as much endangered as its business and manufactures, if the government ever wholly usurped the place of private companies.

Feelings and opinions are recruited, the heart is enlarged, and the human mind is developed by no other means than by the reciprocal influence of men upon each other. I have shown that these influences are almost nil in democratic countries. They must therefore be artificially created, and this can only be accomplished by associations.

When the members of an aristocracy adopt a new opinion, or conceive a new sentiment, they give it a station, as it were, beside themselves, upon the lofty platform where they stand; and opinions or sentiments so conspicuous to the eyes of the multitude are easily introduced into the minds or hearts of all around. In democratic countries only the governing power is naturally in a condition to act in this manner; but it is easy to see that such an action on its part is always inadequate, and often dangerous. A government can no more be competent to keep alive and renew the circulation of opinions and feelings amongst a great people, than to manage all the speculations of productive industry. No sooner does a government attempt to go beyond its political sphere and to enter upon this new path than it exercises, even unintentionally, an intolerable tyranny. For a government can only dictate strict rules, the opinions which it favours are rigidly enforced, and it is never easy to discriminate between its advice and its commands. The case will be worse still if the government really believes itself interested in preventing all circulation of ideas; it will then stand motionless, and oppressed by the heaviness of voluntary torpor. Governments therefore should not be the only active powers: associations ought, in democratic nations, to take the place of those powerful private individuals whom the equality of conditions has swept away.

As soon as several of the inhabitants of the United States have taken up an opinion or a feeling which they wish to promote in the world, they look out for mutual assistance; and as soon as they have found each other, they combine. From that moment they are no longer isolated men, but a power seen from afar, whose actions serve for an example, and whose language is listened to. The first time I heard in the United States that a hundred thousand men had bound themselves publicly to abstain from spirituous liquors, it appeared to me more like a joke than something serious, and I did not at first see why these temperate citizens could not content themselves with drinking water by their own firesides. I at last understood that these hundred thousand Americans, alarmed by the progress of drunkenness around them, had made up their minds to support temperance. They acted just in the same way as a man of high rank might dress very plainly, in order to inspire the humbler orders with a contempt of luxury. It is probable that if these hundred thousand men had lived in France each of them would singly have written to the government begging it to watch the public-houses all over the kingdom.

Nothing, in my opinion, more deserves our attention than the intellectual and moral associations of America. The political and industrial associations of that country strike us forcibly; but the others elude our observation, or if we notice them, we understand them imperfectly because we have hardly ever seen anything of the kind. It must, however, be acknowledged that they are as necessary to the American people as the political ones, and perhaps more so.

In democratic countries the science of association is the key science; the progress of all the rest depends upon the progress it has made.

Amongst the laws which rule human societies there is one which seems to be more precise and clear than all others. If men are to remain civilized, or to become so, the art of associating together must grow and improve, in step with the increasing equality of conditions.

HOW DEMOCRACY AFFECTS THE RELATIONS OF MASTERS AND SERVANTS

An American who had traveled for a long time in Europe once said to me, "The English treat their servants with a stiffness and imperiousness of manner which surprise us; but on the other hand the French sometimes treat their attendants with a degree of familiarity or of politeness which we cannot conceive. It looks as if they were afraid to give orders: the posture of the superior and the inferior is ill-maintained." The remark was a just one, and I have often made it myself. I have always considered England the country in the world where, in our time, the bond of domestic service is drawn most tightly, and France as the country where it is most relaxed. Nowhere have I seen masters stand so high or so low as these two countries. Between these two extremes are the Americans. Such is the fact as it appears upon the surface of things: to discover the causes of that fact, it is necessary to explore the matter thoroughly.

No societies have ever yet existed in which social conditions have been so equal that there were neither rich nor poor, and consequently neither masters nor servants. Democracy does not prevent the existence of these two classes, but it changes their dispositions, and modifies their relations.

From *Democracy in America,* pt. 2, bk. 3, chap. 5.

In aristocratic societies, servants form a distinct class, the members of which are no more dissimilar among themselves than are the masters. A settled order is soon established. In both classes a scale is formed, with numerous distinctions or marked gradations of rank, and generations succeed each other without any change of position. These two classes are ranked one above the other, always distinct, but regulated by analogous principles. This aristocratic constitution exerts no less powerful an influence on the ideas and manners of servants than on those of masters; and, although the effects are different, the same cause may easily be traced.

Both classes constitute small nations within the larger nation, and certain permanent notions of right and wrong are ultimately engendered amongst them. The different acts of human life are viewed in one particular and unchanging light. In the society of servants as in that of masters, men exercise a great influence over each other. They acknowledge settled rules, and in the absence of law they are guided by a sort of public opinion; their habits are settled, and their conduct is subject to a certain control.

These men, whose destiny it is to obey, certainly do not understand fame, virtue, honesty and honour in the same way as their masters. But they have a pride, a virtue, and an honesty pertaining to their condition; and they have a notion, if I may use the expression, of a sort of servile honour. Because a class is mean, it must not be supposed that all who belong to it are mean-hearted; to think so would be a great mistake. However lowly it may be, he who is foremost there, and who has no notion of quitting it, occupies an aristocratic position which inspires him with lofty feelings, pride, and self-respect, that fit him for the higher virtues and actions above the common.

Amongst aristocratic nations it was by no means rare to find men of noble and vigorous minds in the service of the great, who felt no sense of servitude, and who submitted to the will of their masters without any fear of their displeasure.

But this was hardly ever the case amongst the inferior ranks of domestic servants. It may be imagined that anyone who occupies the lowest rank in the order of menials stands very low indeed. The French created a word on purpose to designate the servants of the aristocracy—they call them 'lackeys.' This word lackey served as the strongest expression, when all others were exhausted, to designate human meanness. Under the old French monarchy, to denote by a single expression a low-spirited contemptible fellow, it was usual to say that he had the *soul of a lackey;* the term was enough to convey all that was intended.

The permanent inquality of conditions not only gives servants certain peculiar virtues and vices, but it places them in a peculiar relation with respect to their masters. In aristocratic societies the poor man is familiarized from his childhood with the notion of being commanded. To whichever side he turns his eyes the image of hierarchy and obedience meet his view. Hence in those countries the master readily obtains prompt, complete, respectful, and easy obedience from his servants, because they revere in him not only their master but the class of masters. He weighs down their will by the whole weight of the aristocracy. He orders their actions—to a certain extent he even directs their thoughts. In aristocracies the master often exercises, even without being aware of it, an amazing sway over the opinions, the habits and the manners of those who obey him, and his influence extends even further than his authority.

In aristocratic communities, there are not only hereditary families of servants as well as of masters, but the same families adhere for several generations to the same families of masters (like two parallel lines which neither meet nor separate), and this considerably modifies the mutual relations of these two classes of persons. Thus, although in aristocratic society the master and servant have no natural resemblance—although, on the contrary, they are placed at an immense distance on the scale of human beings by their fortune, education, and opinions—yet time ultimately binds them together. They are connected by a long series of common reminiscences, and however different they may be, they grow alike; whilst in democracies, where they are naturally almost alike, they always remain strangers to each other. Amongst an aristocratic people the master gets to look upon his servants as an inferior and secondary part of himself, and he often takes an interest in their lot by a last stretch of egotism.

Servants, on their part, are not averse to regard themselves in the same light. They sometimes identify themselves with the person of the master, so that they become an appendage to him in their own eyes as well as in his. In aristocracies a servant fills a subordinate position which he cannot get out of; above him is another man, holding a superior rank which he cannot lose. On one side are obscurity, poverty, obedience for life; on the other and also for life, fame, wealth, and command. The two conditions are always distinct and always in propinquity; the tie that connects them is as lasting as they are themselves.

In this predicament the servant ultimately detaches his notion of interest from his own person; he deserts himself as it were, or rather he transports himself into the character of his master, and thus assumes an imaginary personality. He complacently invests himself with the wealth of those who command him; he shares their fame, exalts himself by their rank, and feeds his mind with borrowed greatness, to which he attaches more importance than those who fully and really possess it. There is something touching, and at the same time ridiculous, in this strange confusion of two different states of being. These passions of masters, when they pass into the souls of menials, assume the natural dimensions of the place they occupy—they are contracted and lowered. What was pride in the former becomes puerile vanity and paltry ostentation in the latter. The servants of a great man are commonly most punctilious as to the marks of respect due to him, and they attach more importance to his slightest privileges than he does himself. In France a few of these old servants of the aristocracy are still to be met with here and there; they have survived their race, which will soon disappear with them altogether.

In the United States I never saw any one at all like them. The Americans are not only unacquainted with the kind of man, but it is hardly possible to make them understand that such ever existed. It is scarcely less difficult for them to conceive it than for us to form a correct notion of what a slave was amongst the Romans, or a serf in the Middle Ages. All these men were in fact, though in different degrees, results of the same cause: they are all disappearing from our sight in the obscurity of the past, together with the social condition to which they owed their origin.

Equality of conditions turns servants and masters into new

beings, and places them in new relative positions. When social conditions are nearly equal, men are constantly changing their situations in life: there is still a class of menials and a class of masters, but these classes are not always composed of the same individuals, still less of the same families; and those who command are no more permanently secure than those who obey. As servants do not form a separate people, they have no habits, prejudices, or manners peculiar to themselves: they are not remarkable for any particular turn of mind or moods of feeling. They know no vices or virtues of their condition, but they partake of the education, the opinions, the feelings, the virtues and the vices of their contemporaries; and they are honest men or scoundrels in the same way as their masters are.

The conditions of servants are no less equal than those of masters. As there are no marked ranks or fixed subordination amongst them, they will not display either the meanness or the greatness which characterize the aristocracy of menials as well as all other aristocracies. I never saw a man in the United States who reminded me of that class of élite servants which we still remember in Europe, neither did I ever meet with such a thing as a lackey: all traces of the one and of the other have disappeared.

In democracies servants are not only equal amongst themselves, but it may be said that they are in a way the equals of their masters. This requires explanation in order to be rightly understood. At any moment a servant may become a master, and he aspires to rise to that condition: the servant is therefore not a different man from the master. Why then has the former a right to command, and what compels the latter to obey?—the free and temporary consent of both their wills. Neither of them is by nature inferior to the other; they only become so for a time by agreement. Within the terms of this agreement, the one is a servant, the other a master: beyond it they are two citizens—two men.

I beg the reader particularly to observe that this is not only the notion which servants themselves entertain of their own condition. Domestic service is looked upon by masters in the same light, and the precise limits of authority and obedience are as clearly settled in the mind of the one as in that of the other.

When the greater part of the community have long attained a

condition nearly alike, and when equality is an old and acknowledged fact, the public mind, which is never affected by exceptions, assigns certain general limits to the value of man, above or below which no man can long remain. It is in vain that wealth and poverty, authority and obedience, accidentally interpose great distances between two men; public opinion, founded upon the usual order of things, puts them on a common level, and creates a kind of imaginary equality between them, in spite of the real inequality of their conditions. This all-powerful opinion penetrates eventually even into the hearts of those whose interest might lead them to resist it; it affects their judgments whilst it subdues their will.

In their inmost convictions the master and the servant no longer perceive any deep-seated difference between them, and they neither hope nor fear to meet with any such at any time. They are therefore neither subject to disdain nor to anger, and they discern in each other neither humility nor pride. The master holds the contract of service to be the only source of his power, and the servant regards it as the only cause of his obedience. They do not quarrel about their reciprocal situations, but each knows his own and keeps it.

In the French army the common soldier is recruited from nearly the same classes as the officer, and may rise to become an officer himself; out of the ranks he considers himself entirely equal to his military superiors, and in point of fact he is so. But when under arms he does not hesitate to obey, and his obedience is no less prompt, precise, and ready, for being voluntary and defined. This example may give a notion of what takes place between the master and the servant in democratic communities. It would be preposterous to suppose that those warm and deep-seated affections which are sometimes kindled in the domestic service of aristocracy will ever spring up between these two men, or that they will exhibit strong instances of self-sacrifice. In aristocracies masters and servants live apart, and frequently their only contact is through a third person, yet they commonly stand firmly by one another. In democratic countries the master and the servant are close together: they are in daily personal contact, but their minds do not meet; they have common occupations, hardly ever common interests.

DEMOCRACY AND THE EQUALITY
OF THE SEXES

No free communities ever existed without morals; and . . . morals are the work of woman. Consequently, whatever affects the condition of women, their habits and their opinions, has great political importance in my eyes. Amongst almost all Protestant nations young women are far more the mistresses of their own actions than they are in Catholic countries. This independence is still greater in Protestant countries like England which have retained or acquired the right of self-government; the spirit of freedom is then infused into the domestic circle by political habits and by religious opinions. In the United States the doctrines of Protestantism are combined with great political freedom and a most democratic state of society, and nowhere are young women surrendered so early or completely to their own guidance.

Long before an American girl arrives at the age of marriage, her emancipation from maternal control begins. She has scarcely ceased to be child, when she already thinks for herself, speaks with freedom, and acts on her own impulse. The wider world beyond the home is not concealed from her. It is constantly displayed before her, and she is taught to look at it firmly and calmly. Thus the vices and dangers of society are revealed early to her. As she sees them clearly, she views them without illusions, and braves them without fear; for she is full of reliance on her own strength, and her reliance seems to be shared by all who are about her.

An American girl scarcely ever displays that virginal bloom in the midst of young desires, or that innocent and ingenuous grace which usually mark the European woman in the transition from girlhood to youth. Rarely does an American woman at any age display childish timidity or ignorance. Like the young women of Europe, she seeks to please, but she knows precisely the cost of pleasing. If she does not abandon herself to evil, at least she knows that it exists; she is remarkable rather for purity of manners than for chastity of mind.

From *Democracy in America*, pt. 2, bk. 3, chaps. 9 and 12.

I have been frequently surprised and almost frightened at the singular skill and happy boldness with which young women in America contrive to manage their thoughts and their language amidst all the difficulties of stimulating conversation; a philosopher would have stumbled at every step along the narrow path which they trod without accidents and without effect. It is easy indeed to perceive that, even amidst the independence of early youth, an American woman is always mistress of herself: she indulges in all permitted pleasures, without yielding herself up to any of them, and her reason never allows the reins of self-guidance to drop, though it often seems to hold them loosely.

In France, where remnants of every age are still so strangely mingled in the opinions and tastes of the people, women commonly receive a reserved, retired, and almost conventual education, as they did in aristocratic times. And then they are suddenly abandoned, without a guide and without assistance, in the midst of all the disorder inseparable from democratic society.

The Americans are more consistent. They have found out that in a democracy the independence of individuals cannot fail to be very great, youth premature, tastes ill-restrained, customs fleeting, public opinion often unsettled and powerless, paternal authority weak, and marital authority contested. Under these circumstances, believing that they had little chance of repressing in woman the most vehement passions of the human heart, they held that the surer way was to teach her the art of combating those passions for herself. As they could not prevent her virtue from being exposed to frequent danger, they determined that she should know how best to defend it; and more reliance was placed on the free vigour of her will, than on safeguards which have been shaken or overthrown. Instead then of inculcating mistrust of herself, they constantly seek to enhance her confidence in her own strength of character. As it is neither possible nor desirable to keep a young woman in perpetual and complete ignorance, they hasten to give her a precocious knowledge on all subjects. Far from hiding the corruptions of the world from her, they prefer that she should see them at once and train herself to shun them; and they hold it of more importance to protect her conduct than to be over-scrupulous of her innocence.

Although the Americans are a very religious people, they do

not rely on religion alone to defend the virtue of woman; they seek to arm her reason also. In this they have followed the same method as in several other respects: they first make the most vigorous efforts to bring individual independence to exercise a proper control over itself, and they do not call in the aid of religion until they have reached the utmost limits of human strength.

I am aware that an education of this kind is not without danger; I am sensible that it tends to invigorate the judgment at the expense of the imagination, and to make cold and virtuous women instead of affectionate wives and agreeable companions to man. Society may be more tranquil and better regulated, but domestic life often has fewer charms. These however are secondary evils, which may be braved for the sake of higher interests. At the stage at which we have now arrived the time for choosing is no longer within our control; a democratic education is indispensable, to protect women from the dangers with which democratic institutions and manners surround them. . . .

I have shown how democracy destroys or modifies the different inequalities which originate in society: but is this all or does it not ultimately affect that great inequality of man and woman which has seemed, up to the present day, to be eternally based in human nature? I believe that the social changes which bring nearer to the same level the father and son, the master and servant, and superiors and inferiors generally speaking, will raise woman and make her more and more the equal of man. But here, more than ever, I feel the necessity of making myself clearly understood, for there is no subject on which the coarse and lawless fancies of our age have taken a freer range.

There are people in Europe who, making no distinction between the different characteristics of the sexes, would make men and women not only equal but alike. They would give to both the same functions, impose on both the same duties, and grant to both the same rights; they would mix them in all things—their occupations, their pleasures, their business. It may readily be seen that by thus attempting to make one sex equal to the other, both are degraded; and from so preposterous a medley of the works of nature, nothing could ever result but weak men and disorderly women.

It is not thus that the Americans understand that kind of democratic equality which may be established between the sexes. They admit, that as nature has established such wide differences between the physical and moral constitution of man and woman, its manifest intention was to make different use of their differing abilities. And they contend that improvement does not consist in making beings so dissimilar do pretty nearly the same things, but in getting each of them to fulfil their respective tasks in the best possible manner. The Americans have applied to the sexes the great principle of political economy which dominates the industrial age, by carefully dividing the duties of man from those of woman, in order that the great work of society may be the better carried on.

In no country has such constant care been taken as in America to trace two clearly distinct lines of action for the two sexes, and to make them keep pace one with the other, but in two pathways which are always different. American women never manage the outward concerns of the family, or conduct a business, or take a part in political life; nor are they, on the other hand, ever compelled to perform the rough labour of the fields, or to make any of those laborious exertions which demand the exertion of physical strength. No families are so poor as to form an exception to this rule. If on the one hand an American woman cannot escape from the quiet circle of domestic employments, on the other she is never forced to go beyond it. Hence it is that the women of America, who often exhibit a masculine strength of understanding and a manly energy, generally preserve great delicacy of personal appearance and always retain the manners of women, although they sometimes show that they have the hearts and minds of men.

Nor have the Americans ever supposed that one consequence of democratic principles is the subversion of marital power, or the confusion of the natural authorities in families. They hold that every association must have a head in order to accomplish its object, and that the natural head of the conjugal association is man. They do not therefore deny him the right of directing his partner; and they maintain that in the smaller association of husband and wife, as well in the great social community, the object of democracy is to regulate and legalize the powers which are necessary, not to subvert all power.

This opinion is not peculiar to one sex, and contested by the other: I never observed that the women of America consider conjugal authority a usurpation of their rights, nor that they thought themselves degraded by submitting to it. It appeared to me, on the contrary, that they attach a sort of pride to the voluntary surrender of their own will, and make it their boast to bend themselves to the yoke, not to shake it off. Such at least is the feeling expressed by the most virtuous of their sex; the others are silent, and in the United States it is not the practice for a guilty wife to clamour for the rights of women, whilst she is trampling on her holiest duties.

It has often been remarked that in Europe a certain degree of contempt lurks even in the flattery which men lavish upon women: although a European frequently affects to be the slave of woman, it may be seen that he never sincerely thinks her his equal. In the United States men seldom compliment women, but they daily show how much they esteem them. They constantly display an entire confidence in the understanding of a wife, and a profound respect for her freedom. They have decided that her mind is just as fitted as that of a man to discover the plain truth, and her heart as firm to embrace it, and they have never sought to place her virtue, any more than his, under the shelter of prejudice, ignorance, and fear.

It would seem that in Europe, where man so easily submits to political rule by women, they are nevertheless denied some of the greatest prerogatives of the human species, and considered as seductive but imperfect beings. And (what may well provoke astonishment) women ultimately look upon themselves in the same light, and almost consider it a privilege that they are entitled to show themselves futile, feeble, and timid. The women of America claim no such privileges.

Again it may be said that in our morals we have reserved strange immunities to man so that there is as it were one rule for him, and another for his partner. And, according to the opinion of the public, the very same act may be punished alternately as a crime, or only as a fault. The Americans do not make this iniquitous division of duties and rights; amongst them the seducer is as much dishonoured as his victim.

It is true that the Americans rarely lavish upon women those eager attentions which are commonly paid them in Europe. But their conduct to women always implies that they suppose them to be virtuous and refined; and such is the respect entertained for the moral freedom of the sex, that in the presence of a woman the most guarded language is used, lest her ear should be offended by an expression. In America a young unmarried woman may, alone and without fear, undertake a long journey.

The legislators of the United States, who have mitigated almost all the penalties of criminal law, still make rape a capital offence, and no crime is visited with more inexorable severity by public opinion. As the Americans can conceive nothing more precious than a woman's honour, and nothing which ought so much to be respected as her independence, they hold that no punishment is too severe for the man who deprives her of them against her will. In France, where the same offence is visited with far milder penalties, it is frequently difficult to get a verdict from a jury against the prisoner. Is this a consequence of contempt for decency or contempt for women? I cannot but believe that it is a contempt for both.

Thus the Americans do not think that man and woman have either the duty or the right to do the same things, but they show an equal regard for both their respective roles; and though their lot is different, they consider both of them beings of equal value. They do not expect a woman's courage to be of exactly the same kind or put to the same uses as a man's, but they never doubt her courage. And if they hold that man and his partner ought not always to exercise their intellect and understanding in the same manner, they at least believe the understanding of the one to be as sound as that of that of the other, and her intellect to be as clear. Thus, then, whilst they have allowed the social inferiority of woman to subsist, they have done all they could to raise her morally and intellectually to the level of man; and in this respect they appear to me to have excellently understood the true principle of democratic improvement.

As for myself, I do not hesitate to avow, that, although the women of the United States are confined within the narrow circle of domestic life, and their situation is in some respects one of extreme dependence, I have nowhere seen women occupying a loftier position; and if I were asked, now that I am drawing to the close of this work in which I have spoken of so many important things done by the Americans, to what the singular prosperity and growing strength of that people ought mainly to be attributed, I should reply—to the superiority of their women.

WAR AND DEMOCRATIC ARMIES

The same interests, the same fears, the same passions which deter democratic nations from revolutions, deter them also from war; the spirit of military glory and the spirit of revolution are weakened at the same time and by the same causes. The ever-increasing numbers of men of property who are lovers of peace, the growth of personal wealth which war so rapidly consumes, the mildness of manners, the gentleness of heart, those tendencies to pity which are engendered by the equality of conditions, that coolness of understanding which renders men comparatively insensible to the violent and poetical excitement of arms—all these causes concur to quench the military spirit. I think it may be admitted as a general and constant rule that, amongst civilized nations, the warlike passions will become more rare and less intense in proportion as social conditions become more equal.

War is nevertheless an occurrence to which all nations are subject, democratic nations as well as others. Whatever taste they may have for peace, they must hold themselves in readiness to repel aggression, or in other words they must have an army.

Fortune, which has conferred so many peculiar benefits upon the inhabitants of the United States, has placed them in the midst of a wilderness, where they have, so to speak, no neighbors. A few thousand soldiers are sufficient for their wants, but this is peculiar to America, not to democracy.

The equality of conditions, and the manners as well as the institutions resulting from it, do not exempt a democratic people from the necessity of standing armies, and their armies always

From *Democracy in America,* pt. 2, bk. 3, chap. 22.

exercise a powerful influence over their fate. It is therefore of singular importance to inquire what are the natural instincts of the men of whom these armies are composed.

Amongst aristocratic nations, especially amongst those in which birth is the only source of rank, the same inequality exists in the army as in the nation. The officer is noble, the soldier is a serf. The one is naturally called upon to command, the other to obey. In aristocratic armies, the private soldier's ambition is therefore circumscribed within very narrow limits. Nor has the ambition of the officer an unlimited range. An aristocratic corps not only forms a part of the scale of ranks in the nation, but it contains a scale of ranks within itself. The members of whom it is composed are placed one above another, in a particular and unvarying manner. Thus one man is born to the command of a regiment, another to that of a company; when once they have reached the utmost object of their hopes, they stop of their own accord, and remain content with their lot.

There is, besides, a strong cause which, in aristocracies, weakens the officer's desire of promotion. Amongst aristocratic nations, an officer, independently of his rank in the army, also occupies an elevated rank in society; the former is almost always in his eyes only an appendage to the latter. A nobleman who embraces the profession of arms follows it less from motives of ambition than from a sense of the duties imposed on him by his birth. He enters the army in order to find an honourable employment for the idle years of his youth, and to be able to bring back to his home and his peers some honourable recollections of military life. But his principal object is not to obtain by that profession either property, distinction, or power, for he possesses these advantages in his own right, and enjoys them without leaving his home.

In democratic armies all the soldiers may become officers, which makes the desire for promotion general, and immeasurably extends the bounds of military ambition.

The officer, on his part, sees nothing which naturally and necessarily stops him at one grade more than at another; and each grade has immense importance in his eyes, because his rank in society almost always depends on his rank in the army. Amongst democratic nations it often happens that an officer has no property but his pay, and no distinction but that of military honours: consequently as often as his duties change, his fortune changes, and he becomes, as it were, a new man. What was only an appendage to his position in aristocratic armies, has thus become the main point, the basis of his whole condition.

Under the old French monarchy officers were always called by their titles of nobility; they are now always called by the title of their military rank. This little change in the forms of language suffices to show that a great revolution has taken place in the constitution of society and in that of the army.

In democratic armies the desire for advancement is almost universal: it is ardent, tenacious, perpetual; it is strengthened by all other desires, and only extinguished with life itself. But it is easy to see, that of all armies in the world, those in which advancement must be slowest in time of peace are the armies of democratic countries. As the number of commissions is naturally limited, whilst the number of competitors is almost unlimited, and as the strict law of equality applies to all alike, none can make rapid progress—many can make no progress at all. Thus the desire for advancement is greater, and the opportunities for advancement fewer, there than elsewhere. All the ambitious spirits of a democratic army consequently ardently desire war, because war makes vacancies, and warrants the violation of that law of seniority which is the sole privilege natural to democracy.

We thus arrive at this singular consequence, that of all armies those which most ardently desire war are democratic armies, and of all nations those most fond of peace are democratic nations. And what makes these facts still more extraordinary is that these contrary effects are produced at the same time by the principle of equality.

4

THE CULTURAL CONSEQUENCES
OF DEMOCRACY

PHILOSOPHICAL METHOD AMONG THE AMERICANS

I think that in no country in the civilized world is less attention
paid to philosophy than in the United States. The Americans have
no philosophical school of their own; and they care but little for
all the schools into which Europe is divided, the very names of
which are scarcely known to them.

Nevertheless it is easy to perceive that almost all the inhabitants of the United States conduct their understanding in the
same manner, and govern it by the same rules; that is to say, that
without ever having taken the trouble to define the rules of a
philosophical method, they are in possession of one, common to
the whole people.

To evade the bondage of system and habit, of family-maxims,
class-opinions, and, in some degree, of national prejudices; to
accept tradition only as a means of information, and existing facts
only as a lesson used in doing otherwise and doing better; to seek
the reason of things for oneself, and in oneself alone; to tend to
results without being bound to means, and to aim at the substance
through the form—such are the principal characteristics of what I
shall call the philosophical method of the Americans.

But if I go further, and if I seek amongst these characteristics
that which predominates over and includes almost all the rest, I
discover that in most of the operations of the mind each American
appeals to the individual exercise of his own understanding alone.

America is therefore one of the countries in the world where

From *Democracy in America*, pt. 2, bk. 1, chap. 1.

philosophy is least studied, and where the precepts of Descartes are best applied. Nor is this surprising. The Americans do not read the works of Descartes, because their social condition deters them from speculative studies; but they follow his maxims, because this very social condition naturally disposes their understanding to adopt them.

In the midst of the continual movement which agitates a democratic community, the tie which unites one generation to another is relaxed or broken; every man readily loses the trace of the ideas of his forefathers or does not care about them.

Nor can men living in this state of society derive their belief from the opinions of the class to which they belong; for, so to speak, there are no longer any classes, or those which still exist are composed of such mobile elements that they can never exercise a real control over their members.

As to the influence which the intelligence of one man has on that of another, it must necessarily be very limited in a country where the citizens, placed on the footing of a general similitude, are all closely seen by each other; and where, as no signs of incontestable greatness or superiority are perceived in any one of them, they are constantly brought back to their own reason as the most obvious and proximate source of truth. It is not only confidence in this or that man which is then destroyed, but the taste for trusting the *ipse dixit* of any man whatsoever. Every one shuts himself up in his own breast, and affects from that point to judge the world.

The practice which obtains amongst the Americans of fixing the standard of their judgment in themselves alone, leads them to other habits of mind. As they perceive that they succeed without assistance in resolving all the little difficulties which their practical life presents, they readily conclude that everything in the world may be explained, and that nothing in it transcends the limits of the understanding. Thus they fall to denying what they cannot comprehend, which leaves them but little faith for whatever is extraordinary, and an almost insurmountable distaste for whatever is supernatural. As it is on their own testimony that they are accustomed to rely, they like to discern the object which engages their attention with extreme clearness; they therefore strip off as much as possible all that covers it, they rid themselves of whatever separates them from it, they remove whatever conceals it from sight, in order to view it more closely and in the broad light of day. This disposition of the mind soon leads them to feel contempt for forms, which they regard as useless and inconvenient veils placed between them and the truth.

The Americans then have not needed to extract their philosophical method from books; they have found it in themselves. The same thing may be said of what has taken place in Europe.

This same method has only been established and made popular in Europe in proportion as the condition of society has become more equal, and men have grown more like each other. Let us consider for a moment the connection of the periods in which this change may be traced.

In the sixteenth century the Reformers subjected some of the dogmas of the ancient faith to the scrutiny of private judgment; but they still withheld from it the discussion of all the rest. In the seventeenth century, Bacon in the natural sciences, and Descartes in the study of philosophy in the strict sense of the term, abolished recognized formulas, destroyed the power of tradition, and overthrew the authority of the schools. The philosophers of the eighteenth century, generalizing at length the same principle, undertook to submit to the private judgment of each man all the objects of his belief. . . .

The philosophical method here designated may have been engendered in the sixteenth century. It may have been more accurately defined and more extensively applied in the seventeenth. But neither in the one nor in the other could it be commonly adopted. Political laws, the condition of society, and the habits of mind which are derived from these causes, were as yet opposed to it.

It was discovered at a time when men were beginning to equalize and assimilate their conditions. It could only be generally followed in ages when those conditions had at length become nearly equal, and men nearly alike.

The philosophical method of the eighteenth century is then not only French, but it is democratic; and this explains why it was so readily accepted throughout Europe, where it has contributed so powerfully to change the face of society. It is not because the French have changed their former opinions and altered their former manners that they have convulsed the world, but because they were the first to generalize and bring to light a philosophical method, by the assistance of which it became easy to attack all that was old, and to open a path to all that was new.

If it be asked why, at the present day, this same method is more rigorously followed and more frequently applied by the French than by the Americans, although the principle of equality be no less complete, and of more ancient date, amongst the latter people, the fact may be attributed to two circumstances which it is essential to have clearly understood in the first instance.

It must never be forgotten that religion gave birth to Anglo-American society. In the United States religion is therefore commingled with all the habits of the nation and all the feelings of patriotism, whence it derives a peculiar strength. To this powerful reason, another of no less intensity may be added: in America religion has, as it were, laid down its own limits. Religious institutions have remained wholly distinct from political institutions, so that former laws have been easily changed whilst former belief has remained unshaken. Christianity has therefore retained a strong hold on the public mind in America; and, I would more particularly remark, that its sway is not only that of a philosophical doctrine which has been adopted upon inquiry, but of a religion which is believed without discussion. In the United States Christian sects are infinitely diversified and perpetually modified, but Christianity itself is a fact so irresistibly established, that no one undertakes either to attack or to defend it. The Americans, having admitted the principal doctrines of the Christian religion without inquiry, are obliged to accept in like manner a great number of moral truths originating in it and connected with it. Hence the activity of individual analysis is restrained within narrow limits, and many of the most important of human opinions are removed from the range of its influence.

The second circumstance to which I have alluded is the following: the social condition and the constitution of the Americans are democratic, but they have not had a democratic revolution. They arrived upon the soil they occupy in nearly the condition in which we see them at the present day; and this is of very considerable importance.

There are no revolutions which do not shake existing belief, enervate authority, and throw doubts over commonly received ideas. The effect of all revolutions is therefore more or less to surrender men to their own guidance, and to open to the mind of every man a void and almost unlimited range of speculation. When equality of conditions succeeds a protracted conflict between the different classes of which the elder society was composed, envy, hatred and mistrust of fellow-men, pride and exaggerated self-confidence are apt to prevail in men's minds for a time. This, independently of equality itself, tends strongly to divide men—to lead them to mistrust the judgment of others, and to seek the light of truth nowhere but in their own understandings. Everyone then attempts to be his own sufficient guide, and makes it his boast to form his own opinions on all subjects. Men are no longer bound together by ideas, but by interests; and it would seem as if human opinions were reduced to a sort of intellectual dust, scattered on every side, unable to collect, unable to cohere.

Thus, that independence of mind which equality supposes to exist, is never so great, nor ever appears so excessive, as at the time when equality is beginning to establish itself, and in the course of that painful labour by which it is established. That sort of intellectual freedom which equality may give ought therefore to be very carefully distinguished from the anarchy which revolution brings. Each of these two things must be separately considered, in order not to conceive exaggerated hopes or fears of the future.

I believe that the men who will live under the new forms of society will make frequent use of their private judgment; but I am far from thinking that they will often abuse it. This is attributable to a cause of more general application to all democratic countries, and which, in the long run, must needs restrain in them the independence of individual speculation within fixed, and sometimes narrow, limits.

I shall proceed to point out this cause in the next chapter.

THE PRINCIPAL SOURCE OF BELIEF AMONG DEMOCRATIC NATIONS

At different periods dogmatic beliefs are more or less abundant. They arise in different ways, and may change their object or form; but under no circumstances will dogmatic belief cease to exist. Or, in other words, men will never cease to hold some implicit opinions without subjecting them to actual discussion. If everyone undertook to form his own opinions and to seek for truth by isolated paths struck out by himself alone, it is not to be supposed that any considerable number of men would ever unite in any common belief.

But obviously without such common belief no society can prosper—indeed no society can subsist. For without ideas held in common, there is no common action, and without common action, there may still be men, but there is no social body. In order that society should exist, and, *a fortiori,* that a society should prosper, it is necessary that all the minds of the citizens should be rallied and held together by certain predominant ideas. And this cannot be the case unless each of them sometimes draws his opinions from the common source, and consents to accept certain matters of belief at the hands of the community.

If I now consider man in isolation, I find that dogmatic belief is no less indispensable to him in order to live alone than it is to enable him to co-operate with his fellow-creatures. If man were forced to demonstrate to himself all the truths of which he makes daily use, his task would never end. He would exhaust his strength in preparatory exercises, without advancing beyond them. As, from the shortness of his life, he has not the time, nor, from the limits of his intelligence, the capacity, to accomplish this, he is reduced to take upon trust a number of facts and opinions which he has not had either the time or the power to verify himself, but which men of greater ability have sought out, or which the world adopts. On this groundwork he raises for himself the structure of his own thoughts; nor is he led to proceed in this

From *Democracy in America,* pt. 2, bk. 1, chap. 2.

manner by choice, so much as he is constrained by the inflexible law of his condition.

There is no philosopher in the world so great that he does not believe a million of things on the faith of other people, and suppose a great many more truths than he demonstrates.

This is not only necessary but desirable. A man who undertook to inquire into everything for himself could devote to each thing but little time and attention. His task would keep his mind in perpetual unrest, which would prevent him from penetrating to the depth of any truth, or of grappling his mind indissolubly to any conviction. His intellect would be at once independent and powerless. He must therefore make his choice from amongst the various objects of human belief, and he must adopt many opinions without discussion, in order to search the better into that smaller number which he sets apart for investigation. It is true that whoever receives an opinion on the word of another does so far enslave his mind; but it is a salutary servitude which allows him to make a good use of freedom.

A principle of authority must then always occur, under all circumstances, in some part or other of the moral and intellectual world. Its place is variable, but a place it necessarily has. The independence of individual minds may be greater, or it may be less: unbounded it cannot be. Thus the question is, not to know whether any intellectual authority exists in the ages of democracy, but simply where it resides and by what standard it is to be measured. . . .

When the ranks of society are unequal, and men unlike each other in condition, there are some individuals invested with all the power of superior intelligence, learning, and enlightenment, whilst the multitude is sunk in ignorance and prejudice. Men living at these aristocratic periods are therefore naturally induced to shape their opinions by the superior standard of a person or a class of persons, whilst they are averse to recognize the infallibility of the mass of the people.

The contrary takes place in ages of equality. The nearer the citizens are drawn to the common level of an equal and similar condition, the less prone does each man become to place implicit faith in a certain man or a certain class of men. But his readiness to believe the multitude increases, and opinion is more than ever mistress of the world. Not only is common opinion the only guide which private judgment retains amongst a democratic people, but amongst such a people it possesses a power infinitely beyond what it has elsewhere. At periods of equality men have no faith in one another, by reason of their common resemblance; but this very resemblance gives them almost unbounded confidence in the judgment of the public; for it would not seem probable, as they are all endowed with equal means of judging, but that the greater truth should go with the greater number.

When the inhabitant of a democratic country compares himself individually with all those about him, he feels with pride that he is the equal of any one of them; but when he comes to survey the totality of his fellows, and to place himself in contrast to so huge a body, he is instantly overwhelmed by the sense of his own insignificance and weakness.

The same equality which renders him independent of each of his fellow-citizens, taken severally, exposes him alone and unprotected to the influence of the greater number.

The public has therefore among a democratic people a singular power, of which aristocratic nations could never so much as conceive an idea; for it does not persuade to certain opinions, but it enforces them, and infuses them into the faculties by a sort of enormous pressure of the minds of all upon the reason of each.

In the United States the majority undertakes to supply a multitude of ready-made opinions for the use of individuals, who are thus relieved from the necessity of forming opinions of their own. Everybody there adopts great numbers of theories, on philosophy, morals, and politics, without inquiry, upon public trust; and if we look to it very narrowly, it will be perceived that religion herself holds her sway there, much less as a doctrine of revelation than as a commonly received opinion.

The fact that the political laws of the Americans are such that the majority rules the community with sovereign sway, materially increases the power which that majority naturally exercises over the mind. For nothing is more customary in man than to recognize superior wisdom in the person of his oppressor. This political omnipotence of the majority in the United States doubtless augments the influence which public opinion would obtain without it over the mind of each member of the community; but the foundations of that influence do not rest upon it. They must be sought for in the principle of equality itself, not in the more or less popular institutions which men living under that condition may give themselves. The intellectual dominion of the greater number would probably be less absolute amongst a democratic people governed by a king than in the sphere of a pure democracy, but it will always be extremely absolute; and by whatever political laws men are governed in the ages of equality, it may be foreseen that faith in public opinion will become a species of religion there, and the majority its ministering prophet.

Thus intellectual authority will be different, but it will not be diminished; and far from thinking that it will disappear, I augur that it may readily acquire too much preponderance, and confine the action of private judgment within narrower limits than are suited either to the greatness or the happiness of the human race. In the principle of equality I very clearly discern two tendencies; the one leading the mind of every man to untried thoughts, the other inclined to prohibit him from thinking at all. And I perceive how, under the dominion of certain laws, democracy would extinguish that liberty of mind to which a democratic social condition is favourable; so that, after having broken all the bondage once imposed on it by ranks or by men, the human mind would be closely fettered to the general will of the greatest number.

WHY THE AMERICANS ARE MORE ADDICTED TO PRACTICAL THAN TO THEORETICAL SCIENCE

Those who cultivate the sciences amongst a democratic people are always afraid of losing their way in visionary speculation. They mistrust systems; they adhere closely to facts and the study of facts with their own senses. As they do not easily defer to the mere name of any fellow-man, they are never inclined to rest upon any man's authority; but, on the contrary, they are un-

From *Democracy in America,* pt. 2, bk. 1, chap. 10.

remitting in their efforts to point out the weaker points of their neighbors' opinions. Scientific precedents have very little weight with them; they are never long detained by the subtilty of the schools, nor ready to accept big words for sterling coin; they penetrate, as far as they can, into the principal parts of the subject which engages them, and they expound them in the vernacular tongue. Scientific pursuits then follow a freer and a safer course, but a less lofty one.

The mind may, as it appears to me, divide science into three parts.

The first comprises the most theoretical principles, and those more abstract notions, whose application is either unknown or very remote.

The second is composed of those general truths, which still belong to pure theory, but lead nevertheless by a straight and short road to practical truths.

Methods of application and means of execution make up the third.

Each of these different portions of science may be separately cultivated, although reason and experience show that none of them can prosper long, if it be absolutely cut off from the two others.

In America the purely practical part of science is admirably understood, and careful attention is paid to the theoretical portion which is immediately requisite to application. On this head the Americans always display a clear, free, original, and inventive power of mind. But hardly any one in the United States devotes himself to the essentially theoretical and abstract portion of human knowledge. In this respect the Americans carry to excess a tendency which is, I think, discernible, though in a less degree, amongst all democratic nations.

Nothing is more necessary to the culture of the higher sciences, or of the more elevated departments of science, than meditation; and nothing is less suited to meditation than the structure of democratic society. We do not find there, as amongst an aristocratic people, one class which clings to a state of repose because it is well off; and another, which does not venture to stir because it despairs of improving its condition. Everyone is active: some in quest of power, others of gain. In the midst of this universal tumult—this incessant conflict of jarring interests—this continual stride of men after fortune—where is that calm to be found which is necessary for the deeper products of the intellect? How can the mind dwell upon any single point, when everything whirls around it, and man himself is swept and beaten onwards by the heady current which rolls all things in its course? . . .

Men who live in democratic communities not only seldom indulge in meditation, but they naturally entertain very little esteem for it. A democratic state of society and democratic institutions plunge the greater part of men in constant active life; and the habits which are suited to an active life, are not always suited to a contemplative one. The man of action is frequently obliged to content himself with the best he can get, because he would never accomplish his purpose if he chose to carry every detail to perfection. He has perpetually occasion to rely on ideas which he has not had leisure to search to the bottom; for he is much more frequently aided by the opportunity of an idea than by its strict accuracy; and, in the long run, he risks less in making use of some false principles, than in spending his time in establishing all his principles on the basis of truth. The world is not led by long or learned demonstrations: a rapid glance at particular incidents, the daily study of the fleeting passions of the multitude, the accidents of the time, and the art of turning them to account, decide all its affairs.

In the ages in which active life is the condition of almost everyone, men are therefore generally led to attach an excessive value to the rapid bursts and superficial conceptions of the intellect; and, on the other hand, to depreciate below their true standard its slower and deeper labours. This opinion of the public influences the judgment of the men who cultivate the sciences; they are persuaded that they may succeed in those pursuits without meditation, or deterred from such pursuits as demand it.

There are several methods of studying the sciences. Amongst a multitude of men you will find a selfish, mercantile, and trading taste for the discoveries of the mind, which must not be confounded with that disinterested passion which is kindled in the heart of the few. A desire to utilize knowledge is one thing; the pure desire to know is another. I do not doubt that in a few minds and far between, an ardent, inexhaustible love of truth springs up,

self-supported, and living in ceaseless fruition without ever attaining the satisfaction which it seeks. This ardent love it is—this
proud, disinterested love of what is true—which raises men to the
abstract sources of truth, to draw their mother-knowledge
thence....

The future will prove whether these passions, at once so rare
and so productive, come into being and into growth as easily in
the midst of democratic as in aristocratic communities. For myself, I confess that I am slow to believe it.

In aristocratic society, the class which gives the tone to opinion, and has the supreme guidance of affairs, being permanently
and hereditarily placed above the multitude, naturally conceives a
lofty idea of itself and of man. It loves to invent for him noble
pleasures, to carve out splendid objects for his ambition. Aristocracies often commit very tyrannical and very inhuman actions;
but they rarely entertain grovelling thoughts; and they show a
kind of haughty contempt of little pleasures, even whilst they indulge in them. The effect is greatly to raise the general pitch of
society. In aristocratic ages vast ideas are commonly entertained
of the dignity, the power, and the greatness of man. These opinions exert their influence on those who cultivate the sciences, as
well as on the rest of the community. They facilitate the natural
impulse of the mind to the highest regions of thought, and they
naturally prepare it to conceive a sublime—nay, almost a
divine—love of truth.

Men of science at such periods are consequently carried away
by theory; and it even happens that they frequently conceive an
inconsiderate contempt for the practical part of learning. "Ar-
chimedes," says Plutarch, "was of so lofty a spirit, that he never
condescended to write any treatise on the manner of constructing
all these engines of offence and defence. And as he held this
science of inventing and putting together engines, and all arts
generally speaking which tended to any useful end in practice, to
be vile, low, and mercenary, he spent his talents and his studious
hours in writing of those things only whose beauty and subtlety
had in them no admixture of necessity." Such is the aristocratic
aim of science: in democratic nations it cannot be the same.

The greater part of the men who constitute these nations are
extremely eager in the pursuit of present and material gratifica-

tion. As they are always dissatisfied with the position which they occupy, and are always free to leave it, they think of nothing but the means of changing their fortune, or of increasing it. To minds thus predisposed, every new method which leads by a shorter road to wealth, every machine which spares labour, every instrument which diminishes the cost of production, every discovery which facilitates pleasures or augments them, seems to be the grandest effort of the human intellect. It is chiefly from these motives that a democratic people addicts itself to scientific pursuits—that it understands, and that it respects them. In aristocratic ages, science is more particularly called upon to furnish gratification to the mind; in democracies, to the body.

You may be sure that the more a nation is democratic, enlightened, and free, the greater will be the number of these interested promoters of scientific genius, and the more will discoveries immediately applicable to productive industry confer gain, fame, and even power on their authors. For in democracies the working class takes a part in public affairs; and public honours, as well as pecuniary remuneration, may be awarded to those who deserve them.

In a community thus organized it may easily be conceived that the human mind may be led insensibly to the neglect of theory; and that it is urged, on the contrary, with unparalleled vehemence to the applications of science, or at least to that portion of theoretical science which is necessary to those who make such applications. In vain will some innate propensity raise the mind towards the loftier spheres of the intellect; interest draws it down to the middle zone. There it may develop all its energy and restless activity, there it may engender all its wonders. These very Americans, who have not discovered one of the general laws of mechanics, have introduced into navigation a new machine which is changing the face of the world.

Certainly I do not contend that the democratic nations of our time are destined to witness the extinction of the transcendent luminaries of man's intelligence, nor even that no new lights will ever start into existence. At the age at which the world has now arrived, and amongst so many cultivated nations, perpetually excited by the fever of productive industry, the bonds which connect the different parts of science together cannot fail to strike the observation; and the taste for practical science itself, if it be enlightened, ought to lead men not to neglect theory. In the midst of such numberless attempted applications of so many experiments, repeated every day, it is almost impossible that general laws should not frequently be brought to light, so that great discoveries would be frequent, though great inventors rare.

I believe, moreover, in the high calling of scientific minds. If the democratic principle does not, on the one hand, induce men to cultivate science for its own sake, on the other it enormously increases the number of those who do cultivate it. Nor is it credible that, from amongst so great a multitude, no speculative genius should from time to time arise, inflamed by the love of truth alone. Such a one, we may be sure, would dive into the deepest mysteries of nature, whatever be the spirit of his country or his age. He requires no assistance in his genius—enough that it is not obstructed.

All that I mean to say is this: permanent inequality of conditions leads men to confine themselves to the arrogant and sterile research of abstract truths; whilst the social condition and the institutions of democracy prepare them to seek the immediate and useful practical results of the sciences. This tendency is natural and inevitable: it is curious, and it may be necessary to point it out.

If those who are called upon to guide the nations of our time clearly discerned from afar these new tendencies, which will soon be irresistible, they would understand that, possessing education and freedom, men living in democratic ages cannot fail to improve the industrial part of science; and that henceforward all the efforts of the constituted authorities ought to be directed to support the highest branches of learning, and to foster the nobler passion for science itself. In the present age the human mind must be coerced into theoretical studies. It runs of its own accord to practical applications; and instead of perpetually guiding it towards minute examination of secondary effects, it is well to divert it from them sometimes, in order to raise it up to the contemplation of primary causes.

Because the civilization of ancient Rome perished in consequence of the invasion of the barbarians, we are perhaps too apt to think that civilization cannot perish in any other manner. If the light by which we are guided is ever extinguished, it will dwindle by degrees, and expire of itself. By dint of close adherence to mere applications, principles would be lost sight of; and when the principles were wholly forgotten, the methods derived from them would be ill pursued. New methods could no longer be invented, and men would continue to apply, without intelligence, and without art, scientific processes no longer understood.

When Europeans first arrived in China, three hundred years ago, they found that almost all the arts had reached a certain degree of perfection there; and they were surprised that a people which had attained this point should not have gone beyond it. At a later period they discovered some traces of the higher branches of science which were lost. The nation was absorbed in productive industry; the greater part of its scientific processes had been preserved, but science itself no longer existed there. This served to explain the strangely motionless state in which they found the minds of this people. The Chinese, in following the track of their forefathers, had forgotten the reasons by which the latter had been guided. They still used the formula, without asking for its meaning; they retained the instrument, but they no longer possessed the art of altering or renewing it. The Chinese, then, had lost the power of change; for them to improve was impossible. They were compelled, at all times and in all points, to imitate their predecessors, lest they should stray into utter darkness, by deviating for an instant from the path already laid down for them. The spring of human knowledge was all but dry; and though the stream still ran on, it could neither swell its waters, nor alter its channels.

THE SPIRIT IN WHICH THE AMERICANS
CULTIVATE THE ARTS

The general mediocrity of fortunes, the absence of superfluous wealth, the universal desire of comfort, and the constant efforts by which everyone attempts to procure it, make the taste for the useful predominate over the love of the beautiful in the heart of

From *Democracy in America*, pt. 2, bk. 1, chap. 11.

man. Democratic nations, amongst which all these things exist, will therefore cultivate the arts which serve to render life easy, in preference to those whose object is to adorn it. They will habitually prefer the useful to the beautiful, and they will require that the beautiful should be useful. . . .

In countries in which riches as well as power are concentrated and retained in the hands of the few, the use of the greater part of this world's goods belongs to a small number of individuals, who are always the same. Necessity, public opinion, or moderate desires exclude all others from the enjoyment of them. As this aristocratic class remains fixed at the pinnacle of greatness on which it stands, without diminution or increase, it is always subject to the same wants and affected by them in the same manner. The men of whom it is composed naturally derive from their superior and hereditary position a taste for what is extremely well-made and lasting. This affects the general way of thinking of the nation in relation to the arts. If often occurs, among such a people, that even the peasant will rather go without the objects he covets than procure them in a state of imperfection. In aristocracies, then, the handicraftsmen work for only a limited number of very fastidious customers: the profit they hope to make depends principally on the perfection of their workmanship.

Such is no longer the case when, all privileges being abolished, ranks are intermingled, and men are for ever rising or sinking upon the ladder of society. Amongst a democratic people a number of citizens always exist whose patrimony is divided and decreasing. They have contracted, under more prosperous circumstances, certain wants, which remain after the means of satisfying such wants are gone; and they are anxiously looking out for some surreptitious method of providing for them. On the other hand, there are always in democracies a large number of men whose fortune is on the increase, but whose desires grow much faster than their fortunes, and who gloat upon the gifts of wealth in anticipation, long before they have the means to command them. Such men are eager to find some short cut to these gratifications, already almost within their reach. From the combination of these two causes the result is, that in democracies there are always a multitude of individuals whose wants are above their

means, and who are very willing to put up with imperfect satisfaction, rather than abandon the object of their desires.

The craftsman readily understands these passions, for he himself partakes in them: in an aristocracy he would seek to sell his
workmanship at a high price to the few; he now conceives that the
more expeditious way of getting rich is to sell them at a low price
to all. But there are only two ways of lowering the price of commodities. The first is to discover some better, shorter, and more
ingenious method of producing them: the second is to manufacture a larger quantity of goods, nearly similar, but of less value.
Amongst a democratic population, all the intellectual faculties of
the workman are directed to these two objects: he strives to invent methods which may enable him not only to work better, but
quicker and cheaper; or, if he cannot succeed in that, to diminish
the intrinsic qualities of the thing he makes, without rendering it
wholly unfit for the use for which it is intended. When none but
the wealthy had watches, they were almost all very good ones:
few are now made which are worth much, but everybody has one
in his pocket. Thus the democratic principle not only tends to
direct the human mind to the useful arts, but it induces the artisan
to produce with great rapidity a quantity of imperfect commodities, and the consumer to content himself with these commodities. . . .

⌊ When I arrive in a country where I find some of the finest
productions of the arts, I learn from this fact nothing of the social
condition or of the political constitution of the country. But if I
perceive that the productions of the arts are generally of an inferior quality, very abundant and very cheap, I am convinced
that, amongst the people where this occurs, privilege is on the
decline, and that ranks are beginning to intermingle, and will soon
be indistinguishable.⌉

The craftsmen of democratic ages endeavour not only to bring
their useful productions within the reach of the whole community, but they strive to give to all their commodities attractive
qualities which they do not in reality possess. In the confusion of
all ranks every one hopes to appear what he is not, and makes
great exertions to succeed in this object. This sentiment indeed,
which is but too natural to the heart of man, does not originate in

the democratic principle; but that principle applies it to material objects. To mimic virtue is of every age; but the hypocrisy of luxury belongs more particularly to the ages of democracy.

To satisfy these new cravings of human vanity, the arts have recourse to every species of imposture, and these devices sometimes go so far as to defeat their own purpose. Imitation diamonds are now made which may be easily mistaken for real ones; as soon as the art of fabricating false diamonds has reached so high a degree of perfection that they cannot be distinguished from real ones, it is probable that both one and the other will be abandoned, and become mere pebbles again.

This leads me to speak of those arts which are called the fine arts, by way of distinction. I do not believe that it a necessary effect of a democratic social condition and of democratic institutions to diminish the number of men who cultivate the fine arts; but these causes exert a very powerful influence on the manner in which these arts are cultivated. Many of those who had already contracted a taste for the fine arts are impoverished: on the other hand, many of those who are not yet rich begin to conceive that taste, at least by imitation; and the number of consumers increases, but opulent and fastidious consumers become more scarce. Something analogous to what I have already pointed out in the useful arts then takes place in the fine arts; the productions of artists are more numerous, but the merit of each production is diminished. No longer able to soar to what is great, they cultivate what is pretty and elegant, and appearance is more attended to than reality.

In aristocracies a few great pictures are produced; in democratic countries, a vast number of insignificant ones. In the former, statues are raised of bronze; in the latter, they are modelled in plaster.

When I arrived for the first time at New York, by that part of the Atlantic Ocean which is called the Narrows, I was surprised to perceive along the shore, at some distance from the city, a considerable number of little palaces of white marble, several of which were built after the models of ancient architecture. When I went the next day to inspect more closely the building which had particularly attracted my notice, I found that its walls were of whitewashed brick, and its columns of painted wood. All the edifices which I had admired the night before were of the same kind.

The social condition and the institutions of democracy impart, moreover, certain peculiar tendencies to all the imitative arts which it is easy to point out. They frequently turn them from depicting the soul to focus them exclusively on depicting the body, and they substitute the representation of motion and sensation for that of sentiment and thought. In a word, they put the Real in the place of the Ideal.

I doubt whether Raphael studied the minutest intricacies of the mechanism of the human body as thoroughly as the draftsmen of our own time. He did not attach the same importance to rigorous accuracy on this point as they do, because he aspired to surpass nature. He sought to make of man something which should be superior to man, and to embellish beauty's self. David and his scholars were, on the contrary, as good anatomists as they were good painters. They wonderfully depicted the models which they had before their eyes, but they rarely imagined anything beyond them. They followed nature with fidelity, whilst Raphael sought for something better than nature. They have left us an exact picture of man; but he reveals in his works a glimpse of the Divinity.

This remark as to the manner of treating a subject is no less applicable to the choice of it. The painters of the Middle Ages generally sought far above themselves, and away from their own time, for mighty subjects, which left to their imagination an unbounded range. Our painters frequently employ their talents in the exact imitation of the details of private life, which they have always before their eyes; and they are for ever copying trivial objects, the originals of which are only too abundant in nature.

LITERARY CHARACTERISTICS OF DEMOCRATIC AGES

Although America is perhaps in our days the civilized country in which literature is least attended to, a large number of persons are nevertheless to be found there who take an interest in the prod-

From *Democracy in America*, pt. 2, bk. 1, chap. 13.

ucts of the mind, and who make them, if not the study of their lives, at least the charm of their leisure hours. But England supplies these readers with the larger portion of the books which they require. Almost all important English books are republished in the United States. The literary genius of Great Britain still darts its rays into the recesses of the forests of the New World. There is hardly a pioneer's hut which does not contain a few odd volumes of Shakespeare. I remember that I read the feudal play of Henry V for the first time in a log house.

Not only do the Americans constantly draw upon the treasures of English literature, but it may be said with truth that they find the literature of England growing on their own soil. The larger part of that small number of men in the United States who are engaged in the composition of literary works are English in substance, and still more so in form. Thus they transport into the midst of democracy the ideas and literary fashions which are current amongst the aristocratic nation they have taken for their model. They paint with colours borrowed from foreign manners; and as they hardly ever represent the country they were born in as it really is, they are seldom popular there.

The citizens of the United States are themselves so convinced that it is not for them that books are published, that before they can make up their minds upon the merit of one of their authors, they generally wait till his fame has been ratified in England, just as in pictures the author of an original is held to be entitled to judge of the merit of a copy.

The inhabitants of the United States have then at present, properly speaking, no literature. The only authors whom I acknowledge as American are the journalists. They indeed are not great writers, but they speak the language of their countrymen, and make themselves heard by them. Other authors are aliens; they are to the Americans what the imitators of the Greeks and Romans were to us at the revival of learning, an object of curiosity, not of general sympathy. They amuse the mind, but they do not act upon the manners of the people.

I have already said that this state of things is very far from originating in democracy alone, and that the causes of it must be sought for in several peculiar circumstances independent of the democratic principle. If the Americans, retaining the same laws and social condition, had had a different origin, and had been transported into another country, I do not question that they would have had a literature. Even as they now are, I am convinced that they will ultimately have one; but its character will be different from that which marks the American literary productions of our time, and that character will be peculiarly its own. Nor is it impossible to trace this character beforehand.

I suppose an aristocratic people amongst whom letters are cultivated; the labours of the mind, as well as the affairs of state, are conducted by a ruling class in society. The literary as well as the political career is almost entirely confined to this class, or to those nearest to it in rank. These premises suffice to give me a key to all the rest.

When a small number of the same men are engaged at the same time upon the same objects, they easily concert with one another, and agree upon certain leading rules which are to govern them each and all. If the object which attracts the attention of these men is literature, the productions of the mind will soon be subjected by them to precise canons, from which it will no longer be allowable to depart. If these men occupy an hereditary position in the country, they will be naturally inclined, not only to adopt a certain number of fixed rules for themselves, but to follow those which their forefathers laid down for their own guidance; their code will be at once strict and traditional. As they are not necessarily engrossed by the cares of daily life—as they have never been so, any more than their fathers were before them—they have learned to take an interest, for several generations back, in the labours of the mind. They have learned to understand literature as an art, to love it in the end for its own sake, and to feel a scholar-like satisfaction in seeing men conform to its rules. Nor is this all: the men of whom I speak began and will end their lives in easy or in affluent circumstances; hence they have naturally conceived a taste for choice gratifications, and a love of refined and delicate pleasures. Nay more, a kind of indolence of mind and heart, which they frequently contract in the midst of this long and peaceful enjoyment of so much welfare, leads them to put aside, even from their pleasures, whatever might be too startling or too acute. They had rather be amused, than intensely excited; they wish to be interested, but not to be carried away.

Now let us fancy a great number of literary performances executed by the men, or for the men, whom I have just described, and we shall readily conceive a style of literature in which everything will be regular and pre-arranged. The slightest work will be carefully touched in its least details; art and labour will be conspicuous in everything; each kind of writing will have rules of its own, from which it will not be allowed to swerve, and which distinguish it from all others. Style will be thought of almost as much importance as thought; and the form will be no less considered than the matter: the diction will be polished, measured, and uniform. The tone of the mind will be always dignified, seldom very animated; and writers will care more to perfect what they produce, than to multiply their productions. It will sometimes happen, that the members of the literary class, always living amongst themselves and writing for themselves alone, will lose sight of the rest of the world, which will infect them with a false and laboured style; they will lay down minute literary rules for their exclusive use, which will insensibly lead them to deviate from common sense, and finally to transgress the bounds of nature. By dint of striving after a mode of parlance different from the vulgar, they will arrive at a sort of aristocratic jargon, which is hardly less remote from pure language than is the coarse dialect of the people. Such are the natural perils of literature amongst aristocracies. Every aristocracy which keeps itself entirely aloof from the people becomes impotent—a fact which is as true in literature as it is in politics.

Let us now turn the picture and consider the other side of it: let us transport ourselves into the midst of a democracy, not unprepared by ancient traditions and present culture to partake in the pleasures of the mind. Ranks are there intermingled and indistinguishable; knowledge and power are both infinitely subdivided, and, if I may use the expression, scattered on every side. Here then is a motley multitude, whose intellectual wants are to be supplied. These new votaries of the pleasures of the mind have not all received the same education; they do not possess the same degree of culture as their fathers, nor any resemblance to them—nay, they perpetually differ from themselves, for they live in a state of incessant change of place, feelings, and fortunes. The mind of each member of the community is therefore unattached to that of his fellow-citizens by tradition or by common habits; and they have never had the power, the inclination, nor the time to concert together. It is however from the bosom of this heterogeneous and agitated mass that authors spring; and from the same source their profits and their fame are distributed.

I can without difficulty understand that, under these circumstances, I must expect to meet in the literature of such a people with but few of those strict conventional rules which are recognised by readers and by writers in aristocratic ages. If it should happen that the men of some one period were agreed upon any such rules, that would prove nothing for the following period; for, amongst democratic nations, each new generation is a new people. Amongst such nations, then, literature will not easily be subjected to strict rules, and it is impossible that any such rules should ever be permanent.

In democracies it is by no means the case that all the men who cultivate literature have received a literary education; and most of those who have some tinge of belles-lettres, are either engaged in politics, or in a profession which only allows them to taste occasionally and by stealth the pleasures of the mind. . . . They prefer books which may be easily procured, quickly read, and which require no learned researches to be understood. They ask for beauties, self-proffered, and easily enjoyed; above all, they must have what is unexpected and new. Accustomed to the struggle, the crosses, and the monotony of practical life, they require rapid emotions, startling passages—truths or errors brilliant enough to rouse them up, and to plunge them at once, as if by violence, into the midst of a subject.

Why should I say more? or who does not understand what is about to follow, before I have expressed it? Taken as a whole, literature in democratic ages can never present, as it does in the periods of aristocracy, an aspect of order, regularity, science, and art; its form will, on the contrary, ordinarily be slighted, sometimes despised. Style will frequently be fantastic, incorrect, overburdened, and loose—almost always vehement and bold. Authors will aim at rapidity of execution, more than at perfection of detail. Small productions will be more common than bulky books:

there will be more wit than erudition, more imagination than profundity; and literary performances will bear marks of an untutored and rude vigour of thought—frequently of great variety and singular fecundity. The object of authors will be to astonish rather than to please, and to stir the passions more than to charm the taste.

Here and there, indeed, writers will doubtless occur who will choose a different track, and who will, if they are gifted with superior abilities, succeed in finding readers, in spite of their defects or their better qualities; but these exceptions will be rare, and even the authors who shall so depart from the received practice in the main subject of their works, will always relapse into it in some lesser details.

I have just depicted two extreme conditions: the transition by which a nation passes from the former to the latter is not sudden but gradual, and marked with shades of very various intensity. In the passage which conducts a lettered people from the one to the other, there is almost always a moment at which the literary genius of democratic nations has its confluence with that of aristocracies, and both seek to establish their joint sway over the human mind. Such epochs are transient, but very brilliant: they are fertile without exuberance, and animated without confusion. French literature of the eighteenth century may serve as an example.

I should say more than I mean, if I were to assert that the literature of a nation is always subordinate to its social condition and its political constitution. I am aware that, independently of these causes, there are several others which confer certain characteristics on literary productions; but these appear to me to be the chief....

The Trade of Literature

Democracy not only infuses a taste for letters among the trading classes, but introduces a trading spirit into literature.

In aristocracies, readers are fastidious and few in number; in

From *Democracy in America,* pt. 2, bk. 1, chap. 14.

democracies, they are far more numerous and far less difficult to please. The consequence is, that among aristocratic nations no one can hope to succeed without immense exertions, and that these exertions may bestow a great deal of fame, but can never earn much money; whilst among democratic nations, a writer may flatter himself that he will obtain at a cheap rate a meagre reputation and a large fortune. For this purpose he need not be admired, it is enough that he is liked.

The ever-increasing crowd of readers, and their continual craving for something new, ensures the sale of books which nobody much esteems.

In democratic periods the public frequently treat authors as kings do their courtiers; they enrich, and they despise them. What more is needed by the venal souls which are born in courts, or which are worthy to live there?

Democratic literature is always infested with a tribe of writers who look upon letters as a mere trade; and for some few great authors who adorn it, you may reckon thousands of idea-mongers.

The Effect of Democracy on Language

It is not to the written, but to the spoken language that attention must be paid, if we would detect the modifications which the idiom of an aristocratic people may undergo when it becomes the language of a democracy.

Englishmen of education, and more competent judges than I can be myself of the nicer shades of expression, have frequently assured me that the language of the educated classes in the United States is notably different from that of the educated classes in Great Britain. They complain, not only that the Americans have brought into use a number of new words—the difference and the distance between the two countries might suffice to explain that much—but that these new words are more especially taken from the jargon of parties, the mechanical arts, or the language of

From *Democracy in America,* pt. 2, bk. 1, chap. 16.

trade. They assert, in addition to this, that old English words are often used by the Americans in new senses and lastly, that the inhabitants of the United States frequently intermingle their phraseology in the strangest manner, and sometimes place words together which are always kept apart in the language of the mother-country. These remarks, which were made to me at various times by persons who appeared to be worthy of credit, led me to reflect upon the subject; and my reflections brought me, by theoretical reasoning, to the same point at which my informants had arrived by practical observation.

In aristocracies, language must naturally partake of that state of repose in which everything remains. Few new words are coined, because few new things are made; and even if new things were made, they would be designated by known words, whose meaning has been determined by tradition . . . Democratic nations love change for its own sake; and this is seen in their language as much as in their politics. Even when they do not need to change words, they sometimes feel a wish to transform them.

The genius of a democratic people is not only shown by the great number of words they bring into use, but also by the nature of the ideas these new words represent. Amongst such a people the majority lays down the law in language as well as in everything else; its prevailing spirit is as manifest in that as in other respects. But the majority is more engaged in business than in study—in political and commercial interests, than in philosophical speculation or literary pursuits. Most of the words coined or adopted for its use will therefore bear the mark of these habits; they will mainly serve to express the wants of business, the passions of party, or the details of the public administration. . . .

The most common expedient employed by democratic nations to make an innovation in language consists in giving some unwonted meaning to an expression already in use. This method is very simple, prompt, and convenient; no learning is required to use it aright, and ignorance itself rather facilitates the practice, but that practice is most dangerous to the language. When a demcratic people doubles the meaning of a word in this way, they sometimes render the signification which it retains as ambiguous as that which it acquires. An author begins by a slight deflection of a known expression from its primitive meaning, and he adapts it, thus modified, as well as he can to his subject. A second writer twists the sense of the expression in another way; a third takes possession of it for another purpose; and as there is no common appeal to the sentence of a permanent tribunal which may definitively settle the signification of the word, it remains in an ambiguous condition. The consequence is that writers hardly ever appear to dwell upon a single thought, but they always seem to point their aim at a knot of ideas, leaving the reader to judge which of them has been hit.

This is a deplorable consequence of democracy. I had rather that the language should be made hideous with words imported from the Chinese, the Tartars, or the Hurons, than that the meaning of a word in our own language should become indeterminate. Harmony and uniformity are only secondary beauties in composition: many of these things are conventional, and, strictly speaking, it is possible to forgo them; but without clear phraseology there is no good language.

The principle of equality necessarily introduces several other changes into language.

In aristocratic ages, when each nation tends to stand aloof from all others and likes to have distinct characteristics of its own, it often happens that several peoples which have a common origin become nevertheless estranged from each other; so that, without ceasing to understand the same language, they no longer all speak it in the same manner. In these ages each nation is divided into a certain number of classes, which see but little of each other and do not intermingle. Each of these classes contracts, and invariably retains, habits of mind peculiar to itself, and adopts by choice certain words and certain terms, which afterwards pass from generation to generation, like their estates. The same idiom then comprises a language of the poor and a language of the rich, a language of the citizen and a language of the nobility, a learned language and a vulgar one. The deeper the divisions, and the more impassable the barriers of society become, the more must this be the case. I would lay a wager that amongst the castes of India there are amazing variations of language, and that there is almost as much difference between the language of the Pariah and that of the Brahmin as there is in their dress.

When, on the contrary, men, being no longer restrained by ranks, meet on terms of constant intercourse—when castes are destroyed, and the classes of society are recruited and intermixed with each other—all the words of a language are mingled. Those which are unsuitable to the greater number perish: the remainder form a common store, whence everyone chooses pretty nearly at random. Almost all the different dialects which divided the idioms of European nations are manifestly declining: there is no *patois* in the New World, and it is disappearing every day from the old countries.

The influence of this revolution in social conditions is as much felt in style as it is phraseology. Not only does everyone use the same words, but a habit springs up of using them without discrimination. The rules which style had set up are almost abolished: the line ceases to be drawn between expressions which seem by their very nature vulgar, and others which appear to be refined. Persons springing from different ranks of society carry the terms and expressions they are accustomed to use with them into whatever circumstances they may pass; thus the origin of words is lost like the origin of individuals, and there is as much confusion in language as there is in society. . . .

I shall not quit this topic without touching on a feature of democratic languages which is perhaps more characteristic of them than any other. It has already been shown that democratic nations have a taste, and sometimes a passion, for general ideas, and that this arises from their peculiar merits and defects. This liking for general ideas is displayed in democratic languages by the continual use of generic terms or abstract expressions, and by the manner in which they are employed. This is the great merit and the great imperfection of these languages.

Democratic nations are passionately addicted to generic terms or abstract expressions, because these modes of speech enlarge thought, and assist the operations of the mind by enabling it to include several objects in a small compass. . . .

I cannot better illustrate what I mean than by my own example.

I have frequently used the word "equality" in an absolute sense—nay, I have personified equality in several places; thus I have said that equality does such and such things, or refrains from doing others. It may be affirmed that the writers of the age of Louis XIV would not have used these expressions: they would never have thought of using the word equality without applying it to some particular object; and they would rather have renounced the term altogether than have consented to make a living personage of it.

These abstract terms which abound in democratic languages, and which are used on every occasion without attaching them to any particular fact, enlarge and obscure the thoughts they are intended to convey; they render the mode of speech more succinct, and the idea contained in it less clear. But with regard to language, democratic nations prefer obscurity to labour.

Indeed I am not sure whether this loose style does not have some secret charm for those who speak and write amongst these nations. As the men who live there are frequently left to the efforts of their individual powers of mind, they are almost always a prey to doubt: and as their situation in life is for ever changing, they are never held fast to any of their opinions by the certain tenure of their fortunes. Men living in democratic countries are, then, apt to entertain unsettled ideas, and they require loose expressions to convey them. As they never know whether the idea they express to-day will be appropriate to the new position they may occupy to-morrow, they naturally acquire a liking for abstract terms. An abstract term is like a box with a false bottom; you may put in it what ideas you please, and take them out again without being observed.

Amongst all nations, generic and abstract terms form the basis of language. I do not, therefore, affect to expel these terms from democratic languages; I simply remark, that men have an especial tendency, in the ages of democracy, to multiply words of this kind—to take them always by themselves in their most abstract acceptation, and to use them on all occasions, even when the nature of the discourse does not require them.

CHARACTERISTICS OF HISTORIANS IN DEMOCRATIC AGES

Historians who write in aristocratic ages are wont to refer all occurrences to the particular will or temper of certain individuals; and they are apt to attribute the most important revolutions to very slight accidents. They trace out the smallest causes with sagacity, and frequently leave the greatest unperceived.

Historians who live in democratic ages exhibit precisely opposite characteristics. Most of them attribute hardly any influence to the individual over the destiny of the race, nor to citizens over the fate of a people; but, on the other hand, they assign great general causes to all petty incidents. These contrary tendencies explain each other.

When the historian of aristocratic ages surveys the theatre of the world, he at once perceives a very small number of prominent actors, who manage the whole piece. These great personages, who occupy the front of the stage, attract the historian's attention and fix it on themselves; and whilst the historian is bent on penetrating the secret motives which make them speak and act, he forgets about the rest. The importance of the things which some men are seen to do, gives him an exaggerated estimate of the influence which one man may possess, and naturally leads him to think that in order to explain the impulses of the multitude it is necessary to refer them to the particular influence of some one individual.

When, on the contrary, all the citizens are independent of one another, and each of them is individually weak, no-one is seen to exert a great, or still less, a lasting power, over the community. At first sight, individuals appear to be absolutely devoid of any influence over it; and society would seem to advance alone by the free and voluntary concurrence of all the men who compose it. This naturally prompts the mind to search for that general reason which operates upon so many men's faculties at the same time, and turns them simultaneously in the same direction.

I am very well convinced, that even amongst democratic nations, the genius, the vices, or the virtues of certain individuals retard or accelerate the natural current of a people's history; but

From *Democracy in America*, pt. 2, bk. 1, chap. 20.

causes of this secondary and fortuitous nature are infinitely more various, more concealed, more complex, less powerful, and consequently less easy to trace in periods of equality than in ages of aristocracy, when the task of the historian is simply to detach from the mass of general events the particular influences of one man or of a few men. In the former case the historian is soon wearied by the toil; his mind loses itself in this labyrinth. And, in his inability clearly to discern or conspicuously to point out the influence of individuals, he denies their existence. He prefers talking about the characteristics of race, the physical conformation of the country, or the genius of civilization—which abridges his own labours, and satisfies his reader far better at less cost.

M. de Lafayette says somewhere in his Memoirs that the exaggerated system of general causes affords surprising consolations to second-rate statesmen. I would add that its effects are no less consoling to second-rate historians; it can always furnish a few mighty reasons to extricate them from the most difficult part of their work, and it indulges the indolence or incapacity of their minds, whilst it confers upon them the honours of deep thinking.

For myself, I am of opinion that at all times one great portion of the events of this world are attributable to general facts, and another to special inflences. These two kinds of cause are always in operation; only their proportion varies. General facts serve to explain more things in democratic than in aristocratic ages, and fewer things are then assignable to special influences. At periods of aristocracy the reverse takes place: special influences are stronger, general causes weaker—unless indeed we consider as a general cause the fact itself of the inequality of conditions, which allows some individuals to baffle the natural tendencies of all the rest.

Historians who seek to describe what occurs in democratic societies are right, therefore, in assigning much to general causes, and in devoting their chief attention to discovering them; but they are wrong in wholly denying the special influence of individuals, because they cannot easily trace or follow it.

Historians who live in democratic ages are not only prone to assign a great cause to every incident, but they are also given to connect incidents together, so as to deduce a system from them.

In aristocratic ages, as the attention of historians is constantly drawn to individuals, the connection of events escapes them; or rather, they do not believe in any such connection. To them the clue of history seems every instant crossed and broken by the step of man. In democratic ages, on the contrary, as the historian sees much more of actions than of actors, he may easily establish some kind of sequency and methodical order amongst the former.

Ancient literature, which is so rich in fine historical compositions, does not contain a single great historical system, whilst the poorest of modern literatures abound with them. It would appear that the ancient historians did not make sufficient use of those general theories which our historical writers are ever ready to carry to excess.

Those who write in democratic ages have another more dangerous tendency. When the traces of individual action upon nations are lost, it often happens that the world goes on moving, though the moving agent is no longer discoverable. As it becomes extremely difficult to discern and to analyse the reasons which, acting separately on the volition of each member of the community, concur in the end to produce movement in the whole mass, men are led to believe that this movement is involuntary, and that societies unconsciously obey some superior force ruling over them. But even when the general fact which governs the private volition of all individuals is supposed to be discovered upon the earth, the principle of human free-will is not secure. A cause sufficiently extensive to affect millions of men at once, and sufficiently strong to bend them all together in the same direction, may well seem irresistible: having seen that mankind do yield to it, the mind is close upon the inference that mankind cannot resist it.

Historians who live in democratic ages, then, not only deny that the few have any power of acting upon the destiny of a people, but they deprive the people themselves of the power of modifying their own condition, and they subject them either to an inflexible Providence, or to some blind necessity. According to them, each nation is indissolubly bound by its position, its origin, its precedents, and its character, to a certain lot which no efforts can ever change. They involve generation in generation, and thus, going back from age to age, and from necessity to necessity, up to the origin of the world, they forge a close and enormous chain, which girds and binds the human race. To their minds it is not enough to show what events have occurred: they would fain show that events could not have occurred otherwise. They take a nation arrived at a certain stage of its history, and they affirm that it could not but follow the track which brought it thither. It is easier to make such an assertion, than to show by what means the nation might have adopted a better course.

In reading the historians of aristocratic ages, and especially those of antiquity, it would seem that, to be master of his lot and to govern his fellow-creatures, man requires only to be master of himself. In perusing the historical volumes which our age has produced, it would seem that man is utterly powerless over himself and over all around him. The historians of antiquity taught how to command: those of our time teach only how to obey; in their writings the author often appears great, but humanity is always diminutive.

If this doctrine of necessity, which is so attractive to those who write history in democratic ages, passes from authors to their readers, till it infects the whole mass of the community and gets possession of the public mind, it will soon paralyze the activity of modern society, and reduce Christians to the level of the Turks.

I would moreover observe, that such principles are peculiarly dangerous at the present day. Our contemporaries are only too prone to doubt human free-will, because each of them feels himself confined on every side by his own weakness; but they are still willing to acknowledge the strength and independence of men united in society. Let not this principle be lost sight of; for the great object in our time is to raise the faculties of men, not to complete their prostration.

5

THE ANCIEN RÉGIME
AND THE ORIGINS
OF THE FRENCH REVOLUTION

THE NATURE OF THE PROBLEM

No nation had ever before embarked on so resolute an attempt as that of the French in 1789 to break with the past, to make, as it were, a scission in their life line and to create an unbridgeable gulf between all they had hitherto been and all they now aspired to be. With this in mind they took a host of precautions so as to make sure of importing nothing from the past into the new régime, and saddled themselves with all sorts of restrictions in order to differentiate themselves in every possible way from the previous generation; in a word, they spared no pains in their endeavor to obliterate their former selves.

I have always felt that they were far less successful in this curious attempt than is generally supposed in other countries and than they themselves at first believed. For I am convinced that though they had no inkling of this, they took over from the old régime not only most of its customs, conventions, and modes of thought, but even those very ideas which prompted our revolutionaries to destroy it; that, in fact, though nothing was further from their intentions, they used the debris of the old order for building up the new. Thus if we wish to get a true understanding of the French Revolution and its achievement, it is well to disregard for the moment the France of today and to look back to the France that is no more. This is what I have aimed at doing in the present book, and I must admit that it proved to be a far less easy task than I had expected when I first embarked on it.

From *The Old Régime and the French Revolution*, Foreword.

The early monarchy, the Middle Ages, and the Renaissance have been the subject of exhaustive treatises and painstaking research work; thus we are well acquainted not only with the historical events but also with the legislative systems, customs, and ideologies of the French government and people in these periods. But nobody so far has thought fit to study the eighteenth century with the same meticulous care. True, we imagine we know all about the French social order of the period, for the good reason that its surface glitter holds our gaze and we are familiar not only with the life stories of its outstanding figures but also, thanks to the many brilliant critical studies now available, with the works of the great writers who adorned that age. But we have only vague, often quite wrong conceptions of the manner in which public business was transacted and institutions functioned; of the exact relations between the various classes in the social hierarchy; of the situation and sentiments of that section of the population which as yet could neither make itself heard nor seen; and, by the same token, of the ideas and mores basic to the social structure of eighteenth-century France.

I have tried to strike to the heart of this phase of the *ancien régime,* so near to us in time, but overshadowed so completely by the Revolution. With this in view I have not merely reread those well-known books which made literary history in the eighteenth century, but given much time to studying records that, while less known and rightly regarded as of minor importance, throw perhaps more light on the true spirit of the age. I have given special attention to the public documents in which Frenchmen voiced their opinions and aspirations on the eve of the Revolution. The minutes of the meetings of the "Estates" and, later, of the provincial assemblies were particularly enlightening. Above all, I have made use of the *cahiers* (written instructions given to the deputies by their constituents) drawn up in 1789 by the three Orders of the State. This long series of manuscript volumes constitutes, as it were, the swan song of the old régime, the ultimate expression of its ambitions, its last will and testament.

But I have also had recourse to other, no less rewarding sources of information. In a country where a strong central administration has gained control of all the national activities there are few trends of thought, desires or grievances, few interests or propensities that do not sooner or later make themselves known to it, and in studying its records we can get a good idea not only of the way in which it functioned but of the mental climate of the country as a whole. Were a foreigner given free access to the confidential files of the Ministry of the Interior and those of our prefectures, he would soon come to know more about present-day France than we know ourselves. In the eighteenth century, as readers of this book will not fail to note, the government of France was already highly centralized and all-powerful; indeed, the range of its activities was prodigious. We find it constantly coming to the rescue of individuals in difficulties, issuing permits or vetoes, as the case might be; lavish of promises and subsidies. Its influence made itself felt at every turn, not only in the management of public affairs but also in the private lives of citizens and families. Moreover, as there was no danger of publicity, no one felt any qualms about informing it of his personal troubles, even when these reflected no credit on himself. I have devoted much time to studying such records of this order as have survived in Paris and in several provinces.

In their archives I found (as indeed I had expected) a living memorial of the spirit of the old régime, the ways men thought and felt, their habits and their prejudices. For in them everyone expressed his views with total frankness and voiced his inmost thoughts. Thus I had access to a mine of information which was not available to contemporaries, since these archives were kept rigorously secret.

The more closely I studied these documents, the more I was struck by the innumerable resemblances between the France of that period and nineteenth-century France. Men had, it seemed, already many of the sentiments and opinions which I had always regarded as products of the Revolution, and in the same way many of the customs commonly thought to stem from it exclusively had already entered into our mores. It would seem, in fact, that the peculiarities of our modern social system are deeply rooted in the ancient soil of France. The nearer my researches brought me to that fateful year 1789, the more clearly did I see the spirit which sponsored the conception, birth, and fruition of the

Revolution gaining ground, and little by little all its salient features taking form under my eyes. For it was not merely foreshadowed in the years preceding it; it was an immanent reality, a presence on the threshold. These records disclose not only the reasons of the events accompanying its outbreak but also, and perhaps even more clearly, those of its aftereffects on the destinies of France. The Revolution had, indeed, two distinct phases: one in which the sole aim of the French nation seemed to be to make a clean sweep of the past; and a second, in which attempts were made to salvage fragments from the wreckage of the old order. For many of the laws and administrative methods which were suppressed in 1789 reappeared a few years later, much as some rivers after going underground re-emerge at another point, in new surroundings.

In the work I now present to the public my aim is, firstly, to indicate the reasons why it was in France rather than elsewhere that the Great Revolution, stirrings of which were perceptible in almost all European countries, came to a head; secondly, why it presented itself as an almost natural outcome of the very social order it made such haste to destroy; and, lastly, why the monarchy which had weathered so many storms in the past collapsed so suddenly and catastrophically.

How, Though Its Objectives Were Political, the French Revolution Followed the Lines of a Religious Revolution and Why This Was So

Whereas all social and political revolutions had so far been confined to the countries in which they took their rise, the French Revolution aspired to be world-wide and its effect was to erase all the old national frontiers from the map. We find it uniting or dividing men throughout the world, without regard to national traditions, temperaments, laws, and mother tongues, sometimes leading them to regard compatriots as foes and foreigners as their kinsmen. Or, perhaps, it would be truer to say that it created a

From *The Old Régime*, pt. 1, chap. 3.

common intellectual fatherland whose citizenship was open to men of every nationality and in which racial distinctions were obliterated.

In all the annals of recorded history we find no mention of any *political* revolution that took this form; its only parallel is to be found in certain *religious* revolutions. Thus when we seek to study the French Revolution in the light of similar movements in other countries and at other periods, it is to the great religious revolutions we should turn.

Schiller rightly points out in his *History of the Thirty Years' War* that one of the most striking effects of the reformation that took place in the sixteenth century was the bringing together of races which knew next to nothing of each other and the creation of a novel sense of fellow feeling between them. So it was that when Frenchmen were fighting against Frenchmen, the English intervened, while men hailing from remote Baltic hinterlands advanced into the heart of Germany to defend the cause of Germans of whose very existence they had until then been almost unaware. Foreign wars tended to assume the nature of civil wars, while in civil wars foreigners came to take a hand. Former interests were superseded by new interests, territorial disputes by conflicts over moral issues, and all the old notions of diplomacy were thrown into the melting pot—much to the horror and dismay of the professional politicians of the age. Precisely the same thing happened in Europe after 1789.

Thus the French Revolution, though ostensibly political in origin, functioned on the lines, and assumed many of the aspects, of a religious revolution. Not only did it have repercussions far beyond French territory, but like all great religious movements it resorted to propaganda and broadcast a gospel. This was something quite unprecedented: a political revolution that sought proselytes all the world over and applied itself as ardently to converting foreigners as compatriots. Of all the surprises that the French Revolution launched on a startled world, this surely was the most astounding. But there was more to it than that; let us try to carry our analysis a stage further and to discover if this similarity of effects may not have stemmed, in fact, from an underlying similarity of causes.

Common to all religions is an interest in the human personality, the man-in-himself irrespective of the trappings foisted on him by local traditions, laws, and customs. The chief aim of a religion is to regulate both the relations of the individual man with his Maker and his rights and duties towards his fellow men on a universal plane, independently, that is to say, of the views and habits of the social group of which he is a member. The rules of conduct thus enjoined apply less to the man of any given nation or period than to man in his capacity of son, father, master, servant, neighbor. Since these rules are based on human nature, pure and simple, they hold good for men in general all the world over. To this is due the fact that religious revolutions have often ranged so far afield and seldom been confined, like political revolutions, to their country of origin or even to a single race. Moreover, when we look more deeply into the matter, we find that the more a religion has the universal, abstract qualities described above, the vaster is its sphere of influence and the less account it takes of differences of laws, local conditions, and temperaments.

The pagan religions of antiquity were always more or less linked up with the political institutions and the social order of their environment, and their dogmas were conditioned to some extent by the interests of the nations, or even the cities, where they flourished. A pagan religion functioned within the limits of a given country and rarely spread beyond its frontiers. It sometimes sponsored intolerance and persecutions, but very seldom embarked on missionary enterprises. This is why there were no great religious revolutions in the Western World before the Christian era. Christianity, however, made light of all the barriers which had prevented the pagan religions from spreading, and very soon won to itself a large part of the human race. I trust I shall not be regarded as lacking in respect for this inspired religion if I say it partly owed its triumph to the fact that, far more than any other religion, it was catholic in the exact sense, having no links with any specific form of government, social order, period, or nation.

The French Revolution's approach to the problems of man's existence here on earth was exactly similar to that of the religious revolutions as regards his afterlife. It viewed the "citizen" from an abstract angle, that is to say as an entity independent of any particular social order, just as religions view the individual, without regard to nationality or the age he lives in. It did not aim merely at defining the rights of the French citizen, but sought also to determine the rights and duties of men in general towards each other and as members of a body politic.

It was because the Revolution always harked back to universal, not particular, values and to what was the most "natural" form of government and the most "natural" social system that it had so wide an appeal and could be imitated in so many places simultaneously.

No previous political upheaval, however violent, had aroused such passionate enthusiasm, for the ideal the French Revolution set before it was not merely a change in the French social system but nothing short of a regeneration of the whole human race. It created an atmosphere of missionary fervor and, indeed, assumed all the aspects of a religious revival—much to the consternation of contemporary observers. It would perhaps be truer to say that it developed into a species of religion, if a singularly imperfect one, since it was without a God, without a ritual or promise of a future life. Nevertheless, this strange religion has, like Islam, overrun the whole world with its apostles, militants, and martyrs.

It must not be thought, however, that the methods employed by the Revolution had no precedents or that the ideas it propagated were wholly new. In all periods, even in the Middle Ages, there had been leaders of revolt who, with a view to effecting certain changes in the established order, appealed to the universal laws governing all communities, and championed the natural rights of man against the State. But none of these ventures was successful; the firebrand which set all Europe ablaze in the eighteenth century had been easily extinguished in the fifteenth. For doctrines of this kind to lead to revolutions, certain changes must already have taken place in the living conditions, customs, and mores of a nation and prepared men's minds for the reception of new ideas.

There are periods in a nation's life when men differ from each other so profoundly that any notion of "the same law for all" seems to them preposterous. But there are other periods when it is enough to dangle before their eyes a picture, however indistinct and remote, of such a law and they promptly grasp its meaning and hasten to acclaim it. In fact, the most extraordinary thing about the Revolution is not that it employed the methods which led to its success or that certain men should have conceived the ideas which supplied its driving force. What was wholly novel was that so many nations should have simultaneously reached a stage in their development which enabled those methods to be successfully employed and that ideology to be so readily accepted.

WHAT DID THE FRENCH REVOLUTION ACCOMPLISH?

The aim of the Revolution was not, as once was thought, to destroy the authority of the Church and religious faith in general. Appearances notwithstanding, it was essentially a movement for political and social reform and, as such, did not aim at creating a state of permanent disorder in the conduct of public affairs or (as one of its opponents bitterly remarked) at "methodizing anarchy." On the contrary, it sought to increase the power and jurisdiction of the central authority. Nor was it intended, as some have thought, to change the whole nature of our traditional civilization, to arrest its progress, or even to make any vital changes in the principles basic to the structure of society in the Western World. If we disregard various incidental developments which briefly modified its aspect at different periods and in different lands, and study it as it was essentially, we find that the chief permanent achievement of the French Revolution was the suppression of those political institutions, commonly described as feudal, which for many centuries had held unquestioned sway in most European countries. The Revolution set out to replace them with a new social and political order, at once simple and more uniform, based on the concept of the equality of all men.

This in itself was enough to constitute a thorough-paced revolution since, apart from the fact that the old feudal institutions still entered into the very texture of the religious and political institutions of almost the whole of Europe, they had also given rise

From *The Old Régime*, pt. 1, chap. 5.

to a host of ideas, sentiments, manners, and customs which, so to speak, adhered to them. Thus nothing short of a major operation was needed to excise from the body politic these accretions and to destroy them utterly. The effect was to make the Revolution appear even more drastic than it actually was; since what it was destroying affected the entire social system.

Radical though it may have been, the Revolution made far fewer changes than is generally supposed, as I shall point out later. What in point of fact it destroyed, or is in process of destroying—for the Revolution is still operative—may be summed up as everything in the old order that stemmed from aristocratic and feudal institutions, was in any way connected with them, or even bore, however faintly, their imprint. The only elements of the old régime that it retained were those which had always been foreign to its institutions and could exist independently of them. Chance played no part whatever in the outbreak of the Revolution; though it took the world by surprise, it was the inevitable outcome of a long period of gestation, the abrupt and violent conclusion of a process in which six generations had played an intermittent part. Even if it had not taken place, the old social structure would nonetheless have been shattered everywhere sooner or later. The only difference would have been that instead of collapsing with such brutal suddenness it would have crumbled bit by bit. At one fell swoop, without warning, without transition, and without compunction, the Revolution effected what in any case was bound to happen, if by slow degrees.

Such then was the achievement of the Revolution, and it may appear surprising that even the most clear-sighted contemporaries should have missed the point of an event whose purport seems so clear to us today. Even Burke failed to understand it. "You wish to correct the abuses of your government," he said to the French, "but why invent novelties? Why not return to your old traditions? Why not confine yourselves to a resumption of your ancient liberties? Or, if it was not possible to recover the obliterated features of your original constitution, why not look towards England? There you have found the ancient common law of Europe." Burke did not see that what was taking place before his eyes was a revolution whose aim was precisely to abolish that "ancient common law of Europe," and that there could be no question of putting the clock back.

But why did the storm that was gathering over the whole of Europe break in France and not elsewhere, and why did it acquire certain characteristics in France which were either absent in similar movements in other countries, or if present, assumed quite different forms?

WHY FEUDALISM HAD COME TO BE MORE DETESTED IN FRANCE THAN IN ANY OTHER COUNTRY

At first sight it may appear surprising that the Revolution, whose primary aim, as we have seen, was to destroy every vestige of the institutions of the Middle Ages, should not have broken out in countries where those institutions had the greatest hold and bore most heavily on the people instead of those in which their yoke was relatively light.

At the close of the eighteenth century serfdom had not yet been completely abolished anywhere in Germany; indeed, in most parts of that country the peasants were still literally bound to the land, as they had been in the Middle Ages. The armies of Frederick II and Maria Theresa were composed almost entirely of men who were serfs on the medieval pattern.

In most German states in 1788 the peasant was not allowed to quit his lord's estate; if he did so, he was liable to be tracked down wherever he was and brought back in custody. He was subject to the jurisdiction of his lord, who kept a close eye on his private life and could punish him for intemperance or idleness. He could neither better his social position, change his occupation, nor even marry without his master's consent, and a great number of his working hours had to be spent in his master's service. The system of compulsory labor, known in France as the *corvée*, was in full force in Germany, and in some districts entailed no less than three days' work a week. The peasant was expected to keep the buildings on his lord's estate in good repair and to carry the

From *The Old Régime*, pt. 2, chap. 1

produce of the estate to market; he drove his lord's carriage and carried his messages. Also he had to spend some years of his youth in his lord's household as a member of the domestic staff. However, it was possible for the serf to become a landowner, though his tenure was always hedged round with restrictions. He had to cultivate his land in a prescribed manner, under his lord's supervision, and could neither alienate nor mortgage it without permission. In some cases he was compelled to sell its produce, in others forbidden to sell it; in any case he was bound to keep the land under cultivation. Moreover, his children did not inherit his entire estate, some part of it being usually withheld by his lord.

It must not be thought that I am describing ancient or obsolete laws; these provisions can be found even in the code drawn up by Frederick the Great and put in force by his successor at the very time when the French Revolution was getting under way.

In France such conditions had long since passed away; the peasants could move about, buy and sell, work, and enter into contracts as they liked. Only in one or two eastern provinces, recent annexations, some last vestiges of serfdom lingered on; everywhere else it had wholly disappeared. Indeed, the abolition of serfdom had taken place in times so remote that its very date had been forgotten. However, as a result of recent research work it is now known that as early as the thirteenth century serfdom had ceased to exist in Normandy.

Meanwhile another revolution, of a different order, had done much to improve the status of the French peasant; he had not merely ceased to be a serf, he had also become a landowner. Though this change had far-reaching consequences, it is apt to be overlooked, and I propose to devote some pages to this all-important subject.

Until quite recently it was taken for granted that the splitting up of the landed estates in France was the work of the Revolution, and the Revolution alone; actually there is much evidence in support of the contrary view. Twenty years or more before the Revolution we find complaints being made that land was being subdivided to an unconscionable extent. "The practice of partitioning inheritances," said Turgot, writing at about this time, "has gone so far that a piece of land which just sufficed for a single family is now parceled out between five or six sons. The result is that the heirs and their families soon find that they cannot depend on the land for their livelihood and have to look elsewhere." And some years later Necker declared that there was "an inordinate number" of small country estates in France.

In a confidential report made to an Intendant shortly before the Revolution I find the following observations: "Inheritances are being subdivided nowadays to an alarming extent. Everybody insists on having his share of the land, with the result that estates are broken up into innumerable fragments, and this process of fragmentation is going on all the time." One might well imagine these words to have been written by one of our contemporaries.

I have been at great pains to make, as it were, a cadastral survey (i.e., of the distribution of land) of the old régime and have to some extent, I think, succeeded. Under the provisions of the law of 1790, which imposed a tax on land, each parish was required to draw up a return of all the privately owned land within its boundaries. Most of these documents are lost, but I discovered some in certain villages and on comparing them with their modern equivalents have found that in these villages the number of landowners was as high as half, often two thirds, of the present number. These figures are impressive, and all the more so when we remember that the population of France has risen by over twenty-five per cent since that time.

Then, as in our own day, the peasant's desire for owning land was nothing short of an obsession and already all the passions to which possession of the soil gives rise in present-day France were active. "Land is always sold above its true value," a shrewd contemporary observer remarked, "and this is due to the Frenchman's inveterate craving to become a landowner. All the savings of the poorer classes, which in other countries are invested in private companies or the public funds, are used for buying land."

When Arthur Young visited France for the first time, among a multitude of new experiences, none impressed him more than the extent to which ownership of the soil was vested in innumerable peasant proprietors; half the cultivable land was owned by them. "I had no idea," he often says, "that such a state of affairs existed anywhere"—and in fact none such existed outside France.

There had once been many peasant proprietors in England, but by now their number had greatly dwindled. Everywhere in Germany and in all periods a limited number of free peasants had enjoyed full ownership of the land they worked. The special, often highly peculiar laws regulating the cultivator's ownership of land are set forth in the oldest German *Books of Customs,* but this type of ownership was always exceptional, there never were many of these small landed proprietors.

It was chiefly along the Rhine that at the close of the eighteenth century German farmers owned the land they worked and enjoyed almost as much freedom as the French small proprietor; and it was there, too, that the revolutionary zeal of the French found its earliest adepts and took most permanent effect. On the other hand, the parts of Germany which held out longest against the current of new ideas were those where the peasants did not as yet enjoy such privileges—and this is, to my mind, a highly suggestive fact.

Thus the prevalent idea that the breakup of the big estates in France began with the Revolution is erroneous; it had started long before. True, the revolutionary government sold the estates owned by the clergy and many of those owned by the nobility; however, if we study the records of these sales (a rather tedious task, but one which I have on occasion found rewarding) we discover that most of the parcels of land were bought by people who already had land of their own. Thus, though estates changed hands, the number of landowners was increased much less than might have been expected. For, to employ the seemingly extravagant, but in this case correct, expression used by Necker, there were already "myriads" of such persons.

What the Revolution did was not to parcel out the soil of France, but to "liberate" it—for a while. Actually these small proprietors had much difficulty in making a living out of the land since it was subject to many imposts from which there was no escaping.

That these charges were heavy is undeniable, but, oddly

enough, what made them seem so unbearable was something that, on the face of it, should have had the opposite effect: the fact that, as in no other part of Europe, our agriculturists had been emancipated from the control of their lords—a revolution no less momentous than that which had made them peasant proprietors.

Although the old régime is still so near to us in time—every day we meet persons born under its auspices—it already seems buried in the night of ages. So vast was the revolution that has intervened that its shadow falls on all that it did not destroy, and it is as if centuries lay between the times we live in and the revolutionary epoch. This explains why so few people know the answer to the quite simple question: How was rural France administered previous to 1789? And indeed it is impossible to give a full and accurate answer without having studied not the literature but the administrative records of the period.

I have often heard it said that though they had long ceased to play a part in the government of the country as a whole, the nobility kept in their hands, right up to the end, the administration of the rural districts; that, in fact, the landed proprietor "ruled" his peasants. This idea, too, seems based on a misconception of the true state of affairs.

In the eighteenth century all that touched the parish, the rural equivalent of the township, was under the control of a board of officials who were no longer agents of the seigneur or chosen by him. Some were nominated by the Intendant of the province, others elected by the local peasantry. Amongst the many functions of these officials were those assessing the tax to be paid by each member of the community, of keeping churches in repair, of building schools, of summoning and presiding over the parish assemblies. They supervised the municipal funds, decided how these were to be expended, and in litigation to which the parish was a party acted as its representatives. Far from controlling the administration of parish affairs the lord had no say at all in them. All members of the parish councils were ex officio public servants or under the control of the central power. . . . As for the lord, he rarely figured as the King's representative in the parish or as an intermediary between him and its inhabitants. He was no longer expected to see to the maintenance of law and order, to call out the militia, to levy taxes, to publish royal edicts, or to distribute the King's bounty in times of shortage. All these rights and duties had passed into the hands of others and the lord was in reality merely one of the inhabitants of the parish, differentiated from the others by certain exemptions and privileges. His social rank was higher, but he had no more power than they. In letters to their subdelegates the Intendents were careful to point out that the lord was only "the first resident."

When we turn from the parish to the larger territorial unit, the canton, we find the same arrangement; the nobles play no part, collectively or individually, in the administration of public affairs. This was peculiar to France; in all other countries what was the chief characteristic of ancient feudalism persisted to some extent and possession of the land carried with it the right to govern the people on it.

England was administered as well as governed by the great landed proprietors. Even in those parts of Germany, for example Prussia and Austria, where the ruling Princes had been most successful in shaking off the control of the nobility in the conduct of affairs of State, they had allowed the nobles to retain to some extent the administration of the rural areas. Though in some places they kept a firm hand on the local lord, they had not, as yet, supplanted him.

The French nobility, however, had long ceased to play any part in public administration, with one exception: the administration of justice. The leading nobles retained the right of delegating to judges appointed by them the trial of certain kinds of suits and still issued police regulations, from time to time, that held good within the limits of their domains. But the central authority had gradually curtailed and subordinated to itself the judicial powers of the landed proprietor; to such an extent that the lords who still exercised them regarded them as little more than a source of revenue.

The same thing had happened to all the special powers of the nobility; on the political side these powers were now defunct and only the pecuniary advantages attaching to them remained (and in some cases had been much increased). At this point something must be said about those lucrative privileges which our forefathers usually had in mind when they spoke of "feudal rights," since it was these that most affected the life of the general public.

It is hard to say today which of these rights were still in force in 1789 and in what they consisted. There had been a vast number of them and by then many had died out or been modified almost out of recognition; indeed, the exact meaning of the terms in which they are described (about which even contemporaries were not very clear) is extremely hard to ascertain today. Nevertheless, my study of works by eighteenth-century experts on feudal law and my researches into local usages have made it clear to me that the rights still functioning in 1789 fell into a relatively small number of categories; others survived, no doubt, but they were operative only in exceptional cases.

Of the old seigneurial *corvée,* or statutory labor obligation, traces remained everywhere, but half obliterated. Most of the toll charges on the roads had been reduced or done away with, though there were few provinces in which some had not survived. Everywhere the resident seigneur levied dues on fairs and markets, and everywhere enjoyed exclusive rights of hunting. Usually he alone possessed dovecotes and pigeons, and it was the general rule that farmers must bring their wheat to their lord's mill and their grapes to his wine press. A universal and very onerous right was that named *lods et ventes*; that is to say an impost levied by the lord on transfers of land within his domain. And throughout the whole of France the land was subject to quitrents, ground rents, dues in money or in kind payable by the peasant proprietor to his lord and irredeemable by the former. Varied as they were, all these obligations had one common feature: they were associated with the soil or its produce, and all alike bore heavily on the cultivator.

The lords spiritual enjoyed similar privileges. For though the Church derived its authority from a different source and had aims and functions quite different from those of the temporal power, it had gradually become tied up with the feudal system and, though never fully integrated into it, was so deeply involved as to seem part and parcel of it.

Bishops, canons, and abbots owned fiefs or quitrents in virtue of their ecclesiastical status, and usually monasteries had seig-neurial rights over the villages on whose land they stood. The monastery had serfs in the only part of France where serfdom had survived, employed forced labor, levied dues on fairs and mar-kets, had the monopoly of the communal wine press, bakehouse, mill, and the stud bull. Moreover, the clergy enjoyed in France—as indeed in all Christian Europe—the right of levying tithes.

The point, however, on which I would lay stress is that exactly the same feudal rights were in force in every European land and that in most other countries of the continent they pressed far more heavily on the population than in France. Take, for exam-ple, the lord's right to forced labor, the *corvée*. It was rarely exercised and little oppressive in France, whereas in Germany it was stringent and everywhere enforced.

Moreover, when we turn to the feudal rights which so much outraged our fathers and which they regarded as opposed not merely to all ideas of justice but to the spirit of civilization itself (I am thinking of the tithe, irredeemable ground rents, perpetual charges, *lods et ventes*, and so forth, all that in the somewhat grandiloquent language of the eighteenth century was styled "the servitude of the land"), we find that all these practices obtained to some extent in England and, indeed, are still found there today. Yet they do not prevent English husbandry from being the best organized and most productive in the modern world; and, what is perhaps still more remarkable, the English nation seems hardly aware of their existence.

Why then did these selfsame feudal rights arouse such bitter hatred in the heart of the French people that it has persisted even after its object has long since ceased to exist? One of the reasons is that the French peasant had become a landowner, and another that he had been completely emancipated from the control of his lord. (No doubt there were other reasons, but these, I think, were the chief ones.)

If the peasant had not owned his land he would hardly have no-ticed many of the charges which the feudal system imposed on all real estate. What could the tithe matter to a man who had no land of his own? He could simply deduct it from the rent. And even restrictions hampering agriculture mean nothing to an agriculturist who is simply cultivating land for the benefit of someone else.

Moreover, if the French peasant had still been under his lord's control, the feudal rights would have seemed much less obnoxious, because he would have regarded them as basic to the constitution of his country.

When the nobles had real power as well as privileges, when they governed and administered, their rights could be at once greater and less open to attack. In fact, the nobility was regarded in the age of feudalism much as the government is regarded by everyone today; its exactions were tolerated in view of the protection and security it provided. True, the nobles enjoyed invidious privileges and rights that weighed heavily on the commoner, but in return for this they kept order, administered justice, saw to the execution of the laws, came to the rescue of the oppressed, and watched over the interests of all. The more these functions passed out of the hands of the nobility, the more uncalled-for did their privileges appear—until at last their mere existence seemed a meaningless anachronism.

I would ask you to picture to yourself the French peasant as he was in the eighteenth century—or, rather, the peasant you know today, for he has not changed at all. His status is different, but not his personality. See how he appears in the records from which I have been quoting: a man so passionately devoted to the soil that he spends all his earnings on buying land, no matter what it costs. To acquire it he must begin by paying certain dues, not to the government but to other landowners of the neighborhood, who are as far removed as he from the central administration and almost as powerless as he. When at long last he has gained possession of this land which means so much to him, it is hardly an exaggeration to say that he sinks his heart in it along with the grain he sows. The possession of this little plot of earth, a tiny part, his very own, of the wide world, fills him with pride and a sense of independence. But now the neighbors aforesaid put in an appearance, drag him away from his cherished fields, and bid him work elsewhere without payment. When he tries to protect his seedlings from the animals they hunt, they tell him to take down his fences, and they lie in wait for him at river crossings to exact a toll. At the market there they are again, to make him pay for the right of selling the produce of his land, and when on his return home he wants to use the wheat he has put aside for his daily needs, he has to take it to their mill to have it ground, and then to have his bread baked in the lord's oven. Thus part of the income from his small domain goes to supporting these men in the form of charges which are imprescriptible and irredeemable. Whatever he sets out to do, he finds these tiresome neighbors barring his path, interfering in his simple pleasures and his work, and consuming the produce of his toil. And when he has done with them, other fine gentlemen dressed in black step in and take the greater part of his harvest. When we remember the special temperament of the French peasant proprietor in the eighteenth century, his ruling interests and passions, and the treatment accorded him, we can well understand the rankling grievances that burst into a flame in the French Revolution.

For even after it had ceased to be a political institution, the feudal system remained basic to the economic organization of France. In this restricted form it was far more hated than in the heyday of feudalism, and we are fully justified in saying that the very destruction of some of the institutions of the Middle Ages made those which survived seem all the more detestable.

ADMINISTRATIVE CENTRALIZATION
UNDER THE ANCIEN RÉGIME

In the bygone years when we still had political assemblies in France I remember hearing one of the speakers referring to the centralization of our country's government as "a glorious achievement of the Revolution, the envy of all Europe." Far be it from me to deny that this centralization was a glorious achievement and that other nations envy us in this respect, but I do deny that it was an achievement of the Revolution. On the contrary, it was a legacy from the old régime and, I may add, the only part of

From *The Old Régime,* pt. 2, chaps. 2 and 6.

the political constitution of that régime which survived the Revolution—for the good reason that it alone could be adapted to the new social system sponsored by the Revolution. . . .

A first glance at the administration of France under the old order gives the impression of a vast diversity of laws and authorities, a bewildering confusion of powers. In all parts of the kingdom we find administrative bodies and officials vested with rights acquired by purchase, which could not be withdrawn from them. There was no co-operation between them and often their functions overlapped to such an extent that they hampered each other or came into conflict when their activities covered the same ground.

The courts of justice indirectly took a hand in legislation; they had the right to frame administrative rules which had the force of law within their jurisdictions. Sometimes they made a stand against the central administration, vigorously censured its procedures and even issued writs against its representatives. Local magistrates drew up police regulations for the towns and boroughs where they resided.

In the towns systems of administration were very varied; the chief officials had different titles and derived their powers from different sources. In some towns there were "Consuls," in others "Syndics," in others Mayors. Some were appointed by the King, others by the seigneur or a princely holder of the appanage. Some were elected annually by their fellow townsmen, others bought the right of governing the latter in perpetuity.

Obviously we here have vestiges of the old system of a multiplicity of powers, but meanwhile there had gradually arisen new or greatly modified methods of local government, which I shall now describe.

At the heart of the realm, very near the throne, an administrative body, vested with high authority and combining in a new manner all the pre-existing powers, had little by little taken form; this was the *conseil du roi* or Royal Council. The Royal Council was composed not of great lords but of men of middle-class or even low extraction: former Intendants and others who had practical experience of public business, and any of its members could be dismissed at the King's will. . . . Though the Council was of ancient origin, most of its functions were of recent date. It was at once the supreme court of appeal (for it could set aside the judgments of all ordinary courts) and the highest administrative authority, for on it depended in the last resort all the "special jurisdictions." Moreover, as a governing council it also possessed, subject to the King's approval, the power of legislation. Most of the new laws were proposed and debated by the Council, which also fixed the sums to be levied by taxation and their distribution. As the highest administrative body in the land it was called on to enact the regulations determining the duties of government officials in their various spheres. It made decisions on all important matters and supervised the work of the subordinate civil authorities. In fact, all the affairs of the realm came before it in the last instance and it gave directives in every field of the administration. . . .

In the same way as the general administration of the country was in the hands of a single group of men, almost the entire management of internal affairs was in the hands of a single official, the Controller-General. . . . It was the Controller-General who had the whip hand in the conduct of public business and he had gradually brought under his control everything that had to do with money, in other words almost the entire administration of the country, and we find him acting as Finance Minister, Minister of the Interior, of Public Works, of Commerce.

Just as the central administration had to all intents and purposes only one executive officer in Paris, so it had only one such representative in each province. True, in the eighteenth century we still find great lords bearing the title of Governors of Provinces, these men being traditional, often hereditary representatives of the feudal monarchy of the past. But though they still were treated with deference, they had ceased to have any power now that all real authority was vested in the Intendants.

The Intendant was a young man of humble extraction, who still had his way to make and was never a native of the province to which he was posted. He did not obtain his office by purchase, by right of birth, or by election, but was chosen by the government from amongst the junior members of the Council and he was always liable to dismissal. In the official jargon of the time he was described as a *commissaire départi*, because he had been "detached" from the Council to act as its provincial agent. Most of the powers possessed by the Council itself were vested in him and he was entitled to use them as he thought fit. Like those of the Council these were both administrative and judicial; he corresponded directly with Ministers and was sole executant of all the measures enacted by the government in the province to which he had been posted. . . .

Anyone who reads letters that passed between the Intendants and their superiors or subordinates cannot fail to be struck by the family likeness between the government officials of the past and those of modern France. They seem to join hands across the abyss made by the Revolution and, indeed, the same may be said of the people they administered. Never, perhaps, has the extent to which systems of government shape the mentality of the governed been so clearly demonstrated.

Long before the Revolution, Ministers of State had made a point of keeping a watchful eye on everything that was happening in the country and of issuing orders from Paris on every conceivable subject. As time went on and with the increasing efficiency of administrative technique, this habit of surveillance became almost an obsession with the central government. Towards the close of the eighteenth century it was impossible to arrange for poor-relief work in the humblest village of a province hundreds of miles from the capital without the Controller-General insisting on having his say about the exact sum to be expended, the site of the workhouse, and the way it was to be managed. When an almshouse was established, he insisted on being supplied with the names of the paupers using it, the dates of their arrival and departure. In 1733 M. d'Argenson observed that "the amount of office work imposed on our heads of departments is quite appalling. Everything passes through their hands, they alone decide what is to be done, and when their knowledge is not as wide as their authority, they have to leave things to subordinate members of their staffs, with the result that the latter have become the true rulers of the country."

The Controller-General did not merely call for reports on matters of public interest; he insisted also on being given detailed information, often of a trivial kind, about private persons. In such cases the Intendant directed his subdelegates to make inquiries and in his report to the Controller-General he repeated verbatim what they had told him, without mentioning that he knew the facts only at second hand.

Owing to this system of centralizing information and controlling everything from Paris, a most elaborate machinery had to be set up for coping with the flood of documents that poured in from all sides, and even so the delays of the administration were notorious. On studying the records I found that it took a year at least for a parish to get permission to repair a church steeple or the priest's house. Oftener than not the time required was much longer: two or three years.

The Council itself took notice of this regrettable state of affairs in one of its minutes (March 29, 1773). "The transaction of public business is delayed to an almost incredible extent by administrative formalities and the public has all too often just cause for complaint. Nevertheless," the writer makes haste to add, "all these formalities are indispensable." . . .

Already characteristic of the French civil service was its intense dislike for all outsiders, whether of noble or of middle-class extraction, who showed a wish to take a hand, on their own initiative, in public affairs. Any independent group, however small, which seemed desirous of taking action otherwise than under the aegis of the administration filled it with alarm, and the tiniest free association of citizens, however harmless its aims, was regarded as a nuisance. The only corporate bodies tolerated were those whose members had been hand-picked by the administration and which were under its control. Even big industrial concerns were frowned upon. In a word, our administration resented the idea of private citizens' having any say in the control of their own enterprises, and preferred sterility to competition. . . .

During the eighteenth century the central power had not as yet developed the healthy, robust constitution which it has today. All the same, since by then it had succeeded in eliminating all intermediate authorities and since there was a vast gulf between the government and the private citizen, it was accepted as being the only source of energy for the maintenance of the social system, and as such, indispensable to the life of the nation.

This is borne out even in the writings of its bitterest adversaries. In the long period of rankling unrest and rising discontent preceding the Revolution all sorts of schemes were worked up for the establishment of a new social order and a new method of government. The ends proposed by the reformers varied greatly, but the means were always the same. They wished to make use of the central power, as it stood, for shattering the whole social structure and rebuilding it on lines that seemed to them desirable. For, to their thinking, only the central authority could bring this "ideal State" into being, and there should be no limit to its might, as there was none to its right. The one thing needed was to persuade it to exercise its power in the right direction. . . .

Such notions were not confined to books; they had taken root in people's minds and were implicit in their ways of living; in fact, they entered into the very texture of everyday life throughout the country.

It never occurred to anyone that any large-scale enterprise could be put through successfully without the intervention of the State. Even the cultivators—and the French cultivator has always had a shrewd mistrust of his would-be mentors—came to believe that the government was largely to blame for the backwardness of agriculture in France because it did not give the peasants adequate assistance and advice. In the recriminatory tone of a letter written by a farmer to an Intendant we sense something of the spirit of the impending revolution. "Why does government not appoint inspectors to tour the provinces once a year and examine the condition of the crops and explain to the cultivators how to improve them, how to rear their cattle, fatten them and sell them, and at what places they can count on the best markets? These inspectors should draw good salaries and the farmer producing the best crops in each district should be given a badge of merit." (This idea of touring inspectors and badges of merit would certainly have tickled an English farmer of the day!) . . .

The government having stepped into the place of Divine Providence in France, it was but natural that everyone, when in difficulties, invoked its aid. We find a vast number of petitions which, though the writers professed to be speaking on behalf of the public, were in reality intended to further their small private interests. The files in which they figure are perhaps the only places in which all the various classes of prerevolutionary France rub shoulders, so to speak. They make depressing reading. We find peasants applying for compensation for the loss of their cattle or their homes; wealthy landowners asking for financial aid for the improvement of their estates; manufacturers petitioning the Intendant for monopolies protecting them from competition. Often, too, businessmen report to the Intendant confidentially that their affairs are in a bad way and request him to approach the Controller-General for a loan to tide them over this emergency. (It would seem, in fact, that special funds were earmarked for such eventualities.) Sometimes even members of the nobility did not disdain to play the part of suppliants, the only difference being that their letters were more grandiloquently phrased than those of the common herd. . . .

In times of dearth—and these were frequent in the eighteenth century—everyone expected the Intendant to come to the rescue as a matter of course. For the government was held responsible for all the misfortunes befalling the community; even when these were "acts of God," such as floods or droughts, the powers-that-be were blamed for them.

For all these reasons we need not be surprised at the remarkable ease with which centralization was re-established in France at the beginning of the nineteenth century. Though the men of '89 had overthrown the ancient edifice, its foundations had been laid immutably in the minds of all Frenchmen, even its destroyers; thus there was little trouble in reestablishing it not only rapidly but in a more stable, shockproof form.

How Paternal Government, as It Is Called Today, Had Been Practiced under the Ancien Régime

Under the feudal system the lord, while possessing extensive powers, had no less imperative duties, one of these being to succor the needy within his domain. A last vestige of this ancient

From *The Old Régime*, pt. 2, chaps. 2 and 3.

obligation, which once obtained throughout Europe, can be found in the Prussian Code of 1795, where we read that "the lord must see to it that poor peasants are given education. As far as possible he should provide means of livelihood for such of his vassals as have no land, and if any are reduced to poverty he must come to their aid."

In France, however, no such law had existed for a long while; having been divested of his power, the lord no longer felt bound by his traditional obligations. And no local authority, no poor relief committee or parish council had taken them over. Now that nobody was bound by law to see to the welfare of the poor in rural areas, the central government had, somewhat venturesomely, accepted sole responsibility for this duty. Every year the Council allotted to each province a sum of money taken from the public funds for poor relief. This was divided up by the Intendant between the parishes under his control and it was to him that the cultivator had to apply in time of need. It was he, too, who made distributions of wheat or rice when the crops had failed. Each year the Council issued orders for the setting up in various places (specified by itself) of poor-houses, in which impoverished peasants were given work at a low wage. For obvious reasons a system of relief operating from such a distance was bound to be capricious, sometimes misdirected, and always quite inadequate.

However, the central government did not limit itself to coming to the rescue of the peasantry when times were hard; it aspired to teach them how to become rich and to help them to make their land pay, even if this meant using what was little short of compulsion. Pamphlets on agricultural science were issued periodically by the Intendants and their subdelegates, farmers' associations were founded and prizes awarded; moreover, nurseries, whose seed grains were available to all, were maintained at considerable expense. Still one cannot help feeling that it would have been more to the point to have lightened some of the fiscal burdens under which the agriculturist was laboring and equalized their incidence. But as far as one can see, no such idea ever crossed the minds of the authorities.

Sometimes the Council tried to force workers to make more money, willy-nilly. Dozens of laws were passed ordering artisans to use "improved" methods and to manufacture certain specified kinds of goods. Since the Intendants were unable to cope with the work involved in the enforcement of all these regulations "Inspectors-General of Industry" were appointed who toured the provinces to make sure they were complied with.

We find decrees prohibiting the growing of certain crops on land which the Council declared unsuitable for them; thus vine-growers were ordered to uproot their vines when these were planted—according to the omniscient Council—on a bad soil. In short, the central power had taken to playing the part of an indefatigable mentor and keeping the nation in quasi-paternal tutelage.

Municipal autonomy survived the feudal system, and long after the lords had ceased to administer the country districts French towns retained the right of governing themselves. Indeed, until almost the end of the seventeenth century some towns were still to all intents and purposes small democratic republics, their officials being elected by the townsfolk and answerable to them alone. In short, there was an active municipal life in which all took part, and the communities of French towns still prided themselves on their ancient rights and set much store in their independence.

It was not until 1692 that free municipal elections were everywhere abolished. In that year appointments to municipal posts were, to use the official jargon of the day, "put in offices," which meant that the King now sold to certain members of the community the right of governing in perpetuity their fellow citizens.

This dealt a serious blow not only to the independence but also to the prosperity of the towns. True, the system of making public offices purchasable may often work well enough where judicial posts are concerned, since the criterion of a good judge is his incorruptibility and the purchaser of such a post may be presumed to be a man of substance. But the system of selling offices has always had disastrous effects when applied to administrative and executive posts, the chief qualifications for which are a sense of responsibility combined with zeal and a habit of obedience. The monarchical government had no illusions on the subject and took good care not to apply to its own personnel the system foisted on the towns. Thus, for example, it never put up to sale the post of Intendant or subdelegate.

A circumstance on which historians may justly pour scorn is that this vast, not to say revolutionary, innovation had no political aim in view. True, Louis XI had curtailed the townsfolk's rights because they savored of democracy, which he regarded as a danger to the throne; Louis XIV, however, when he abolished them altogether, had no such fear. This is proved by the fact that he was quite willing to sell back their rights to such towns as could raise the sums required. In fact, he was less concerned with destroying local autonomy than with making money out of it. If the result in many cases was the extinction of the municipal freedom of the past, this was merely incidental to his financial policy and, one almost might say, unintended. Strangest of all, this curious process went on for eighty years, during which period towns were invited on no less than seven occasions to buy the right of electing their executive officials; then, after they had tasted for a while the pleasure of self-government, the right was withdrawn and sold back to them once more. This was always done for the same reason, and often the central government made no secret of it. Thus in the preamble to the Edict of 1722 we read: "Given the present financial stringency, we must needs employ the most effective methods of reducing it." The methods in question were certainly effective, but ruinous for those on whom the burden fell. "I am appalled," wrote an Intendant to the Controller-General in 1764, "by the huge sums that this town has disbursed from time to time to repurchase the right of choosing its own officials. Had the money been employed on works of public utility, all the townsfolk would have greatly benefited; as it is, they have had to bear the brunt of expenditure entailed by these offices and the privileges they carry with them." To my thinking, this was the most shameful feature of the old régime. . . .

Municipal government in the eighteenth century had everywhere degenerated into a petty oligarchy. . . . The Assembly now consisted of members of the middle class, representatives of the business corporations, and contained very few artisans. Not so easily hoodwinked as many have imagined, the "common people" ceased to take any active part in local government and lost all interest in it. Time and again the authorities tried to re-awaken that fine spirit of local patriotism which had worked such wonders in the Middle Ages—but without success. The ordinary citizen seemed wholly indifferent to the interests of the town he lived in.... A few families kept a watchful eye on their own interests, out of sight of the public and feeling no responsibilities toward less privileged citizens. Everywhere in France the local governments were stricken with this disease, and all Intendants drew attention to it. But the only remedy they could think of was to tighten the central government's control over the local authorities....

When we turn from towns to villages we find other powers, other methods; but the same subordination. I have found much evidence in support of the view that during the Middle Ages the inhabitants of each French village formed a commonalty independent in many ways of the seigneur. No doubt he requisitioned their services, watched over and governed them; but the village held property in common and had exclusive ownership of it. The villagers elected their own officials and governed themselves on democratic lines....

I well remember my surprise when I was for the first time examining the records of an intendancy with a view to finding out how much a parish was administered under the old order. For in the organization of this small community, despite its poverty and servile state, I discovered some of the features which had struck me so much in the rural townships of North America: features which I then had—wrongly—thought peculiar to the New World. Neither had permanent representatives, that is to say a town council in the strict sense of the term, and both were administered by officials acting separately, under instructions from the whole community. General assemblies were convened from time to time in both and at these the townsfolk, acting in concert, elected their own officials and passed orders on matters affecting the interests of the community. In short, the French and the American systems resembled each other—in so far as a dead creature can be said to resemble one that is very much alive.

For these two systems of local government, though their ways soon parted, had in fact a common origin. Transported overseas from feudal Europe and free to develop in total independence, the rural parish of the Middle Ages became the township of New England. Emancipated from the seigneur, but controlled at every turn by an all-powerful government, it took in France the form which we shall now describe.

During the eighteenth century the number and the titles of parish officials varied from province to province. Old records show that they once had been most numerous where there was a vigorous communal life and fewest where it had decayed. By the eighteenth century their number had been reduced to two in most parishes; one being styled the Collector and the other, usually, the Syndic. Theoretically these officials were still elected by the community, but in practice they had everywhere become agents of the central power rather than representatives of the community. The Collector saw to the levying of the impost known as the *taille,* under the personal supervision of the Intendant. The Syndic, briefed daily for this purpose by the subdelegate, represented him in all matters concerning public order and the central administration, and was his chief executive as regards the militia, public works, and the enforcement of the laws....

Once elected, these parochial officials were treated without the least consideration and were forced to truckle to the whims, however absurd, of the lowest representative of the central government, the subdelegate. Often he imposed fines on them and sometimes even had them sentenced to imprisonment; for the laws ordinarily protecting individuals from highhanded treatment of this order did not here apply. In a report dated 1750 made by an Intendant we find him saying: "I have had sentences of imprisonment passed on some of the principal persons in villages that have been prating about their 'grievances,' and made these villages defray the expenses of the visit of the mounted constabulary. So I have had no trouble in bringing them to heel." Indeed, appointment to any of these local official posts was regarded less as an honor than as a calamity to be avoided at all costs.

Nonetheless, the peasants clung to these last vestiges of the old order and local self-government; indeed, even today it is the only form of freedom which, by and large, means much to them. A

French peasant may be willing enough to leave the government of the nation as a whole in the hands of an autocratic central power, but he bitterly resents the idea of not having a say in the local administration of his village. Thus even the hollowest of forms has retained "old-world" glamour!

What has been said about the towns and parishes applies to all corporate bodies which were self-contained and owned property collectively. Under the old régime, as nowadays, there was in France no township, borough, village, or hamlet, however small, no hospital, factory, convent, or college which had a right to manage its own affairs as it thought fit or to administer its possessions without interference. Then, as today, the central power held all Frenchmen in tutelage. The term "paternal government" had not yet been invented, but the reality already existed.

How in France, More Than in Any Other European Country, the Provinces Had Come under the Domination of the Capital City

It is not the geographical position of a capital, nor its size or wealth, that gives it political supremacy over the rest of the country; that depends, rather, on the nature of the country's government.

London, for example, though its population is as great as that of some entire kingdoms, has not so far had any determinant influence on the political destinies of Great Britain. Nor does any citizen of the United States imagine that the populace of New York can shape the course of the American Union—not even the residents in New York State would advance any such claim. Nevertheless, present-day New York can boast of a population as large as that of Paris at the outset of the Revolution.

During the Wars of Religion the population of Paris stood in the same proportion to that of the rest of France as it stood in 1789; yet its voice was not decisive in national affairs. And at the time

From *The Old Régime*, pt. 2, chap. 7.

of the Fronde insurrection Paris was still no more than the largest town in France. But by 1789 things were very different; it is no exaggeration to say that Paris *was* France. . . .

The government saw only the most obvious aspect of what was taking place in France, that aspect being the steady growth of the metropolis. From day to day Paris was extending her boundaries and the authorities feared that the proper administration of so big a city might soon become impracticable. . . . Six times during his reign Louis XIV tried to check the growth of Paris, yet all-powerful as he proved himself in many other fields, he failed in this. Meanwhile the capital's authority over the rest of France was being enlarged even more rapidly than the city's area, this being due less to what was being done within its walls than to what was taking place outside them. For throughout this period local autonomy was everywhere becoming a dead letter; the characteristic traits of the ancient provinces were steadily being ironed out and the last traces of an independent public life obliterated. . . .

Some have been surprised at the extraordinary ease with which the Constituent Assembly annihilated at one fell swoop all the historic divisions of France—the provinces—and split up the kingdom into eighty-three well-defined units—the departments—almost as if they were partitioning not an ancient kingdom but the virgin soil of the New World. Nothing surprised and, indeed, shocked the rest of Europe more than this. "It is the first time," Burke said, "that we have seen men hack their native land to pieces in so barbarous a manner." But though it might seem that living bodies were being mutilated, actually the "victims" were already corpses.

During the same period as that in which Paris was coming to dominate the entire country another change was taking place within the city itself, a change which all historians do well to take into account. Besides being at once a business and commercial center, a city of pleasure seekers and consumers, Paris had now developed into a manufacturing city—a change which, in conjunction with the political ascendancy of Paris described above, was destined to have great and dangerous consequences. . . .

Though the statistical records of the old régime are far from trustworthy, we are justified, I think, in saying that during the sixty years preceding the Revolution the number of workers employed in Paris more than doubled, while in the same period the general population of the city rose by hardly a third.... Thus Paris had mastered France, and the army that was soon to master Paris was mustering its forces.

HOW FRANCE HAD BECOME THE COUNTRY IN WHICH MEN WERE MOST LIKE EACH OTHER

One of the things which cannot fail to strike an attentive student of the social system under the old order is that it had two quite contradictory aspects. On the one hand, we get an impression that the people composing it, at least those belonging to the upper and the middle classes—the only ones that is to say who catch the eye—were all exactly like each other. Nevertheless, we also find that this seemingly homogeneous mass was still divided within itself into a great number of watertight compartments, small, self-contained units, each of which watched vigilantly over its own interests and took no part in the life of the community at large.

If we bear in mind the number of these minute gradings and the fact that nowhere else in the world were citizens less inclined to join forces and stand by each other in emergencies, we can see how it was that a successful revolution could tear down the whole social structure almost in the twinkling of an eye. All the flimsy barriers between the various compartments were instantaneously laid low, and out of the ruins there arose a social order closer knit and less differentiated, perhaps, than any that the Western World had ever known.

I have pointed out how local differences between the various provinces had long since been obliterated throughout practically the entire kingdom; this had greatly contributed to making Frenchmen everywhere so much like each other. Behind such diversities as still existed the unity of the nation was making itself

From *The Old Régime,* pt. 2, chap. 8.

felt, sponsored by that new conception: "the same laws for all."
For as the eighteenth century advances, we find an ever increasing number of edicts, Orders in Council, and royal mandates imposing the same regulations and the same procedures on all parts of the kingdom. Not only the governing class but also the governed endorsed this concept of a standardized legislative system valid everywhere. Indeed, it underlies all the successive projects of reform put forward during the three decades preceding the Revolution. Two centuries earlier any such projects would have been quite literally unthinkable.

Not only did the provinces come to resemble each other more and more, but within each province members of the various classes (anyhow those above the lowest social stratum) became ever more alike, differences of rank notwithstanding. This is borne out conspicuously by the *cahiers* (written instructions given to the deputies) presented by the different Orders at the meeting of the Estates-General in 1789. Allowing for the fact that the parties who drew up these memoranda had strongly conflicting interests, they seem remarkably alike in tenor.

When we turn to the proceedings of the earliest Estates-General we find a very different picture: the middle class and the nobility then had more common interests, more points of contact, and displayed much less antipathy towards each other—even if they still gave the impression of belonging to different races. Though with the passing years the privileges which made a cleavage between these two important sections of the community had not merely been maintained but in some respects intensified, the lapse of time had worked towards a certain leveling out of their differences in all else.

For during several centuries the French nobility had been getting steadily poorer. "Despite its privileges," a man of gentle birth, writing in 1755, laments, "the nobility is being starved out, and all its wealth passing into the hands of the Third Estate." Yet the laws protecting property owned by the nobility had not been modified and to all appearances its economic position was unchanged. Nonetheless, the more its power declined, the poorer it became.

It would seem that in all human institutions, as in the human body, there is a hidden source of energy, the life principle itself, independent of the organs which perform the various functions needed for survival; once this vital flame burns low, the whole organism languishes and wastes away, and though the organs seem to function as before, they serve no useful purpose. The French nobility still had entails (Burke, indeed, observed that in his day entails were commoner and more binding in France than in England), the law of primogeniture, the right to perpetual dues on the land, and, in fact, all their vested interests had been left intact. They had been released from the costly obligation of defraying their own expenses on active service in the army and, nevertheless, had retained their immunity from taxation; that is to say they still profited by the exemption after being relieved of the obligation. Moreover, they now enjoyed several financial advantages unknown to their ancestors. And yet, in proportion as both the instinct and the practice of leadership declined among them, their wealth passed out of their hands. This gradual impoverishment of the French nobility was largely due to the breaking up of the great landed estates.... The nobleman had sold his land, plot by plot, to the peasants, keeping only the seigneurial dues which safeguarded the semblance, but not the reality, of his overlordship. In several French provinces—for example the Limousin, of which Turgot gives us so good a description—the erstwhile seigneurs eked out a hand-to-mouth existence; they had hardly any land of their own, and dues and quitrents were almost their only source of income.

"In this *généralité*," wrote an Intendant at the beginning of the century, "there are still several thousand noble families, but not fifteen of them have an income of twenty thousand *livres* a year." The position is lucidly summed up in a note handed by the Intendant of Franche-Comté to his successor (in 1750). "The nobles in these parts are worthy folk but very poor, and as proud as they are poor. Their prestige has sadly declined. It is not bad policy to keep them in this state, for thus they are obliged to have recourse to us and to carry out our wishes. They have formed a closed society, to belong to which a man must prove his right to four quarterings on his escutcheon. It meets only once a year, and it is not officially recognized; merely tolerated. The Intendant is always present at this society. On such occasions, after dining and attending Mass in a body, these worthy gentlemen go home, some on foot, and some on old, worn-out hacks. It's quite a comical sight—as you will see for yourself.''

This gradual impoverishment of the nobility was not peculiar to France. It was taking place in all parts of the continent where the feudal system was in process of dying out without being replaced by a new form of aristocracy. In German territory, along the Rhine, the decadence of the indigenous nobility was particularly marked and attracted much attention. England was the one exception. There the old nobility had not only retained but greatly increased its wealth; its members were still the richest and most influential of the King's subjects. True, new families were coming to the fore, but their wealth was no greater than that of the ancient houses.

In France the commoners alone seemed to be taking over the wealth that was being lost by the nobility, to be growing fat at their expense. Yet there was no law preventing the middle-class man from ruining himself or helping him to amass a fortune. All the same he steadily grew wealthier and frequently became as rich as, sometimes richer than, the nobleman. Moreover, his wealth often took the same form; though usually residing in a town, he owned land in the country and sometimes even bought up entire seigneurial estates.

Education and a similar style of living had already obliterated many of the distinctions between the two classes. The bourgeois was as cultivated as the nobleman and his enlightenment came from the same source. Both had been educated on literary and philosophic lines, for Paris, now almost the sole fountainhead of knowledge for the whole of France, had cast the minds of all in the same mold and given them the same equipment. No doubt it was still possible at the close of the eighteenth century to detect shades of difference in the behavior of the aristocracy and that of the bourgeoisie; for nothing takes longer to acquire than the surface polish which is called good manners. But basically all who ranked above the common herd were of a muchness; they had the same ideas, the same habits, the same tastes, the same kinds of amusements; read the same books and spoke in the same way. They differed only in their rights.

I doubt if this leveling-up process was carried so far in any other country, even in England, where the different classes, though solidly allied by common interests, still differed in mentality and manners. For political freedom, though it has the admirable effect of creating reciprocal ties and a feeling of solidarity between all the members of a nation, does not necessarily make them resemble each other. It is only government by a single man that in the long run irons out diversities and makes each member of a nation indifferent to his neighbor's lot.

How, Though in Many Respects so Similar, the French Were Split Up into Small, Isolated, Self-regarding Groups

Let us now turn to the other side of the picture and observe how these same Frenchmen who had so much in common were kept apart from each other to an extent hitherto unknown in France; perhaps unparalleled in any other country.

When the feudal system first struck root in Europe, the nobility (to use the term that subsequently came into currency) did not immediately, so far as we can judge, assume the form of a caste. Composed of all the leading men in the nation, it was no more than an aristocracy (in the exact sense of the term) during its early phase. There is no occasion here to go deeply into the question and I confine myself to pointing out that by the Middle Ages it had developed into a caste, by which I mean that membership in it was essentially a matter of birth and had become hereditary.

True, it retained one of the chief functions of an aristocracy, that of being a governing body; but birth alone decided who should be the leaders of the nation. Those who were not of noble blood were automatically excluded from the magic circle, and

From *The Old Régime*, pt. 2, chaps. 9 and 10.

though they might hold posts of some importance in the administration, these were always of a subordinate nature.

Wherever feudalism established itself on the continent it led to the formation of a caste of this description; in England, exceptionally, it gave rise to an aristocracy. I have always been surprised that a circumstance that renders England so different from all other modern nations and which alone explains the peculiarities of her laws, history, and traditions has not received more attention from historians and statesmen—and that long familiarity has made Englishmen themselves so unaware of it. Some have had glimpses of this fact and alluded to it briefly; but never, to my knowledge, has it been adequately dealt with by observers of the English scene. Thus when Montesquieu visited England in 1739, he wrote to a friend, "Here am I in a land that is quite unlike any other European country"—but he let it go at that.

It was not merely parliamentary government, freedom of speech, and the jury system that made England so different from the rest of contemporary Europe. There was something still more distinctive and more far-reaching in its effects. England was the only country in which the caste system had been totally abolished, not merely modified. Nobility and commoners joined forces in business enterprises, entered the same professions, and—what is still more significant—intermarried. The daughter of the greatest lord in the land could marry a "new" man without the least compunction.

For when we seek to discover whether the caste system, with its age-old conventions and social barriers, has been definitively eradicated in any country, the acid test is that country's marriage customs. Even in modern France, after sixty years of democracy, we often find the old prejudices surviving. Though persons of high rank and parvenus may seem to fraternize in other respects, intermarriage between the classes is still discountenanced.

One often hears it said that the English nobility has proved itself more adroit, more worldly wise, more accessible to new ideas than any other. It would be truer to say that for a long time past there has been no nobility in England, if we use the term "nobility" in the sense it has elsewhere.

Though this curious revolution (for such in fact it was) is hidden in the mists of time, we can detect traces of it in the English language. For several centuries the word "gentleman" has had in England a quite different application from what it had when it originated, and, similarly, there is no equivalent for its French antithesis, the word *roturier*. It would have been impossible to translate into English, even in 1664 when Molière wrote it, the line:

"Et tel que l'on le voit, il est bon gentilhomme."

A study of the connection between the history of language and history proper would certainly be revealing. Thus if we follow the mutations in time and place of the English word "gentleman" (a derivative of our *gentilhomme*), we find its connotation being steadily widened in England as the classes draw nearer to each other and intermingle. In each successive century we find it being applied to men a little lower in the social scale. Next, with the English, it crosses to America. And now in America it is applicable to all male citizens, indiscriminately. Thus its history is the history of democracy itself.

In France, however, there has been no question of enlarging the application of the word *gentilhomme,* which as a matter of fact has, since the Revolution, dropped out of common use. This is because it has always been employed to designate the members of a caste—a caste that has never ceased to exist in France and is still as exclusive as it was when the term was coined many centuries ago.

I will, indeed, go further and say that this caste has become more and more exclusive and that a tendency diametrically opposed to what we have observed in England has been operative in France. For while the bourgeois and the nobleman were becoming more and more alike in many ways, the gap between them was steadily widening, and these two tendencies, far from counteracting each other, often had the opposite effect. . . .

When we study such records of the proceedings of the Estates-General in the fourteenth century as have survived, we cannot fail to be struck by the place assigned to the Third Estate in these assemblies and the power it exercised. Doubtless, from the point of view of his mental and moral equipment the fourteenth-century bourgeois was much inferior to his eighteenth-century counterpart; nevertheless, the middle class as a body were accorded a higher, more responsible position in those early days. Their right to participate in the government of the country was taken for granted, their opinions always carried weight in political assemblies and often were preponderant, and the other classes never forgot that theirs was a force to be reckoned with.

But most striking of all is the fact that the nobility and the Third Estate found it so much easier in those days than at any later time to co-operate in the management of public affairs.... By the eighteenth century, nobleman and bourgeois never met except by chance in private life. And by then the two classes were not merely rivals, they were foes.

What seems peculiar to France is that at the very time when the nobility, *qua* Order, was losing its political power, the nobleman as an individual was granted privileges he had never hitherto enjoyed and was even extending those he had already. It seemed as if individuals were enriching themselves at the expense of the Order as a corporate body. More and more the nobility was being divested of its right to rule, but by the same token the nobles enjoyed more and more the exclusive prerogative of being the chief servitors of their supreme overlord, the King. It was easier for a man of humble extraction to become a high official under Louis XIV than it was under Louis XVI.... Each privilege, once granted, became hereditary and inalienable. Thus in the course of ceasing to be an aristocracy, the nobility tended more and more to become a caste, thriving on vested rights.

The privilege most resented by the general public, that of exemption from taxation, became progressively more valuable from the fifteenth century up to the Revolution. For its value obviously kept pace with the steady increase in the financial burdens imposed on the mass of the people. When (under Charles VII) a mere 1,200,000 *livres* were brought in by the tax known as the *taille,* the advantages of exemption were relatively slight. But when, under Louis XVI, the sum raised by taxation was eighty millions the value of the privilege was enormous. So long as the *taille* was the only impost to which the rest of the population was subject, the nobleman's immunity attracted little attention. But when taxes of this order were multiplied under a host of names and in various forms; when four other imposts were assimilated to the *taille;* and when obligations unknown in the Middle Ages— notably forced labor requisitioned by the Crown for public works and compulsory service in the militia—were superadded, with a complete disregard for equality, keen resentment was felt for the privileged position of the nobility. True, the inequality, though great, was not so bad as it seemed, since the nobleman was often affected indirectly, through his tenants, by taxes from which ostensibly he was exempted. But in such cases injustice that is glaring causes more irritation than actual injury. . . .

Although inequality of taxation prevailed all over Europe, there were few countries in which it had become so flagrant and so much detested as in France. In a great part of Germany taxation was mostly indirect, and even as regards direct taxation the nobles did not escape altogether, their privilege often consisting merely in being assessed at a somewhat lower rate than other taxpayers. Moreover, there were some taxes falling on the nobility alone; these took the place of the unpaid military service which otherwise would have been exacted from them.

Of all the various ways of making men conscious of their differences and of stressing class distinctions unequal taxation is the most pernicious, since it creates a permanent estrangement between those who benefit and those who suffer by it. Once the principle is established that noblemen and commoners are not to be taxed at the same rates, the public is reminded of the distinction drawn between them year by year when the imposts are assessed and levied. Thus on these occasions each member of the privileged class takes notice of the practical interest he has in differentiating himself from the masses and in stiffening the barriers between himself and them.

Since so many debates on public affairs concern an existing tax or the imposition of a new one, it is obvious that when one section of the community is exempt and another subject to it, they will rarely see eye to eye or wish to meet together and exchange ideas. Thus little or no effort is required to keep them apart, there being no incentives or any inclination to act in concert.

In his flattering picture of the old French constitution Burke mentioned as a point in favor of the French nobility the ease with which a commoner could obtain a title by securing one of the official posts that automatically ennobled their holders. Here, to his thinking, was something analogous to the "open" aristocracy of England. No doubt Louis XI had distributed titles lavishly, but his aim was to lower the prestige of the nobility. If his successors were equally lavish of titles, this was for a different motive: that of raising money. Necker tells us that in his day no less than four thousand official posts carried titles with them. Nothing of this sort was to be seen in any other country on the continent; yet the parallel drawn by Burke between France and England was due to a misconception of the facts.

The reason why the English middle class, far from being actively hostile to the aristocracy, inclined to fraternize with it was not so much that the aristocracy kept open house as that its barriers were ill defined; not so much that entrance into it was easy as that you never knew when you had got there. The result was that everyone who hovered on its outskirts nursed the agreeable illusion that he belonged to it and joined forces with it in the hope of acquiring prestige or some practical advantage under its aegis.

But the barriers between the French nobility and the other classes, though quite easily traversed, were always fixed and plain to see; so conspicuous, indeed, as to exasperate those against whom they were erected. For once a man had crossed them he was cut off from all outside the pale by privileges injurious both to their pockets and their pride.

Far from reducing the dislike of the nobility felt by their "inferiors" the practice of ennobling commoners had the opposite effect. The envy with which the newly made nobleman inspired his former equals intensified their sense of being unfairly treated. This explains why the Third Estate in its petitions for radical changes always shows more animosity towards the recent creations than towards the old nobility, and far from asking that the ways of access to the privileged class should be more widely open to commoners, constantly demands that they be narrowed.

In no other period of French history was it so easy to acquire a title as in 1789, yet never had the gap between the middle class and the nobility been so great. Not only did the nobles refuse to tolerate in their electoral body anything that savored in the least of the bourgeoisie, but the bourgeois showed an equal distaste for anything and anyone of high extraction. In some provinces newly ennobled men were given the cold shoulder by the former because they were not thought high-born enough, and by the latter because they were already too much so! (This happened, we are told, to that famous man Lavoisier.)

When we turn from the nobility to the middle class we find a very similar state of affairs; the bourgeois was almost as aloof from the "common people" as the noble from the bourgeois.

Under the old régime nearly all the middle class preferred to live in the towns, and there were two causes for this preference: the privileges of the nobility and the *taille*. The lord who lived on his estate usually displayed a certain bonhomie towards his peasants—in fact, they got on very well together—but he made no secret of his disdain for his middle-class neighbors. This disdain had continuously increased, keeping pace with the decline of his political influence, and in fact because of it. For one thing, now that he no longer held the reins of power, there was no need to humor people who might have aided him in his public duties; and also (as has often been remarked) he tried to console himself for the loss of real power by an exaggerated insistence on such prerogatives as still were his. Even when he lived away from his estate, this did not make things any more agreeable for his neighbors; on the contrary, they felt all the more aggrieved, since privileges flaunted by a deputy seemed still more odious.

Yet I am inclined to think that the *taille* and the other imposts linked up with it were more to blame. It would be easy to explain, relatively briefly, why the incidence of the *taille* and the taxes assimilated to it made itself felt more strongly in rural districts than in towns. But for my present purpose it is enough to point out that the urban middle class, acting as a group, had many means of reducing the impact of the *taille* and sometimes of escaping it altogether; whereas an isolated member of that class, living in the country on his own land, had no such means of escape. One of the chief advantages of the town dwellers was that they were not concerned with collecting the *taille*—an obligation dreaded even more than that of having to pay it. Indeed, there was no post under the old régime (or, for that matter, any other that I know of) so unenviable as that of the rural tax collector.... No one living in a French village (except members of the nobility) was exempted from this duty; many rich commoners left their lands and moved to the nearest town so as to avoid it. All the records I have studied bear out Turgot's statement that "the obligation to collect the *taille* was changing all rural landowners, noblemen excepted, into town dwellers." (This, by the way, is one of the reasons why there are so many more towns, small towns especially, in France than in most other European countries.)...

Segregated from the peasantry by his place of residence and still more by his way of living, the bourgeois was usually estranged from them no less by a conflict of interests. There were many justified complaints about the privileges enjoyed by the nobility in the matter of taxation, but there were equal grounds for complaint as regards the middle class. For thousands of official posts existed which carried with them partial or total exemption from the burdens imposed on the general public: one post exonerated its holder from service in the militia, another from forced labor, another from the *taille*. Where is there a parish, asked a writer of the day, which does not contain, apart from nobles and ecclesiastics, a number of citizens who have secured immunity from taxation in virtue of the official posts they hold or public duties they perform? One of the reasons which led now and again to the abolition of certain official posts earmarked for the middle class was the diminution of revenue caused by so many exemptions from payment of the *taille*. I am convinced that the number of persons thus exempted was as great among the bourgeoisie as among the nobility, and indeed often greater.

While enraging all who did not share in them, these odious prerogatives inspired their possessors with a pride as inordinate as it was shortsighted. Throughout the eighteenth century the hostility of the urban middle class towards the peasantry living around the towns and the jealousy of the latter were common knowledge. "Every town," wrote Turgot, "is bent on promoting its own interests at the expense of the rural districts in its vicinity." Elsewhere he says, addressing his subdelegates, "You have often been obliged to check the tendency of the towns to overstep their lawful rights in dealing with the rural population within their spheres of influence." . . .

To complete the picture, let us now examine the middle class in itself, quite apart from the common people, in the same way as we examined the nobility separately from the middle class. The first thing to catch our notice in this small section of the nation is the immense number of separate elements of which it was composed. Like those substances once thought indivisible in which modern scientists, the more closely they examine them, find more and more separate particles, the French bourgeoisie, while seemingly a uniform mass, was extremely composite. Thus I find that the notabilities of a quite small town were split up into no less than thirty-six distinct groups. Small as they were, these groups kept trying still further to narrow themselves down by expelling all such elements as seemed in any way out of sympathy with their aims. Indeed, this exclusiveness was carried to such a pitch that some of these groups comprised only three or four members. But this made them all the more vocal, the more determined to assert themselves. Each group was differentiated from the rest by its right to petty privileges of one kind or another, even the least of which was regarded as a token of its exalted status. Thus they were constantly wrangling over questions of precedence, so much so that the Intendant and the courts were often at a loss for a solution of their differences. "At last an order has been passed that the holy water is to be given to the judges of the presidial court before being given to members of the town corporation. The parlement had been unable to come to a decision, so the King took the matter up in Council and has decided it himself. It was high time, too, as the whole town was in a ferment." When a group was not given the precedence it claimed in the general assembly of notables, it ceased to attend, preferring to withdraw from public affairs altogether rather than to stomach such an affront to its dignity.

These disputes about questions of prestige between small groups of men gave many occasions for the display of that personal vanity which seems innate in Frenchmen—to the exclusion of the honest pride of the self-respecting citizen. Most of the corporate bodies of which I have been speaking were in existence as far back as the sixteenth century, but in those early days their members, after having settled among themselves such matters as concerned their group interests, made a point of conferring with all the other inhabitants of the town or city when matters affecting the community at large were to be discussed. By the eighteenth century, however, these groups had withdrawn to a great extent from this wider sphere of action, since municipal business was much reduced in volume and transacted by specially empowered officials. Thus each of these small groups lived only for itself and, quite literally, minded its own business.

That word "individualism," which we have coined for our own requirements, was unknown to our ancestors, for the good reason that in their days every individual necessarily belonged to a group and no one could regard himself as an isolated unit. Nevertheless, each of the thousands of small groups of which the French nation was then composed took thought for itself alone; in fact, there was, so to speak, a group individualism which prepared men's minds for the thorough-paced individualism with which nowadays we are familiar.

What is still more singular is that all these men, split up into compact groups though they were, had become so similar as to be almost interchangeable; that is to say anyone might have moved out of his group into another without one's noticing any difference in his practices or personality. Moreover, had anyone with a gift for psychology delved into their inmost feelings, he would have found that these very men regarded the flimsy barriers dividing people so much alike as contrary both to the public interest and to common sense and that already, theoretically anyhow, these ancestors of ours were all for unity. Each set store on his status as member of a particular group because he saw others asserting their personalities in this way; yet all were quite ready to sink their differences and to be integrated into a homogenous whole, provided no one was given a privileged position and rose above the common level....

It was no easy task bringing together fellow citizens who had lived for many centuries aloof from, or even hostile to, each other and teaching them to co-operate in the management of their own affairs. It had been far easier to estrange them than it now was to reunite them, and in so doing France gave the world a memorable example. Yet, when sixty years ago the various classes which under the old order had been isolated units in the social system came once again in touch, it was on their sore spots that they made contact and their first gesture was to fly at each other's throats. Indeed, even today, though class distinctions are no more, the jealousies and antipathies they caused have not died out.

How the Lot of the French Peasant Was Sometimes Worse in the Eighteenth Century Than It Had Been in the Thirteenth

In the eighteenth century the peasant was no longer at the mercy of petty feudal overlords, nor did he often receive harsh treatment from the government. He enjoyed civil liberty and had land of his own. Nevertheless, the other classes looked down on him and he was, in fact, more isolated from the rest of the community than the peasant of any other place or period. This was a new, peculiar form of oppression and its consequences merit close and special study. . . .

    Hardly any of the gentry—except those whom poverty compelled to remain on their estates—still lived in the country. When a member of the upper class was thus marooned on his estate, his relations with the peasantry around him were of a kind that no rich landowner, I imagine, had ever entertained in earlier days. Now that he had ceased to hold a dominant position he was no longer at pains, as he would once have been, to help "his" peasants, to further their interests, and to give them good advice. Moreover, since he was not subject to the same taxes as they, he could not easily enter into their feelings on this score and associate himself with grievances he did not share. In short, they

From *The Old Régime*, pt. 2, chap. 12.

were no longer his subjects and protégés, but he was not as yet their fellow citizen—a state of affairs unique in history.

This led to what might be called a spiritual estrangement more prevalent and more pernicious in its way than mere physical absenteeism. For in his dealings with his tenants the landowners who lived on his estate often developed sentiments and views that would, were he an absentee, have been those of his agent. Like an agent he came to regard his tenants as mere rent-payers and exacted from them the uttermost farthing to which the law, or ancient usage, still entitled him, the result being that the collection of such feudal dues as still existed was apt to seem even more galling to the peasants than it had been in the heyday of feudalism.

Always short of money and often deep in debt, he usually lived with extreme economy in his country home, his one idea being to save up all he could for the winter season in town. The common people, with their knack of hitting on the telling word, had a good name for these squireens, that of the smallest bird of prey; they called them "the hobbyhawks." I am dealing here with classes as a whole, to my mind the historian's proper study, and am quite willing to admit there were exceptions. No one, indeed, would think of denying that during this period many rich landowners did much for the welfare of the peasants, though they were under no obligation to do so and their own interests were not in any way involved. But these were the laudable few who swam against the stream and successfully resisted the forces urging them towards indifference and their former vassals towards hatred.

It is often said that some of our Kings and Ministers of State— notably Louis XIV and Richelieu—were mainly responsible for this desertion of their country homes by the nobility. Nor can it be denied that almost all our Kings during the last three centuries of the monarchy made it their policy to detach the nobles from the people, to lure them to the Court, and to encourage them to take service under the King. This was specially the case in the seventeenth century, when the King saw in them a threat to his power. . . .

Nevertheless, we must beware of assuming that the desertion of the countryside by those who at the time were still regarded as the leaders of the nation was due to the direct influence of certain French Kings. Its principal and permanent cause was not that it was encouraged by various monarchs, but, rather, the slow, persistent action of our institutions. This is proved by the fact that when, in the eighteenth century, the government tried to put a stop to this unhealthy tendency, it could not even prevent its gaining ground. The more the nobles lost their ancient rights without being granted any new ones and local freedoms died out, the more the upper-class migration to the cities intensified. Indeed, it was no longer necessary to offer inducements to the nobles to quit their estates; they had no wish to stay on them since they found country life profoundly boring.

What I have been saying of the nobles applies equally to all rich landowners in France. Centralization was now the order of the day and all the well-to-do and cultured residents of the country districts were moving to the towns. In this context I would suggest that one of the consequences of extreme centralization is that agriculture ceases to be progressive and the peasant blindly keeps to the old methods of cultivation—thus confirming a famous remark of Montesquieu's: "The soil is productive less by reason of its natural fertility than because the people tilling it are free." But to develop this idea would take me too far afield.

I have already drawn attention to the fact that everywhere the middle class was migrating from the country to the towns, whose atmosphere was more congenial. This is borne out by all the records of the period. From them we learn that only one generation of rich peasants is usually to be found in country districts, for no sooner has an industrious farmer put a little money aside than he tells his son to quit the plow and move to the nearest town, where he buys for him some petty official post....

Thus not only was the peasant almost entirely deprived of any contacts with the upper classes; he was also separated even from those of his own class who might have been able to befriend and to advise him. For once such persons had achieved a certain culture or prosperity they turned their backs on him. He was, in fact, cold-shouldered on all sides and treated like a being of a peculiar species. This was not (or anyhow not to the same degree) the case in any other great civilized country of Europe, and even in France it was a new development. The fourteenth-century peasants had been at once more oppressed and better cared for; the great seigneurs may have sometimes treated them harshly, but they never abandoned them to their own resources.

The eighteenth-century French village was a community of poor, benighted rustics; its local officials were as little educated and as much looked down on as the ordinary villagers; its Syndic could not read; its tax collector was incapable of compiling, unaided, the returns which so vitally affected his neighbors' incomes and his own. Not only had the seigneur lost all control over local affairs, but he had come to the point of regarding any participation in them as beneath his dignity. It was for the Syndic to assess the *taille,* to call up the militia, to recruit and direct the forced labor gangs—servile functions unworthy of the lord. The villages were left entirely to the tender mercies of the central government, and since it was at a great distance and had nothing to fear from them, its primary concern was to use them as a source of revenue. . . .

. . . Only with the utmost difficulty did members of the upper classes succeed in glimpsing something of the feelings of the common people, and particularly those of the peasants. For the peasant's upbringing and way of living gave him an outlook on the world at large peculiar to himself, incomprehensible to others. And whenever the poor and the rich come to have hardly any common interests, common activities, and common grievances, the barriers between their respective mentalities become insuperable, they are sealed books to each other even if they spend all their lives side by side. This may help to explain the singular fact that at the very moment when the Revolution was knocking at the door so few apprehensions of any kind were felt by members of the upper and the middle classes, and why they went on blithely discoursing on the virtues of the people, their loyalty, their innocent pleasures, and so forth. Such was the blindness, at once grotesque and tragic, of these men who would not see!

Before going further let us pause for a moment to reflect on one of the laws of Divine Providence which, behind these "petty details" (as they seemed to be at the time), was shaping human destiny in that momentous phase of our history.

The French nobility had stubbornly held aloof from the other classes and had succeeded in getting themselves exempted from most of their duties to the community, fondly imagining they could keep their lofty status while evading its obligations. At first it seemed they had succeeded, but soon a curious internal malady attacked them, whose effect was, so to speak, to make them gradually crumple up, though no external pressure of any kind was brought to bear. The more their immunities increased, the poorer they became. On the other hand, the middle class (of being merged into which they were so much afraid) grew steadily richer and more enlightened without their aid and, in fact, at their expense. Thus the nobles, who had refused to regard the bourgeois as allies or even fellow citizens, were forced to envisage them as their rivals, before long as their enemies, and finally as their masters. A power external to themselves had released them from the tasks of protecting, instructing, and succoring their vassals, and at the same time had left intact their pecuniary and honorific privileges. So they imagined that all was well, and that as they still were given pride of place in the social hierarchy, they were still the nation's leaders. Moreover, they were still surrounded by men to whom legal documents referred as their "subjects," others being described as their vassals, their tenants, or their farmers. In reality, however, they led nobody; they were alone, and when an attack was launched on them, their sole recourse was flight.

Though the nobility and the middle class followed divergent paths, in one respect they were alike; for the bourgeois ended up by being as isolated from the people as any nobleman. Far from showing any concern for the peasants, he shut his eyes to their misfortunes instead of making common cause with them in an attempt to correct social disabilities in which he shared; he deliberately sponsored new forms of injustice that benefited him personally; indeed, he was quite as eager to secure preferential treatment for himself as any noble to retain his privileges. The peasantry, from whom he stemmed, had come to seem to him an alien, incomprehensible race of men. It was only after he had put arms in their hands that he realized he had kindled passions such as he had never dreamed of, passions which he could neither restrain nor guide, and of which, after being their promoter, he was to be the victim.

No doubt there will always be some to express amazement at the catastrophic downfall of that great house of France which at one time seemed destined to bring all Europe within its orbit. Yet those who, studying its history, read between the lines will have no difficulty in understanding how this happened. Almost all the vices, miscalculations, and disastrous prejudices I have been describing owed their origin, their continuance, and their proliferation to a line of conduct practiced by so many of our Kings, that of dividing men so as the better to rule them.

But once the bourgeois had been completely severed from the noble, and the peasant from both alike, and when a similar differentiation had taken place within each of these three classes, with the result that each was split up into a number of small groups almost completely shut off from each other, the inevitable consequence was that, though the nation came to seem a homogeneous whole, its parts no longer held together. Nothing had been left that could obstruct the central government, but, by the same token, nothing could shore it up. This is why the grandiose edifice built up by our Kings was doomed to collapse like a card castle once disturbances arose within the social order on which it was based.

6

THE DYNAMICS
OF REVOLUTION

HOW, AROUND THE MIDDLE OF THE EIGHTEENTH CENTURY, MEN OF LETTERS TOOK THE LEAD IN POLITICS

I now leave behind the circumstances remote in time and of a general order which prepared the way for the great revolution, and come to the particular, more recent events which finally determined its place of origin, its outbreak, and the form it took.

For a long while the French had been the most literary-minded of all the nations of Europe, but so far our writers had not displayed that intellectual brilliance which won them world-wide fame toward the middle of the eighteenth century. True, they did not play an active part in public affairs, as English writers did; on the contrary, never had they kept so steadily aloof from the political arena. In a nation teeming with officials none of the men of letters held posts of any kind, none was invested with authority.

Nevertheless, they did not (like most of their German contemporaries) resolutely turn their backs on politics and retire to a world apart, of *belles lettres* and pure philosophy. On the contrary, they were keenly interested in all that concerned the government of nations; this, one might almost say, was an obsession with them. . . .

The political programs advocated by our eighteenth-century writers varied so much that any attempt to synthesize them or deduce a single coherent theory of government from them would be labor lost. Nonetheless, if, disregarding details, we look to the

From *The Old Régime*, pt. 3, chap. 1.

directive ideas, we find that all these various systems stemmed from a single concept of a highly general order, their common source, and that our authors took this as their premise before venturing on their personal, often somewhat eccentric solutions of the problem of good government. Thus, though their ways diverged in the course of their researches, their starting point was the same in all cases; and this was the belief that what was wanted was to replace the complex of traditional customs governing the social order of the day by simple, elementary rules deriving from the exercise of the human reason and natural law.

When we look closely into it we find that the political philosophy of these writers consists to all intents and purposes in ringing the changes on this one idea. It was no new one; it had haunted men's imaginations off and on for three millennia, but never until now had it succeeded in making itself accepted as a basic principle. How was it that at this particular point of time it could root itself so firmly in the minds of the writers of the day? Why, instead of remaining as in the past the purely intellectual concept of a few advanced thinkers, did it find a welcome among the masses and acquire the driving force of a political passion to such effect that general and abstract theories of the nature of human society not only became daily topics of conversation among the leisure class but fired the imagination even of women and peasants? And why was it that men of letters, men without wealth, social eminence, responsibilities, or official status, became in practice the leading politicians of the age, since despite the fact that others held the reins of government, they alone spoke with accents of authority? These questions I shall now try to answer, and at the same time I shall draw attention to the remarkable, not to say formidable, influence these men's writings (which at first sight might seem to concern the history of our literature alone) had on the Revolution, and, indeed, still have today.

It was not by mere chance that our eighteenth-century thinkers as a body enounced theories so strongly opposed to those that were still regarded as basic to the social order; they could hardly be expected to do otherwise when they contemplated the world around them. The sight of so many absurd and unjust privileges, whose evil effects were increasingly felt on every hand though their true causes were less and less understood, urged or, rather, forced them towards a concept of the natural equality of all men irrespective of social rank. When they saw so many ridiculous, ramshackle institutions, survivals of an earlier age, which no one had attempted to co-ordinate or to adjust to modern conditions and which seemed destined to live on despite the fact that they had ceased to have any present value, it was natural enough that thinkers of the day should come to loathe everything that savored of the past and should desire to remold society on entirely new lines, traced by each thinker in the sole light of reason.

Their very way of living led these writers to indulge in abstract theories and generalizations regarding the nature of government, and to place a blind confidence in these. For living as they did, quite out of touch with practical politics, they lacked the experience which might have tempered their enthusiasms. Thus they completely failed to perceive the very real obstacles in the way of even the most praiseworthy reforms, and to gauge the perils involved in even the most salutary revolutions. That they should not have had the least presentiment of these dangers was only to be expected, since as a result of the total absence of any political freedom, they had little acquaintance with the realities of public life, which, indeed, was *terra incognita* to them. Taking no personal part in it and unable to see what was being done by others in that field, they lacked even the superficial acquaintance with such matters which comes to those who live under a free régime, can see what is happening, and hear the voice of public opinion even though they themselves take no part whatever in the government of the country. As a result, our literary men became much bolder in their speculations, more addicted to general ideas and systems, more contemptuous of the wisdom of the ages, and even more inclined to trust their individual reason than most of those who have written books on politics from a philosophic angle.

When it came to making themselves heard by the masses and appealing to their emotions, this very ignorance served them in good stead. If the French people had still played an active part in politics (through the Estates-General) or even if they had merely continued to concern themselves with the day-to-day administration of affairs through the provincial assemblies, we may be sure that they would not have let themselves be carried away so easily by the ideas of the writers of the day; any experience, however slight, of public affairs would have made them chary of accepting the opinions of mere theoreticians.

Similarly, if, like the English, they had succeeded in gradually modifying the spirit of their ancient institutions without destroying them, perhaps they would not have been so prompt to clamor for a new order. As it was, however, every Frenchman felt he was being victimized; his personal freedom, his money, his self-respect, and the amenities of his daily life were constantly being tampered with on the strength of some ancient law, some medieval usage, or the remnants of some antiquated servitude. Nor did he see any constitutional remedy for this state of affairs; it seemed as if the choice lay between meekly accepting everything or destroying the whole system.

Nevertheless, in the nation-wide debacle of freedom we had preserved one form of it; we could indulge, almost without restriction, in learned discussions on the origins of society, the nature of government, and the essential rights of man. All who were chafing under the yoke of the administration enjoyed these literary excursions into politics; indeed, the taste for them spread even into sections of the community whose temperaments or upbringing would have normally discouraged them from abstract speculations. But there was no taxpayer aggrieved by the injustices of the *taille* who did not welcome the idea that all men should be equal; no farmer whose land was devastated by a noble neighbor's rabbits who did not rejoice at hearing it declared that privilege of any kind whatever was condemned by the voice of reason. Thus the philosopher's cloak provided safe cover for the passions of the day and the political ferment was canalized into literature, the result being that our writers now became the leaders of public opinion and played for a while the part which normally, in free countries, falls to the professional politician. And as things were, no one was in a position to dispute their right to leadership.

A powerful aristocracy does not merely shape the course of public affairs, it also guides opinion, sets the tone for writers, and lends authority to new ideas. By the eighteenth century the

French nobility had wholly lost this form of ascendancy, its prestige had dwindled with its power, and since the place it had occupied in the direction of public opinion was vacant, writers could usurp it with the greatest ease and keep it without fear of being dislodged.

Still more remarkable was the fact that this very aristocracy whose place the writers had taken made much of them. So completely had our nobility forgotten that new political theories, once they are generally accepted, inevitably rouse popular passions and bear fruit in deeds, that they regarded even the doctrines most hostile to their prerogatives, and in fact to their very existence, as mere flights of fancy, entertaining *jeux d'esprit*. So they, too, took a hand in the new, delightful game and, while clinging to their immunities and privileges, talked lightheartedly of the "absurdity" of all the old French customs.

Astonishment has often been expressed at this singular blindness of the upper classes of the old régime and the way they compassed their own downfall. Yet how could they have known better? Political freedom is no less indispensable to the ruling classes to enable them to realize their perils than to the rank and file to enable them to safeguard their rights. More than a century had elapsed since the last traces of free public life had disappeared in France, and those most directly interested in the maintenance of the old constitution had not been forewarned by any sound or sign of an impending breakdown. Since outwardly nothing had changed, they had no fears for its stability. In a word, their point of view was that of their fathers, they could not move with the times. In the 1789 *cahiers* [see p. 164 above] we find the nobility still harping as much on the "encroachments" of the royal power as if they were living in the fifteenth century. And that ill-starred King, Louis XVI, at the very moment when he was about to be engulfed by the flood tide of democracy, continued (as Burke has aptly pointed out) to regard the aristocracy as the chief danger to the throne and mistrusted it as much as if he were back in the days of the "Fronde." On the other hand, he, like his ancestors, saw in the middle class and the people the staunchest supporters of the Crown.

But what must seem still more extraordinary to us, given our experience of the aftermath of so many revolutions, is that the possibility of a violent upheaval never crossed our parents' minds. No one breathed a word of it, no one even dreamed of it. The small disturbances which, when there is political freedom, inevitably take place from time to time in even the most stable social systems are a constant reminder of the risk of large-scale cataclysms and keep the authorities on the *qui vivre*. But in the eighteenth century, on the very eve of the Revolution, there had been as yet no warning that the ancient edifice was tottering.

I have closely studied the *cahiers* drawn up by the three Orders before the meeting of the Estates-General—by all three Orders, be it noted—nobility and clergy as well as the Third Estate. In the course of plowing my way through these voluminous documents I made many notes: here was a request for the amendment of a law, here for the suppression of a custom, and so forth. When I had reached the end of my labors and made a list of these various proposals I realized with something like consternation that what was being asked for was nothing short of the systematic, simultaneous abolition of *all* existing French laws and customs. There was no blinking the fact that what the authors of these *cahiers* jointly sponsored was one of the vastest, most catastrophic revolutions the world had ever known. Yet the men who were to be its victims had not the least presentiment of this; they nursed the foolish hope that a sudden, radical transformation of a very ancient, highly intricate social system could be effected almost painlessly, under the auspices of reason and by its efficacy alone. Theirs was a rude awakening! They would have done better to recall an ancient dictum formulated by their ancestors, four centuries before, in the rather crabbed language of the day: "Claim too great freedom, too much license, and too great subjection shall befall you!"

Given their long exclusion from any form of public life, it is not surprising that the nobility and bourgeoisie should have developed this singular obtuseness. But it is decidedly surprising that those who were at the helm of public affairs—statesmen, Intendants, the magistrates—should have displayed little more foresight. No doubt many of these men had proved themselves highly competent in the exercise of their functions and had a good grasp of all the details of public administration; yet, as for true statecraft—that is to say clear perception of the way society is evolving, an awareness of the trends of mass opinion and an ability to forecast the future—they were as much at sea as any ordinary citizen. For it is only in an atmosphere of freedom that the qualities of mind indispensable to true statesmanship can mature and fructify....

In England writers on the theory of government and those who actually governed co-operated with each other, the former setting forth their new theories, the latter amending or circumscribing these in the light of practical experience. In France, however, precept and practice were kept quite distinct and remained in the hands of two quite independent groups. One of these carried on the actual administration while the other set forth the abstract principles on which good government should, they said, be based; one took the routine measures appropriate to the needs of the moment, the other propounded general laws without a thought for their practical application; one group shaped the course of public affairs, the other that of public opinion.

Thus alongside the traditional and confused, not to say chaotic, social system of the day there was gradually built up in men's minds an imaginary ideal society in which all was simple, uniform, coherent, equitable, and rational in the full sense of the term. It was this vision of the perfect State that fired the imagination of the masses and little by little estranged them from the here-and-now. Turning away from the real world around them, they indulged in dreams of a far better one and ended up by living, spiritually, in the ideal world thought up by the writers.

The French Revolution has often been regarded as a consequence of the American and there is no denying that the latter had considerable influence on it. But it was due less to what actually took place in the United States than to ideas then prevalent in France. To the rest of Europe the American Revolution seemed merely a novel and remarkable historical event; whereas the French saw in it a brilliant confirmation of theories already familiar to them. Elsewhere it merely shocked and startled; for the French it was conclusive proof that they were in the right. Indeed, the Americans seemed only to be putting into practice ideas which had been sponsored by our writers, and to be making our dreams their realities. . . .

Our men of letters did not merely impart their revolutionary ideas to the French nation; they also shaped the national temperament and outlook on life. In the long process of molding men's minds to their ideal pattern their task was all the easier since the French had had no training in the field of politics, and they thus had a clear field. The result was that our writers ended up by giving the Frenchman the instincts, the turn of mind, the tastes, and even the eccentricities characteristic of the literary man. And when the time came for action, these literary propensities were imported into the political arena.

When we closely study the French Revolution we find that it was conducted in precisely the same spirit as that which gave rise to so many books expounding theories of government in the abstract. Our revolutionaries had the same fondness for broad generalizations, cut-and-dried legislative systems, and a pedantic symmetry; the same contempt for hard facts; the same taste for reshaping institutions on novel, ingenious, original lines; the same desire to reconstruct the entire constitution according to the rules of logic and a preconceived system instead of trying to rectify its faulty parts. The result was nothing short of disastrous; for what is a merit in the writer may well be a vice in the statesman and the very qualities which go to make great literature can lead to catastrophic revolutions.

How the Desire for Reforms Took Precedence over the Desire for Freedom

It is a remarkable fact that of all the ideas and aspirations which led up to the Revolution the concept and desire of political liberty, in the full sense of the term, were the last to emerge, as they were also the first to pass away.

Though for some time past the entire edifice of government has been under fire and threatening to collapse, the issue of freedom

From *The Old Régime*, pt. 3, chap. 3.

had not yet been raised. Voltaire hardly gave it a thought; his three-year stay in England had familiarized him with political freedom, but failed to make him like it. What delighted him in that country was the skeptical philosophy so freely voiced there; the English political system appealed to him but little and he had a sharper eye for its defects than for its merits. In his letters about England, which rank among his finest works, Parliament is hardly mentioned. The truth was that he envied the English above all for their freedom to write as they liked, while their political freedom left him indifferent and he quite failed to realize that the former could not have survived for long without the latter.

Towards the middle of the eighteenth century a group of writers known as the "Physiocrats" or "Economists," who made the problems of public administration their special study, came on the scene. Though the Economists figure less prominently than our philosophers in histories of the period and perhaps did less than they towards bringing about the Revolution, I am inclined to think it is from their writings that we learn most of its true character. In dealing with the problems of government the philosophers confined themselves for the most part to general ideas and purely abstract theories; the Economists, while never losing sight of theory, paid more heed to practical politics. Whereas the philosophers depicted imaginary utopias, the Economists sometimes pointed out what could and should be done in the existing world. Their chief targets of attack were those institutions which the Revolution was destined to sweep away forever; not one of them found favor in their eyes. Those, on the other hand, which we now regard as creations of the Revolution were anticipated and warmly advocated by them. Indeed, the germinal ideas of practically all the permanent changes effected by the Revolution can be found in their works.

What is more, their writings had the democratic-revolutionary tenor characteristic of so much modern thought. For they attacked not only specific forms of privilege but any kind of diversity whatsoever; to their thinking all men should be equal even if equality spelled servitude, and every obstacle to the achievement of this end should be done away with immediately. For contractual engagements they had no respect, and no concern for private rights. Indeed, private rights were, in their eyes, negligible; only the public interest mattered. Though most of them were amiable, well-meaning persons, men of substance, conscientious public servants or able administrators, such was their enthusiasm for the cause they sponsored that they carried their theories to fanatical lengths.

Our Economists had a vast contempt for the past. "The nation has been governed," Letronne declared, "on wrong lines altogether; one has the impression that everything was left to chance." Starting out from this premise, they set to work, and there was no French institution, however venerable and well founded, for whose immediate suppression they did not clamor if it hampered them to even the slightest extent or did not fit in with their neatly ordered scheme of government. One Economist proposed the abolition of all the existing territorial divisions of France and the renaming of the provinces forty years before this was actually done by the Constituent Assembly.

It is a curious fact that when they envisaged all the social and administrative reforms subsequently carried out by our revolutionaries, the idea of free institutions never crossed their minds. True, they were all in favor of the free exchange of commodities and a system of *laissez faire* and *lassez passer* in commerce and industry; but political liberty in the full sense of the term was something that passed their imagination or was promptly dismissed from their thoughts if by any chance the idea of it occurred to them. To begin with, anyhow, the Economists were thoroughly hostile to deliberative assemblies, to secondary organizations vested with local powers, and, generally speaking, to all those counterpoises which have been devised by free peoples at various stages of their history to curb the domination of a central authority. "Any system of opposing forces within a government," Quesnay wrote, "is highly objectionable." And a friend of his observed that "all theories of a 'balance of power' within the State are the merest moonshine." . . .

Political freedom had been so long extinct in France that people had almost entirely forgotten what it meant and how it functioned. Indeed, its few surviving relics and the institutions seemingly created to substitute for it tended to give an unfavorable impression of the whole idea of political freedom and its corollaries. For most of the provincial assemblies that had survived were run on antiquated lines, still imbued with the medieval spirit, and, far from promoting social progress, impeded it. Likewise the parlements, the only representative political bodies that still existed, not only failed to check the evil practices of the central government but often prevented it from carrying out beneficial measures.

The Economists saw no hope of effecting the revolutionary changes they had in mind with this obsolete machinery, and the idea of recognizing the nation as sole arbiter of its own destinies and entrusting to it the execution of their plans was little to their taste. For how could a whole nation be persuaded to accept and to put through a program of reform so vast and so intricate? To their thinking the simplest, most practical solution was to enlist the support of the royal power.

This was a "new" power since it neither stemmed from the Middle Ages nor bore any mark of them, and despite its shortcomings the Economists saw in it great possibilities. Like them it favored equality among men and uniformity of law throughout the land. Again like them it had a strong aversion for all the ancient powers deriving from feudalism or associated with aristocracy. Nowhere else in Europe could they see a system of government so solidly established and so efficient, and it seemed to them a singularly happy chance that in France they had such an implement ready to their hand. In fact, had it been customary, as it is today, to see the hand of Providence in everything, they would have called it providential. "The present situation in France," Letronne observed complacently, "is vastly superior to that of England, for here reforms changing the whole social structure can be put through in the twinkling of an eye, whereas in England such reforms can always be blocked by the system of party government." ...

In the mid-eighteenth century the French people, if consulted, would have shown no more enthusiasm than the Economists for liberty; it was something they had quite lost touch with, indeed the very idea of freedom meant nothing to them. ... Twenty years later things were very different. By now the idea of freedom had found its way into the minds of Frenchmen and was appealing to them more and more. There were many symptoms of this change of heart. The provinces began to show a desire to administer their own affairs once again and the feeling that every French citizen had the right to take a share in the government of his country was gaining ground. Memories of the old Estates-General were revived; this, in fact, was the only feature of its early history to which the nation looked back without repugnance. Aware of the trend of popular feeling, the Economists found themselves obliged to allow for some free institutions in their program of nation-wide unification.

When the parlements were abolished in 1771, the selfsame public which had so often suffered from their abuses of justice was much perturbed by their disappearance. For there was a general feeling that with them had fallen the last barrier still capable of holding in check the monarch's absolute power.... The French now wanted something more than ameliorations in the existing system; they wished to get the administration into their own hands. And it was clear that the gigantic revolution that now was getting under way would be carried out not merely with the consent but with the active help of the populace at large.

I am convinced that from this moment the far-reaching political upheaval which was to sweep away without distinction both what was worst and what was best in the old system became inevitable. A nation so unused to acting for itself was bound to begin by wholesale destruction when it launched into a program of wholesale reform. An absolute monarch would have been a far less dangerous innovator. Personally, indeed, when I reflect on the way the French Revolution, in destroying so many institutions, ideas, and customs inimical to freedom, abolished so many others which were indispensable to freedom, I cannot help feeling that had this revolution, instead of being carried out by the masses on behalf of the sovereignty of the people, been the work of an enlightened autocrat, it might well have left us better fitted to develop in due course into a free nation. In any case, what I have said above should, I think, be borne in mind by those who wish to understand the nature of the Revolution and the course it took.

By the time their ancient love of freedom reawakened in the

hearts of the French, they had already been inoculated with a set of ideas as regards the way the country should be governed that were not merely hard to reconcile with free institutions but practically ruled them out. They had come to regard the ideal social system as one whose aristocracy consisted exclusively of government officials and in which an all-powerful bureaucracy not only took charge of affairs of State but controlled men's private lives. Desirous though they were of being free, they were unwilling to go back on the ideology described above and merely tried to adjust it to that of freedom.

This they proposed to do by combining a strong central administration with a paramount legislative assembly: the bureaucratic system with government by the electorate. The nation as a whole had sovereign rights, while the individual citizen was kept in strictest tutelage; the former was expected to display the sagacity and virtues of a free race, the latter to behave like an obedient servant.

It was this desire of grafting political liberty onto institutions and an ideology that were unsuited, indeed adverse to it, but to which the French had gradually become addicted—it was this desire of combining freedom with the servile state that led during the last sixty years to so many abortive essays of a free régime followed by disastrous revolutions. The result has been that, wearied of those vain attempts and the efforts involved, many Frenchmen have lost their taste for freedom and come to think that, after all, an autocratic government under which all men are equal has something to be said for it. This is why the political views of the modern Frenchman are far more similar to those of the Economists than to those of his forebears, the men of '89.

HOW PROSPERITY HASTENED THE OUTBREAK OF THE REVOLUTION

There can be no question that the exhaustion of the kingdom under Louis XIV began at the very time when that monarch's arms were triumphant throughout Europe. Indeed, the first

From *The Old Régime,* pt. 3, chap. 4.

symptoms of an economic decline made their appearance in the years of his most spectacular successes; France was ruined long before she had ceased to be victorious. . . .

Some thirty or forty years before the Revolution, however, a change came over the scene. There were stirrings of a kind hitherto unknown throughout the social system, at first so faint as to be almost imperceptible, but steadily becoming more and more apparent. Year by year these movements spread, at an increasing tempo, until the whole nation seemed to be in the throes of a rebirth. But a rebirth in no literal sense, for what was coming to life was not the France of long ago, and the new spirit animating the nation made short work of all that it resuscitated. For the minds of men were in a ferment, every Frenchman was dissatisfied with his lot and quite decided to better it. And this rankling discontent made him at once impatient and fiercely hostile to the past; nothing would content him but a new world utterly different from the world around him.

Before long the government itself was infected by this spirit; to all appearances the administrative system remained as it has always been but within there was a change of heart. The laws were not altered but differently enforced. . . . The Intendant of 1780 had the same functions, the same subordinates, the same despotic power as his predecessor, but his aims were not the same. The Intendant of an earlier day busied himself chiefly with keeping his province well in hand, levying the militia, and, above all, collecting the *taille*. The 1780 Intendant had quite other interests; he was always trying to think up plans for increasing the wealth of his province. Roads, canals, industries, and commerce were his chief preoccupations. . . .

Parallel with these changes in the mentality of the rulers and the ruled there was an advance as rapid as it was unprecedented in the prosperity of the nation. This took the usual forms: an increase in the population and an even more spectacular increase in the wealth of individuals. The American war did not check this upward movement; though the State fell yet more heavily in debt, private persons went on making fortunes; also, they worked harder than in the past, showed more initiative and resourcefulness. . . . A study of comparative statistics makes it clear that in none of the decades immediately following the Revolution did our national prosperity make such rapid forward strides as in the two preceding it. Only the thirty-seven years of constitutional monarchy, which were for us a time of peace and plenty, are in any way comparable in this respect with the reign of Louis XVI.

At first sight it seems hard to account for this steady increase in the wealth of the country despite the as yet unremedied shortcomings of the administration and the obstacles with which industry still had to contend. Indeed, many of our politicians, being unable to explain it, have followed the example of Molière's physician, who declared that no sick man could recover "against the rules of medicine"—and simply denied its existence. That France could prosper and grow rich, given the inequality of taxation, the vagaries of local laws, internal customs barriers, feudal rights, the trade corporations, the sales of offices, and all the rest, may well seem hardly credible. Yet the fact remains that the country did grow richer and living conditions improved throughout the land, and the reason was that though the machinery of government was ramshackle, ill regulated, inefficient, and though it tended to hinder rather than to further social progress, it had two redeeming features which sufficed to make it function and made for national prosperity. Firstly, though the government was no longer despotic, it still was powerful and capable of maintaining order everywhere; and secondly, the nation possessed an upper class that was the freest, most enlightened of the day and a social system under which every man could get rich if he set his mind to it and keep intact the wealth he had acquired. . . .

It is a singular fact that this steadily increasing prosperity, far from tranquilizing the population, everywhere promoted a spirit of unrest. The general public became more and more hostile to every ancient institution, more and more discontented; indeed, it was increasingly obvious that the nation was heading for a revolution.

Moreover, those parts of France in which the improvement in the standard of living was most pronounced were the chief centers of the revolutionary movement. Such records of the Ile-de-France region as have survived prove clearly that it was in the districts in the vicinity of Paris that the old order was soonest and most drastically superseded. In these parts the freedom and wealth of the peasants had long been better assured than in any other *pays d'élection.* Well before 1789 the system of forced labor (as applied to individuals) had disappeared in this region. The *taille* had become less onerous and was more equitably assessed then elsewhere....

Around the Loire estuary, in the Poitou fenlands, and the *landes* of Brittany the methods of the past were kept to more tenaciously than in any other part of France. Yet it was in these regions that civil war blazed up after the outbreak of the Revolution and the inhabitants put up the most passionate and stubborn resistance to it.

Thus it was precisely in those parts of France where there had been most improvement that popular discontent ran highest. This may seem illogical—but history is full of such paradoxes. For it is not always when things are going from bad to worse that revolutions break out. On the contrary, it oftener happens that when a people which has put up with an oppressive rule over a long period without protest suddenly finds the government relaxing its pressure, it takes up arms against it. Thus the social order overthrown by a revolution is almost always better than the one immediately preceding it, and experience teaches us that, generally speaking, the most perilous moment for a bad government is one when it seeks to mend its ways. Only consummate statecraft can enable a King to save his throne when after a long spell of oppressive rule he sets to improving the lot of his subjects. Patiently endured so long as it seemed beyond redress, a grievance comes to appear intolerable once the possibility of removing it crosses men's minds. For the mere fact that certain abuses have been remedied draws attention to the others and they now appear more galling; people may suffer less, but their sensibility is exacerbated. At the height of its power feudalism did not inspire so much hatred as it did on the eve of its eclipse. In the reign of Louis XVI the most trivial pinpricks of arbitrary power caused more resentment than the thoroughgoing despotism of Louis XIV. The brief imprisonment of Beaumarchais shocked Paris more than the *dragonnades* of 1685.

In 1780 there could no longer be any talk of France's being on the downgrade; on the contrary, it seemed that no limit could be set to her advance. And it was now that theories of the perfectibility of man and continuous progress came into fashion. Twenty years earlier there had been no hope for the future; in 1780 no anxiety was felt about it. Dazzled by the prospect of a felicity undreamed of hitherto and now within their grasp, people were blind to the very real improvement that had taken place and eager to precipitate events.

HOW THE SPIRIT OF REVOLT WAS PROMOTED BY WELL-INTENTIONED EFFORTS TO IMPROVE THE PEOPLE'S LOT

For a hundred and forty years the French people had played no part on the political stage and this had led to a general belief that they could never figure there. So inert did the working class appear that it was assumed to be not only dumb but hard of hearing, with the result that when at long last the authorities began to take an interest in the masses, they talked about them in their presence, as if they were not there. Indeed, there seems to have been an impression that only the upper classes could use their ears and the sole danger was that of failing to make oneself understood by them.

Thus the very men who had most to fear from the anger of the masses had no qualms about publicly condemning the gross injustice with which they had always been treated. They drew attention to the monstrous vices of the institutions which pressed most heavily on the common people and indulged in highly colored descriptions of the living conditions of the working class and the starvation wages it received. And by thus championing the cause of the under-privileged they made them acutely conscious of their wrongs. The people of whom I now am speaking, be it noted, were not our literary men but members of the government, high officials, the privileged few.

When thirteen years before the Revolution the King attempted

From *The Old Régime,* pt. 3, chaps. 5, 6, and 7.

to abolish forced labor, his preamble to the measure ran as follows: "Outside a few provinces...almost all the roads in the kingdom have been made by the unpaid labor of the poorest of our subjects. Thus the whole burden has fallen on those who till the soil and make relatively little use of the highways; it is the landed proprietors, nearly all of them privileged persons, who stand to gain, since the value of their estates is enhanced by the making of these roads. When the poor man is constrained to bear the brunt, unaided, of keeping the roads in order and forced to give his time and toil without remuneration, the one and only means he has of avoiding poverty and hunger is being taken from him and he is being forced to work for the benefit of the rich."

When an attempt was made at the same time to do away with the injustices and restrictions of the guild system, the King issued a declaration to the effect that "the right to work is a man's most sacred possession and any law that tampers with it violates a natural right and should be treated as null and void. The existing trade and craft corporations are unnatural and oppressive organizations stemming from self-regarding motives, greed, and a desire to domineer." It was indiscreet enough to utter such words, but positively dangerous to utter them in vain. For some months later the guild system and forced labor were reinstated....

During his entire reign Louis XVI was always talking about reform, and there were few institutions whose destruction he did not contemplate before the Revolution broke and made an end of them. But after eliminating from the constitution some of its worst features he made haste to reinstate them; in fact, he gave an impression of merely wanting to loosen its foundations and leaving to others the task of laying it low.

Some of the reforms he personally put through made overhasty, ill-considered changes in ancient and respected usages, changes which in certain cases violated vested rights. They prepared the ground for the Revolution not so much because they removed obstacles in its way but far more because they taught the nation how to set about it. Paradoxically enough, what made things worse was that the King and his Ministers were inspired by purely altruistic ideals; for by showing that methods of violence can be employed with good intentions by people of good will, they set a dangerous precedent....

The suppression of the trade and craft corporations, followed by their partial restoration, had entirely changed the old relations between worker and employer. But this relationship did not merely take a different form; it now was ill defined and irksome to all concerned. The employers' authority had been undermined but the quasi-paternal control of the State was not yet solidly established, and between the conflicting claims of the government and his employer the artisan hardly knew where he stood; from which of the two he should take orders, and which could be counted on to protect his interests. This condition of uncertainty, not to say anarchy, to which the working class in all the towns of France had been reduced had far-reaching consequences when the people began once again to make their voice heard in the political arena....

But it was above all the drastic reform of the administration (in the widest sense of the term) which took place in 1787 that not only threw public affairs into confusion but had repercussions on the private life of every Frenchman.

I have already drawn attention to the fact that...in nearly three quarters of France, the entire administration was in the hands of a single man, the Intendant, and that not only his will was law, but he came to his decisions alone, without seeking any outside advice. In 1787, however, a provincial assembly was associated with the Intendant and in effect it took over the entire administration of the district formerly under his sole charge. In the same way an elected municipal committee took over in the villages the functions of the parish council and, in most cases, of the Syndic.

Totally unlike the old system of administration and changing out of recognition both the manner in which public business was transacted and, more, the social status of private citizens, the new system (so the King decreed) was to come into force everywhere simultaneously and under practically the same form; that is to say without the least respect for ancient customs, local usages, or the particular conditions of each province. So deeply had this notion of standardized administration, destined to be a characteristic of the Revolution, already permeated the monarchical government which it was soon to sweep away.

It was easy then to see how large a part is played by habit in the functioning of political institutions and how much more easily a nation can cope with complicated, well-nigh unintelligible laws to which it is accustomed than with a simpler legal system that is new. . . .

. . . the administration of the country slowed down, sometimes coming to a standstill, and all public life lapsed into a state of suspended animation. Thus the Provincial Assembly of Lorraine spoke of "a total stagnation in the conduct of public affairs" (a lament that was echoed by several other assemblies), adding that "all good citizens are much distressed by this." . . .

When the Revolution broke out, that part of the government which, though subordinate, keeps every citizen constantly aware of its existence and affects his daily life at every turn, had just been thrown into confusion; the public administration had made a clean sweep of all its former representatives and embarked on a quite new program. Radical as they were, these reforms did not seem to have jeopardized the State itself, but every Frenchman was affected by them, if only in a minor way. He felt that his life had somehow been disorganized, that he must cultivate new habits, and if a businessman, that his activities would now be handicapped. True, routine of a kind still prevailed in the conduct of affairs of vital importance to the nation, but already no one knew from whom he should take orders, to whom he should apply, or how to solve those small private problems which crop up almost daily in the life of every member of a social group.

Thus the nation as a whole was now in a state of unstable equilibrium, at the mercy of that final stroke of destiny which was to have such tremendous effects and to produce the most formidable social cataclysm the world had ever seen.

How, Given These Facts, the Revolution
Was a Foregone Conclusion

My object in this final chapter is to bring together some of those aspects of the old régime which were depicted piecemeal in the

From *The Old Régime,* pt. 3, chap. 8.

foregoing pages and show how the Revolution was their natural, indeed inevitable, outcome.

When we remember that it was in France that the feudal system, while retaining the characteristics which made it so irksome to, and so much resented by, the masses, had most completely discarded all that could benefit or protect them, we may feel less surprise at the fact that France was the place of origin of the revolt destined so violently to sweep away the last vestiges of that ancient European institution.

Similarly, if we observe how the nobility after having lost their political rights and ceased, to a greater extent than in any other land of feudal Europe, to act as leaders of the people had nevertheless not only retained but greatly increased their fiscal immunities and the advantages accruing to them individually; and if we also note how, while ceasing to be the ruling class, they had remained a privileged, closed group, less and less (as I have pointed out) an aristocracy and more and more a caste—if we bear these facts in mind, it is easy to see why the privileges enjoyed by this small section of the community seemed so unwarranted and so odious to the French people and why they developed that intense jealousy of the "upper class" which rankles still today.

Finally, when we remember that the nobility had deliberately cut itself off both from the middle class and from the peasantry (whose former affection it had alienated) and had thus become like a foreign body in the State: ostensibly the high command of a great army, but actually a corps of officers without troops to follow them—when we keep this in mind, we can easily understand why the French nobility, after having so far weathered every storm, was stricken down in a single night.

I have shown how the monarchical government, after abolishing provincial independence and replacing local authorities by its nominees in the three quarters of the country, had brought under its direct management all public business, even the most trivial. I have also shown how, owing to the centralization of power, Paris, which had until now been merely the capital city, had come to dominate France—or, rather, to embody in itself the whole kingdom. These two circumstances, peculiar to France, suffice to explain why it was that an uprising of the people could overwhelm so abruptly and decisively a monarchy that for so many centuries had successfully withstood so many onslaughts and, on the very eve of its downfall, seemed inexpungable even to the men who were about to destroy it.

In no other country of Europe had all political thought been so thoroughly and for so long stifled as in France; in no other country had the private citizen become so completely out of touch with public affairs and so unused to studying the course of events, so much so that not only had the average Frenchman no experience of "popular movements" but he hardly understood what "the people" meant. Bearing this in mind, we may find it easier to understand why the nation as a whole could launch out into a sanguinary revolution, with those very men who stood to lose most by it taking the lead and clearing the ground for it.

Since no free institutions and, as a result, no experienced and organized political parties existed any longer in France, and since in the absence of any political groups of this sort the guidance of public opinion, when its first stirrings made themselves felt, came entirely into the hands of the philosophers, that is to say the intellectuals, it was only to be expected that the directives of the Revolution should take the form of abstract principles, highly generalized theories, and that political realities would be largely overlooked. Thus, instead of attacking only such laws as seemed objectionable, the idea developed that *all* laws indiscriminately must be abolished and a wholly new system of government, sponsored by these writers, should replace the ancient French constitution.

Moreover, since the Church was so closely bound up with the ancient institutions now to be swept away, it was inevitable that the Revolution, in overthrowing the civil power, should assail the established religion. As a result, the leaders of the movement, shaking off the controls that religion, law, and custom once had exercised, gave free rein to their imagination and indulged in acts of an outrageousness that took the whole world by surprise. Nevertheless, anyone who had closely studied the condition of the country at the time might well have guessed that there was no enormity, no form of violence from which these men would shrink.

In one of his eloquent pamphlets Burke made no secret of his consternation. What particularly surprised him was there was no one anywhere who could stand surety for the smallest group of his fellow citizens or even for a single man, the consequence being that anyone could be arrested in his home without protest or redress, whether the offense alleged against him were royalism, "moderatism," or any other political deviation.

Burke failed to realize how things were in the kingdom which the monarchy (whose downfall he deplored) had bequeathed to its new masters. Under the old order the government had long since deprived Frenchmen of the possibility, and even the desire, of coming to each other's aid. When the Revolution started, it would have been impossible to find, in most parts of France, even ten men used to acting in concert and defending their interests without appealing to the central power for aid. Thus once that central power had passed from the hands of the royal administration into those of irresponsible sovereign assemblies and a benevolent government had given place to a ruthless one, the latter found nothing to impede it or hold up its activities even momentarily. The same conditions which had precipitated the fall of the monarchy made for the absolutism of its successor.

Never had religious tolerance, the lenient use of power and kindness toward one's neighbor been preached so earnestly and, to all appearances, so generally practiced as in the eighteenth century. Even the rules of war, last resort of the will to violence, had been humanized. Yet it was in this humanitarian climate that the most inhuman of revolutions took its rise. Nor must it be thought that these amiable sentiments were merely feigned; once the Revolution had run its headlong course, these same feelings came to the fore again and promptly made their presence felt not only in legislation but in all the doings of the new government.

This contrast between theory and practice, between good intentions and acts of savage violence, which was a salient feature of the French Revolution, becomes less startling when we remember that the Revolution, though sponsored by the most civilized classes of the nation, was carried out by its least educated and most unruly elements. For, since the members of the cultured elite had formed a habit of keeping to themselves, were unused to acting together, and had no hold on the masses, the latter became masters of the situation almost from the start. Even where the people did not govern *de facto* and directly, they set the tone of the administration. And in view of the conditions in which these men had been living under the old régime, it was almost a foregone conclusion how they now would act.

Actually it was to these very conditions that our peasantry owed some of their outstanding qualities. Long enfranchised and owning some of the land he worked, the French peasant was largely independent and had developed a healthy pride and much common sense. Inured to hardships, he was indifferent to the amenities of life, intrepid in the face of danger, and faced misfortune stoically. It was from this simple, virile race of men that those great armies were raised which were to dominate for many years the European scene. But their very virtues made them dangerous masters. During the many centuries in which these men had borne the brunt of nation-wide misgovernment and lived as a class apart, they had nursed in secret their grievances, jealousies, and rancors and, having learned toughness in a hard school, had become capable of enduring or inflicting the very worst.

It was in this mood that gripping the reins of power, the French people undertook the task of seeing the Revolution through. Books had supplied them with the necessary theories, and they now put these into practice, adjusting the writers' ideas to their lust for revenge.

Readers of this book who have followed carefully my description of eighteenth-century France will have noticed the steady growth amongst the people of two ruling passions, not always simultaneous or having the same objectives. One of these, the more deeply rooted and long-standing, was an intense, indomitable hatred of inequality. This inequality forced itself on their attention, they saw signs of it at every turn; thus it is easy to understand why the French had for so many centuries felt a desire, inveterate and uncontrollable, utterly to destroy all such institutions as had survived from the Middle Ages and, having cleared the ground, to build up a new society in which men were as much alike and their status as equal as possible, allowing for the innate differences between individuals. The other ruling passion, more recent and less deeply rooted, was a desire to live not only on an equal footing but also as free men.

Toward the close of the old régime these two passions were equally sincerely felt and seemed equally operative. When the Revolution started, they came in contact, joined forces, coalesced, and reinforced each other, fanning the revolutionary ardor of the nation to a blaze. This was in '89, that rapturous year of bright enthusiasm, heroic courage, lofty ideals—untempered, we must grant, by the reality of experience: a historic date of glorious memory to which the thoughts of men will turn with admiration and respect long after those who witnessed its achievement, and we ourselves, have passed away. At the time the French had such proud confidence in the cause they were defending, and in themselves, that they believed they could reconcile freedom with equality and interspersed democratic institutions everywhere with free institutions. Not only did they shatter that ancient system under which men were divided into classes, corporations, and castes, and their rights were even more unequal than their social situations, but by the same token they did away with all the more recent legislation, instituted by the monarchy, whose effect was to put every Frenchman under official surveillance, with the government as his mentor, overseer, and, on occasion, his oppressor. Thus centralization shared the fate of absolute government.

But when the virile generation which had launched the Revolution had perished or (as usually befalls a generation engaging in such ventures) its first fine energy had dwindled; and when, as was but to be expected after a spell of anarchy and "popular" dictatorship, the ideal of freedom had lost much of its appeal and the nation, at a loss where to turn, began to cast round for a master—under these conditions the stage was set for a return to one-man government. Indeed, never had conditions been more favorable for its establishment and consolidation, and the man of genius destined at once to carry on and to abolish the Revolution was quick to turn them to account.

Actually there had existed under the old régime a host of institutions which had quite a "modern" air and, not being incompatible with equality, could easily be embodied in the new social order—and all these institutions offered remarkable facilities to despotism. They were hunted for among the wreckage of the old order and duly salvaged. These institutions had formerly given rise to customs, usages, ideas, and prejudices tending to keep men apart, and thus make them easier to rule. They were revived and skillfully exploited; centralization was built up anew, and in the process all that had once kept it within bounds was carefully eliminated. Thus there arose, within a nation that had but recently laid low its monarchy, a central authority with powers wider, stricter, and more absolute than those which any French King had ever wielded. Rash though this venture may have been, it was carried through with entire success for the good reason that people took into account only what was under their eyes and forgot what they had seen before. Napoleon fell but the more solid parts of his achievement lasted on; his government died, but his administration survived, and every time that an attempt is made to do away with absolutism the most that could be done has been to graft the head of Liberty onto a servile body.

On several occasions during the period extending from the outbreak of the Revolution up to our time we find the desire for freedom reviving, succumbing, then returning, only to die out once more and presently blaze up again. This presumably will be the lot for many years to come of a passion so undisciplined and untutored by experience; so easily discouraged, cowed and vanquished, so superficial and short-lived. Yet during this same period the passion for equality, first to entrench itself in the hearts of Frenchmen, has never given ground; for it links up with feelings basic to our very nature. For while the urge to freedom is forever assuming new forms, losing or gaining strength according to the march of events, our love of equality is constant and pursues the object of its desire with a zeal that is obstinate and often blind, ready to make every concession to those who give it satisfaction. Hence the fact that the French nation is prepared to tolerate in a government that favors and flatters its desire for equality practices and principles that are, in fact, the tools of despotism.

To those who study it as an isolated phenomenon the French Revolution can but seem a dark and sinister enigma; only when we view it in the light of the events preceding it can we grasp its true significance. And, similarly, without a clear idea of the old régime, its laws, its vices, its prejudices, its shortcomings, and its greatness, it is impossible to comprehend the history of the sixty years following its fall. Yet even this is not enough; we need also to understand and bear in mind the peculiarities of the French temperament.

When I observe France from this angle I find the nation itself far more remarkable than any of the events in its long history. It hardly seems possible that there can ever have existed any other people so full of contrasts and so extreme in all their doings, so much guided by their emotions and so little by fixed principles, always behaving better, or worse, than one expected of them. At one time they rank above, at another below, the norm of humanity; their basic characteristics are so constant that we can recognize the France we know in portraits made of it two or three thousand years ago, and yet so changeful are its moods, so variable its tastes that the nation itself is often quite as much startled as any foreigner at the things it did only a few years before. Ordinarily the French are the most routine-bound of men, but once they are forced out of the rut and leave their homes, they travel to the ends of the earth and engage in the most reckless ventures. Undisciplined by temperament, the Frenchman is always readier to put up with the arbitrary rule, however harsh, of an autocrat than with a free, well-ordered government by his fellow citizens, however worthy of respect they be. At one moment he is up in arms against authority and the next we find him serving the powers-that-be with a zeal such as the most servile races never display. So long as no one thinks of resisting, you can lead him on a thread, but once a revolutionary movement is afoot, nothing can restrain him from taking part in it. That is why our rulers are so often taken by surprise; they fear the nation either too much or not enough, for though it is never so free that the possibility of enslaving it is ruled out, its spirit can never be broken so completely as to prevent its shaking off the yoke of an oppressive government. The Frenchman can turn his hand to anything, but he excels in war alone and he prefers fighting against odds, preferring dazzling feats of arms and spectacular successes to achievements of the more solid kind. He is more prone to heroism than to humdrum virtue, apter for genius than for good sense, more inclined to think up grandiose schemes than to carry through great enterprises. Thus the French are at once the most brilliant and the most dangerous of all European nations, and the best qualified to become, in the eyes of other peoples, an object of admiration, of hatred, of compassion, or alarm—never of indifference.

France alone could have given birth to revolution so sudden, so frantic, and so thoroughgoing, yet so full of unexpected changes of direction, of anomalies and inconsistencies. But for the antecedent circumstances described in this book the French would never have embarked on it; yet we must recognize that though their effect was cumulative and overwhelming, they would not have sufficed to lead to such a drastic revolution elsewhere than in France.

From the Revolution to Napoleon

As time passed on, and the *ancien régime* faded in the distance, the people grew more and more resolved not to return to it. The phenomenon was remarkable. The Revolution seemed to become dear to the nation in proportion to the suffering which it inflicted. From the writings of the time it is evident that it was this which most astonished the enemies of the Revolution. When they contrasted the evils that it produced with the attachment that it retained, France seemed to them to have become raving mad.

These opposite effects, however, were due to one cause.

Men suffered more and more from the Revolution the longer the bad government which had risen out of it lasted, while this very duration made the habits that it had planted take root, and increased the number and variety of the interests which it sustained. As the nation advanced, barrier after barrier rose up behind and impeded a return. Most Frenchmen had taken an active share in affairs since the beginning of the Revolution, and had

From the two completed chapters of the sequel to *The Old Régime* in *Memoir, Letters and Remains,* pp. 281–94.

attested their adherence to it by public acts; they felt almost themselves responsible for the calamities that had ensued. This responsibility seemed to strengthen with the increase and duration of the evils. Thus the Reign of Terror gave to many, even of its victims, an unconquerable aversion to the re-establishment of old rights, the owners of which would have so many injuries to resent.

Something like this has been witnessed in every revolution. Even the most oppressive render a return to a former state intolerable to the nation, if they only last long enough. Our revolution, besides, did not oppress the whole country in an equal degree; some suffered little by it, and among those even who bore the burden many had found considerable advantages mixed with the evils that it had caused. I believe that the comfort of the lower classes was much less disturbed than is commonly supposed. At least they had great alleviations of their misfortunes. Great numbers of workmen having willingly, or by compulsion, joined the army, those who remained in France obtained much higher pay. Wages rose in spite of public and private calamities, for the working class diminished still more quickly than the demand for their services. . . .

As for the peasantry, I need not repeat that they were able to purchase much land at a low price. It is impossible to set down precisely in figures the gain that they made, but it is well known that it was considerable. All the world knows that the Revolution abolished many heavy and vexatious taxes, such as tithes, feudal dues, forced labour, the salt-tax, some of which were never re-imposed, and others only partially, and at a much later period. Today we can scarcely imagine how hateful many of those taxes were to the people, either on account of their oppressiveness, or from the ideas with which they were connected. . . .

Another fact, which has not sufficiently been noticed, is the less direct and regular, but not less real benefit conferred by the Revolution on many poor debtors. Their debts were not actually abolished in law, but soon afterwards they were reduced in fact by the issue of paper money.

It is now known that in many provinces in France the number of small proprietors was considerable, even before 1789. There is reason for thinking (although the fact cannot be absolutely proved) that most of these small landowners were involved in debt, for at that time they bore the chief burden of taxation. Even now, when the weight of contributing to the revenue is laid on all equally, that class still falls most into debt. The possessors of small encumbered estates nearly filled the towns, for France has always been a country abounding more in vanity and in wants than in wealth. We must note that before the Revolution, as in our own day, the farmers formed a numerous class, because our farms are in general small. The rapid depreciation of paper-money operated universally, as if all securities had been thrown into the fire, and rents reduced to nothing. The disorder of the times, and, still more, the weakness of the administration, prevented even the debt to the State from being regularly or fully paid. The financial records of the Republic show that neither the old taxes which were retained nor the new ones that were imposed were ever completely collected. The State was maintained by means of *assignats,* by payment in kind, and by the spoils of Europe. M. Thibeaudeau said with reason in his memoirs, "that the discredit of *assignats,* while it ruined the great proprietors and annuitants, made the fortunes of the peasants and farmers."

"The country," wrote in 1795 M. Mallet-Dupan, whom I have already quoted, "grows rich by the poverty of the towns; fabulous profits are made in it. A sack of flour pays the farmer's rent. The peasantry have become calculating and speculating; they fight with each other for the lands of *émigrés,* and pay no taxes."

A foreigner, evidently a man of talent, who was travelling in France at this period, wrote in his journal, "In France, at the present day, the rich aristocracy is the aristocracy of farmers and peasants."

It is true that the peasant had to set against these advantages some oppressions incident to the times, the billetting of soldiers and requisitions in kind; but these partial and momentary evils did not prevent his enjoying the benefits of the Revolution. On the contrary, he became more and more attached to them, and he bore these annoyances as he bore storms and floods, for which a good estate is never abandoned, though they make the owner long for a fair season that will enable him to turn it to good account.

When one considers the means by which the originators of our first revolution succeeded in gaining the hearts of the agricultural classes, and with what substantial gifts they obtained the enthusiastic suffrage of the small farmers and lower classes (that is, of the masses) for their work, in spite of the misery and desolation of the period, one wonders at the simplicity of some democrats in our own day who thought that it would be easy to persuade a highly civilized people to submit patiently to the inconvenience inseparable from a great political change, by the bribe of freedom instead of that of plunder and profit.

The middle class, especially that of the towns, who began the revolution, was, of the victorious party, the class that had chiefly to bear the burden. Its personal sufferings were greater, and its substantial losses relatively almost as great as those of the nobles. Its trade was partially, its manufactures were totally destroyed. The small Government employments, and many other privileges belonging to it, were abolished, but the events which ruined it made it the governing class. The power of the State passed to it immediately, the fortune of the State soon followed. The greater part of the innovations which were suddenly produced by the violent and disorderly tyranny of the Revolution had been expected, extolled, and longed-for all through the eighteenth century. They satisfied the judgment and charmed the imagination even of those with whose interests they interfered. The only fault found with these innovations was that they had cost too dear. Even the price that had been paid rendered some of them still more precious. Much as France, therefore, feared and suffered, there was always one thing which seemed worse than present pain and anxiety; it was a return to the past.

Some ingenious modern writers have undertaken the defence of the *Ancien Régime*. My first remark is that it is a small proof of the excellence of a government when men wait to praise it till they have ceased to believe in the possibility of its restoration. But I judge of it, not from my own ideas, but from the feelings that it inspired in those who endured and overthrew it. All through the course of that cruel and tyrannical revolution I see hatred towards the *Ancien Régime* surpass in the heart of every Frenchman every other hatred, and so deeply rooted as to survive the object

of its abhorrence, and from a passing impulse become a permanent instinct....

... Divided between fears of the royalists and of the Jacobins,
the mass of the nation sought for an escape. The Revolution was
loved, but the Republic was feared lest it should bring back the
royalists or the Jacobins. We may even say that each of these
passions nourished the other; it was because the French set great
value upon certain benefits conferred upon them by the Revolution, that they felt all the more keenly the inconvenience that
would result from a government which should interfere with their
enjoyment of them. Of all the privileges that they had won or
obtained during the last ten years, the only one that they were
willing to surrender was liberty! They were ready to give up the
liberty which the Revolution has only promised, to enjoy at length
in peace the other advantages that it had given to them.

All parties, indeed, reduced, cold, and weary, longed to rest for
a time in a despotism of any kind, provided that it were exercised
by a stranger, and weighed upon their rivals as heavily as on
themselves. This stroke finishes the picture. When great political
parties begin to cool in their attachments, without softening their
antipathies, and at last reach the point of wishing less to succeed
than to prevent the success of their adversaries, one must prepare
for slavery—the master is near. It was easy to see that this master
could rise only from the army.

It is interesting to follow throughout the different phases of this
long revolution, the gradual advance of the army towards
sovereign power. In the beginning, the army was dispersed by an
unarmed populace, or, rather, fell to pieces in the rapid changes
of public opinion. For a long time it stood aloof from all internal
affairs. The population of Paris usurped the power of making and
unmaking the rulers of France. Still the revolution went on. The
enthusiasm which it had inspired faded; the able men who had directed its course in the Assembly retired or died. The government
relaxed; public opinion, stern in the early days of the Revolution,
became weak, anarchy spread in every direction. Meanwhile
the army acquired organisation, experience and fame; great
generals emerged from it. It retained a common object and common passions, while the nation had them no more. In short, the

military and the civilians grew into two entirely distinct societies, within the same period and in the heart of the same nation. The chain that bound the one was drawn closer, while that which united the other relaxed its hold.

On the 13th Vendémiaire, 1795, the army, for the first time since 1789, took part in internal affairs. It caused the victory of the Convention, and the discomfiture of the middle class in Paris.

In 1797, on the 18th Fructidor, it assisted the Directory in the conquest, not only of Paris, but of the legislative body, or rather of the whole country, by which that body had been chosen. On the 30th Prairial, 1799, it refused to support the very Directors whom it held responsible for its own reverses, and they fell before the Assembly. . . .

The Directory, after having governed without opposition and almost without control, having interfered with everything, having tried everything, with the absolute power bestowed on it by the events of Fructidor, seemed gradually to expire of itself, and without an effort. (June, 1799; in the language of that time, 30th Prairial, an VII.) The same legislative body that it had decimated, in part recomposed, and always treated as its slave, regained the mastery and resumed the government. But soon the victor knew not what to do with his conquest. Hitherto the administrative machinery had worked irregularly, now it seemed to stand still. It was evident that Assemblies, which are of admirable use sometimes in strengthening, and at other times in moderating the government, are more incapable than the worst governments of directing public affairs.

No sooner had the sovereign power returned to the *corps législatif,* than universal debility pervaded the administration throughout the country. Anarchy spread from private individuals to officials. No one resisted—no one obeyed. It was like a disbanding army. The taxes, instead of being ill paid, were not paid at all. In every direction, conscripts preferred highway-robbery to rejoining the army. At one time it seemed as if not only order, but civilization itself, were to be overturned. Neither persons, nor property, nor even the high-roads were safe. In the correspondence of the public functionaries with the Government, still preserved in the national archives, is a description of these calamities; for, as a minister of that time said, "The accounts given to the nation should be reassuring; but in the retreat, not exposed to the public eye, where the Government deliberates, everything ought to be told."

I have before me one of these secret reports, that of the Minister of Police, dated the 30th Fructidor, an VII. (the 16th of September, 1799), on the condition of the country. I gather from it, that, at that time, of the eighty-six departments into which France (properly so called, for I except the recent acquisitions by conquest) was divided, forty-five were abandoned to disorder and civil war. Troops of brigands forced open the prisons, assassinated the police, and set the convicts at liberty; the receivers of taxes were robbed, killed, or maimed; municipal officers murdered, landowners imprisoned for ransom or taken as hostages, lands laid waste and diligences stopped. Bands of two hundred, of three hundred, and of eight hundred men overspread the country. Gangs of conscripts resisted everywhere, arms in hand, the authorities whose duty it was to enrol them. The laws were disobeyed in all quarters; by some to follow the impulse of their passions—by others to follow the practices of their religion; some profited by the state of affairs to strip travellers—others to ring the long-silent church-bells, or to carry the banners of the Catholic faith through the desecrated churchyards. . . . After the 13th Vendémiaire, no government was possible without the army. Soon after, there could be no government except through the army. Having reached this point, it chose to assume the government itself. One step induced the other. Long before they were really masters, the soldiery adopted the tone and habits of command. . . .

The friends of the Republic, who perceived the growing influence of the army, consoled themselves by considering that the military had always exhibited ultrarepublican passions, by which it seemed still to be violently agitated, while they had disappeared in the rest of the nation. What they took for love of the Republic was chiefly love for the Revolution. In fact, the army was the only class in France of which every member, without exception, had gained by the revolution, and had a personal interest in supporting it. Every officer owed his rank to it, and every soldier his hopes of becoming an officer. The army was, in truth, the Revo-

lution roused and in arms. When it still wildly exclaimed,—
"Long live the Republic!" it was only as a challenge to the *ancien
régime,* whose adherents cried,—"Long live the King!" In reality
it cared nothing for the liberties of the nation. Hatred to foreigners, and a love of his native land, are in general the only elements of the soldier's patriotism, even in free countries; still more
must this have been the case in a nation in the then state of
France. The army, like almost every other army in the world,
could make nothing of the slow and complicated movements of a
representative government; it detested and despised the Assembly, because it was incapable of understanding any power that
was not strong and simple, and all that it wanted was national
independence and victories.

The recent revolution having thus prepared the way, it must not
be supposed that a clear idea was formed of what was coming.
There are moments when the world resembles one of our theatres
before the curtain rises. We know that we shall see a new play.
We already hear the preparations on the stage; the actors are
close to us, but we cannot see them, and we know not what the
piece is to be. In like manner, especially toward the end of the
year 1799, the approach of a revolution was heard in every direction, though none knew whence it was to come. It appeared to be
impossible for the existing state of things to continue, and seemed
equally impossible to escape from it. In every correspondence of
the time is this sentence: "things cannot remain as they are"—no
more is added. Even imagination was exhausted. Men were tired
of hoping and predicting. France abandoned herself to her fate;
filled with dread, but overcome by languor, she looked wearily
from side to side to see if no one could come to her aid. It was
evident that this deliverer must rise from the army. Who could it
be? Some named Pichegru, some Moreau, others thought that it
would be Bernadotte.

"Retired into the country in the heart of the Bourbonnais,"
writes M. Fiévée in his memoirs, "one fact only recalled me to
politics; every peasant whom I met in the fields, the vineyards, or
the forest stopped me to ask if there were any news of General
Bonaparte, and why he did not return to France; I was never
asked any question concerning the Directory."

7

THE REVOLUTION OF 1848
AND ITS AFTERMATH

The July Monarchy:
Triumph of the Bourgeoisie

Our history from 1789 to 1830, if viewed from a distance and as a whole, affords as it were the picture of a struggle to the death between the Ancien Régime, its traditions, memories, hopes, and men, as represented by the aristocracy, and New France under the leadership of the middle class. The year 1830 closed the first period of our revolutions, or rather of our revolution: for there is but one, which had remained always the same in the face of varying fortunes, of which our fathers witnessed the commencement, and of which we, in all probability, shall not live to behold the end. In 1830 the triumph of the middle class had been definite and so thorough that all political power, every franchise, every prerogative, and the whole government was confined and, as it were, heaped up within the narrow limits of this one class, to the statutory exclusion of all beneath them and the actual exclusion of all above. Not only did it thus alone rule society, but it may be said to have formed it. It ensconced itself in every vacant place, prodigiously augmented the number of places, and accustomed itself to live almost as much upon the Treasury as upon its own industry.

No sooner had the Revolution of 1830 become an accomplished fact, than there ensued a great lull in political passion, a sort of general subsidence, accompanied by a rapid increase in public wealth. The particular spirit of the middle class became the gen-

From the *Recollections,* pt. 1, chap. 1.

eral spirit of the government; it ruled the latter's foreign policy as well as affairs at home: an active, industrious spirit, often dishonourable, generally sober, occasionally reckless through vanity or egoism, but timid by temperament, moderate in all things, except in its love of ease and comfort, and wholly undistinguished. It was a spirit which, mingled with that of the people or of the aristocracy, can do wonders; but which, by itself, will never produce more than a government shorn of both virtue and greatness. Master of everything in a manner that no aristocracy had ever been or may ever hope to be, the middle class, when called upon to assume the government, took it up as a trade; it entrenched itself behind its power, and before long, in their egoism, each of its members thought much more of his private business than of public affairs, and of his personal enjoyment than of the greatness of the nation.

Posterity, which sees none but the more dazzling crimes, and which in general loses sight of mere vices, will never perhaps know to what extent the government of that day, towards its close, assumed the ways of a trading company, which conducts all its transactions with a view to the profits accruing to the shareholders. These vices were due to the natural instincts of the dominant class, to the absoluteness of its power, and also to the character of the time. Possibly also King Louis-Philippe had contributed to their growth. . . .

The End of the July Monarchy

In this political world thus constituted and conducted, what was most lacking, particularly towards the end, was political life itself. It could neither come into being nor be maintained within the legal circle which the Constitution had traced for it: the old aristocracy was vanquished, the people excluded. As all business was discussed among members of one class, in the interest and in the spirit of that class, there was no battlefield for contending parties to meet upon. This singular homogeneity of position, of

From the *Recollections*, pt. 1, chaps. 1 and 2.

interests, and consequently of views, reigning in what M. Guizot had once called the legal country, deprived the parliamentary debates of all originality, of all reality, and therefore of all genuine passion. I have spent ten years of my life in the company of truly great minds, who were in a constant state of agitation without succeeding in heating themselves, and who spent all their perspicacity in vain endeavours to find subjects upon which they could seriously disagree.

— On the other hand, the dominance which King Louis-Philippe had acquired in public affairs, which never permitted the politicians to stray very far from that Prince's ideas lest they should at the same time be removed from power, reduced the different colours of parties to the merest shades, and debates to the splitting of straws. I doubt whether any parliament (not excepting the Constituent Assembly—I mean the true one, that of 1789) ever contained more varied and brilliant talents than did ours during the closing years of the July Monarchy. Nevertheless, I am able to declare that these great orators were tired to death of listening to one another, and, what was worse, the whole country was tired of listening to them. It grew unconsciously accustomed to look upon the debates in the Chambers as exercises of the intellect rather than as serious discussions, and upon all the differences between the various parliamentary parties—the majority, the left centre, or the dynastic opposition—as domestic quarrels between children of one family trying to trick one another. A few glaring instances of corruption, discovered by accident, led it to presuppose a number of hidden cases, and convinced it that the whole of the governing class was corrupt; whence it conceived for the latter a silent contempt, which was generally taken for confiding and contented submission.

The country was at that time divided into two unequal parts, or rather zones: in the upper, which alone was intended to contain the whole of the nation's political life, there reigned nothing but languor, impotence, stagnation, and boredom; in the lower, on the contrary, political life began to make itself manifest by means of feverish and irregular signs, of which the attentive observer was easily able to seize the meaning.

I was one of these observers; and although I was far from imagining that the catastrophe was so near at hand and destined to be so terrible, I felt a distrust springing up and gradually growing in my mind, and the idea taking root more and more that we were making strides towards a fresh revolution. This marked a great change in my thoughts, since the general appeasement and flatness that followed the July Revolution had led me to believe for a long time that I was destined to spend my life amid an enervated and peaceful society. Indeed, anyone who had only examined the inside of the fabric of government would have had the same conviction. Everything there seemed combined to produce with the machinery of liberty a preponderance of royal power which verged upon despotism; and, in fact, this result was produced almost without effort by the regular and tranquil movement of the machine. King Louis-Philippe was persuaded that, so long as he did not himself lay hand upon that fine instrument, and allowed it to work according to rule, he was safe from all peril. His only occupation was to keep it in order, and to make it work according to his own views, forgetful of society, upon which this ingenious piece of mechanism rested; he resembled the man who refused to believe that his house was on fire, because he had the key in his pocket. I had neither the same interests nor the same cares, and this permitted me to see through the mechanism of institutions and the agglomeration of petty everyday facts, and to observe the state of morals and opinions in the country. There I clearly observed the appearance of several of the portents that usually denote the approach of revolutions, and I began to believe that in 1830 I had taken for the end of the play what was nothing more than the end of the act.

A short unpublished document which I composed at the time, and a speech which I delivered early in 1848, will bear witness to these pre-occupations of my mind.

A number of my friends in Parliament met together in October 1847, to decide upon the policy to be adopted during the ensuing session. It was agreed that we should issue a programme in the form of a manifesto, and the task of drawing it up was deputed to me. Later, the idea of this publication was abandoned, but I had already written the document. I have discovered it among my papers, and I give the following extracts. After commenting on the symptoms of languor in Parliament, I continued:

... The time will come when the country will find itself once again divided between two great parties. The French Revolution, which abolished all privileges and destroyed all exclusive rights, has allowed one to remain, that of landed property. Let not the landlords deceive themselves as to the strength of their position, nor think that the rights of property form an insurmountable barrier because they have not as yet been surmounted; for our times are unlike any others. When the rights of property were merely the origin and beginning of a number of other rights, they were easily defended, or rather, they were never attacked; they then formed the surrounding wall of society, of which all other rights were the outposts; no blows reached them. But today, when the rights of property are nothing more than the last remnants of an overthrown aristocratic world; when they alone are left intact, isolated privileges amid the universal levelling of society; when they are no longer protected behind a number of still more controversible and odious rights, the situation is changed, and they alone are left daily to resist the direct and unceasing impact of democratic opinion. . . .

... Before long, the political struggle will be restricted to those who have and those who have not; property will form the great field of battle; and the principal political questions will turn upon the major or minor modifications to be introduced into the rights of landlords. We shall then have once more among us great public agitations and great political parties.

How is it that these premonitory symptoms escape the general view? Can anyone believe that it is by accident, through some passing whim of the human mind, that we see appearing on every side these curious doctrines, bearing different titles, but all characterized in their essence by their denial of the rights of property, and all tending, at least, to limit, diminish, and weaken the exercise of these rights? Who can fail here to recognise the final symptom of the old democratic disease of the time, whose crisis would seem to be at hand?

I was still more urgent and explicit in the speech which I delivered in the Chamber of Deputies on the 29th of January 1848, and which appeared in the *Moniteur* of the 30th.

I quote the principal passages:

... I am told that there is no danger because there are no riots; I am told that, because there is no visible disorder on the surface of society, there is no revolution at hand.

Gentlemen, permit me to say that I believe you are deceiving yourselves. True, there is no actual disorder; but it has entered deeply into men's minds. See what is passing in the breasts of the working classes, who, I grant, are at present quiet. No doubt they are not disturbed by political passion, properly so-called, to the same extent that they have been; but can you not see that their passions, instead of political, have become social? Do you not see that there are gradually forming in their breasts opinions and ideas which are destined not only to upset this or that law, ministry, or even form of government, but society itself, until it totters upon the foundations on which it rests to-day? Do you not listen to what they say to themselves each day? Do you not hear them repeating unceasingly that all that is above them is incapable and unworthy of governing them; that the present distribution of goods throughout the world is unjust; that property rests on a foundation which is not an equitable foundation? And do you not realize that when such opinions take root, when they spread in an almost universal manner, when they sink deeply into the masses, they are bound to bring with them sooner or later, I know not when nor how, a most formidable revolution?

This, gentlemen, is my profound conviction: I believe that we are at this moment sleeping on a volcano. I am profoundly convinced of it. ...

... I was saying just now that this evil would, sooner or later, I know not how nor whence it will come, bring with it a most serious revolution: be assured that that is so.

When I come to investigate what, at different times, in different periods, among different peoples, has been the effective cause that has brought about the downfall of the governing classes, I perceive this or that event, man, or accidental or superficial cause; but, believe me, the real reason, the effective reason which causes men to lose their power is, that they have become unworthy to retain it.

Think, gentlemen, of the old Monarchy: it was stronger than you are, stronger in its origin; it was able to lean more than you do upon ancient customs, ancient habits, ancient beliefs; it was stronger than you are, and yet it has fallen to dust. And why did it fall? Do you think it was by some particular mischance? Do you think it was by the act of some man, by the deficit, the oath in the Tennis Court, Lafayette, Mirabeau? No, gentlemen; there was another reason: the class that was then the governing class had become, through its indifference, its selfishness and its vices, incapable and unworthy of governing the country.

That was the true reason.

Well, gentlemen, if it is right to have this patriotic concern at all times, how much more is it not right to have it in our own? Do you not feel, by some intuitive instinct which is not capable of analysis, but which is undeniable, that the earth is quaking once again in Europe? Do you not feel.... what shall I say?... as it were a gale of revolution in the air? This gale, no one knows whence it springs, whence it blows, nor, believe me, whom it will carry with it; and it is in such times as these that you remain calm before the degradation of public morality—for the expression is not too strong.

I speak without bitterness; I am even addressing you without any party spirit; I am attacking men against whom I feel no vindictiveness. But I am obliged to communicate to my country my firm and decided conviction. Well then, my firm and decided conviction is this: that public morality is being degraded, and that the degradation of public morality will shortly, very shortly, perhaps, bring down upon you a new revolution. Is the life of kings held by stronger threads? Are these more difficult to snap than those of other men? Can you say to-day that you are certain of to-morrow? Do you know what may happen in France a year hence, or even a month or a day hence? You do not know; but what you must know is that the storm is looming on the horizon, that it is coming towards us. Will you allow it to take you by surprise?

Gentlemen, I implore you not to do so. I do not ask you, I implore you. I would gladly throw myself on my knees before you, so strongly do I believe in the reality and the seriousness of the danger, so convinced am I that my warnings are no empty rhetoric. Yes, the danger is great. Allay it while there is yet time; correct the evil by efficacious remedies, by attacking it not in its symptoms but in itself.

Legislative changes have been spoken of. I am greatly disposed to think that these changes are not only very useful, but necessary; thus, I believe in the need of electoral reform, in the urgency of parliamentary reform; but I am not, gentlemen, so mad as not to know that no laws can affect the destinies of nations. No, it is not the mechanism of laws that produces great events, gentlemen, but the inner spirit of the government. Keep the laws as they are, if you wish. I think you would be very wrong to do so; but keep them. Keep the men, too, if it gives you any pleasure. I raise no objection so far as I am concerned. But, in God's name, change the spirit of the government; for, I repeat, that spirit will lead you to the abyss.

These gloomy predictions were received with ironical cheers from the majority. The Opposition applauded loudly, but more from party feeling than conviction. The truth is that no one as yet believed seriously in the danger which I was prophesying, although we were so near the catastrophe. The inveterate habit contracted by all the politicians, during this long parliamentary farce, of over-colouring the expression of their opinions and grossly exaggerating their thoughts had deprived them of all power of appreciating what was real and true. For several years the majority had every day been declaring that the Opposition was imperilling society; and the Opposition repeated incessantly that the Ministers were ruining the Monarchy. These statements had been made so constantly on both sides, without either side greatly believing in them, that they ended by not believing in them at all, at the very moment when the event was about to justify both of them. Even my own friends themselves thought that I had overshot the mark, and that my facts were a little blurred by rhetoric.

I remember that, when I stepped from the rostrum, Dufaure took me on one side, and said, with that sort of parliamentary intuition which is his only talent:

"Your speech was a success, but you would have succeeded much more if you had not gone so far beyond the feeling of the Assembly and tried to frighten us."

And now that I am face to face with myself, searching in my memory to discover whether I was actually myself so much alarmed as I seemed, the answer is no, and I readily recognise that the event justified me more promptly and more completely than I foresaw (a thing which may sometimes have happened to other political prophets, better qualified to predict than I was). No, I did not expect such a revolution as we were destined to have; and who could have expected it? I did, I believe, perceive more clearly than the others the general causes which were making for the event, but I did not observe the accidents which were to precipitate it. Meantime the days which still separated us from the catastrophe passed rapidly by. . . .

It is not one of the least curious characteristics of this singular revolution that the incident which led to it was brought about and almost longed for by the men whom it eventually precipitated from power, and that it was only foreseen and feared by those who were to triumph by its means.

Here let me for a moment resume the chain of history, so that I may the more easily attach to it the thread of my personal recollections.

It will be remembered that, at the opening of the session of 1848, King Louis-Philippe, in his Speech from the Throne, had described the authors of the banquets as men excited by blind or hostile passions. This was bringing Royalty into direct conflict with more than one hundred members of the Chamber. This insult, which added anger to all the ambitious passions which were already disturbing the hearts of the majority of these men, ended by making them lose their reason. A violent debate was expected, but did not take place at once. The earlier discussions on the Address were calm: the majority and the Opposition both restrained themselves at the beginning, like two men who feel that they have lost their tempers, and who fear lest while in that condition they should perpetrate some folly in word or deed.

But the storm of passion broke out at last, and continued with unaccustomed violence. The extraordinary heat of these debates was already redolent of civil war for those who knew how to scent revolutions from afar.

The spokesmen of the moderate section of the Opposition were led, in the heat of debate, to assert that the right of assembling at the banquets was one of our most undeniable and essential rights; that to question it, was equivalent to trampling liberty itself underfoot and to violating the Charter, and that those who did so unconsciously made an appeal, not to discussion, but to arms. On his side M. Duchâtel, who ordinarily was very dexterous in debate, displaying in this circumstance a consummate want of tact. He absolutely denied the right of assembly, and yet would not say clearly that the Government had made up its mind to prohibit thenceforth any manifestations of the kind. On the contrary, he seemed to invite the Opposition to try the experiment once more, so that the question might be brought before the Courts. His colleague, M. Hébert, the Minister of Justice, was still more tactless, but this was his habit. I have always observed that lawyers never make statesmen, but I have never met anyone who was less of a statesman than M. Hébert. He remained the Public-Prosecutor down to the marrow of his bones; he had all the mental and physical characteristics of that office. You must imagine a little wizened, sorry face, shrunk at the temples, with a pointed forehead, nose and chin, cold, bright eyes, and thin, in-drawn lips. Add to this a long quill generally held across the mouth, and looking at a distance like a cat's bristling whiskers, and you have a portrait of a man, than whom I have never seen anyone more resembling a carnivorous animal. At the same time, he was neither stupid nor even ill-natured; but he was by nature hot-headed and unyielding; he always overshot his goal, for want of knowing when to turn aside or stop still; and he fell into violence without intending it, and from sheer want of discrimination. It showed how little importance M. Guizot attached to conciliation, that under the circumstances he sent a speaker of this stamp to the rostrum; his language while there was so outrageous and so provoking that Barrot, quite beside himself and almost without knowing what he was doing, exclaimed, in a voice half stifled with rage, that the ministers of Charles X, Polignac and Peyronnet, had never dared to talk like that. I remember that I shuddered involuntarily in my seat when I heard this naturally moderate man exasperated into recalling, for the first time, the terrible memories of the Revolution of 1830, holding it up in some sort of example, and unconsciously suggesting the idea of repeating it.

The result of this heated discussion was a sort of challenge to mortal combat exchanged between the Government and the Opposition, the scene of the duel to be the law-courts. It was tacitly agreed that the challenged party should meet at one final banquet; that the authorities, without interfering to prevent the meeting, should prosecute its organizers, and that the courts should pronounce judgment.

The debates on the Address were closed, if I remember rightly, on the 12th of February, and it is really from this moment that the Revolutionary movement burst out. The Constitutional Opposition, which had for many months been constantly pushed on by the Radical party, was from this time forward led and directed not so much by the members of that party who occupied seats in the Chamber of Deputies (the greater number of these had become lukewarm and, as it were, enervated in the Parliamentary atmosphere), as by the younger, bolder, and more irresponsible men who wrote for the democratic press. This change was especially apparent in two principal facts which had an overwhelming influence upon events—the programme of the banquet and the arraignment of Ministers.

On the 20th of February, there appeared in almost all the Opposition newspapers, by way of a programme for the approaching banquet, what was really a proclamation calling upon the entire population to join in an immense political demonstration, calling the schools together and inviting the National Guard itself to attend the ceremony in a body. It read like a decree emanating from the Provisional Government which was to be set up three days later. The Cabinet, which had already been blamed by many of its followers for tacitly authorising the banquet, considered that it was justified in backtracking. It officially announced that it forbade the banquet, and that it would prevent it by force.

It was this declaration of the Government which provided the field for the battle. I am in a position to state, although it sounds hardly credible, that the programme which thus suddenly turned the banquet into an insurrection was resolved upon, drawn up and published without the participation or the knowledge of the members of Parliament who considered themselves to be still leading the movement which they had created. The programme was the hurried work of a nocturnal gathering of journalists and Radicals, and the leaders of the Dynastic Opposition heard of it at the same time as the public, by reading it in the papers in the morning.

And see how uncertain is the course of human affairs! M. Odilon Barrot, who disapproved of the programme as much as anyone, dared not disclaim it for fear of offending the men who, till then, had seemed to be moving with him; and then, when the Government, alarmed by the publication of this document, prohibited the banquet, M. Barrot, finding himself brought face to face with civil war, drew back. He himself gave up this dangerous demonstration; but at the same time that he was making this concession to the men of moderation, he granted to the extremists the impeachment of Ministers. He accused the latter of violating the Constitution by prohibiting the banquet, and thus furnished an excuse to those who were about to take up arms in the name of the violated Constitution.

Thus the principal leaders of the Radical Party, who thought that a revolution would be premature, and who did not yet desire it, had considered themselves obliged, in order to differentiate themselves from their allies in the Dynastic Opposition, to make very revolutionary speeches and fan the flame of insurrectionary passion. On the other hand, the Dynastic Opposition, which had had enough of the banquets, had been forced to persevere in this bad course so as not to present an appearance of retreating before the defiance of the Government. And finally, the mass of the Conservatives, who believed in the necessity of great concessions and were ready to make them, were driven by the violence of their adversaries and passions of some of their chiefs to deny even the right of meeting in private banquets and to refuse the country any hopes of reform.

One has to have spent a long time in politics to understand the extent to which men push each other away from their own plans and how the destinies of the world unfold through the consequences, but often the contrary consequences, of the intentions which produce them, like a kite which flies by the opposing forces of the wind and the string.

CAUSES OF THE FEBRUARY REVOLUTION

And so the Monarchy of July had fallen, fallen without a struggle, and before rather than beneath the blows of the victors, who were as astonished at their triumph as were the vanquished at their defeat. I have often, since the Revolution of February, heard M. Guizot and even M. Molé and M. Thiers declare that this event should only be attributed to a surprise and regarded as a mere accident, a bold and lucky stroke and nothing more. I have always felt tempted to answer them in the words which Molière's Misanthrope uses to Oronte:

> Pour en juger ainsi, vous avez vos raisons;

for these three men had conducted the affairs of France, under the guidance of King Louis-Philippe, for eighteen years, and it was difficult for them to admit that it was the King's bad government which had prepared the catastrophe which hurled him from the Throne.

As for me, I have not the same motives for forming an opinion, and I could hardly persuade myself to be of theirs. I am not prepared to say that accidents played no part in the February Revolution. On the contrary, they played a great one; but they were not the only thing.

I have come across men of letters who have written history without taking part in public affairs, and politicians who have only concerned themselves with producing events without thinking of describing them. I have observed that the first are always inclined to find general causes, whereas the latter, living in the midst of disconnected daily facts, are prone to imagine that everything is attributable to particular incidents, and the wires which they pull are the same that move the world. Both should be considered mistaken.

For my part I hate those absolute systems which make all the events of history depend on great first causes linked to each other by a chain of fate and which thus, so to speak, omit men from the history of mankind. To my mind they seem narrow under their

From the *Recollections*, pt. 2, chap. 1.

pretence of broadness, and false beneath their air of mathematical exactness. I believe (*pace* the writers who have invented these sublime theories in order to feed their vanity and ease their work) that many important historical facts can only be explained as the results of accidental circumstances, and that many others remain inexplicable. In the end chance, or rather the entanglement of secondary causes which we call chance because we do not know how to unravel them, plays a large part in all we observe taking place on the world's stage. But I firmly believe that chance accomplishes nothing that has not been prepared in advance. Antecedent facts, the nature of institutions, turns of mind, the state of manners and morals—these are the materials with which chance constructs those impromptu events which surprise and alarm us.

The Revolution of February, in common with all other great events of this class, sprang from general causes, impregnated, if I am permitted the expression, by accidents; and it would be as superficial a judgment to ascribe it necessarily to the former or exclusively to the latter.

The industrial revolution which, during the past thirty years, had turned Paris into the principal manufacturing city of France and attracted within its walls an entire new population of workmen (to whom the works of the fortifications had added another population of labourers at present deprived of work) tended more and more to inflame this multitude. Add to this the democratic disease of envy, which was silently permeating it; the economic and political theories which were beginning to make their way and which strove to prove that human misery was the work of laws and not of Providence, and that poverty could be suppressed by changing the conditions of society; the contempt into which the governing class, and especially the men who led it, had fallen, a contempt so general and so profound that it paralyzed the resistance even of those who were most interested in maintaining the power that was being overthrown; the centralization which reduced the whole revolutionary movement to the overmastering of Paris and the seizing of the machinery of government; and lastly, the mobility of all things, institutions, ideas, men and customs, in a fluctuating state of society which had, in less than sixty years, undergone the shock of seven great revolutions, without counting a multitude of smaller, secondary upheavals. These were the general causes without which the Revolution of February would have been impossible. The principal accidents which led to it were the passions of the dynastic Opposition, which brought about a riot in proposing a reform; the suppression of this riot, first over-violent, and then abandoned; the sudden disappearance of the old Ministry, unexpectedly snapping the threads of power, which the new ministers, in their confusion, were unable either to seize upon or to reunite; the mistakes and disorder of mind of these ministers, so powerless to re-establish that which they had been strong enough to overthrow; the vacillation of the generals; the absence of the only Princes who possessed either personal energy or popularity; and above all, the senile imbecility of King Louis-Philippe, his weakness, which no one could have foreseen, and which still remains almost incredible, after the event has proved it.

I have sometimes asked myself what could have produced this sudden and unprecedented depression in the King's mind. Louis-Philippe had spent his life in the midst of revolutions, and certainly lacked neither experience, courage, nor readiness of mind, although these qualities all failed him so completely on that day. In my opinion, his weakness was due to his excessive surprise; he was overwhelmed with consternation before he had grasped the meaning of things. The Revolution of February was *unforeseen* by all, but by him more than any other; he had been prepared for it by no warning from the outside, for since many years his mind had withdrawn into that sort of haughty solitude into which in the end the intellect almost always settles down of princes who have long lived happily, and who, mistaking luck for genius, refuse to listen to anything, because they think that there is nothing left for them to learn from anybody. Besides, Louis-Philippe had been deceived, as I have already said that his ministers were, by the misleading light cast by antecedent facts upon present times. One might draw a strange picture of all the errors which have thus been begotten, one by the other, without resembling each other. We see Charles I driven to tyranny and violence at the sight of the progress which the spirit of opposition had made in England during the gentle reign of his father; Louis

XVI determined to suffer everything because Charles I had
perished by refusing to endure anything; Charles X provoking the
Revolution, because he had with his own eyes beheld the weakness of Louis XVI; and lastly, Louis-Philippe, who had more
perspicacity than any of them, imagining that, in order to remain
on the Throne, all he had to do was to observe the letter of the law
while violating its spirit, and that, provided he himself kept within
the bounds of the Charter, the nation would never exceed them.
To warp the spirit of the Constitution without changing the letter;
to set the vices of the country in opposition to each other; gently
to drown revolutionary passion in the love of material enjoyment:
such was the idea of his whole life. Little by little, it had become,
not his leading, but his sole idea. He had wrapped himself in it, he
had lived in it; and when he suddenly saw that it was a false idea,
he became like a man who is awakened in the night by an
earthquake, and who, feeling his house crumbling in the darkness, and the very ground seeming to yawn beneath his feet,
remains distracted amid this unforeseen and universal ruin.

I am arguing very much at my ease today concerning the
causes that brought about the events of the 24th of February; but
on the afternoon of that day I had many other things in my head: I
was thinking of the events themselves, and sought less for what
had produced them than for what was to follow.

I returned slowly home. I explained in a few words to Madame
de Tocqueville what I had seen, and sat down in a corner to think.
I cannot remember ever feeling my soul so full of sadness. It was
the second revolution I had seen accomplish itself, before my
eyes, within seventeen years!

On the 30th of July 1830, at daybreak, I had met carriages of
King Charles X on the outer boulevards of Versailles, with
escutcheons already obliterated, proceeding at a foot pace, in
single file, like a funeral, and I was unable to restrain my tears at
the sight. This time my impressions were of another kind, but
even keener. Both revolutions had afflicted me; but how much
more bitter were the impressions caused by the last! I had until
the end felt a remnant of hereditary affection for Charles X; but
that King fell for having violated rights that were dear to me, and I
had every hope that my country's freedom would be revived

rather than extinguished by his fall. But now this freedom seemed dead; the Princes who were fleeing were nothing to me, but I felt that the cause I had at heart was lost.

I had spent the best days of my youth amid a society which seemed to increase in greatness and prosperity as it increased in liberty; I had conceived the idea of a balanced, regulated liberty, held in check by religion, custom and law; the attractions of this liberty had touched me; it had become the passion of my life; I felt that I could never be consoled for its loss, and that I must renounce all hope of its recovery.

I had gained too much experience of mankind to be able to content myself with empty words; I knew that, if one great revolution is able to establish liberty in a country, a number of succeeding revolutions make all regular liberty impossible for very many years.

I could not yet know what would issue from this latest revolution, but I was already convinced that it could give rise to nothing that would satisfy me; and I foresaw that, whatever might be the lot reserved for our posterity, our own fate was to drag on our lives miserably amid alternate reactions of licence and oppression.

I began to pass in review the history of our last sixty years, and I smiled bitterly when I thought of the illusions formed at the conclusion of each period in this long revolution; the theories on which these illusions had been fed; the sapient dreams of our historians, and all the ingenious and deceptive systems by the aid of which it had been endeavoured to explain a present which was still incorrectly seen, and a future which was not seen at all.

The Constitutional Monarchy had succeeded the Ancien Régime; the Republic, the Monarchy; the Empire, the Republic; the Restoration, the Empire; and then came the July Monarchy. After each of these successive changes it was said that the French Revolution, having accomplished what was presumptuously called its work, was finished; this had been said and it had been believed. Alas! I myself had hoped it under the Restoration, and again after the fall of the Government of the Restoration; and here is the French Revolution beginning over again, for it is still the same one. As we go on, its end seems farther off and shrouded in greater darkness. Shall we ever—as we are assured by other prophets, perhaps as delusive as their predecessors—shall we ever attain a more complete and more far-reaching social transformation than our fathers foresaw and desired, and than we ourselves are able to foresee; or are we not destined simply to end in a condition of intermittent anarchy, the well-known chronic and incurable complaint of old races? As for me, I am unable to say; I do not know when this long voyage will be ended; I am weary of seeing the shore in each successive mirage, and I often ask myself whether the *terra firma* we are seeking does really exist, and whether we are not doomed to rove upon the seas for ever.

THE CLASS CHARACTER OF REVOLUTIONS

I spent the whole afternoon walking about Paris. Two things in particular struck me: the first was, I will not say the mainly, but the uniquely and exclusively popular character of the revolution that had just taken place; the omnipotence it had given to the people properly so-called—that is to say, the classes who work with their hands—over all others. The second was the comparative absence of malignant passion, or, as a matter of fact, of any keen passion—an absence which at once made it clear that the lower orders had suddenly become masters of Paris.

Although the working classes had often played the leading part in the events of the First Revolution, they had never been the sole leaders and masters of the State, either *de facto* or *de jure;* it is doubtful whether the Convention contained a single man of the people; it was composed of *bourgeois* and men of letters. The war between the Mountain and the Girondists was conducted on both sides by members of the middle class, and the triumph of the former never brought power down into the hands of the people alone. The July Revolution was effected by the people, but the middle class had stirred it up and led it, and secured the principal benefits of it. The Revolution of February, on the contrary, seemed to be made entirely outside the *bourgeoisie* and against it.

From the *Recollections,* pt. 2, chap. 2.

In this great clash, the two parts of which society in France is mainly composed had, in a way, been thrown more completely asunder, and the mass of the people, which had stood alone, remained in sole possession of power. Nothing more novel had been known in our annals. Similar revolutions had taken place, it is true, in other countries and other times; for the history of our own age, however new and unexpected it may seem, always belongs at bottom to the old history of humanity, and what we call new facts are oftenest nothing more than facts forgotten. Florence, in particular, towards the close of the Middle Ages, had presented on a small scale a spectacle analogous to ours; the noble class had first been succeeded by the bourgeois class, and then one day the latter was, in its turn, expelled from the government, and a *gonfalonier* was seen marching barefoot at the head of the people, and thus leading the Republic. But in Florence this popular revolution was the result of transient and special causes, while with us it was brought about by causes very permanent and of a kind so general that, after stirring up France, it was to be expected that it would excite all the rest of Europe. This time it was not only a question of the triumph of a party; the aim was to establish a social science, a philosophy, I might almost say a religion, fit to be learned and followed by all mankind. This was the really new portion of the old picture.

Throughout this day, I did not see in Paris a single one of the former agents of the public authority: not a soldier, not a gendarme, not a policeman; the National Guard itself had disappeared. The people alone bore arms, guarded the public buildings, watched, gave orders, punished; it was an extraordinary and terrible thing to see in the sole hands of those who possessed nothing all this immense town, so full of riches, or rather this great nation: for, thanks to centralization, he who reigns in Paris governs France. Hence the terror of all the other classes was extreme; I doubt whether at any period of the Revolution it had been so great, and I should say that it was only to be compared to that which the civilized cities of the Roman Empire must have experienced when they suddenly found themselves in the power of the Goths and Vandals. As nothing like this had ever been seen before, many people expected acts of unexampled violence. For my part I did not once partake of these fears. What I saw led me to predict strange disturbances in the near future—singular crises. But I never believed that the rich would be pillaged; I knew the men of the people in Paris too well not to know that their first movements in times of revolution are usually generous, and that they are best pleased to spend the days immediately following their triumph in boasting of their victory, laying down the law, and playing at being great men. During that time it generally happens that some government or other is set up, the police returns to its post, and the judge to his bench; and when at last our great men consent to step down to the better known and more vulgar ground of petty and malicious human passion, they are no longer able to do so, and reduced to live simply like honest men. Besides, we have spent so many years in insurrections that there has arisen among us a kind of morality peculiar to times of disorder, and a special code for days of rebellion. According to these exceptional laws, murder is tolerated and havoc permitted, but theft is strenuously forbidden; although this, whatever one may say, does not prevent a good deal of robbery from occurring upon those days, for the simple reason that society in a state of rebellion cannot be different from that at any other time, and it will always contain a number of rascals who, as far as they are concerned, scorn the morality of the main body, and despise its point of honour when they are unobserved. What reassured me still more was the reflection that the victors had been as much surprised by success as their adversaries were by defeat: their passions had not had time to take fire and become intensified in the struggle; the Government had fallen undefended by others, or at least keenly censured, by the very men who at heart most deeply regretted its fall.

For a year past the dynastic Opposition and the republican Opposition had been living in fallacious intimacy, acting in the same way from different motives. The misunderstanding which had facilitated the revolution tended to mitigate its after effects. Now that the Monarchy had disappeared, the battle-field seemed empty; the people no longer clearly saw what enemies remained for them to pursue and strike down; the former objects of their anger, themselves, were no longer there; the clergy had never been completely reconciled to the new dynasty, and witnessed its ruin without regret; the old nobility were delighted at it, whatever the ultimate consequences might be: the first had suffered through the system of intolerance of the middle classes, the second through their pride: both either despised or feared their government.

For the first time in sixty years, the priests, the old aristocracy and the people met in a common sentiment—a feeling of revenge, it is true, and not of affection; but even that is a great thing in politics, where a community of hatred is almost always the foundation of friendships. The real, the only vanquished were the middle class; but even they had little to fear. Their reign had been exclusive rather than oppressive; corrupt, but not violent; they were despised rather than hated. Moreover, the middle class never forms a compact body in the heart of the nation, a part very distinct from the whole; it always participates a little with all the others, and in some places merges into them. This absence of homogeneity and of exact limits makes the government of the middle class weak and uncertain, but it also makes it intangible, and, as it were, invisible to those who desire to strike it when it is no longer governing.

From all these united causes proceeded that languor of the people which had struck me as much as its omnipotence, a languor which was the more discernible in that it contrasted strangely with the turgid energy of the language used and the terrible recollections which it evoked. The lukewarm passions of the time were made to speak in the bombastic language of '93, and one heard cited at every moment the name and example of the illustrious ruffians whom no-one possessed either the energy or even a sincere desire to resemble.

It was the Socialistic theories which I have already described as the philosophy of the Revolution of February that later kindled genuine passion, embittered jealousy, and ended by stirring up war between the classes. If the actions at the beginning were less disorderly than might have been feared, on the very morrow of the Revolution there was displayed an extraordinary agitation, an unequalled disorder, in the ideas of the people.

From the 25th of February onwards, a thousand strange systems came issuing pell-mell from the minds of innovators, and spread among the troubled minds of the crowd. Everything still remained standing except Royalty and Parliament; yet it seemed as though the shock of the Revolution had reduced society itself to dust, and as though a competition had been opened for the new form that was to be given to the edifice about to be erected in its place. Everyone came forward with a plan of his own: one printed it in the papers, another on the placards with which the walls were soon covered, a third proclaimed his loud-mouthed in the open air. One aimed at destroying inequality of fortune, another inequality of education, a third undertook to do away with the oldest of all inequalities, that between man and woman. Cures were offered for poverty, and remedies for the disease of work which has tortured humanity since the first days of its existence.

These theories were of very varied natures, often opposed and sometimes hostile to one another; but all of them, aiming lower than the government and striving to reach society itself, on which government rests, adopted the common name of Socialism.

Socialism will always remain the essential characteristic and the most redoubtable remembrance of the February Revolution. The Republic will only appear to the on-looker to have come upon the scene as a means, not as an end.

It does not come within the scope of these Recollections that I should seek for the causes which gave a socialistic character to the Revolution of February, and I will content myself with saying that the discovery of this new facet of the French Revolution was not of a nature to cause so great surprise as it did. Had it not long been perceived that the people had continually been improving and raising its condition, that its importance, its education, its desires, its power had been constantly increasing? Its prosperity had also grown greater, but less rapidly, and was approaching the limit which it hardly ever passes in societies of the old type, where there are many men and but few places. How should the poor and humbler and yet powerful classes not have dreamt of escaping from their poverty and inferiority by means of their power, especially in an epoch when our view of another world has become dimmer, and the miseries of this world become more visible and seem more intolerable? They had been working to this end for the last sixty years. The people had first endeavoured to help itself by changing every political institution, but after each change it found that its lot was in no way improved, or was only improving with a slowness quite incompatible with the eagerness of its desire. Inevitably, it had sooner or later to discover that that which held it fixed in its position was not the constitution of the government but the unalterable laws that constitute society itself; and it was natural that it should be brought to ask itself if it had not both the power and the right to alter those laws, as it had altered all the rest. And to speak more specially of property, which is, as it were, the foundation of our social order—all the privileges which covered it and which, so to speak, concealed the privilege of property having been destroyed, and the latter remaining the principal obstacle to equality among men, and appearing to be the only sign of inequality—was it not necessary, I will not say that it should be abolished in its turn, but at least that the thought of abolishing it should occur to the minds of those who did not enjoy it?

This natural restlessness in the minds of the people, this inevitable perturbation of its thoughts and its desires, these needs, these instincts of the crowd formed in a certain sense the fabric upon which the political innovators embroidered so many monstrous and grotesque figures. Their work may be regarded as ludicrous, but the material on which they worked is the most serious that it is possible for philosophers and statesmen to contemplate.

Will Socialism remain buried in the disdain with which the Socialists of 1848 are so justly covered? I put the question without making any reply. I do not doubt that the laws concerning the constitution of our modern society will in the long run undergo modification: they have already done so in many of their principal parts. But will they ever be destroyed and replaced by others? It seems to me to be impracticable. I say no more, because—the more I study the former condition of the world and see the world of our own day in greater detail, the more I consider the prodigious variety to be met with not only in laws, but in the principles of law, and the different forms even now taken and retained, whatever one may say, by the rights of property on this earth—the more I am tempted to believe that what we call necessary institutions are often no more than institutions to which we have grown accustomed, and that in matters of social constitution the field of possibilities is much more extensive than men living in their various societies are ready to imagine.

BLUNDERS OF THE REVOLUTIONARIES

There have certainly been more wicked revolutionaries than those of 1848, but I doubt if there were ever any more stupid; they neither knew how to make use of universal suffrage nor how to do without it. If they had held the elections immediately after the 24th of February, while the upper classes were still bewildered by the blow they had just received, and the people more amazed than discontented, they would perhaps have obtained an assembly after their hearts; if, on the other hand, they had boldly seized the dictatorship, they might have been able for some time to retain it. But they trusted themselves to the nation, and at the same time did all that was most likely to set the latter against them; they threatened it while placing themselves in its power; they alarmed it by the recklessness of their proposals and the violence of their language, while inviting it to resistance by the feebleness of their actions; they pretended to lay down the law to it at the very time that they were placing themselves at its disposal. Instead of opening out their ranks after the victory, they jealously closed them up, and seemed, in one word, to be striving to solve this insoluble problem, namely, how to govern through the majority and yet against its inclination.

Following the examples of the past without understanding them, they foolishly imagined that to summon the crowd to take part in political life was sufficient to attach it to their cause; and that to popularize the Republic, it was enough to give the public rights without offering them any profits. They forgot that their predecessors, when they gave every peasant the vote, at the same time did away with tithes, abolished statute labour and the other

From the *Recollections*, pt. 2, chap. 5.

seignorial privileges, and divided the property of the nobles among the peasants; whereas they were not in a position to do anything of the kind. In establishing universal suffrage they thought they were summoning the people to the assistance of the Revolution: they were only giving them arms against it. Nevertheless, I am far from believing that it was impossible to arouse revolutionary passions, even in the country districts. In France, every agriculturist owns some portion of the soil, and most of them are more or less involved in debt; it was not, therefore, the landlords that should have been attacked, but the creditors; not the abolition promised of the rights of property, but the abolition of debts. The demagogues of 1848 did not think of this scheme; they showed themselves much clumsier than their predecessors, but no less dishonest, for they were as violent and unjust in their desires as the others in their acts. Only, to commit violent and unjust acts, it is not enough for a government to have the will, or even the power; the habits, ideas, and passions of the time must lend themselves to the committal of them.

As the party which held the reins of government saw its candidates rejected one after the other, it displayed great vexation and rage, complaining now sadly and now rudely of the electors, whom it treated as ignorant, ungrateful blockheads, and enemies of their own good; it lost its temper with the whole nation; and, its impatience exhausted by the latter's coldness, it seemed ready to say with Molière's Arnolfe, when he addresses Agnès:

Pourquoi ne m'aimer pas, madame l'impudente?

One thing was not ridiculous, but really ominous and terrible; and that was the appearance of Paris on my return. I found in the capital a hundred thousand armed workmen formed into regiments, out of work, dying of hunger, but with their minds crammed with vain theories and visionary hopes. I saw society cut into two: those who possessed nothing, united in a common greed; those who possessed something, united in a common terror. There were no bonds, no sympathy between these two great sections; everywhere the idea of an inevitable and immediate struggle seemed at hand. Already the *bourgeois* and the *peuple* (for the old nicknames had been resumed) had come to blows, with varying fortunes, at Rouen, Limoges, Paris; not a day passed but the owners of property were attacked or menaced in either their capital or income: they were asked to employ labour without selling the produce; they were expected to remit the rents of their tenants when they themselves possessed no other means of living. They gave way as long as they could to this tyranny, and endeavoured at least to turn their weakness to account by publishing it. I remember reading in the papers of that time this advertisement, among others, which still strikes me as a model of vanity, cowardice, and stupidity harmoniously mingled:

"Mr Editor," it read, "I make use of your paper to inform my tenants that, desiring to put into practice in my relations with them the principles of fraternity that should guide all true democrats, I will hand to those of my tenants who apply for it a formal receipt for their next quarter's rent."

Meanwhile, a gloomy despair had spread through the middle class thus threatened and oppressed, and imperceptibly this despair was changing into courage. I had always believed that it was useless to hope to settle the movement of the Revolution of February peacefully and gradually, and that it could only be stopped suddenly, by a great battle fought in the streets of Paris. I had said this immediately after the 24th of February; and what I now saw persuaded me that this battle was not only inevitable but imminent, and that it would be well to seize the first opportunity to deliver it.

The National Assembly met at last on the 4th of May; it was doubtful until the last moment whether it would meet at all. I believe, in fact, that the more ardent of the demagogues were often tempted to do without it, but they dared not; they remained crushed beneath the weight of their own dogma of the sovereignty of the people.

LOUIS NAPOLEON'S COUP OF 2 DECEMBER 1851

When the representatives of the people learned, on waking that morning, that several of their colleagues were arrested, they ran to the assembly. The doors were guarded by the Chasseurs de Vin-

From a letter to the Editor, the *Times*, 11 December 1851.

cennes, a corps of troops recently returned from Africa, and long accustomed to the violence of rule in Algeria; and, moreover, stimulated by a donation of 5f. distributed to every soldier who was in Paris that day. The representatives, nevertheless, presented themselves to go in, having at their head one of their Vice-Presidents, M. Daru. This gentleman was violently struck by the soldiers, and the representatives who accompanied him were driven back at the point of the bayonet. Three of them, M. de Talhouet, Etienne, and Duparc, were slightly wounded. Several others had their clothes pierced. Such was the commencement.

Driven from the doors of the Assembly, the deputies retired to the Mairie of the 10th arrondissement. They were already assembled to the number of about 300, when the troops arrived, blocked up the approaches, and prevented a greater number of representatives from entering the apartment, though no one was at that time prevented from leaving it.

Who, then, were those representatives assembled at the Mairie of the 10th arrondissement, and what did they do there? Every shade of opinion was represented in this extemporaneous Assembly. But eight-tenths of its members belonged to the different Conservative parties which had constituted the majority. This Assembly was presided over by two of its Vice-Presidents, M. Vitet and M. Benoist d'Azy. M. Daru was arrested in his own house; the fourth Vice-President, the illustrious General Bedeau, had been seized that morning in his bed, and handcuffed like a robber.... The Assembly, thus constituted, began by voting a decree in the following terms:—...

"Louis Napoleon Bonaparte is deprived of all authority as President of the Republic. The citizens are enjoined to withhold their obedience. The executive power has passed in full right to the National Assembly. The Judges of the High Court of Justice are enjoined to meet immediately, under pain of forfeiture, to proceed to the judgment of the President and his accomplices; consequently, all the officers and functionaries of power and of public authority are bound to obey all requisitions made in the name of the National Assembly, under pain of forfeiture and of high treason.

Done and decreed unanimously in public sitting, this 2nd of December, 1851.''...

These decrees had scarcely been signed by all the members present, and deposited in a place of safety, when a band of soldiers, headed by their officers, sword in hand, appeared at the door, without, however, daring to enter the apartment. The Assembly awaited them in perfect silence. The President alone raised his voice, read the decrees which had just been passed to the soldiers, and ordered them to retire. The poor fellows, ashamed of the part they were compelled to play, hesitated. The officers, pale and undecided, declared that they should go for further orders. They retired, contenting themselves with blockading the passages leading to the apartment. The Assembly, not being able to go out, ordered the windows to be opened, and caused the decrees to be read to the people and the troops in the street below, especially that decree which, in pursuance of the 68th Article of the Constitution, pronounced the deposition and impeachment of Louis Napoleon.

Soon, however, the soldiers reappeared at the door, preceded this time by two *Commissaires de Police*. These men entered the room, and amid the unbroken silence and total immobility of the Assembly, summoned the representatives to disperse. The President ordered them to retire themselves. One of the Commissaires was agitated, and faltered; the other broke out in invectives. The President said to him, "Sir, we are here the lawful authority and sole representatives of law and of right. We know that we cannot oppose to you material force, but we will leave this chamber only under constraint. We will not disperse. Seize us, and convey us to prison." "All, all!" exclaimed the members of the Assembly. After much hesitation, the *Commissaires de Police* decided to act. They caused the two Presidents to be seized by the collar. The whole body then rose, and, arm-in-arm, two-and-two, they followed the Presidents, who were led off. In this order we reached the street, and were marched across the city, without knowing whither we were going.

Care had been taken to circulate a report among the crowd and the troops that a meeting of Socialist and Red Republican deputies had been arrested. But when the people beheld among those who were thus dragged through the mud of Paris on foot, like a gang of malefactors, men the most illustrious by their talents and their virtues,—ex-ministers, ex-ambassadors, generals, admirals, great orators, great writers, surrounded by the bayonets of the line, a shout was raised, *"Vive l'Assemblée Nationale."* The representatives were attended by these shouts until they reached the barracks of the Quai d'Orsay, where they were shut up. Night was coming on, and it was wet and cold. Yet the Assembly was left two hours in the open air, as if the Government did not deign to remember its existence. The representatives here made their last roll-call in presence of their shorthand-writer, who had followed them. The number present was 218, to whom were added about twenty more in the course of the evening, consisting of members who had voluntarily caused themselves to be arrested. Almost all the men known to France and to Europe, who formed the majority of the Legislative Assembly, were gathered together in this place....

When two hours had elapsed, this assemblage was driven into barrack-rooms upstairs, where most of them spent the night, without fire, and almost without food, stretched upon the boards. It only remained to carry off to prison these honourable men, guilty of no crime but the defence of the laws of their country. For this purpose the most distressing and ignominious means were selected. The cellular vans, in which convicts are conveyed to prison, were brought up. In these vehicles were shut up the men who had served and honoured their country, and they were conveyed like three bands of criminals, some to the fortress of Mont Valerien, some to the Prison Mazas in Paris, and the remainder to Vincennes. The indignation of the public compelled the Government two days afterwards to release the greater number of them; some are still in confinement, unable to obtain either their liberty or their trial....

Such are the indignities offered to persons. Let me now review the series of general crimes. The liberty of the press is destroyed to an extent unheard of even in the time of the Empire. Most of the journals are suppressed; those which appear cannot say a word on politics or even publish any news....

Such is the state of the public journals. Let us now see the condition of personal liberty. I say, again, that personal liberty is more trampled on than ever it was in the time of the Empire. A decree of the new Power gives the prefects the right to arrest, in their respective departments, whomsoever they please; and the prefects, in their turn, send blank warrants of arrest, which are literally *lettres de cachet,* to the sub-prefects under their orders. The Provisional Government of the Republic never went so far. Human life is as little respected as human liberty. I know that war has its dreadful necessities, but the disturbances which have recently occurred in Paris have been put down with a barbarity unprecedented in our civil contests; and when we remember that this torrent of blood has been shed to consummate the violation of all laws, we cannot but think that sooner or later it will fall back upon the heads of those who shed it. As for the appeal to the people, to which Louis Napoleon affects to submit his claims, never was a more odious mockery offered to a nation. The people is called upon to express its opinion, yet not only is public discussion suppressed, but even the knowledge of facts. The people is asked its opinion, but the first measure taken to obtain it is to establish military terrorism throughout the country, and to threaten with deprivation every public agent who does not approve in writing what has been done.

Such, Sir, is the condition in which we stand. Force overturning law, trampling on the liberty of the press and of the person, deriding the popular will, in whose name the Government pretends to act,—France torn from the alliance of free nations to be yoked to the despotic monarchies of the Continent,—such is the result of this *coup d'état.*

8

SOCIAL CONTROL:
INDIVIDUALISM, ALIENATION,
AND DEVIANCE

SOCIAL CONTROL UNDER THE ANCIEN RÉGIME

Our eighteenth-century government seems to have made a fetish of tinkering with the laws of the land; new regulations followed on each other's heels so rapidly that executive officers could not keep track of them and were often at a loss how to act. We even find town officials protesting to the Controller-General himself against the incessant changes in the field of municipal legislation. "In the sphere of finance alone there are now such frequent changes that a municipal officer who wished to keep abreast of them would have to devote his whole time to this task, and neglect his other duties."

Even where the actual wording of a law was not altered, the manner of putting it into execution varied from day to day. A study of confidential records of this period throws a singularly revealing light on the methods of the administration under the old régime at the time when there no longer existed any political assemblies or newspapers to act as a check on the caprices and the erratic, often misdirected activities of high officials and their staffs. Reading these documents, we are not surprised at the contempt which then was felt for the laws of the land, even by those whose duty it was to put them into effect.

We find few Orders in Council in which reference is not made to existing laws, often of very recent origin, which had been promulgated but never put into practice. In point of fact, there were no royal edicts or decrees, no letters patent duly embodied

From *The Old Regime,* pt. 2, chap. 6.

in the code book that did not lend themselves to a host of different interpretations when it was a matter of applying them to particular cases. Letters from the Controller-General and the Intendants show that government was always read to countenance deviations from the orders issued by it. It rarely did violence to a law, but from time to time, in special cases, it allowed a law to be discreetly turned if this made for the smooth running of public affairs.

Thus when a public works contractor was seeking exemption from certain toll dues, an Intendant wrote as follows to his superior: "It is obvious that on a strict interpretation of the edicts and decrees cited above, no man in the kingdom can claim exemption from these dues. All the same, it is well known to all experienced government officials that these sweeping provisions are like the penalties imposed: although one finds them in almost all edicts, declarations, and decrees establishing taxes, that does not mean there may not be exceptions." There we have the old régime in a nutshell: rigid rules, but flexibility, not to say laxity, in their application.

Were we in fact to try to form an opinion of the way France was governed at this time in the light of the laws that then existed, we should be led to the most preposterous conclusions. Thus in 1757 the King issued an edict to the effect that any author publishing tracts or books "contrary to religion" was to be sentenced to death, and this fate would befall not only the printers of such works but also the booksellers and itinerant peddlers vending them to the public. One might well fancy one was back in the age of St. Dominic. Actually this was the very period when Voltaire was being hailed on all sides as a leading light of French literature!

One often hears people lamenting the modern Frenchman's outspoken contempt for the laws of his country; but when could the French have learned to respect them? It might almost be said that under the old régime everything was calculated to discourage the law-abiding instinct. It was the normal thing for a man filing a petition to ask that in his case a departure should be made from the strict letter of the law, and petitioners showed as much boldness and insistence in such requests as if they were claiming their legal rights. Indeed, whenever the authorities fell back on the letter of the law, this was only a polite expedient for rejecting a petition. The population was still submissive to authority, but this was more a matter of habit than of law-abiding disposition. When their passions were roused (as sometimes happened), the least incident became the signal for an outbreak of mob violence, and usually such movements were followed by summary and brutal reprisals, not by trials of the offenders. . . .

To the mind of the great majority of people only the government was capable of maintaining order in the land. The populace had a salutary dread of the mounted police, and of them alone, while the landed proprietors regarded them as the only force in which they could feel some confidence. The mounted policeman was, in fact, the embodiment of law and order, not merely its chief defender. "No one," we read in the minutes of the Provincial Assembly of Guienne, "can have failed to notice how the mere sight of a mounted policeman is enough to bring to heel even the most truculent disturbers of the peace." For this reason, every man of property wanted to have a detachment of mounted police posted at his door, and the records of the intendancies are full of such requests. No one seemed to have had the faintest inkling that the protector might one day become the master.

One of the features of English life which most impressed our émigrés was the absence of any military police. . . . All were surprised, and some saw it as a piece of typically English obtuseness. The comments of a Frenchman, no fool but a man whose upbringing had not prepared him for what he was to see in England, are enlightening. "It is the literal truth that the average Englishman consoles himself for having been robbed with the reflection that at any rate his country has no mounted police! However great his indignation at a breach of the public peace, the Englishman can console himself for the fact that the offenders are enabled to return to the bosom of society, scoundrels though they are, by the thought that anyhow the letter of the law has been respected. However, these mistaken notions are not shared by all; an enlightened few refuse to entertain them—and counsels of wisdom will certainly prevail in the long run."

Obviously it never occurred to him that these "eccentricities" were bound up with the whole British concept of freedom. . . .

SOCIAL CONTROL IN THE
NEW ENGLAND TOWNSHIPS

Nothing is more striking to a European traveller in the United States than the absence of what we term the Government, or the Administration. Written laws exist in America, and one sees that they are daily executed; but although everything is in motion, the hand which gives the impulse to the social machine can nowhere be discovered. Nevertheless, as all peoples are obliged to have recourse to certain grammatical forms which are the foundation of human language in order to express their thoughts, so all communities are obliged to secure their existence by submitting to a certain dose of authority, without which they fall a prey to anarchy. This authority may be distributed in several ways, but it must always exist somewhere.

There are two methods of diminishing the force of authority in a nation:

The first is to weaken the supreme power in its very principle, by forbidding or preventing society from acting in its own defence under certain circumstances. To weaken authority in this manner is what is generally termed in Europe to lay the foundations of freedom.

The second manner of diminishing the influence of authority does not consist in stripping society of any of its rights, nor in paralysing its efforts, but in distributing the exercise of its privileges in various hands, and in multiplying functionaries, to each of whom the degree of power necessary for him to perform his duty is entrusted. There may be nations whom this distribution of social powers might lead to anarchy; but in itself it is not anarchical. The action of authority is indeed thus rendered less irresistible, and less perilous, but it is not totally suppressed.

The revolution of the United States was the result of a mature and dignified taste for freedom, and not of a vague or ill-defined craving for independence. It contracted no alliance with the turbulent passions of anarchy; but its course was marked, on the contrary, by an attachment to whatever was lawful and orderly.

From *Democracy in America*, pt. 1, chap. 5.

It was never assumed in the United States that the citizen of a free country has a right to do whatever he pleases; on the contrary, social obligations were there imposed upon him more various than anywhere else. No idea was ever entertained of attacking the principles, or of contesting the rights of society; but the exercise of its authority was divided, to the end that the office might be powerful and the officer insignificant, and that the community should be at once regulated and free. In no country in the world does the law hold so considerable a place as in America; and in no country is the right of applying it vested in so many hands. The administrative power in the United States presents nothing either central or hierarchical in its constitution, which accounts for its passing unperceived. The power exists, but its representative is not to be perceived.

We have already seen that the independent townships of New England protect their own private interests; and the municipal magistrates are the persons to whom the execution of the laws of the State is most frequently entrusted. Besides the general laws, the State sometimes passes general police regulations; but more commonly the townships and town-officers, conjointly with the justices of the peace, regulate the minor details of social life, according to the necessities of the different localities, and promulgate such enactments as concern the health of the community, and the peace as well as morality of the citizens. Lastly, these municipal magistrates provide, of their own accord and without any delegated powers, for those unforeseen emergencies which frequently occur in society.

It results from what we have said, that in the State of Massachusetts the administrative authority is almost entirely restricted to the township, but that it is distributed among a great number of individuals. In the French commune there is properly but one official functionary, namely, the Maire; and in New England we have seen that there are nineteen. These nineteen functionaries do not in general depend upon one another. The law carefully prescribes a circle of action to each of these magistrates; and within that circle they have an entire right to perform their functions independently of any other authority. Above the township scarcely any trace of a series of official dignities is to be found. It sometimes happens that the county officers alter a decision of the townships, or town magistrates, but in general the authorities of the county have no right to interfere with the authorities of the township, except in such matters as concern the county.

The magistrates of the township, as well as those of the county, are bound to communicate their acts to the central government in a very small number of predetermined cases. But the central government is not represented by an individual whose business it is to publish police regulations and ordinances enforcing the execution of the laws; to keep up a regular communication with the officers of the township and the county; to inspect their conduct, to direct their actions, or to reprimand their faults. There is no point which serves as a centre to the radii of the administration.

What, then, is the uniform plan on which the government is conducted, and how is the compliance of the counties and their magistrates, or the townships and their officers, enforced? In the States of New England the legislative authority embraces more subjects than it does in France; the legislator penetrates to the very core of the administration; the law descends to the most minute details; the same enactment prescribes the principle and the method of its application, and thus imposes a multitude of strict and rigorously defined obligations on the secondary functionaries of the State. The consequence of this is, that if all the secondary functionaries of the administration conform to the law, society in all its branches proceeds with the greatest uniformity: the difficulty remains of compelling the secondary functionaries of the administration to conform to the law. It may be affirmed, that, in general, society has only two methods of enforcing the execution of the laws at its disposal: a discretionary power may be entrusted to a superior functionary of directing all the others, and of cashiering them in case of disobedience; or the courts of justice may be authorized to inflict judicial penalties on the offender: but these two methods are not always available.

The right of directing a civil officer presupposes that of cashiering him if he does not obey orders, and of rewarding him by promotion if he fulfils his duties with propriety. But an elected magistrate can neither be cashiered nor promoted. All elective functions are inalienable until their term is expired. In fact, the elected magistrate has nothing either to expect or to fear from his constituents: and when all public offices are filled by ballot, there can be no series of official dignities, because the double right of commanding and of enforcing obedience can never be vested in the same individual, and because the power of issuing an order can never be joined to that of inflicting a punishment or bestowing a reward.

The communities therefore in which the secondary functionaries of the government are elected, are perforce obliged to make great use of judicial penalties as a means of administration. This is not evident at first sight; for those in power are apt to look upon the institution of elective functionaries as one concession, and the subjection of the elected magistrate to the judges of the land as another. They are equally averse to both these innovations; and as they are more pressingly solicited to grant the former than the latter, they accede to the election of the magistrate, and leave him independent of the judicial power. Nevertheless, the second of these measures is the only thing that can possibly counterbalance the first: and it will be found that an elective authority which is not subject to judicial power will, sooner or later, either elude all control or be destroyed. The courts of justice are the only possible medium between the central power and the administrative bodies: they alone can compel the elected functionary to obey, without violating the rights of the elector. The extension of judicial power in the political world ought therefore to be in the exact ratio of the extension of elective offices: if these two institutions do not go hand in hand, the State must fall into anarchy or into subjection.

It has always been remarked that habits of legal business do not render men apt to the exercise of administrative authority. The Americans have borrowed from the English, their fathers, the idea of an institution which is unknown upon the continent of Europe: I allude to that of the Justices of the Peace.

The Justice of the Peace is a sort of *mezzo termine* between the magistrate and the man of the world, between the civil officer and the judge. A justice of the peace is a well-informed citizen, though he is not necessarily versed in the knowledge of the laws. His office simply obliges him to execute the police regulations of society; a task in which good sense and integrity are of more avail than legal science. The justice introduces into the administration a certain taste for established forms and publicity, which renders him a most unserviceable instrument of despotism; and on the other hand, he is not blinded by those superstitions which render legal officers unfit members of a government. The Americans have adopted the system of the English justices of the peace, but they have deprived it of that aristocratic character which is discernible in the mother-country. The Governor of Massachusetts appoints a certain number of justices of the peace in every county, whose functions last seven years. He further designates three individuals from amongst the whole body of justices who form in each county what is called the Court of Sessions. The justices take a personal share in public business; they are sometimes intrusted with administrative functions in conjunction with elected officers; they sometimes constitute a tribunal, before which the magistrates summarily prosecute a refractory citizen, or the citizens inform against the abuses of the magistrate. But it is in the Court of Sessions that they exercise their most important functions. This court meets twice a year in the county town; in Massachusetts it is empowered to enforce the obedience of the greater number of public officers. It must be observed, that in the State of Massachusetts the Court of Sessions is at the same time an administrative body, properly so called, and a political tribunal. It has been asserted that the county is a purely administrative division. The Court of Sessions presides over that small number of affairs which, as they concern several townships, or all the townships of the county in common, cannot be entrusted to any one of them in particular. In all that concerns county business, the duties of the Court of Sessions are purely administrative; and if in its investigations it occasionally borrows the forms of judicial procedure, it is only with a view to its own information, or as a guarantee to the community over which it presides. But when the administration of the township is brought before it, it always acts as a judicial body, and in some few cases as an official assembly.

The first difficulty is to procure the obedience of an authority as entirely independent of the general laws of the State as the township is. We have stated that assessors are annually named by the town-meetings to levy the taxes. If a township attempts to evade the payment of the taxes by neglecting to name its assessors, the Court of Sessions condemns it to a heavy penalty. The fine is levied on each of the inhabitants; and the sheriff of the county, who is the officer of justice, executes the mandate. Thus it is that in the United States the authority of the Government is mysteriously concealed under the forms of a judicial sentence; and its influence is at the same time fortified by that irresistible power with which men have invested the formalities of law. . . .

. . . Townships and a local activity exist in every State; but in no part of the confederation is a township to be met with precisely similar to those of New England. . . . The laws differ, and their outward features change, but their character does not vary. If the township and the county are not everywhere constituted in the same manner, it is at least true that in the United States the county and the township are always based upon the same principle, namely, that every one is the best judge of what concerns himself alone, and the most proper person to supply his private wants. The township and the county are therefore bound to take care of their special interests: the State governs, but it does not interfere with their administration. . . .

The first consequence of this doctrine has been to cause all the magistrates to be chosen either by or at least from amongst the citizens. As the officers are everywhere elected or appointed for a certain period, it has been impossible to establish the rules of a dependent series of authorities; there are almost as many independent functionaries as there are functions, and the executive power is disseminated in a multitude of hands. Hence arose the indispensable necessity of introducing the control of the courts of justice over the administration, and the system of pecuniary penalties, by which the secondary bodies and their representatives are constrained to obey the laws. This system obtains from one end of the Union to the other.

RESPECT FOR THE LAW IN THE UNITED STATES

It is not always feasible to consult the whole people, either directly or indirectly, in the formation of the law; but it cannot be denied that when such a measure is possible, the authority of the law is very much augmented. This popular origin, which impairs the excellence and the wisdom of legislation, contributes prodigiously to increase its power. There is an amazing strength in the expression of the determination of a whole people; and when it declares itself, the imagination of those who are most inclined to contest it, is overawed by its authority. The truth of this fact is very well known by parties; and they consequently strive to make out a majority whenever they can. If they have not the greater numbers of voters on their side, they assert that the true majority abstained from voting; and if they are foiled even there, they have recourse to the body of those persons who had no votes to give.

In the United States, except slaves, servants, and paupers in the receipt of relief from the townships, there is no class of persons who do not exercise the elective franchise, and who do not indirectly contribute to make the laws. Those who design to attack the laws must consequently either modify the opinion of the nation or trample upon its decision.

A second reason, which is still more weighty, may be further adduced; in the United States every one is personally interested in enforcing the obedience of the whole community of the law; for as the minority may shortly rally the majority to its principles, it is interested in professing that respect for the decrees of the legislator, which it may soon have occasion to claim for its own. However irksome an enactment may be, the citizen of the United States complies with it, not only because it is the work of the majority, but because it originates in his own authority; and he regards it as a contract to which he is himself a party.

In the United States, then, that numerous and turbulent multitude does not exist, which always looks upon the law as its natural enemy, and accordingly surveys it with fear and with distrust. It is impossible, on the other hand, not to perceive that all classes display the utmost reliance upon the legislation of their

From *Democracy in America,* pt. 1, chap. 14.

country, and that they are attached to it by a kind of parental affection.

I am wrong, however, in saying all classes; for as in America the European scale of authority is inverted, the wealthy are there placed in a position analogous to that of the poor in the Old World, and it is the opulent classes which frequently look upon the law with suspicion. I have already observed that the advantage of democracy is not, as has been sometimes asserted, that it protects the interests of the whole community, but simply that it protects those of the majority. In the United States, where the poor rule, the rich have always some reason to dread the abuses of their power. This natural anxiety of the rich may produce a sullen dissatisfaction, but society is not disturbed by it; for, the same reason which induces the rich to withhold their confidence in the legislative authority, makes them obey its mandates: their wealth, which prevents them from making the law, prevents them from withstanding it. Amongst civilized nations revolts are rarely excited except by such persons as have nothing to lose by them; and if the laws of a democracy are not always worthy of respect, at least they always obtain it: for those who usually infringe the laws have no excuse for not complying with the enactments they have themselves made, and by which they are themselves benefited, whilst the citizens whose interest might be promoted by the infraction of them, are induced, by their character and their station, to submit to the decisions of the legislature, whatever they may be. Besides which, the people in America obeys the law not only because it emanates from the popular authority, but because that authority may modify it in any points which may prove vexatious; a law is observed because it is a self-imposed evil in the first place, and an evil of transient duration in the second.

ANOMIE IN FRANCE ON THE EVE OF THE REVOLUTION

The suppression of the trade and craft corporations, followed by their partial restoration, had entirely changed the old relations

From *The Old Régime*, pt. 3, chap. 7.

between worker and employer. But this relationship did not merely take a different form; it now was ill defined and irksome to all concerned. The employers' authority had been undermined but the quasi-paternal control of the State was not yet solidly established, and between the conflicting claims of the government and his employer the artisan hardly knew where he stood; from which of the two he should take orders, and which could be counted on to protect his interests. This condition of uncertainty, not to say anarchy, to which the working class in all the towns of France had been reduced had far-reaching consequences when the people began once again to make their voice heard in the political arena.

A year before the Revolution the King issued an edict over-hauling the entire judicial system. Several new jurisdictions were introduced, a number of others abolished, and all the rules defin-ing the powers of the various courts were altered. Now, as I have already pointed out, the number of persons engaged in trying cases or executing orders passed by the courts was at this time immense; one might almost say that the whole middle class was concerned in one way or another with the administration of jus-tice. Thus the changes made in the judicial system of the country had a disturbing effect on both the social status and the pecuniary situation of thousands of families; they felt as if the ground had been cut from under their feet. The inconvenience caused to liti-gants by the edict was hardly less; as a result of these sweeping changes none could be sure what law applied to his special case and which court was competent to try it.

But it was above all the drastic reform of the administration (in the widest sense of the term) which took place in 1787 that not only threw public affairs into confusion but had repercussions on the private life of every Frenchman.

I have already drawn attention to the fact that in all *pays d'élection,* that is to say in nearly three quarters of France, the entire administration was in the hands of a single man, the In-tendant, and that not only his will was law, but he came to his decisions alone, without seeking any outside advice. In 1787, however, a provincial assembly was associated with the In-tendant and in effect it took over the entire administration of the district formerly under his sole charge. In the same way an elected municipal committee took over in the villages the functions of the parish council and, in most cases, of the Syndic.

Totally unlike the old system of administration and changing out of recognition both the manner in which public business was transacted and, more, the social status of private citizens, the new system (so the King decreed) was to come into force everywhere simultaneously and under practically the same form; that is to say without the least respect for ancient customs, local usages, or the particular conditions of each province. So deeply had this notion of standardized administration, destined to be a characteristic of the Revolution, already permeated the monarchical government which it was soon to sweep away.

It was easy then to see how large a part is played by habit in the functioning of political institutions and how much more easily a nation can cope with complicated, well-nigh unintelligible laws to which it is accustomed than with a simpler legal system that is new. . . .

The administration of the country slowed down, sometimes coming to a standstill, and all public life lapsed into a state of suspended animation. Thus the Provincial Assembly of Lorraine spoke of "a total stagnation in the conduct of public affairs" (a lament that was echoed by several other assemblies), adding that "all good citizens are much distressed by this." . . .

When the Revolution broke out, that part of the government which, though subordinate, keeps every citizen constantly aware of its existence and affects his daily life at every turn, had just been thrown into confusion; the public administration had made a clean sweep of all its former representatives and embarked on a quite new program. Radical as they were, these reforms did not seem to have jeopardized the State itself, but every Frenchman was affected by them, if only in a minor way. He felt that his life had somehow been disorganized, that he must cultivate new habits, and if a businessman, that his activities would now be handicapped. True, routine of a kind still prevailed in the conduct of affairs of vital importance to the nation, but already no one knew from whom he should take orders, to whom he should apply, or how to solve those small private problems which crop up almost daily in the life of every member of a social group.

Thus the nation as a whole was now in a state of unstable equilibrium, at the mercy of that final stroke of destiny which was to have such tremendous effects and to produce the most formidable social cataclysm the world had ever seen.

INDIVIDUALISM IN DEMOCRATIC COUNTRIES

Individualism is a novel expression, to which a novel ideal has given birth. Our fathers were only acquainted with egotism. Egotism is a passionate and exaggerated love of self, which leads a man to connect everything with his own person, and to prefer himself to everything in the world. Individualism is a mature and calm feeling, which disposes each member of the community to sever himself from the mass of his fellow-creatures; and to draw apart with his family and his friends; so that, after he has thus formed a little circle of his own, he willingly leaves society at large to itself. Egotism originates in blind instinct: individualism proceeds from erroneous judgment more than from depraved feelings; it originates as much in the deficiencies of the mind as in the perversity of the heart.

Egotism blights the germ of all virtue: individualism, at first, only saps the virtues of public life; but, in the long run, it attacks and destroys all others, and is at length absorbed in downright egotism. Egotism is a vice as old as the world, which does not belong to one form of society more than to another: individualism is of democratic origin, and it threatens to spread in the same ratio as the equality of conditions.

Amongst aristocratic nations, as families remain for centuries in the same condition, often on the same spot, all generations become as it were contemporaneous. A man almost always knows his forefathers, and respects them: he thinks he already sees his remote descendants, and he loves them. He willingly imposes duties on himself towards the former and the latter; and he will frequently sacrifice his personal gratifications to those who went before and to those who will come after him.

Aristocratic institutions have, moreover, the effect of closely

From *Democracy in America*, pt. 2, bk. 2, chaps. 2, 3, 4, and 8.

binding every man to several of his fellow-citizens. As the classes of an aristocratic people are strongly marked and permanent, each of them is regarded by its own members as a sort of lesser country, more tangible and more cherished than the country at large. As in aristocratic communities all the citizens occupy fixed positions, one above the other, the result is that each of them always sees a man above himself whose patronage is necessary to him, and below himself another man whose co-operation he may claim.

Men living in aristocratic ages are therefore almost always closely attached to something placed out of their own sphere, and they are often disposed to forget themselves. It is true that in those ages the notion of human fellowship is faint, and that men seldom think of sacrificing themselves for mankind; but they often sacrifice themselves for other men. In democratic ages, on the contrary, when the duties of each individual to society are much more clear, devoted service to any one man becomes more rare; the bond of human affection is extended, but it is relaxed.

Amongst democratic nations new families are constantly springing up, others are constantly falling away, and all that remain change their condition; the woof of time is every instant broken, and the track of generations effaced. Those who went before are soon forgotten; of those who will come after no one has any idea: the interest of man is confined to those in close propinquity to himself.

As each class approximates to other classes, and intermingles with them, its members become indifferent and as strangers to one another. Aristocracy had made a chain of all the members of the community, from the peasant to the king: democracy breaks that chain, and severs every link of it.

As social conditions become more equal, the number of persons increases who, although they are neither rich enough nor powerful enough to exercise any great influence over their fellow-creatures, have nevertheless acquired or retained sufficient education and fortune to satisfy their own wants. They owe nothing to any man, they expect nothing from any man; they acquire the habit of always considering themselves as standing alone, and they are apt to imagine that their whole destiny is in their own hands.

Thus not only does democracy make every man forget his ancestors, but it hides his descendants, and separates his contemporaries, from him; it throws him back for ever upon himself alone, and threatens in the end to confine him entirely within the solitude of his own heart.

Individualism Stronger at the Close of a Democratic Revolution Than at Other Periods

The period when the construction of democratic society upon the ruins of an aristocracy has just been completed, is especially that at which this separation of men from one another, and the egotism resulting from it, most forcibly strike the observation. Democratic communities not only contain a large number of independent citizens, but they are constantly filled with men who, having entered but yesterday upon their independent condition, are intoxicated with their new power. They entertain a presumptuous confidence in their strength, and as they do not suppose that they can henceforward ever have occasion to claim the assistance of their fellow-creatures, they do not scruple to show that they care for nobody but themselves.

An aristocracy seldom yields without a protracted struggle, in the course of which implacable animosities are kindled between the different classes of society. These passions survive the victory, and traces of them may be observed in the midst of the democratic confusion which ensues.

Those members of the community who were at the top of the late gradations of rank cannot immediately forget their former greatness; they will long regard themselves as aliens in the midst of the newly composed society. They look upon all those whom this state of society has made their equals as oppressors, whose destiny can excite no sympathy; they have lost sight of their former equals, and feel no longer bound by a common interest to their fate: each of them, standing aloof, thinks that he is reduced to care for himself alone. Those, on the contrary, who were formerly at the foot of the social scale, and who have been brought up to the common level by a sudden revolution, cannot enjoy their newly acquired independence without secret uneasiness; and if they meet with some of their former superiors on the same footing as themselves, they stand aloof from them with an expression of triumph and of fear.

It is, then, commonly at the outset of democratic society that citizens are most disposed to live apart. Democracy leads men not to draw near to their fellow-creatures; but democratic revolutions lead them to shun each other, and perpetuate in a state of equality the animosities which the state of inequality engendered.

The great advantage of the Americans is that they have arrived at a state of democracy without having to endure a democratic revolution; and that they are born equal, instead of becoming so.

That the Americans Combat the Effects of Individualism by Free Institutions

When the members of a community are forced to attend to public affairs, they are necessarily drawn from the circle of their own interests, and snatched at times from self-observation. As soon as a man begins to participate in public affairs, he begins to perceive that he is not so independent of his fellow-men as he had at first imagined, and, that, in order to obtain their support, he must often lend them his co-operation.... Under a free government, as most public offices are elective, men...constantly feel that they cannot do without the population which surrounds them. Men learn at such times to think of their fellow-men from ambitious motives; and they frequently find it, in a manner, their interest to forget themselves....

It is difficult to draw a man out of his own circle to interest him in the destiny of the state, because he does not clearly understand what influence the destiny of the state can have upon his own lot. But if it be proposed to make a road cross the end of his estate, he will see at a glance that there is a connection between this small public affair and his greatest private affairs; and he will discover, without its being shown to him, the close tie which unites private to general interest. Thus, far more may be done by entrusting to the citizens the administration of minor affairs than by surrendering to them the control of important ones, towards interesting them in the public welfare, and convincing them that they constantly stand in need one of the other in order to provide for it. A brilliant achievement may win for you the favour of a people at one stroke; but to earn the love and respect of the population which surrounds you, a long succession of little services rendered and of obscure good deeds,—a constant habit of kindness, and an established reputation for disinterestedness,—will be required. Local freedom, then, which leads a great number of citizens to value the affection of their neighbours and of their kindred, perpetually brings men together, and forces them to help one another, in spite of the propensities which sever them.

In the United States the more opulent citizens take great care not to stand aloof from the people; on the contrary, they constantly keep on easy terms with the lower classes: they listen to them, they speak to them every day. They know that the rich in democracies always stand in need of the poor; and that in democratic ages you attach a poor man to you more by your manner than by benefits conferred. The magnitude of such benefits, which sets off the difference of conditions, causes a secret irritation to those who reap advantage from them; but the charm of simplicity of manners is almost irresistible: their affability carries men away, and even their want of polish is not always displeasing. This truth does not take root at once in the minds of the rich. They generally resist it as long as the democratic revolution lasts, and they do not acknowledge it immediately after that revolution is accomplished. They are very ready to do good to the people, but they still choose to keep them at arm's length; they think that is sufficient, but they are mistaken. They might spend fortunes thus without warming the hearts of the population around them;—that population does not ask them for the sacrifice of their money, but of their pride.

It would seem as if every imagination in the United States were upon the stretch to invent means of increasing the wealth and satisfying the wants of the public. The best-informed inhabitants of each district constantly use their information to discover new truths which may augment the general prosperity; and, if they have made any such discoveries, they eagerly surrender them to the mass of the people. . . .

It would be unjust to suppose that the patriotism and the zeal which every American displays for the welfare of his fellow-citizens are wholly insincere. Although private interest directs the greater part of human actions in the United States, as well as elsewhere, it does not regulate them all. I must say that I have often seen Americans make great and real sacrifices to the public welfare; and I have remarked a hundred instances in which they hardly ever failed to lend faithful support to each other. The free institutions which the inhabitants of the United States possess, and the political rights of which they make so much use, remind every citizen, and in a thousand ways, that he lives in society. They every instant impress upon his mind the notion that it is the duty as well as the interest of men to make themselves useful to their fellow-creatures; and as he sees no particular ground of animosity to them, since he is never either their master or their slave, his heart readily leans to the side of kindness. Men attend to the interests of the public, first by necessity, afterwards by choice: what was intentional becomes an instinct; and by dint of working for the good of one's fellow-citizens, the habit and the taste for serving them is at length acquired.

The Americans Combat Individualism by the Principle of Enlightened Self-Interest

When the world was managed by a few rich and powerful individuals, these persons loved to entertain a lofty idea of the duties of man. They were fond of professing that it is praiseworthy to forget oneself, and that good should be done without hope of reward, as it is by the Deity himself. Such were the standard opinions of that time in morals.

I doubt whether men were more virtuous in aristocratic ages than in others; but they were incessantly talking of the beauties of virtue, and its utility was only studied in secret. But since the imagination takes less lofty flights and every man's thoughts are centred in himself, moralists are alarmed by this idea of self-sacrifice, and they no longer venture to present it to the human mind. They therefore content themselves with inquiring whether the personal advantage of each member of the community does not consist in working for the good of all; and when they have hit upon some point on which private interest and public interest meet and amalgamate, they are eager to bring it into notice. Observations of this kind are gradually multiplied: what was only a single remark becomes a general principle; and it is held as a truth that man serves himself in serving his fellow-creatures, and that his private interest is to do good.

I have already shown the means by which the inhabitants of the United States almost always manage to combine their own advantage with that of their fellow-citizens: my present purpose is to point out the general rule which enables them to do so. In the United States hardly anybody talks of the beauty of virtue; but they maintain that virtue is useful, and prove it every day. The American moralists do not profess that men ought to sacrifice themselves for their fellow-creatures *because* it is noble to make such sacrifices; but they boldly aver that such sacrifices are as necessary to him who imposes them upon himself, as to him for whose sake they are made.

They have found out that in their country and their age man is brought home to himself by an irresistible force; and losing all hope of stopping that force, they turn all their thoughts to the direction of it. They therefore do not deny that every man may follow his own interest; but they endeavour to prove that it is the interest of every man to be virtuous. I shall not here enter into the reasons they allege, which would divert me from my subject: suffice it to say that they have convinced their fellow-countrymen.

Montaigne said long ago, "Were I not to follow the straight road for its straightness, I should follow it for having found by experience that in the end it is commonly the happiest and most useful track." The doctrine of enlightened self-interest is not then new, but amongst the Americans of our time it finds universal acceptance: it has become popular there; you may trace it at the bottom of all their actions, you will remark it in all they say. It is as often to be met with on the lips of the poor man as of the rich. In Europe the principle of self-interest is much grosser than it is in America, but at the same time it is less common, and especially it is less avowed; amongst us men still constantly feign great abnegation which they no longer feel.

The Americans, on the contrary, are fond of explaining almost all the actions of their lives by the principle of enlightened self-interest; they show with complacency how an enlightened regard for themselves constantly prompts them to assist each other, and inclines them willingly to sacrifice a portion of their time and property to the welfare of the State.⎮ In this respect I think they frequently fail to do themselves justice; for in the United States, as well as elsewhere, people are sometimes seen to give way to those disinterested and spontaneous impulses which are natural to man: but the Americans seldom allow that they yield to emotions of this kind; they are more anxious to do honour to their philosophy than to themselves. . . .

The principle of enlightened self-interest is not a lofty one, but it is clear and sure. It does not aim at mighty objects, but it attains without excessive exertion all those at which it aims. As it lies within the reach of all capacities, every one can without difficulty apprehend and retain it. By its admirable conformity to human weaknesses, it easily obtains great dominion; nor is that dominion precarious, since the principle checks one personal interest by another, and uses, to direct the passions, the very same instrument which excites them.

The principle of interest rightly understood produces no great acts of self-sacrifice, but it suggests daily small acts of self-denial. By itself it cannot suffice to make a man virtuous, but it disciplines a number of citizens in habits of regularity, temperance, moderation, foresight, self-command; and, if it does not lead men straight to virtue by the will, it gradually draws them in that direction by their habits. If the principle of enlightened self-interest were to sway the whole moral world, extraordinary virtues would doubtless be more rare; but I think that gross depravity would then also be less common. The principle of enlightened self-interest perhaps prevents some men from rising far above the level of mankind; but a great number of other men, who were falling far below it, are caught and restrained by it. Observe some few individuals, they are lowered by it; survey mankind, it is raised.

That Aristocracy May Be Engendered by Industry

It is acknowledged, that when a workman is engaged every day upon the same detail, the whole commodity is produced with greater ease, promptitude, and economy. It is likewise acknowledged, that the cost of the production of manufactured goods is diminished by the extent of the establishment in which they are made, and by the amount of capital employed or of credit. These truths had long been imperfectly discerned, but in our time they have been demonstrated. They have been already applied to many very important kinds of manufactures, and the humblest will gradually be governed by them. I know of nothing in politics which deserves to fix the attention of the legislator more closely than these two new axioms of the science of manufactures.

When a workman is unceasingly and exclusively engaged in the fabrication of one thing, he ultimately does his work with singular dexterity; but at the same time he loses the general faculty of applying his mind to the direction of the work. He every day becomes more adroit and less industrious; so that it may be said of him, that in proportion as the workman improves the man is degraded. What çan be expected of a man who has spent twenty years of his life in making heads for pins? and to what can that mighty human intelligence, which has so often stirred the world, be applied in him, except it be to investigate the best method of making pins' heads? When a workman has spent a considerable portion of his existence in this manner, his thoughts are for ever set upon the object of his daily toil; his body has contracted certain fixed habits, which it can never shake off: in a word, he no longer belongs to himself, but to the calling which he has chosen. It is in vain that laws and manners have been at the pains to level all barriers round such a man, and to open to him on every side a thousand different paths to fortune; a theory of manufactures more powerful than manners and laws binds him to a craft, and frequently to a spot, which he cannot leave: it assigns to him a

From *Democracy in America*, pt. 2, bk. 2, chap. 20.

certain place in society, beyond which he cannot go: in the midst of universal movement, it has rendered him stationary.

In proportion as the principle of the division of labour is more extensively applied, the workman becomes more weak, more narrow-minded and more dependent. The art advances, the artisan recedes. On the other hand, in proportion as it becomes more manifest that the productions of manufactures are by so much the cheaper and better as the manufacture is larger and the amount of capital employed more considerable, wealthy and educated men come forward to embark in manufactures which were heretofore abandoned to poor or ignorant handicraftsmen. The magnitude of the efforts required, and the importance of the results to be obtained, attract them. Thus at the very time at which the science of manufactures lowers the class of workmen, it raises the class of masters.

Whereas the workman concentrates his faculties more and more upon the study of a single detail, the master surveys a more extensive whole, and the mind of the latter is enlarged in proportion as that of the former is narrowed. In a short time the one will require nothing but physical strength without intelligence; the other stands in need of science, and almost of genius, to ensure success. This man resembles more and more the administrator of a vast empire,—that man, a brute.

The master and the workman have then here no similarity, and their differences increase every day. They are only connected as the two rings at the extremities of a long chain. Each of them fills the station which is made for him, and out of which he does not get: the one is continually, closely, and necessarily dependent upon the other, and seems as much born to obey as that other is to command. What is this but aristocracy?

As the conditions of men constituting the nation become more and more equal, the demand for manufactured commodities becomes more general and more extensive; and the cheapness which places these objects within the reach of slender fortunes becomes a great element of success. Hence there are every day more men of great opulence and education who devote their wealth and knowledge to manufactures; and who seek, by opening large establishments, and by a strict division of labour, to meet the fresh demands which are made on all sides. Thus, in proportion as the mass of the nation turns to democracy, that particular class which is engaged in manufactures becomes more aristocratic. Men grow more alike in the one—more different in the other; and inequality increases in the less numerous class, in the same ratio in which it decreases in the community.

Hence it would appear, on searching to the bottom, that aristocracy should naturally spring out of the bosom of democracy.

But this kind of aristocracy by no means resembles those kinds which preceded it. It will be observed at once, that, as it applies exclusively to manufactures and to some manufacturing callings, it is a monstrous exception in the general aspect of society. The small aristocratic societies which are formed by some manufacturers in the midst of the immense democracy of our age, contain, like the great aristocratic societies of former ages, some men who are very opulent, and a multitude who are wretchedly poor. The poor have few means of escaping from their condition and becoming rich; but the rich are constantly becoming poor, or they give up business when they have realized a fortune. Thus the elements of which the class of the poor is composed is fixed; but the elements of which the class of the rich is composed are not so. To say the truth, though there are rich men, the class of rich men does not exist; for these rich individuals have no feelings or purposes in common, no mutual traditions or mutual hopes; there are therefore members, but no body.

Not only are the rich not compactly united amongst themselves, but there is no real bond between them and the poor. Their relative position is not a permanent one; they are constantly drawn together or separated by their interests. The workman is generally dependent on the master, but not on any particular master: these two men meet in the factory, but know not each other elsewhere; and whilst they come into contact on one point, they stand very wide apart on all others. The manufacturer asks nothing of the workman but his labour; the workman expects nothing from him but his wages. The one contracts no obligation to protect, nor the other to defend; and they are not permanently connected either by habit or by duty.

The aristocracy created by business rarely settles in the midst of the manufacturing population which it directs: the object is not to govern that population, but to use it. An aristocracy thus constituted can have no great hold upon those whom it employs; and even if it succeed in retaining them at one moment, they escape the next: it knows not how to will, and it cannot act.

The territorial aristocracy of former ages was either bound by law, or thought itself bound by usage, to come to the relief of its serving-men, and to succour their distresses. But the manufacturing aristocracy of our age first impoverishes and debases the men who serve it, and then abandons them to be supported by the charity of the public. This is a natural consequence of what has been said before. Between the workman and the master there are frequent relations, but no real partnership.

I am of opinion, upon the whole, that the manufacturing aristocracy which is growing up under our eyes, is one of the harshest which ever existed in the world; but at the same time it is one of the most confined and least dangerous. Nevertheless the friends of democracy should keep their eyes anxiously fixed in this direction; for if ever a permanent inequality of conditions and aristocracy again penetrate into the world, it may be predicted that this is the channel by which they will enter.

A Manufacturing City—Manchester

An undulating plain, or rather a collection of little hills. Below the hills a narrow river (the Irwell), which flows slowly to the Irish sea. Two streams (the Meddlock and the Irk) wind through the uneven ground and after a thousand bends, flow into the river. Three canals made by man unite their tranquil, lazy waters at the same point. On this watery land, which nature and art have contributed to keep damp, are scattered palaces and hovels. Everything in the exterior appearance of the city attests the individual powers of man; nothing the directing power of society. At every turn human liberty shows its capricious creative force. There is no trace of the slow continuous action of government.

From *Journeys to England and Ireland*, pp. 93–96.

Thirty or forty factories rise on the tops of the hills I have just described. Their six stories tower up; their huge enclosures give notice from afar of the centralisation of industry. The wretched dwellings of the poor are scattered haphazard around them. Round them stretches land uncultivated but without the charm of rustic nature, and still without the amenities of a town. The soil has been taken away, scratched and torn up in a thousand places, but it is not yet covered with the habitations of men. The land is given over to industry's use. The roads which connect the still-disjointed limbs of the great city, show, like the rest, every sign of hurried and unfinished work; the incidental activity of a population bent on gain, which seeks to amass gold so as to have everything else all at once, and, in the interval, mistrusts the niceties of life. Some of these roads are paved, but most of them are full of ruts and puddles into which foot or carriage wheel sinks deep. Heaps of dung, rubble from buildings, putrid, stagnant pools are found here and there among the houses and over the bumpy, pitted surfaces of the public places. No trace of surveyor's rod or spirit-level. Amid this noisome labyrinth, this great, sombre stretch of brickwork, from time to time one is astonished at the sight of fine stone buildings with Corinthian columns. It might be a medieval town with the marvels of the nineteenth century in the middle of it. But who could describe the interiors of these quarters set apart, home of vice and poverty, which surround the huge palaces of industry and clasp them in their hideous folds. On ground below the level of the river and overshadowed on every side by immense workshops, stretches marshy land which widely spaced muddy ditches can neither drain nor cleanse. Narrow, twisting roads lead down to it. They are lined with one-story houses whose ill-fitting planks and broken windows show them up, even from a distance, as the last refuge a man might find between poverty and death. Nonetheless the wretched people reduced to living in them can still inspire jealousy of their fellow beings. Below some of their miserable dwellings is a row of cellars to which a sunken corridor leads. Twelve to fifteen human beings are crowded pell-mell into each of these damp, repulsive holes. Lines of washing block the roads. A coal fire lights the hovel and fills it with a damp and stuffy heat. No chairs. . . .

Look up and all around this place you will see the huge palaces of industry. You will hear the noise of furnaces, the whistle of steam. These vast structures keep air and light out of the human habitations which they dominate; they envelop them in perpetual fog; here is the slave, there the master; there the wealth of some, here the poverty of most; there the organised effort of thousands produce, to the profit of one man, what society has not yet learnt to give. Here the weakness of the individual seems more feeble and helpless even than in the middle of a wilderness; here the effects, there the causes.

A sort of black smoke covers the city. The sun seen through it is a disc without rays. Under this half daylight 300,000 human beings are ceaselessly at work. A thousand noises disturb this damp, dark labyrinth, but they are not at all the ordinary sounds one hears in great cities.

The footsteps of a *busy* crowd, the crunching wheels of machinery, the shriek of steam from boilers, the regular beat of the looms, the heavy rumble of carts, those are the noises from which you can never escape in the sombre half-light of these streets. You will never hear the clatter of hoofs as the rich man drives back home or out on expeditions of pleasure. Never the gay shouts of people amusing themselves, or music heralding a holiday. You will never see smart folk strolling at leisure in the streets, or going out on innocent pleasure parties in the surrounding country. Crowds are ever hurrying this way and that in the Manchester streets, but their footsteps are brisk, their looks preoccupied, and their appearance sombre and harsh. Day and night the city echoes with street noises. But it is heavily loaded wagons lumbering slowly.

From this foul drain the greatest stream of human industry flows out to fertilise the whole world. From this filthy sewer pure gold flows. Here humanity attains its most complete development and its most brutish; here civilisation works its miracles, and civilised man is turned back almost into a savage.

SOCIAL CONDITIONS IN IRELAND—CONVERSATIONS WITH
A CATHOLIC PRIEST

All the houses in line to my right and my left were made of sun-dried mud and built with walls the height of a man. The roofs of these dwellings were made of thatch so old that the grass which covered it could be confused with the meadows on the neighbouring hills. In more than one place I saw that the flimsy timbers supporting these fragile roofs had yielded to the effects of time, giving the whole thing the look of a molehill on which a passer-by has trod. The houses mostly had neither windows nor chimneys; the daylight came in and smoke came out by the door. If one could see into the houses, it was rare to notice more than bare walls, a ricketty stool and a small peat fire burning slowly and dimly between four flat stones. . . .

The pig in the house. The dunghill. The bare heads and feet. . . .

Further on I saw five or six men full of strength and health nonchalantly lying by the banks of the brook. If I had known less of Ireland, this laziness in the midst of so great poverty would have excited my indignation. But already I understood enough of this unhappy country to realise that there was a ceaseless lack of employment. They cannot earn their bread by the sweat of their brow as God commanded. . . .

The dinner, as may be believed, was short and my host noticing that I did not care for the English custom of remaining drinking at table, said to me: 'I have a few visits to make to some of my parishioners, Sir. If you wish to accompany me, perhaps we will have a chance for a talk along the way, which we would not have here.' I eagerly accepted this proposition, and my host having put his boots on and his stick under his arm, we left together and came into the village where I had already seen those young people idly lying by the brook. I saw them from far off in the same place, but they got up at our approach. 'Then you were not able to find work today,' the priest said to them. 'No,' they replied. 'We went to farmer O'Croly as your honour suggested. But farmer O'Croly himself has just been evicted from his farm by the Lord's agent.'

From *Journeys to England and Ireland*, pp. 155–60.

The priest hunched his shoulders as if he felt a heavy burden placed on them. 'What do you expect, my children,' he said, 'perhaps the day will come when there will be nothing in Ireland but lazy people left to die of hunger. But that time has not yet come. Have confidence in God.'

We left the village street here and took another sunken path on the left which led to another valley. When we had taken a few steps along it, my companion suddenly stopped, struck the ground with his stick, turned round, and said to me, 'Is such a state of things to be borne, Sir? God said to man after his fall that he must earn his bread by the sweat of his brow, but here they go even further than the divine malediction. For you have just seen men who ask for nothing but to work for their living, but cannot succeed in doing so; and when you think that in Ireland more than a million of our fellows are reduced to this extremity, do you not say, as I do, that such a state of things cannot be tolerated much longer?'

'I have heard,' said I in reply, 'that the Marquis of Sligo who, I believe owns large properties in this parish, has come to live in his castle. Do you think that, if he knew what was happening, he would not seek to lessen the extreme distress which at present prevails on his domain?'

'You must be very ill informed about the state of Ireland,' the priest replied, 'to put such a question. Do you not know that the aristocracy is the cause of all our miseries and that it does not soften any of the ills it has created? Sir, do you know what it is that prevents the poor from starving to death in Ireland? It is the poor. A farmer who has only thirty acres and who harvests only a hundred bushels of potatoes, puts aside a fifth of his harvest annually to be distributed among those unfortunates who are the most terribly in need. In Ireland, Sir, it is the poor who provide for the needs of the poor. It is the poor who raise and maintain the schools where the children of the poor are educated. Finally it is the poor who furnish the poor with the means of obtaining the comforts of religion. The starving man presents himself at the door of the cottage without fear; he is sure to receive something to appease his present hunger. But at the doors of the mansions

ιe will only meet liveried lackeys, or dogs better nourished than
ιe, who will drive him roughly away. In order to give alms the
ʾarmer will stint his land of manure and wear rags, and his wife
will sleep on straw and his children not go to school. What will the
ord do all this time? He will take walks in immense grounds
surrounded by high walls. Within his park everything breathes
splendour; outside misery groans, but he does not notice it. His
doormen take care to keep the poor from his sight, and if by
accident he meets one he answers his entreaties by saying, 'I
make it a duty not to encourage begging.' He has big, fat dogs,
and his fellows die at his door. Not only do they not help the poor
in any way, but they profit from their needs to charge enormous
rents which they spend in France or Italy. If for a short time one
returns among us, it is only to evict a farmer who is behind with
the rent and chase him from his home, as happened to poor
O'Croly. Does it seem fair to you, Sir, that this man with 80,000
acres and an income of £40,000 escapes from all the duties of
society, and does not alleviate directly by gifts, or indirectly by
giving work, the misery which he has caused, while the poor man
gives something from his own necessities to relieve miseries
which are not of his causing? Our aristocracy, Sir, has a definite,
permanent interest in making the people poverty-stricken. For
the more wretched the people are, the easier it is to impose hard
conditions of rent for farms. Daily we see great landlords, for a
trifling pecuniary advantage, change the system of farming and
put half the farm-labourers in a district out of work from one
moment to the next.'

'I can just understand,' I said, 'that a Protestant nobleman
living amid a hostile population is not much given to relieving
public distress. But you have some Catholic landowners in Ireland. Should not they give the others an example?'

'Not at all,' said the priest. 'Catholics and Protestants oppress
the people in about the same way. The moment a Catholic becomes a great landowner he conceives the same egotistical dislike
which seems natural to the aristocracy, for the interest of the
people. Like the others he eagerly seizes on all means of enriching himself at the expense of the poor.'

PRISONS: A GRESHAM'S LAW OF CRIME

Whoever has studied the interior of prisons and the moral state of their inmates, has become convinced that communication between these persons renders their moral reformation impossible, and becomes even for them the inevitable cause of an alarming corruption. This observation, justified by the experience of every day, has become in the United States an almost popular truth; and the publicists who disagree most respecting the way of putting the penitentiary system into practice, fully agree upon this point, that no salutary system can possibly exist without the separation of criminals.

For a long time it was believed that, in order to remedy the evil caused by the intercourse of prisoners with each other, it would be sufficient to establish in the prison, a certain number of classifications. But after having tried this plan, its insufficiency has been acknowledged. There are similar punishments and crimes called by the same name, but there are no two beings equal in regard to their morals; and every time that convicts are put together, there exists necessarily a fatal influence of some upon others, because, in the association of the wicked, it is not the less guilty who act upon the more criminal, but the more depraved who influence those who are less so.

We must therefore, impossible as it is to classify prisoners, come to a separation of all.

This separation, which prevents the wicked from injuring others, is also favorable to himself.

Thrown into solitude he reflects. Placed alone, in view of his crime, he learns to hate it; and if his soul be not yet surfeited with crime, and thus have lost all taste for anything better, it is in solitude, where remorse will come to assail him.

[Such was the thought which in the early nineteenth century prompted several states of the Union to build new prisons based on "the penitentiary system." The principle of the system was that prisoners were held in solitary confinement not only to prevent harmful contact between them but to induce them to reflect

From *The Penitentiary System in the United States,* p. 55.

)enitently on their crimes. When the system was applied in ex-
reme form, however, the effects were unanticipated. In the fol-
owing excerpt, Tocqueville and Beaumont describe what hap-
)ened at the State of New York's Auburn prison.]

THE EFFECTS OF SOLITARY CONFINEMENT

The northern wing having been nearly finished in 1821, eighty
)risoners were placed there, and a separate cell was given to
each. This trial, from which so happy a result had been anticipated, was fatal to the greater part of the convicts. In order to
reform them, they had been submitted to complete isolation; but
:his absolute solitude, if nothing interrupts it, is beyond the
strength of man; it destroys the criminal without intermission and
without pity; it does not reform, it kills.

The unfortunates, on whom this experiment was made, fell into
a state of depression, so manifest, that their keepers were struck
with it; their lives seemed in danger, if they remained longer in
this situation; five of them had already succumbed during a single
year; their moral state was no less alarming; one of them had
become insane; another, in a fit of despair, had embraced the
opportunity when the keeper brought him something, to precipitate himself from his cell, running the almost certain chance of
a mortal fall.

Upon similar effects the system was finally judged. The Governor of the State of New York pardoned twenty-six of those in
solitary confinement; the others to whom this favor was not extended, were allowed to leave the cells during day, and to work in
the common workshops of the prison. From this period, (1823)
the system of unmodified isolation ceased entirely to be practiced
at Auburn. Proofs were soon afforded that this system, fatal to
the health of the criminals, was likewise inefficient in producing
their reform. Of twenty-six convicts, pardoned by the governor,
fourteen returned a short time after into the prison, in consequence of new offenses.

From *The Penitentiary System in the United States*, pp. 41–42.

This experiment, so fatal to those who were selected to undergo it, was of a nature to endanger the success of the penitentiary system altogether. After the melancholy effects of isolation, it was to be feared that the whole principle would be rejected: it would have been a natural reaction. The Americans were wiser: the idea was not given up, that the solitude, which causes the criminal to reflect, exercises a beneficial influence; and the problem was, to find the means by which the evil effect of total solitude could be avoided without giving up its advantages. It was believed that this end could be attained, by leaving the convicts in their cells during night, and by making them work during the day, in the common workshops, obliging them at the same time to observe absolute silence.

The Rehabilitation of Prisoners

We have said that his entry into the penitentiary is a critical moment; that of his departure from it is still more so. He suddenly passes from absolute solitude to the ordinary state of society. Is it not to be feared that he will greedily search for those social enjoyments of which he has been deprived so completely? He was dead to the world, and after a loss of several years he reappears in society, to which, it is true, he brings good resolutions, but perhaps also burning passions, the more impetuous, from their being the longer repressed.

This is, perhaps, on the score of reformation, the chief inconvenience of absolute isolation. This system possesses, however, an advantage, which ought not to be passed over in silence; it is, that the prisoners subject to this discipline, do not know each other. This fact avoids serious inconveniences, and leads to happy consequences. There exists always, a tie more or less strong between criminals, who have formed their acquaintance in a common prison, and if they meet again after having gone through their imprisonment, they stand in a reciprocal dependence. Known, mutually, the one is almost forced to assist the other, if the latter will again commit an offense. It would be

From *The Penitentiary System in the United States,* pp. 84–85, 90.

ecessary to have become virtuous in a very elevated degree, in
order not to become again criminal. This rock, generally so fatal
to delivered convicts, is, indeed, in part avoided in the Auburn
system, where the prisoners, seeing without knowing each other,
contract no intimate connection. Yet we are still much more certain of avoiding this danger in the Philadelphia prison, where the
convicts never behold each other's faces.

He who at the expiration of his punishment leaves this prison in
order to re-enter society, cannot find in his former fellowprison-
ers, whom he does not know, any assistance in doing evil. And if
he is willing to pursue an honest course, he meets nobody to
prevent him from doing so. If he wish to commit new offenses, he
stands alone, and as to this point, he is still as isolated in the world
as he was in the prison. If, on the contrary, he is desirous of
commencing a new life, he possesses full liberty to do so....

Perhaps, leaving the prison he is not an honest man, but he has
contracted honest habits. He was an idler; now he knows how to
work. His ignorance prevented him from pursuing a useful occupation; now he knows how to read and to write; and the trade
which he has learnt in the prison furnishes him the means of
existence which formerly he had not. Without loving virtue, he
may detest the crime of which he has suffered the cruel consequences, and if he is not more virtuous he has become at least
more judicious; his morality is not honor, but interest. His religious faith is perhaps neither lively nor deep; but even supposing
that religion has not touched his heart, his mind has contracted
habits of order, and he possesses rules for his conduct in life;
without having a powerful religious conviction, he has acquired a
taste for moral principles which religion affords; finally, if he has
not become in truth better, he is at least more obedient to the
laws, and that is all which society has the right to demand.

THE EFFECTS OF DEGRADING PUNISHMENTS

We have seen...that few states have as yet changed entirely
their system of imprisonment; the number of those which have

From *The Penitentiary System in the United States,* pp. 50–51.

modified their penal laws is still less. Several among them yet possess part of the barbarous laws which they have received from England.

We shall not speak of the Southern states, where slavery still exists. In every place where one-half of the community is cruelly oppressed by the other, we must expect to find in the law of the oppressor, a weapon always ready to strike nature which revolts or humanity that complains. Punishment of death and stripes— these form the whole penal code for the slaves. But if we throw a glance at those states even which have abolished slavery, and which are more advanced in civilization, we shall see this civilization uniting itself, in some, with penal laws full of mildness, and in other, with all the rigor of a code of Draco.

Let us but compare the laws of Pennsylvania with those of New England, which is, perhaps, the most enlightened part of the American Union. In Massachusetts, there are ten different crimes punished by death—among others, rape and burglary. Maine, Rhode Island, and Connecticut, count the same number of capital crimes. Among these laws, some contain the most degrading punishments, such as the pillory; others revolting cruelties, as branding and mutilation. There are also some which order fines equal to confiscations. . . .

Punishments which degrade the guilty, are incompatible with a penitentiary system, the object of which is to reform them. How can we hope to awaken the moral sense of an individual who carries on his body the indelible sign of infamy, when the mutilation of his limbs reminds others incessantly of his crime, or the sign imprinted on his forehead, perpetuates its memory?

Must we not ardently wish that the last traces of such barbarism should disappear from all the United States, and particularly from those which have adopted the penitentiary system, with which they are irreconcilable, and whose existence renders them still more shocking?

How Much Crime Is There?

How shall the number of crimes be proved? By that of the convictions? Several causes, however, may produce more frequent convictions, though the number of crimes be the same.

This may happen, if the police pursue crimes with more activity—a circumstance which generally occurs, if public attention is more actively directed to the subject. In such case the number of crimes is not increased, but more crimes are proved. The same is the case when courts of justice are more exact; which happens always when the penal law is mitigated. Then the number of acquittals diminishes. There are more convictions, though the number of crimes has not varied. The penitentiary system itself, which is intended to diminish the number of crimes, has for its first result, the increase of convictions. In the same degree as magistrates feel repugnant to condemn the guilty, since they know the corrupting influence of the prison which receives them; in the same degree, they show themselves more ready to pronounce a condemnation as soon as they know that the prison, far from being a school of crime, is a place of repentance and reformation.

It is clear from the above that an increase or a decrease in crime is produced sometimes by general causes and sometimes by accidental ones which have no direct connection with the penitentiary system.

From *The Penitentiary System in the United States,* p. 95.

Criminal Statistics: Problems of
International Comparison

If the statistical documents which we possess of Pennsylvania should be applied to the rest of the Union, there are in this country more crimes committed than in France, in proportion to the population. Various causes of another nature explain this result: on the one hand, the colored population, which forms the sixth

From *The Penitentiary System in the United States,* pp. 99–102.

part of the inhabitants of the United States, and which composes half of the inmates of the prisons; and on the other hand, the foreigners pouring in every year from Europe, and who form the fifth and sometimes even the fourth part of the number of convicts.

These two facts, explaining the great number of crimes in the United States, make it not a subject of comparison with the number of offenses in a country where we are met with no similar facts.

If we should deduct from the total number of crimes, those committed by Negroes and foreigners, we should undoubtedly find that the white American population commits less crimes than ours. But proceeding thus, we should fall into another error; in fact, to separate the Negroes from the whole population of the United States, would be equal to deducting the poorer classes of the community with us. That is to say, those who commit the crimes. One obstacle is here avoided only to meet with another; in this respect, the only certain, incontestable fact, which we have remarked in the United States, and which may offer an opportunity for comparison, is the peculiar and extraordinary morality of the women belonging to the white race. Out of one hundred prisoners in the United States, we find but four women; while with us there are twenty in a hundred. Now this morality of the female sex must influence the whole society, because it is upon them that the morality of a family chiefly depends.

At all events, as the elements of comparison are otherwise different, we can on the whole but hazard probabilities.

Difficulties abound if we wish to make approximations of this kind between the two nations. The difference which exists between the penal laws of the United States and ours, adds greatly to them.

In the United States, things are punished as crimes which with us are beyond the reach of the laws. And again, our code punishes offenses which in the United States are not considered as such. Thus, many offenses against religion and morals, such as blasphemy, incest, fornication, drunkenness, etc., are in the United States repressed by severe punishments; with us they are unpunished. Again, our code punishes bankruptcy, against which the laws of the United States have no provisions.

How then can we compare the number of crimes committed in countries the legislation of which is so different? And yet, we must add, that this comparison, were it made exactly, would hardly afford conclusive results: thus, it may well be said, in general, that the number, more or less considerable, of convictions in a country, proves its corruption or its morality. Yet there exist exceptions to this rule, which throw a great uncertainty upon these calculations: thus, in one of the most religious and most moral states of the Union (Connecticut), there are more convictions for offenses against morals than in any other state. To understand this result, it is necessary to remember that crimes of this nature are punished only where they are rare: in societies in which adultery is frequent, it is not punished. No bankrupts are found in the prisons of the United States. Shall we conclude from this that the crime of bankruptcy is never committed there? This would be a strange mistake, because in no country perhaps more bankruptcies take place than there: it is necessary, therefore, in order not to admire on this point the commercial morality of the United States, to know whether a matter is in question which the law regards as a crime. Again, if we know that there are in the United States ten criminals committed for forgery out of one hundred prisoners we are not authorized to take this as a proof of greater corruption in that country than in ours, in which those sentenced for forgery are but two out of the hundred. In the United States the whole population is in some degree commercial, and in addition, there are three hundred and fifty banks, all emitting paper money. The ingenuity of the forger therefore has in that country a much wider field, and much stronger temptation, which is not the case with us, where commerce is but the business of a single class, and where the number of banks is so small.

There is again a difficulty in comparing the crimes committed in the two countries. It is, that in those cases even, in which the legislation of both punishes the same act, it inflicts different punishments; but as the comparison of crimes is made by that of the punishments, it follows that two analogous results, obtained from different bases, are compared together; which is a new source of mistake.

If it is difficult to compare, for any useful purpose, the number and nature of crimes committed in the United States and in France, it is perhaps still more so to compare the number of recommittals, and to arrive by this comparison at a conclusive result, in respect to the prisons of the two countries.

In general, those recommittals only, which bring back the prisoner to the prison where he has been detained the first time, are calculated in the United States. His return to the same prison, is in fact the only means of proving his relapse. In that country, where passports do not exist, nothing is easier than to change one's name. If therefore a delivered convict commits a new crime under a fictitious name, he can very easily conceal his relapse, providing he is not brought back to the prison where he underwent his first punishment. There are, besides, a thousand means of avoiding the chances of being recognized. Nothing is easier than to pass from one state to another, and it is the criminal's interest to do so, whether he intends to commit new crimes, or has resolved to lead an honest life. We find therefore among a hundred criminals convicted in one state, thirty, upon an average, who belong to some neighboring state. This emigration is sufficient to make the proof of recommittals impossible. The tie between the various states being strictly political, there is no central power to which the police officers might refer to obtain information respecting the previous life of an indicted person: so that the courts condemn, almost always, without knowing the true name of the criminal, and still less his previous life. It is clear, therefore, that in such a state of things the number of known recommittals is never that of all the existing ones. The same is not the case with us. There are a thousand ways in France to prove the identity of the indicted and the convicted prisoner, by means of the mutual information which all the agents of the judicial police keep up among themselves. The convictions pronounced by a *cour royal* in the south are known by a court in the north, and the judiciary possesses on this point all the means of investigation which are wanting in the United States. If, therefore, in France, no more recommittals should take place than in the United States, a greater number, nevertheless, would be pub-

icly known. And as the means of proving them in the two coun-
ries are so different, it would be useless to compare the number.

All comparisons of this kind then, between America and
Europe, lead to no satisfactory result. America can be compared
only with herself; yet this comparison is sufficient to shed abundant light upon the question we are considering. We acknowledged the superiority of the new penitentiary system over the old
prisons, when we found that the number of recommittals in the
ancient prisons, compared to all convictions, was in the proportion of one to six, and in the new penitentiaries in the proportion
of only one to twenty.

9

RACE RELATIONS, SLAVERY, AND COLONIALISM

TOCQUEVILLE VERSUS GOBINEAU

I have to beg your pardon, my dear friend, first for not having written as soon as I read your book, and then for having left your latest letter unanswered, despite my better intentions, for ten or twelve days. As for the first omission, it was brought about by a sort of disquiet which reading your book caused me, and by the tangle of praise and criticism I have to send you. As for my fortnight's silence, that was because I had to read very hurriedly some books recalled by the libraries in Paris from which I had borrowed them. Now let us come to the point. I will proceed in the opposite way to most people, and start with the criticisms. They relate to the central idea itself. I will confess frankly that you have not convinced me. All my objections still stand. You are, nevertheless, quite right to defend yourself against the charge of being a materialist. Your doctrine is rather, in fact, a sort of fatalism, or predestination if you like, although it differs from that of St. Augustine, the Jansenists, and the Calvinists (the last are closest to you in the absoluteness with which they adhere to the doctrine) in that you make a close link between predestination and matter. Thus you constantly speak of the regeneration and degeneration of races, of races losing social capabilities or gaining ones they did not have before through an *infusion of new blood*—I think those were your own words. I have to admit to you that this kind of predestination seems to me to be closely akin to pure materialism; and, make no mistake, if the masses, who always

From *Correspondance entre Alexis de Tocqueville et Arthur de Gobineau, 1843–1859* (Paris, Plon, 1908). Trans. SJM.

follow the beaten paths in matters of thought, should accept your doctrine, it would lead them straight from races to individuals, and from social capabilities to any sort of mental capacity. Whether predestination can be directly related to certain biological patterns or to the will of God who wished to make several species within the human genus, and to impose on certain men by reason of the race to which they belong the inability to feel certain feelings, think certain thoughts, behave in certain ways, or possess certain qualities which they can recognize without being able to acquire—none of this has much bearing on my own concern with the practical consequences of these various philosophical doctrines. Both theories result in a great restriction, if not the complete abolition, of human liberty. So I confess that after reading your book I remain as diametrically opposed to these doctrines as I was before. I believe them to be probably false and most certainly pernicious.

Admittedly, among the various families which compose the human race, there are certain peculiar inclinations and aptitudes arising from thousands of different causes. But that these inclinations and aptitudes are insurmountable not only has never been proven but is in itself unprovable, because in order to prove it one would need to know not just the past but also the future. I am sure that Julius Caesar, if he had had the time, would have willingly written a book to show that the savages he met in Britain were not of the same human race as the Romans, and that while the latter were destined by nature to dominate the world, the former were fated to vegetate in an obscure corner. *Tu regere imperio populos, Romane, memento,* said our old friend Vergil. If it were only the broad human families differing amongst themselves in a deep and permanent way in *external appearance* which could be identified with distinctive and enduring traits and traced back to differences of some sort at creation, the doctrine, without being in my opinion any more convincing, would be less improbable and easier to substantiate. But when the doctrine is applied within one of these broad families, like that of the white race for example, the thread of the argument is lost. What in the world is more difficult than to determine from history or tradition when, how, and in what proportions the mixing took place which produced men who now show no visible trace of their origin? These events all took place in remote and barbaric times, from which there remain only vague folk traditions or fragmentary documents. Do you really believe that by choosing this way of explaining the destiny of different peoples you have done much to clarify history? Or that social science has gained in certainty by abandoning the path followed by so many great minds since the world began, of looking for the causes of social events in the influence of particular men, particular emotions, particular ideas, and particular beliefs? If only your doctrine, though no better founded than theirs, were more beneficial to humanity! But it is plainly the opposite. What purpose can it serve to persuade more lowly people, who live in barbarism, indolence, or servitude that, such being the nature of their race, there is nothing they can do to improve their condition, change their habits, or modify their mode of government? Don't you see how from your doctrine inevitably flow all the evils of permanent inborn inequality, pride, violence, contempt for one's fellow men, tyranny and vileness in all their forms? How can you speak to me, my dear friend, of a distinction between *qualities which put moral truths into practice* and what you call *social aptitudes?* What is the difference between them? When you have observed public affairs quite closely and over quite a long time, can you really remain unconvinced that the same means make for success both in the public and private domains; that courage, energy, integrity, farsightedness, and good sense are the true reasons for the prosperity of empires as much as that of families; and that, in short, the destiny of men, whether as individuals or as nations, is what they wish to make it?

I will stop here; please let us allow the discussion to rest there. A world of intellectual difference exists between your doctrine and mine....

ETHNIC STRATIFICATION IN IRELAND

Imagine an aristocracy which was born on the very soil it dominates, or whose origin is lost in the obscurity of past centuries.

From *Journeys to England and Ireland,* pp. 149–51.

Assume that, not being different from the people, they could easily assimilate with them. Give this aristocracy an interest in uniting with the people to resist a power greater than that of the aristocracy or of the people alone, but weaker than that of the people and the aristocracy united together, so that the more rich and enlightened the people are, the more the aristocracy is assured of its preservation, and the more the rights of the aristocracy are respected, the more the people are certain of retaining the enjoyment of theirs. Imagine an aristocracy having the same language, the same manners, the same religion as the people; an aristocracy which would be ahead, but beyond the ken, of the people's understanding; an aristocracy which surpasses the people a little in all respects, but immensely in none. Imagine a middle class gradually increasing in importance in the context of this state of affairs, and by degrees coming to share the power and soon afterwards the privileges of the ancient aristocracy, in such way that money which everybody can hope to obtain, gradually takes the place of birth which depends on God alone. Thus inequality itself will work to forward the wealth of all, for, everybody hoping to come to share the privileges of the few, there would be a universal effort, an eagerness of all minds directed to the acquisition of well-being and wealth. Make of this nation a huge centre of commerce, so that the chances of attaining the wealth with which all the rest can be obtained, multiply infinitely, and ever give the poor a thousand hopes, and so a thousand reasons for remaining satisfied with their lot.

Imagine all these things, and you will have a people among whom the upper classes are more brilliant, more enlightened and wiser, the middle classes richer, the poor classes better off than anywhere else; where the State would be as firm in its plans as if it were governed by one man, as strong and as powerful as if it relied on the free will of all its citizens; where the people would submit to the law as if they had made it themselves, and where order would reign as if it were only the question of carrying out the will of a despot: in fine, where everyone being content with his lot would be proud of his country and would wish to be proud of himself.

Now imagine an aristocracy that was established by a conquest at a time so recent that the memory and the traces of the event were present in all minds. Place the conquest in a century when the conqueror already had almost all the lights of civilisation and the vanquished was still in a state of half savagery, so that both in moral power and in intelligence the conqueror was as far as possible superior to the conquered. Give to these two, who are already so dissimilar and unequal, a different religion, so that the nobility not only distrusts the people, but also hates them, and the people not only hates the nobles but damns them. Far from giving the aristocracy so constituted any particular reason to unite itself with the people, give it a particular reason not to unite with the people in order to remain similar to the nation whence it came, from which it still draws all its strength, and to resemble which is its pride. Instead of giving it a reason to take care of the people, give it a special motive to oppress them, by placing its trust in this foreign support which provides that it should have nothing to fear from the consequences of its tyranny. Give to this aristocracy the exclusive power of government and of self-enrichment. Forbid the people to join its ranks, or, if you do allow that, impose conditions for that benefit which they cannot accept. So that the people, estranged from the upper classes and the object of their enmity, without a hope of bettering their lot, end up by abandoning themselves and thinking themselves satisfied when by the greatest efforts they can extract from their land enough to prevent themselves from dying; and meanwhile the noble, stripped of all that stimulates man to great and generous actions, slumbers in unenlightened egoism.

You would certainly have a terrible state of society, in which the aristocracy would have all the faults and maxims of oppressors; the people all the vices and faint-heartedness of slaves. The law would serve to destroy what it should protect, and violence would protect what elsewhere it seeks to destroy. Religion would seem only to lend its strength to the passions which it should fight, and to exist only to prevent hatreds from being forgotten and men from establishing among them the fraternity it preaches every day.

The two societies I have just described were however both founded on the principle of aristocracy. The two aristocracies of which I have been speaking, have the same origin and manners and almost the same laws. But the one has for centuries given the English one of the best governments that exist in the world; the other has given the Irish one of the most detestable that could ever be imagined.

Aristocracy then can be subjected to particular conditions which modify its nature and its results, so that in judging it one must bear circumstances in mind. The truth is that the aristocratic principle was conditioned in England by particularly happy circumstances, and in Ireland by particularly baneful ones. It would not be fair to make a theoretical judgment about aristocracy on the strength of either of these examples. The rule lies elsewhere.

RACE RELATIONS IN AMERICA

The absolute supremacy of democracy is not all that we meet with in America; the inhabitants of the New World may be considered from more than one point of view. In the course of this work my subject has often led me to speak of the Indians and the Negroes; but I have never been able to stop in order to show what place these two races occupy, in the midst of the democratic people whom I was engaged in describing. . . .

The Negro enters upon slavery as soon as he is born; nay, he may have been purchased in the womb, and have begun his slavery before he began his existence. Equally devoid of wants and of enjoyment, and useless to himself, he learns, with his first notions of existence, that he is the property of another who has an interest in preserving his life, and that the care of it does not devolve upon himself; even the power of thought appears to him a useless gift of Providence, and he quietly enjoys the privileges of his debasement.

If he becomes free, independence is often felt by him to be a heavier burden than slavery; for having learned, in the course of his life, to submit to everything except reason, he is too much unacquainted with her dictates to obey them. A thousand new

From *Democracy in America*, pt. 1, chap. 18.

desires beset him, and he is destitute of the knowledge and energy necessary to resist them: these are master which it is necessary to contend with, and he has learnt only to submit and obey. In short, he sinks to such a depth of wretchedness, that while servitude brutalizes, liberty destroys him.

Oppression has been no less fatal to the Indian than to the Negro race, but its effects are different. Before the arrival of white men in the New World, the inhabitants of North America lived quietly in their woods, enduring the vicissitudes and practising the virtues and vices common to savage nations. The Europeans, having dispersed the Indian tribes and driven them into the deserts, condemned them to a wandering life full of inexpressible sufferings.

Savage nations are only controlled by opinion and by custom. When the North American Indians had lost the sentiment of attachment to their country; when their families were dispersed, their traditions obscured, and the chain of their recollections broken; when all their habits were changed, and their wants increased beyond measure, European tyranny rendered them more disorderly and less civilized than they were before. The moral and physical condition of these tribes continually grew worse, and they became more barbarous as they became more wretched. Nevertheless, the Europeans have not been able to change the character of the Indians; and though they have had power to destroy them, they have never been able to make them submit to the rules of civilized society.

The lot of the Negro is placed on the extreme limit of servitude, while that of the Indian lies on the uttermost verge of liberty; and slavery does not produce more fatal effects upon the first, than independence upon the second. The Negro has lost all property in his own person, and he cannot dispose of his existence without committing a sort of fraud: but the savage is his own master as soon as he is able to act; parental authority is scarcely known to him; he has never bent his will to that of any of his kind, nor learned the difference between voluntary obedience and a shameful subjection; and the very name of law is unknown to him. To be free, with him, signifies to escape from all the shackles of society. As he delights in this barbarous independence, and would rather perish than sacrifice the least part of it, civilization has little power over him.

The Negro makes a thousand fruitless efforts to ingratiate himself with men who repulse him; he conforms to the tastes of his oppressors, adopts their opinions, and hopes by imitating them to form a part of their community. Having been told from infancy that his race is naturally inferior to that of the Whites, he assents to the proposition, and is ashamed of his own nature. In each of his features he discovers a trace of slavery, and, if it were in his power, he would willingly rid himself of everything that makes him what he is.

The Indian, on the contrary, has his imagination inflated with the pretended nobility of his origin, and lives and dies in the midst of these dreams of pride. Far from desiring to conform his habits to ours, he loves his savage life as the distinguishing mark of his race, and he repels every advance to civilization, less perhaps from the hatred which he entertains for it, than from a dread of resembling the Europeans. While he has nothing to oppose to our perfection in the arts but the resources of the desert, to our tactics nothing but undisciplined courage; whilst our well-digested plans are met by the spontaneous instincts of savage life, who can wonder if he fails in this unequal contest?

The Negro, who earnestly desires to mingle his race with that of the European, cannot effect it; while the Indian, who might succeed to a certain extent, disdains to make the attempt. The servility of the one dooms him to slavery, the pride of the other to death.

The American Indians

When the Indians were the sole inhabitants of the wilds from which they have since been expelled, their wants were few. Their arms were of their own manufacture, their only drink was the water of the brook, and their clothes consisted of the skins of animals, whose flesh furnished them with food.

From *Democracy in America*, pt. 1, chap. 18.

The Europeans introduced amongst the savages of North America fire-arms, hard liquor, and iron: they taught them to exchange for manufactured goods, the rough garments which had previously satisfied their untutored simplicity. Having acquired new tastes, without the arts by which they could be gratified, the Indians were obliged to have recourse to the workmanship of the Whites; but in return for their productions the savage had nothing to offer except the rich furs which still abounded in his woods. Hence the chase became necessary, not merely to provide for his subsistence, but in order to procure the only objects of barter which he could furnish to Europe. Whilst the wants of the natives were thus increasing, their resources continued to diminish.

From the moment when an European settlement is formed in the neighbourhood of the territory occupied by the Indians, the beasts of chase take the alarm. Thousands of savages, wandering in the forests and destitute of any fixed dwelling, did not disturb them; but as soon as the continuous sounds of European labour are heard in their neighbourhood, they begin to flee away, and retire to the West, where their instinct teaches them that they will find deserts of immeasurable extent. "The buffalo is constantly receding," says Messrs. Clarke and Cass in their Report of the year 1829; "a few years since they approached the base of the Alleghany; and a few years hence they may even be rare upon the immense plains which extend to the base of the Rocky Mountains." I have been assured that this effect of the approach of the Whites is often felt at two hundred leagues' distance from their frontier. Their influence is thus exerted over tribes whose name is unknown to them; and who suffer the evils of usurpation long before they are acquainted with the authors of their distress.

Bold adventurers soon penetrate into the country the Indians have deserted, and when they have advanced about fifteen or twenty leagues from the extreme frontiers of the Whites, they begin to build habitations for civilized beings in the midst of the wilderness. This is done without difficulty, as the territory of a hunting-nation is ill defined; it is the common property of the tribe, and belongs to no one in particular, so that individual interests are not concerned in the protection of any part of it.

A few European families settled in different situations at a considerable distance from each other, soon drive away the wild animals which remain between their places of abode. The Indians, who had previously lived in a sort of abundance, then find it difficult to subsist, and still more difficult to procure the articles of barter which they stand in need of.

To drive away their game is to deprive them of the means of existence, as effectually as if the fields of our agriculturists were stricken with barrenness; and they are reduced, like famished wolves, to prowl through the forsaken woods in quest of prey. Their instinctive love of their country attaches them to the soil which gave them birth, even after it has ceased to yield anything but misery and death. At length, they are compelled to acquiesce, and to depart: they follow the traces of the elk, the buffalo, and the beaver, and are guided by these wild animals in the choice of their future country. Properly speaking, therefore, it is not the Europeans who drive away the native inhabitants of America; it is famine which compels them to recede; a happy distinction which had escaped the casuists of former times, and for which we are indebted to modern discovery!

It is impossible to conceive the extent of the sufferings which attend these forced emigrations. They are undertaken by a people already exhausted and reduced; and the countries to which the new comers betake themselves are inhabited by other tribes which receive them with jealous hostility. Hunger is in the rear, war awaits them, and misery besets them on all sides. In the hope of escaping from such a host of enemies, they separate; and each individual endeavours to procure the means of supporting his existence in solitude and secrecy, living in the immensity of the desert like an outcast in civilized society. The social tie, which distress had long since weakened, is then dissolved; they have lost their country, and their people soon desert them; their very families are obliterated; the names they bore in common are forgotten, their language perishes, and all traces of their origin disappear. Their nation has ceased to exist, except in the recollection of the antiquaries of America and a few of the learned of Europe.

I should be sorry to have my reader suppose that I am colouring the picture too highly: I saw with my own eyes several of the cases of misery which I have been describing; and I was the witness of sufferings which I have not the power to portray.

At the end of the year 1831, whilst I was on the left bank of the Mississippi at a place named by Europeans Memphis, there arrived a numerous band of Choctaws, (or Chactas, as they are called by the French in Louisiana.) These savages had left their country, and were endeavouring to gain the right bank of the Mississippi, where they hoped to find an asylum which had been promised them by the American Government. It was then the middle of winter, and the cold was unusually severe; the snow had frozen hard upon the ground, and the river was drifting huge masses of ice. The Indians had their families with them; and they brought in their train the wounded and the sick, with children newly born, and old men upon the verge of death. They possessed neither tents nor waggons, but only their arms and some provisions. I saw them embark to pass the mighty river, and never will that solemn spectacle fade from my remembrance. No cry, no sob was heard amongst the assembled crowd: all were silent. Their calamities were of ancient date, and they knew them to be irremediable. The Indians had all stepped into the bark which was to carry them across, but their dogs remained upon the bank. As soon as these animals perceived that their masters were finally leaving the shore, they set up a dismal howl, and, plunging all together into the icy waters of the Mississippi, they swam after the boat....

The Indians, in the little which they have done, have unquestionably displayed as much natural genius as the peoples of Europe in their most important designs; but nations as well as men require time to learn, whatever may be their intelligence and their zeal. Whilst the savages were engaged in the work of civilization, the Europeans continued to surround them on every side, and to confine them within narrower limits; the two races gradually met, and they are now in immediate juxtaposition to each other. The Indian is already superior to his barbarous parent, but he is still very far below his white neighbour. With their resources and acquired knowledge, the Europeans soon appropriated to themselves most of the advantages which the natives might have derived from the possession of the soil: they have settled in the country, they have purchased land at a very low rate or have occupied it by force, and the Indians have been ruined by a competition which they had not the means of resisting. They were isolated in their own country, and their race only constituted a colony of troublesome aliens in the midst of a numerous and domineering people.

Washington said in one of his messages to Congress, "We are more enlightened and more powerful than the Indian nations, we are therefore bound in honour to treat them with kindness and even with generosity." But this virtuous and high-minded policy has not been followed. The rapacity of the settlers is usually backed by the tyranny of the Government. Although the Cherokees and the Creeks are established upon the territory which they inhabited before the settlement of the Europeans, and although the Americans have frequently treated with them as with foreign nations, the surrounding States have not consented to acknowledge them as independent peoples, and attempts have been made to subject these children of the woods to Anglo-American magistrates, laws, and customs. Destitution had driven these unfortunate Indians to civilization, and oppression now drives them back to their former condition: many of them abandon the soil which they had begun to clear, and return to their savage course of life.

If we consider the tyrannical measures which have been adopted by the legislatures of the Southern States, the conduct of their Governors, and the decrees of their courts of justice, we shall be convinced that the entire expulsion of the Indians is the final result to which the efforts of their policy are directed. The Americans of that part of the Union look with jealousy upon the aborigines, they are aware that these tribes have not yet lost the traditions of savage life, and before civilization has permanently fixed them to the soil, it is intended to force them to recede by reducing them to despair. The Creeks and Cherokees, oppressed by the several States, have appealed to the central Government, which is by no means insensible to their misfortunes, and is sincerely desirous of saving the remnants of the natives, and of maintaining them in the free possession of that territory, which the Union is pledged to respect. But the several States oppose so formidable a resistance to the execution of this design, that the Government is obliged to consent to the extirpation of a few barbarous tribes in order not to endanger the safety of the American Union....

...From whichever side we consider the destinies of the aborigines of North America, their calamities appear to be irremediable: if they continue barbarous, they are forced to retire; if they attempt to civilize their manners, the contact of a more civilized community subjects them to oppression and destitution. They perish if they continue to wander from waste to waste, and if they attempt to settle, they still must perish; the assistance of the Europeans is necessary to instruct them, but the approach of the Europeans corrupts and repels them into savage life; they refuse to change their habits as long as their solitudes are their own, and it is too late to change them when they are constrained to submit.

The Spaniards pursued the Indians with blood-hounds, like wild beasts; they sacked the New World with no more temper or compassion than a city taken by storm: but destruction must cease, and frenzy be stayed; the remnant of the Indian population, which had escaped the massacre, mixed with its conquerors, and adopted in the end their religion and their manners. The conduct of the Americans of the United States towards the aborigines is characterized, on the other hand, by a singular attachment to the formalities of law. Provided that the Indians retain their barbarous condition, the Americans take no part in their affairs; they treat them as independent nations, and do not possess themselves of their hunting-grounds without a treaty of purchase: and if an Indian nation happens to be so encroached upon as to be unable to subsist upon its territory, they afford it brotherly assistance in transporting it to a grave sufficiently remote from the land of its fathers.

The Spaniards were unable to exterminate the Indian race by those unparalleled atrocities which brand them with indelible shame, nor did they even succeed in wholly depriving it of its rights; but the Americans of the United States have accomplished this twofold purpose with singular felicity; tranquilly, legally, philanthropically, without shedding blood, and without violating a single great principle of morality in the eyes of the world. It is impossible to destroy men with more respect for the laws of humanity.

BLACKS IN AMERICA

As long as the negro remains a slave, he may be kept in a condition not very far removed from that of the brutes; but, with his liberty, he cannot but acquire a degree of instruction which will enable him to appreciate his misfortunes, and to discern a remedy for them. Moreover, there exists a singular principle of relative justice which is very firmly implanted in the human heart. Men are much more forcibly struck by those inequalities which exist within the circle of the same class, than with those which may be remarked between different classes. It is more easy for them to admit slavery, than to allow several millions of citizens to exist under a load of eternal infamy and hereditary wretchedness. In the North the population of freed negroes feels these hardships and resents these indignities; but its numbers and its powers are small, whilst in the South it would be numerous and strong.

As soon as it is admitted that the whites and the emancipated blacks are placed upon the same territory in the situation of two alien communities, it will readily be understood that there are but two alternatives for the future; the negroes and the whites must either wholly part or wholly mingle. . . . I do not imagine that the white and black races will ever live in any country upon an equal footing. But I believe the difficulty to be still greater in the United States than elsewhere. An isolated individual may surmount the prejudices of religion, of his country, or of his race, and if this individual is a king he may effect surprising changes in society; but a whole people cannot rise, as it were, above itself. A despot who should subject the Americans and their former slaves to the same yoke, might perhaps succeed in commingling their races; but as long as the American democracy remains at the head of affairs, no one will undertake so difficult a task; and it may be foreseen

From *Democracy in America*, pt. 1, chap. 18.

that the freer the white population of the United States becomes, the more isolated will it remain.

I have previously observed that the mixed race is the true bond of union between the Europeans and the Indians; just so the mulattoes are the true means of transition between the white and the negro; so that wherever mulattoes abound, the intermixture of the two races is not impossible. In some parts of America, the European and the negro races are so crossed by one another, that it is rare to meet with a man who is entirely black, or entirely white: when they are arrived at this point, the two races may really be said to be combined; or rather to have been absorbed in a third race, which is connected with both without being identical with either.

Of all the Europeans the English are those who have mixed least with the negroes. More mulattoes are to be seen in the South of the Union than in the North, but still they are infinitely more scarce than in any other European colony: mulattoes are by no means numerous in the United States; they have no force peculiar to themselves, and when quarrels originating in differences of colour take place, they generally side with the whites; just as the lackeys of the great, in Europe, assume the contemptuous airs of nobility to the lower orders.

The pride of origin, which is natural to the English, is singularly augmented by the personal pride which democratic liberty fosters amongst the Americans: the white citizen of the United States is proud of his race, and proud of himself. But if the whites and the negroes do not intermingle in the North of the Union, how should they mix in the South? Can it be supposed for an instant, that an American of the Southern States, placed, as he must for ever be, between the white man with all his physical and moral superiority, and the negro, will ever think of preferring the latter? The Americans of the Southern States have two powerful passions which will always keep them aloof; the first is fear of being assimilated to the negroes, their former slaves; and the second, the dread of sinking below the whites, their neighbours.

If I were called upon to predict what will probably occur at some future time, I should say that the abolition of slavery in the South will, in the common course of things, increase the repugnance of the white population for the men of colour. I found this opinion upon the analogous observation which I already had occasion to make in the North. I there remarked that the white inhabitants of the North avoid the negroes with increasing care, in proportion as the legal barriers of separation are removed by the legislature; and why should not the same result take place in the South? In the North, the whites are deterred from intermingling with the blacks by the fear of an imaginary danger; in the South, where the danger would be real, I cannot imagine that the fear would be less general.

If, on the one hand, it be admitted (and the fact is unquestionable) that the coloured population perpetually accumulates in the extreme South, and that it increases more rapidly than that of the whites; and if, on the other hand, it be allowed that it is impossible to foresee a time at which the whites and the blacks will be so intermingled as to derive the same benefits from society; must it not be inferred, that the blacks and the whites will, sooner or later, come to open strife in the Southern States of the Union? But if it be asked what the issue of the struggle is likely to be, it will readily be understood that we are here left to form a very vague surmise of the truth. The human mind may succeed in tracing a wide circle, as it were, which includes the course of future events; but within that circle a thousand various chances and circumstances may direct it in as many different ways; and in every picture of the future there is a dim spot, which the eye of the understanding cannot penetrate. It appears, however, to be extremely probable, that in the West India Islands the white race is destined to be subdued, and the black population to share the same fate upon the continent.

In the West India Islands the white planters are surrounded by an immense black population; on the continent, the blacks are placed between the ocean and an innumerable people, which already extends over them in a dense mass, from the icy confines of Canada to the frontiers of Virginia, and from the banks of Missouri to the shores of the Atlantic. If the white citizens of North America remain united, it cannot be supposed that the negroes will escape the destruction with which they are menaced; they must be subdued by want or by the sword. But the black population which is accumulated along the coast of the Gulf of Mexico, has a chance of success, if the American Union is dissolved when the struggles between the two races begins. If the Federal tie were broken, the citizens of the South would be wrong to rely upon any lasting succour from their Northern countrymen. The latter are well aware that the danger can never reach them; and unless they are constrained to march to the assistance of the South by a positive obligation, it may be foreseen that the sympathy of colour will be insufficient to stimulate their exertions.

Yet, at whatever period the strife may break out, the whites of the South, even if they are abandoned to their own resources, will enter the lists with an immense superiority of knowledge and of the means of warfare: but the blacks will have numerical strength and the energy of despair upon their side; and these are powerful resources to men who have taken up arms. The fate of the white population of the Southern States will, perhaps, be similar to that of the Moors in Spain. After having occupied the land for centuries, it will perhaps be forced to retire to the country whence its ancestors came, and to abandon to the negroes the possession of a territory, which Providence seems to have more peculiarly destined for them, since they can subsist and labour in it more easily than the whites.

The danger of a conflict between the white and the black inhabitants of the Southern States of the Union,—a danger which, however remote it may be, is inevitable,—perpetually haunts the imagination of the Americans. The inhabitants of the North make it a common topic of conversation, although they have no direct injury to fear from the struggle; but they vainly endeavour to devise some means of obviating the misfortunes which they foresee. In the Southern States the subject is not discussed: the planter does not allude to the future in conversing with strangers; the citizen does not communicate his apprehensions to his friends; he seeks to conceal them from himself: but there is something more alarming in the tacit forebodings of the South, than in the clamorous fears of the Northern States.

This all-pervading disquietude has given birth to an undertaking which is but little known, but which may have the effect of changing the fate of a portion of the human race. From apprehension of the dangers which I have just been describing, a certain number of American citizens have formed a society for the purpose of exporting to the coast of Guinea, at their own expense, such free negroes as may be willing to escape from the oppression to which they are subject.

In 1820, the society to which I allude formed a settlement in Africa, upon the seventh degree of north latitude, which bears the name of Liberia. The most recent intelligence informs us that two thousand five hundred negroes are collected there; they have introduced the democratic institutions of America into the country of their forefathers; and Liberia has a representative system of government, negro jurymen, negro magistrates, and negro priests; churches have been built, newspapers established, and, by a singular change in the vicissitudes of the world, white men are prohibited from sojourning within the settlement.

This is indeed a strange caprice of fortune. Two hundred years have now elapsed since the inhabitants of Europe undertook to tear the negro from his family and his home, in order to transport him to the shores of North America; at the present day, the European settlers are engaged in sending back the descendants of those very negroes, to the continent from which they were originally taken; and the barbarous Africans have been brought into contact with civilization in the midst of bondage, and have become acquainted with free political institutions in slavery. Up to the present time Africa has been closed against the arts and sciences of the whites; but the inventions of Europe will perhaps penetrate into those regions, now that they are introduced by Africans themselves. The settlement of Liberia is founded upon a lofty and a most fruitful idea; but whatever may be its results with regard to the continent of Africa, it can afford no remedy to the New World.

In twelve years the Colonization Society has transported two thousand five hundred negroes to Africa; in the same space of time about seven hundred thousand blacks were born in the United States. If the colony of Liberia were so situated as to be able to receive thousands of new inhabitants every year, and if the negroes were in a state to be sent thither with advantage; if the Union were to supply the society with annual subsidies, and to transport the negroes to Africa in the vessels of the State, it would still be unable to counterpoise the natural increase of population amongst the blacks; and as it could not remove as many men in a year as are born upon its territory within the same space of time, it would fail in suspending the growth of the evil which is daily increasing in the States. The negro race will never leave those shores of the American continent, to which it was brought by the passions and the vices of Europeans; and it will not disappear from the New World as long as it continues to exist. The inhabitants of the United States may retard the calamities which they apprehend, but they cannot now destroy their efficient cause.

I am obliged to confess that I do not regard the abolition of slavery as a means of warding off the struggle of the two races in the United States. The negroes may long remain slaves without complaining; but if they are once raised to the level of free men, they will soon revolt at being deprived of all their civil rights; and as they cannot become the equals of the whites, they will speedily declare themselves as enemies. In the North everything contributed to facilitate the emancipation of the slaves; and slavery was abolished, without placing the free negroes in a position which could become formidable, since their number was too small for them ever to claim the exercise of their rights. But such is not the case in the South. The question of slavery was a question of commerce and manufacture for the slave-owners in the North; for those of the South, it is a question of life and death. God forbid that I should seek to justify the principle of negro slavery, as has been done by some American writers! But I only observe that all the countries which formerly adopted that execrable principle are not equally able to abandon it at the present time.

When I contemplate the condition of the South, I can only discover two alternatives which may be adopted by the white inhabitants of those States; viz. either to emancipate the negroes, and to intermingle with them; or, remaining isolated from them, to keep them in a state of slavery as long as possible. All intermediate measures seem to me likely to terminate, and that shortly, in the most horrible of civil wars, and perhaps in the extirpation of one or other of the two races. Such is the view which the Americans of the South take of the question, and they act consistently with it. As they are determined not to mingle with the negroes, they refuse to emancipate them.

Not that the inhabitants of the South regard slavery as necessary to the wealth of the planter; for on this point many of them agree with their Northern countrymen in freely admitting that slavery is prejudicial to their interests; but they are convinced that, however prejudicial it may be, they hold their lives upon no other tenure. The instruction which is now diffused in the South has convinced the inhabitants that slavery is injurious to the slave-owner, but it has also shown them, more clearly than before, that no means exist of getting rid of its bad consequences. Hence arises a singular contrast; the more the utility of slavery is contested, the more firmly is it established in the laws; and whilst the principle of servitude is gradually abolished in the North, that self-same principle gives rise to more and more rigorous consequences in the South.

The legislation of the Southern States with regard to slaves, presents at the present day such unparalleled atrocities, as suffice to show how radically the laws of humanity have been perverted, and to betray the desperate position of the community in which that legislation has been promulgated. The Americans of this portion of the Union have not, indeed, augmented the hardships of slavery; they have, on the contrary, bettered the physical condition of the slaves. The only means by which the ancients maintained slavery were fetters and death; the Americans of the South of the Union have discovered more intellectual securities for the duration of their power. They have employed their despotism and their violence against the human mind. In antiquity, precautions were taken to prevent the slave from breaking his chains; at the present day measures are adopted to deprive him even of the desire of freedom. The ancients kept the bodies of their slaves in bondage, but they placed no restraint upon the mind and no check upon education; and they acted consistently with their established principle, since a natural termination of slavery then existed, and one day or other the slave might be set free, and become the equal of his master. But the Americans of the South, who do not admit that the Negroes can ever be commingled with themselves, have forbidden them to be taught to read or to write, under severe penalties; and as they will not raise them to their own level, they sink them as nearly as possible to that of the brutes.

The hope of liberty had always been allowed to the slave to cheer the hardships of his condition. But the Americans of the South are well aware that emancipation cannot but be dangerous, when the freed man can never be assimilated to his former master. To give a man his freedom, and to leave him in wretchedness and ignominy, is nothing less than to prepare a future chief for a revolt of the slaves. Moreover, it has long been remarked, that the presence of a free negro vaguely agitates the minds of his less fortunate brethren, and conveys to them a dim notion of their rights. The Americans of the South have consequently taken measures to prevent slave-owners from emancipating their slaves in most cases; not indeed by a positive prohibition, but by subjecting that step to various forms which it is difficult to comply with.

I happened to meet with an old man, in the South of the Union, who had lived in illicit intercourse with one of his negresses, and had had several children by her, who were born the slaves of their father. He had indeed frequently thought of bequeathing to them at least their liberty; but years had elapsed without his being able to surmount the legal obstacles to their emancipation, and in the meanwhile his old-age was come, and he was about to die. He pictured to himself his sons dragged from market to market, and passing from the authority of a parent to the rod of the stranger, until these horrid anticipations worked his expiring imagination into frenzy. When I saw him he was a prey to all the anguish of despair, and he made me feel how awful is the retribution of Nature upon those who have broken her laws.

These evils are unquestionably great; but they are the necessary and foreseen consequence of the very principle of modern slavery. When the Europeans chose their slaves from a race differing from their own, which many of them considered as inferior to the other races of mankind, and which they all repelled with horror from any notion of intimate connexion, they must have believed that slavery would last for ever; since there is no inter-

mediate state which can be durable, between the excessive inequality produced by servitude, and the complete equality which
originates in independence. The Europeans did imperfectly feel
this truth, but without acknowledging it even to themselves.
Whenever they have had to do with negroes, their conduct has
either been dictated by their interest and their pride, or by their
compassion. They first violated every right of humanity by their
treatment of the negro, and they afterwards informed him that
those rights were precious and inviolable. They affected to open
their ranks to the slaves, but the negroes who attempted to penetrate into the community were driven back with scorn; and they
have incautiously and involuntarily been led to admit of freedom
instead of slavery, without having the courage to be wholly iniquitous, or wholly just.

If it be impossible to anticipate a period at which the Americans
of the South will mingle their blood with that of the negroes, can
they allow their slaves to become free without compromising
their own security? And if they are obliged to keep that race in
bondage, in order to save their own families, may they not be
excused for availing themselves of the means best adapted to that
end? The events which are taking place in the Southern States of
the Union, appear to me to be at once the most horrible and the
most natural results of slavery. When I see the order of nature
overthrown, and when I hear the cry of humanity in its vain
struggle against the laws, my indignation does not light upon the
men of our own time who are the instruments of these outrages;
but I reserve my execration for those who, after a thousand years
of freedom, brought back slavery into the world once more.

SLAVERY IN THE FRENCH COLONIES

They, who have hitherto considered the subject of slavery, have,
for the most part, endeavored to show its injustice or to mitigate
its hardships.

From *Report Made to the Chamber of Deputies on the Abolition of Slavery in
the French Colonies* (1840), pp. 5–6, 8–10, 22–23, 53.

The Commission, in the name of which I have the honor to speak, perceived, from the commencement of its labors, that its task was at once more simple and more grand.

It has been sometimes assumed that Negro Slavery had its foundation and justification in nature herself. It has been declared that the slave-trade was a benefit to its unfortunate victims; and that the slave was happier in the tranquillity of bondage, than in the midst of the agitation and the struggles that accompany independence. Thank God, the Commission has no such false and odious doctrines to refute. Europe has long since discarded them. They cannot serve the cause of the colonies, and can only injure those planters who still uphold them.

The Commission has not now to establish the position, that slavery can and ought to cease. This truth is now universally acknowledged, and one which slaveholders themselves do not deny.

The question before us has ceased to be a theoretical one. It is at length comprehended in the field of practical politics. We are not to consider whether slavery is evil, and ought to terminate, but when and how it can best be brought to an end.

Those, who, while they admit that slavery cannot always continue, desire to defer the period of emancipation, say that before breaking the chains of the negroes we must prepare them for independence. The black now escapes almost entirely from the salutary bonds of marriage; he is dissolute, idle, and improvident; in more than one respect he resembles a depraved child rather than a man. The truths of Christianity are almost unknown to him, and of the morals of the Gospel he knows only the name.

Enlighten his religion, reform his habits, establish for him the family relation, extend and fortify his intellect, until his mind can conceive the idea of the future, and acquire the power of forethought. After you have accomplished all these things, you can without fear set him free.

True; but if all these preparations cannot be made in a state of slavery, to exact that they shall have been made before servitude can cease,—is it not in other words to declare that it never shall cease? To insist on giving to a slave the thoughts, the habits, and morals of a free man, is to condemn him to remain always a slave.

Because we have made him unworthy of liberty, can we forever refuse to him and his descendants the right of being free? . . .

All, who have had occasion to reside in our colonies, agree in saying, that the negroes are much disposed to receive and retain religious faith. "The negroes are eager for religion," says the Governor General of Martinique, in one of his last reports.

It seems certain, however, that the negroes have as yet conceived only very obscure and unsettled ideas on the subject of religion. This may be attributed in part to the small number of priests who live in the colonies, to the little zeal of some among them, and to the habitual indifference of the masters on this point. But these are, it must be allowed, only secondary causes; the primary cause is still slavery itself.

This is easily understood, and is explained by what precedes.

In many countries where the Europeans have introduced servitude, the masters have always opposed, openly or in secret, the preaching of the Gospel to the negroes.

Christianity is a religion of free men; and they fear, lest in exciting it in the soul of the slave, they may also awaken there some of the instincts of liberty.

When, on the contrary, they have had occasion to call on the priest for his assistance in preserving order, and introduce him among the laborers, he has had little power, because in the eyes of the slave the priest appeared but as the substitute for the master, and the sanctifier of slavery. In the first case the slaves could not, in the second they would not, receive instruction.

Moreover, how can we succeed in elevating and purifying the mind of one, who feels no responsibility for his own misconduct? How convey the idea of moral dignity to a man, who is nothing in his own eyes? With every exertion, it is hardly possible to enlighten and spiritualize the religion of a slave, whose life is spent in hard and incessant labor, and who is naturally and irrevocably plunged in ignorance by the very tenor of his condition. It is not easy to purify the life of a man, who can never know the principal charms of the conjugal union, who can see in marriage only another slavery in the bosom of bondage. If the subject be carefully examined, we shall be convinced, that in most slave countries, the negro is entirely indifferent to the truths of religion, or at least that he turns Christianity into an exciting and gross superstition.

It would seem then hardly reasonable to believe, that in slavery we can destroy those services to which slavery naturally and necessarily gives birth. The thing is without example in the world. It is only experience of liberty, liberty long possessed, and directed by a power, at once energetic and restrained, which can prompt and form in man the opinions, virtues, and habits, which become a citizen of a free country. The period, which follows the abolition of slavery, has therefore always been a time of uneasiness and social difficulty. This is an inevitable evil; we must resolve to meet it, or make slavery eternal.... Slavery is one of those institutions, which may endure a thousand years, if no one undertakes to enquire why it exists at all, but which it is almost impossible to maintain when that enquiry has once been made....

France has, therefore, by every means in her power encouraged the slave trade for more than a century, and it is only nine years since she ceased to tolerate it. More enlightened and more just, she now wishes to substitute free for forced labor. Science indicates, and many experiments already made, even in the tropical regions, seem to prove, that culture may be easier, more productive, and less burdensome with the labor of enfranchised negroes, than with that of slaves. We may then conclude, that the revolution effected in our islands will be as happy for the planters as for the negroes; and that when it is accomplished, it will cost the proprietor of the soil less to cultivate his fields with a small number of laborers, paid, according to their work, than it costs him now, when he is obliged to purchase, and to support throughout the year a multitude of slaves, a large portion of whom are always unproductive.

On the other hand, it must be acknowledged, that the event of so great a social change will always be attended with uncertainty. Even though the final result of the great experiment should be satisfactory, as there are so many just reasons for believing it will be, the passage from one state to another is never unattended with danger; it is accompanied with inevitable inconvenience; it leads to changes in customs and modes of living always difficult and often burdensome. It is possible, it is even probable, that, for a time, until the negro has been trained by new legislation to habits of labor, the cultivation of estates in the colonies will be less productive by free, than it has been by forced labor; in other words, that wages will be annually more expensive than the purchase and support of slaves are at the present time.

To leave the planters to meet this risk alone would be flagrant iniquity. It is unworthy of the grandeur and the generosity of France, to cause the principles of justice, humanity, and reason, so long unrecognised by her and by her children across the sea, at last to triumph at the cost of these latter alone, taking to herself the honor of so tardy a reparation, and leaving nothing but the expense to her colonists. A great injustice has been committed by both, and both should contribute to repair it. . . .

The majority of the Commission decided that it would be precipitate and dangerous to announce, at this time, the precise moment, when slavery shall cease in our colonies; but they believe that it will be prudent to fix a time when that period shall be named, and also to point out, in general terms, in what manner it shall be accomplished. It is thought that thus the necessary tranquillity of mind may be secured, and the excitement of fear and of exaggerated hope allayed; and that the government may be furnished with competent force safely to effect a revolution, which it is now neither desirable nor possible to prevent.

COLONIALISM IN ALGERIA

What will be the probable result of the action we recommend with respect to the native population? What can we reasonably hope for in this matter? Where do illusions begin to cloud our judgment?

There is no government in existence that is so wise, so benign and so just, that it can instantly reconcile and unite together in intimate association communities that are so fundamentally divided by their history, religion, law and customs. It would be dangerous and virtually futile to delude ourselves on this issue. It

From *Oeuvres complètes*, ed. G. Beaumont 9:442–43. Trans. J. S.

would be foolish to believe that we could succeed in destroying, easily and in a short space of time, the secret hatred that is created and sustained by foreign domination. Thus it is essential, whatever our course of action, to remain strong. This must always be our first principle.

What we can hope for is not to suppress the hostile reaction that our rule inspires, but to lessen it; not to expect that our domination will produce devotion, but that it will appear increasingly tolerable; not to alleviate the repugnance that Moslems always feel towards an alien and Christian power, but to make them discover that this power, in spite of its detested origins, can be useful to them. It would be foolish to believe that we can win the hearts and minds of the natives by our shared ideas and customs, but we can reasonably hope to do this by our shared interests.

We have already seen the creation of this type of bond in many places. If our weapons destroy certain tribes, there are others that our trade has singularly strengthened and enriched, and who both appreciate and understand this fact. Everywhere the reward that the natives can expect from their produce and their labour is greatly increased by our presence. On the other hand, our farmers make frequent use of local labour. The European needs the Arab to farm his estates; the Arab needs the European to earn high wages. It is in this way that there is a natural merging of interests, creating a strong bond between individuals whose education and origins place so far apart. It is in this direction that we must travel, Gentlemen; and it is towards this goal that we must strive.

The Commission is convinced that it is the manner in which we treat the natives that will determine the future of our rule in Africa, the security of our investments and the effectiveness of our army. For, in these matters, questions of humanity and finances are intertwined and overlap. We believe that in the long run good government will lead to lasting peace in the country and to a very significant reduction in our armed forces.

If, on the contrary, without actually saying it, for these things are often done but rarely admitted, we act in such a way that proves that in our eyes the indigenous people of Algeria are only an obstacle to be cast aside and trampled under foot; if we take over these people, not to raise them up towards progress and light, but to suppress and exploit them, this will result in a life and death struggle between the two races. Believe me, Algeria will become, sooner or later, a battleground, a walled arena, where the two races will fight without mercy, and where one or the other will die. Gentlemen, God preserve us from such a destiny!

Let us not repeat, in the middle of the nineteenth century, the history of the conquest of America. Let us not repeat the bloody deeds that the whole of humanity condemns. Realise that we would have a thousand times less excuse than those who in olden days had the misfortune to perpetrate these atrocities; for we lack their fanaticism, and have the advantage of the principles and ideals that the French Revolution has spread throughout the world.

France does not only have free men among her Moslem subjects, Algeria also has a small number of Negro slaves. Can we allow slavery to continue on territory we command? One of our Moslem neighbours, the Bey of Tunis, has abolished slavery in his empire. Can we do less in this respect than he? Gentlemen, do not forget that slavery under the Moslems has not the same character as slavery in our colonies. In the East, this odious institution has lost some of its harshness. But in becoming less severe, it does not become less of an affront to the natural rights of mankind.

10

TOCQUEVILLE'S PROPHECY: CENTRALIZATION, EQUALITY, AND THE PROBLEM OF LIBERTY

FUTURE PROSPECTS OF THE UNITED STATES

The territory now occupied or possessed by the United States of America forms about one-twentieth part of the habitable earth. But extensive as these confines are, it must not be supposed that the Anglo-American race will always remain within them; indeed, it has already far over-stepped them.

There was once a time at which we also might have created a great French nation in the American wilds, to counterbalance the influence of the English upon the destinies of the New World. France formerly possessed a territory in North America, scarcely less extensive than the whole of Europe....

But a combination of circumstances, which it would be tedious to enumerate, have deprived us of this magnificent inheritance. (The foremost of these circumstances is, that nations which are accustomed to free institutions and municipal government are better able than any others to found prosperous colonies. The habit of thinking and governing for oneself is indispensable in a new country, where success necessarily depends, in a great measure, upon the individual exertions of the settlers.) Wherever the French settlers were numerically weak and partially established they have disappeared: those who remain are collected on a small area of land and are now subject to other laws. The 400,000 French inhabitants of Lower Canada constitute, at the present time, the remnant of an old nation lost in the midst of a new people....

From *Democracy in America*, pt. 1, chap. 18.

It cannot be denied that the British race has acquired an amazing preponderance over all the other European races in the New World; and that it is very superior to them in civilization, in industry, and in power. As long as it is only surrounded by desert or thinly-people countries, as long as it encounters no dense populations upon its route, through which it cannot work its way, it will assuredly continue to spread. The lines marked out by treaties will not stop it; but it will everywhere transgress these imaginary barriers. . . .

Thus, in the midst of the uncertain future, one event at least is sure. At a period which may be said to be near, (for we are speaking of the life of a nation,) the Anglo-Americans will alone cover the immense space contained between the Polar regions and the Tropics, extending from the coasts of the Atlantic to the shores of the Pacific Ocean. The territory which will probably be occupied by the Anglo-Americans at some future time, may be calculated to equal three-quarters of Europe in size. . . .

Whatever differences may arise, from peace or from war, from freedom or oppression, from prosperity or want, between the destinies of the different descendants of the great Anglo-American family, they will at least preserve an analogous social condition, and they will hold in common the customs and the opinions to which that social condition has given birth.

In the Middle Ages, the tie of religion was sufficiently powerful to imbue all the different populations of Europe with the same civilization. The British of the New World have a thousand other reciprocal ties; and they live at a time when the tendency to equality is general amongst mankind. The Middle Ages were a period when everything was broken up; when each people, each province, each city, and each family, had a strong tendency to maintain its distinct individuality. At the present time an opposite tendency seems to prevail, and the nations seem to be advancing to unity. Our means of intellectual intercourse unite the most remote parts of the earth; and it is impossible for men to remain strangers to each other, or to be ignorant of the events which are taking place in any corner of the globe. The consequence is that there is less difference, at the present day, between the Europeans and their descendants in the New World, than there was between certain towns in the thirteenth century, which were only separated by a river. If this tendency to assimilation brings foreign nations closer to each other, it must *a fortiori* prevent the descendants of the same people from becoming aliens to each other.

The time will therefore come when one hundred and fifty millions of men will be living in North America, equal in condition, the progeny of one race, owing their origin to the same cause, and preserving the same civilization, the same language, the same religion, the same habits, the same manners, and imbued with the same opinions, propagated under the same forms. The rest is uncertain, but this is certain; and it is a fact new to the world,—a fact fraught with such portentous consequences as to baffle the efforts even of the imagination.

There are, at the present time, two great nations in the world, which seem to tend towards the same end, although they started from different points: I allude to the Russians and the Americans. Both of them have grown up unnoticed; and whilst the attention of mankind was directed elsewhere, they have suddenly assumed a most prominent place amongst the nations; and the world learned their existence and their greatness at almost the same time.

All other nations seem to have nearly reached their natural limits, and only to be charged with the maintenance of their power; but these are still in the act of growth: all the others are stopped, or continue to advance with extreme difficulty; these are proceeding with ease and with celerity along a path to which the human eye can assign no term. The American struggles against the natural obstacles which oppose him; the adversaries of the Russian are men: the former combats the wilderness and savage life; the latter, civilization with all its weapons and its arts: the conquests of the one are therefore gained by the ploughshare; those of the other, by the sword. The Anglo-American relies upon personal interest to accomplish his ends, and gives free scope to the unguided exertions and common sense of the citizens; the Russian centres all the authority of society in a single arm: the principal instrument of the former is freedom; of the latter, servitude. Their starting-point is different, and their courses are not the same; yet each of them seems to be marked out by the will of Heaven to sway the destinies of half the globe.

WHY DEMOCRATIC NATIONS SHOW
A MORE ENDURING LOVE OF EQUALITY
THAN OF LIBERTY

The first and most intense passion which is engendered by the equality of conditions is, I need hardly say, the love of that same equality. . . .

Everybody has remarked, that in our time, and especially in France, this passion for equality is every day gaining ground in the human heart. It has been said a hundred times that our contemporaries are far more ardently and tenaciously attached to equality than to freedom; but, as I do not find that the causes of the fact have been sufficiently analysed, I shall endeavour to point them out.

It is possible to imagine an extreme point at which freedom and equality would meet and be confounded together. Let us suppose that all the members of the community take a part in the government, and that each one of them has an equal right to it. As none is different from his fellows, none can exercise a tyrannical power; men will be perfectly free, because they will all be entirely equal; and they will all be perfectly equal, because they will be entirely free. To this ideal state democratic nations tend. Such is the most complete form that equality can assume upon earth; but there are a thousand others which, without being equally perfect, are no less cherished by those nations.

The principle of equality may be established in civil society without prevailing in the political world. Equal rights may exist of indulging in the same pleasures, of entering the same professions, of frequenting the same places—in a word, of living in the same manner and seeking wealth by the same means, although all men do not take an equal share in the government.

A kind of equality may even be established in the political world, though there should be no political freedom there. A man may be the equal of all his countrymen save one, who is the master of all without distinction, and who selects equally from among them all the agents of his power.

Several other combinations might be easily imagined, by which

From *Democracy in America,* pt. 2, bk. 2, chap. 1.

very great equality would be united to institutions more or less free, or even to institutions wholly without freedom.

Although men cannot become absolutely equal unless they be entirely free, and consequently equality, pushed to its furthest extent, may be confounded with freedom, yet there is good reason for distinguishing the one from the other. The taste which men have for liberty, and that which they feel for equality, are, in fact, two different things; and I am not afraid to add, that, amongst democratic nations, they are two unequal things....

The advantages which freedom brings are only shown by length of time; and it is always easy to mistake the cause in which they originate. The advantages of equality are instantaneous, and they may constantly be traced from their source.

Political liberty bestows exalted pleasures, from time to time, upon a certain number of citizens. Equality every day confers a number of small enjoyments on every man. The charms of equality are every instant felt, and are within the reach of all; the noblest hearts are not insensible to them, and the most vulgar souls exult in them. The passion which equality engenders must therefore be at once strong and general. Men cannot enjoy political liberty unpurchased by some sacrifices, and they never obtain it without great exertions. But the pleasures of equality are self-proffered: each of the petty incidents of life seems to occasion them, and in order to taste them nothing is required but to live.

Democratic nations are at all times fond of equality, but there are certain epochs at which the passion they entertain for it swells to the height of fury. This occurs at the moment when the old social system, long menaced, completes its own destruction after a last intestine struggle, and when the barriers of rank are at length thrown down. At such times men pounce upon equality as their booty, and they cling to it as to some precious treasure which they fear to lose. The passion for equality penetrates on every side into men's hearts, expands there, and fills them entirely. Tell them not that by this blind surrender of themselves to an exclusive passion, they risk their dearest interests: they are deaf. Show them not freedom escaping from their grasp, whilst they are looking another way: they are blind—or rather, they can discern but one sole object to be desired in the universe....

I think that democratic communities have a natural taste for freedom: left to themselves, they will seek it, cherish it, and view any privation of it with regret. But for equality, their passion is ardent, insatiable, incessant, invincible: they call for equality in freedom; and if they cannot obtain that, they still call for equality in slavery. They will endure poverty, servitude, barbarism,—but they will not endure aristocracy.

This is true at all times, and especially true in our own. All men and all powers seeking to cope with this irresistible passion, will be overthrown and destroyed by it. In our age, freedom cannot be established without it, and despotism itself cannot reign without its support.

WHY GREAT REVOLUTIONS WILL
BECOME MORE RARE

A people which has existed for centuries under a system of castes and classes can only arrive at a democratic state of society by passing through a long series of more or less critical transformations, accomplished by violent efforts, and after numerous vicissitudes; in the course of which, property, opinions, and power are rapidly transferred from one hand to another. Even after this great revolution is consummated, the revolutionary habits engendered by it may long be traced, and it will be followed by deep commotion. As all this takes place at the very time at which social conditions are becoming more equal, it is inferred that some concealed relation and secret tie exists between the principle of equality itself and revolution, insomuch that the one cannot exist without giving rise to the other.

On this point reasoning may seem to lead to the same result as experience. Amongst a people whose ranks are nearly equal, no ostensible bond connects men together, or keeps them settled in their station. None of them have either a permanent right or power to command,—none are forced by their condition to obey; but every man, finding himself possessed of some education and

From *Democracy in America*, pt. 2, bk. 3, chap. 21.

some resources, may choose his own path and proceed apart from all his fellow-men. The same causes which make the members of the community independent of each other, continually impel them to new and restless desires, and constantly spur them onwards. It therefore seems natural that, in a democratic community, men, things and opinions should be for ever changing their form and place, and that democratic ages should be times of rapid and incessant transformation.

But is this really the case? does the equality of social conditions habitually and permanently lead men to revolution? does that state of society contain some perturbing principle which prevents the community from ever subsiding into calm, and disposes the citizens to alter incessantly their laws, their principles, and their manners? I do not believe it; and as the subject is important, I beg for the reader's close attention.

Almost all the revolutions which have changed the aspect of nations have been made to consolidate or to destroy social inequality. Remove the secondary causes which have produced the great convulsions of the world, and you will almost always find the principle of inequality at the bottom. Either the poor have attempted to plunder the rich, or the rich to enslave the poor. If then a state of society can ever be founded in which every man shall have something to keep, and little to take from others, much will have been done for the peace of the world.

I am aware that amongst a great democratic people there will always be some members of the community in great poverty, and others in great opulence: but the poor, instead of forming the immense majority of the nation, as is always the case in aristocratic communities, are comparatively few in number, and the laws do not bind them together by the ties of irremediable and hereditary penury.

The wealthy, on their side, are scarce and powerless; they have no privileges which attract public observation; even their wealth, as it is no longer incorporated and bound up with the soil, is impalpable, and as it were invisible. As there is no longer a race of poor men, so there is no longer a race of rich men; the latter spring up daily from the multitude, and relapse into it again. Hence they do not form a distinct class, which may be easily

marked out and plundered; and, moreover, as they are connected
with the mass of their fellow-citizens by a thousand secret ties,
the people cannot assail them without inflicting an injury upon
itself.

Between these two extremes of democratic communities stand
an innumerable multitude of men almost alike, who, without
being exactly either rich or poor, are possessed of sufficient property to desire the maintenance of order, yet not enough to excite
envy. Such men are the natural enemies of violent commotions:
their stillness keeps all beneath them and above them still, and
secures the balance of the fabric of society.

Not indeed that even these men are contented with what they
have gotten, or that they feel a natural abhorrence for a revolution
in which they might share the spoil without sharing the calamity;
on the contrary, they desire, with unexampled ardour, to get rich,
but the difficulty is to know from whom riches can be taken. The
same state of society which constantly prompts desires, restrains
these desires within necessary limits: it gives men more liberty of
changing and less interest in change.

Not only are the men of democracies not naturally desirous of
revolutions, but they are afraid of them. All revolutions more or
less threaten the tenure of property: but most of those who live in
democratic countries are possessed of property—not only are
they possessed of property, but they live in the condition of men
who set the greatest store upon their property.

If we attentively consider each of the classes of which society is
composed, it is easy to see that the passions engendered by
property are keenest and most tenacious amongst the middle
classes. The poor often care but little for what they possess,
because they suffer much more from the want of what they have
not, than they enjoy the little they have. The rich have many
other passions besides that of riches to satisfy; and, besides, the
long and arduous enjoyment of a great fortune sometimes makes
them in the end insensible to its charms. But the men who have an
income, alike removed from opulence and from penury, attach an
enormous value to their possessions. As they are still almost
within the reach of poverty, they see its privations near at hand,
and dread them; between poverty and themselves there is nothing

but a scanty fortune, upon which they immediately fix their apprehensions and their hopes. Every day increases the interest they take in it, by the constant cares which it occasions; and they are the more attached to it by their continual exertions to increase the amount. The notion of surrendering the smallest part of it is insupportable to them, and they consider its total loss as the worst of misfortunes.

Now these eager and apprehensive men of small property constitute the class which is constantly increased by the equality of conditions. Hence, in democratic communities, the majority of the people do not clearly see what they have to gain by a revolution, but they continually and in a thousand ways feel that they might lose by one.

I have shown in another part of this work that the equality of conditions naturally urges men to embark in commercial and industrial pursuits, and that it tends to increase and to distribute real property: I have also pointed out the means by which it inspires every man with an eager and constant desire to increase his welfare. Nothing is more opposed to revolutionary passions than these things. It may happen that the final result of a revolution is favourable to commerce and manufactures; but its first consequence will almost always be the ruin of manufactures and mercantile men, because it must always change at once the general principles of consumption, and temporarily upset the existing proportion between supply and demand.

I know of nothing more opposite to revolutionary manners than commercial manners. Commerce is naturally adverse to all the violent passions; it loves to temporize, takes delight in compromise, and studiously avoids irritation. It is patient, insinuating, flexible, and never has recourse to extreme measures until obliged by the most absolute necessity. Commerce renders men independent of each other, gives them a lofty notion of their personal importance, leads them to seek to conduct their own affairs, and teaches how to conduct them well; it therefore prepares men for freedom, but preserves them from revolutions.

In a revolution the owners of personal property have more to fear than all others; for on the one hand their property is often easy to seize, and on the other it may totally disappear at any moment,—a subject of alarm to which the owners of real property are less exposed, since, although they may lose the income of their estates, they may hope to preserve the land itself through the greatest vicissitudes. Hence the former are much more alarmed at the symptoms of revolutionary commotion than the latter. Thus nations are less disposed to make revolutions in proportion as personal property is augmented and distributed amongst them, and as the numbers of those possessing it is increased.

Moreover, whatever profession men may embrace, and whatever species of property they may possess, one characteristic is common to them all. No one is fully contented with his present fortune,—all are perpetually striving, in a thousand ways to improve it. Consider any one of them at any period of his life, and he will be found engaged with some new project for the purpose of increasing what he has; talk not to him of the interests and the rights of mankind, this small domestic concern absorbs for the time all his thoughts, and inclines him to defer political excitement to some other season. This not only prevents men from making revolutions, but deters men from desiring them. Violent political passions have but little hold on those who have devoted all their faculties to the pursuit of their well-being. The ardour which they display in small matters calms their zeal for momentous undertakings.

From time to time indeed, enterprising and ambitious men will arise in democratic communities, whose unbounded aspirations cannot be contented by following the beaten track. Such men like revolutions and hail their approach; but they have great difficulty in bringing them about, unless unwonted events come to their assistance. No man can struggle with advantage against the spirit of his age and country; and, however powerful he may be supposed to be, he will find it difficult to make his contemporaries share in feelings and opinions which are repugnant to all their feelings and desires.

It is a mistake to believe that, when once the equality of conditions has become the old and uncontested state of society, and has imparted its characteristics to the manners of a nation, men will easily allow themselves to be thrust into perilous risks by an imprudent leader or a bold innovator. Not indeed that they will resist him openly, by well-contrived schemes, or even by a premeditated plan of resistance. They will not struggle energetically against him, sometimes they will even applaud him—but they do not follow him. To his vehemence they secretly oppose their inertia,—to his revolutionary tendencies their conservative interests,—their homely tastes to his adventurous passions,—their good sense to the flights of his genius,—to his poetry their prose. With immense exertion he raises them for an instant, but they speedily escape from him, and fall back, as it were, by their own weight. He strains himself to rouse the indifferent and distracted multitude, and finds at last that he is reduced to impotence, not because he is conquered, but because he is alone.

I do not assert that men living in democratic communities are naturally stationary; I think, on the contrary, that a perpetual stir prevails in the bosom of those societies, and that rest is unknown there; but I think that men bestir themselves within certain limits beyond which they hardly ever go. They are for ever varying, altering, and restoring secondary matters; but they carefully abstain from touching what is fundamental. They love change, but they dread revolutions.

Although the Americans are constantly modifying or abrogating some of their laws, they by no means display revolutionary passions. It may be easily seen, from the promptitude with which they check and calm themselves when public excitement begins to grow alarming, and at the very moment when passions seem most roused, that they dread a revolution as the worst of misfortunes, and that every one of them is inwardly resolved to make great sacrifices to avoid such a catastrophe. In no country in the world is the love of property more active and more anxious than in the United States; nowhere does the majority display less inclination for those principles which threaten to alter, in whatever manner, the laws of property.

I have often remarked that theories which are of a revolutionary nature, since they cannot be put in practice without a complete and sometimes a sudden change in the state of property and persons, are much less favourably viewed in the United States than in the great monarchical countries of Europe: if some

men profess them, the bulk of the people reject them with instinctive abhorrence. I do not hesitate to say that most of the
maxims commonly called democratic in France would be pro-
scribed by the democracy of the United States. This may easily
be understood; in America men have the opinions and passions of
democracy, in Europe we have still the passions and opinions of
revolution.

If ever America undergoes great revolutions, they will be
brought about by the presence of the black race on the soil of the
United States,—that is to say, they will owe their origin, not to
the equality, but to the inequality, of conditions. . . .

Stability of Public Opinion under Democracy

Two things are surprising in the United States,—the mutability of
the greater part of human actions, and the singular stability of
certain principles. Men are in constant motion; the mind of man
appears almost unmoved. When once an opinion has spread over
the country and struck root there, it would seem that no power on
earth is strong enough to eradicate it. In the United States general principles in religion, philosophy, morality, and even politics,
do not vary, or at least are only modified by a hidden and often an
imperceptible process: even the grossest prejudices are obliterated with incredible slowness, amidst the continual friction of
men and things.

I hear it said that it is in the nature and the habits of democracies to be constantly changing their opinions and feelings.
This may be true of small democratic nations, like those of the
ancient world, in which the whole community could be assembled
in a public place and then excited at will by an orator. But I saw
nothing of the kind amongst the great democratic people which
dwells upon the opposite shores of the Atlantic ocean. What
struck me in the United States was the difficulty of shaking the
majority in an opinion once conceived, or of drawing it off from a
leader once adopted. Neither speaking nor writing can accomplish it; nothing but experience will avail, and even experience must be repeated. . . .

Men who are equal in rights, in education, in fortune, or, to
comprise all in one word, in their social condition, have necessar-

ily wants, habits and tastes which are hardly dissimilar. As they look at objects under the same aspect, their minds naturally tend to analogous conclusions; and, though each of them may deviate from his contemporaries and form opinions of his own, they will involuntarily and unconsciously concur in a certain number of received opinions. The more attentively I consider the effects of equality upon the mind, the more am I persuaded that the intellectual anarchy which we witness about us is not, as many men suppose, the natural state of democratic nations. I think it is rather to be regarded as an accident peculiar to their youth, and that it only breaks out at that period of transition when men have already snapped the former ties which bound them together, but are still amazingly different in origin, education, and manners; so that, having retained opinions, propensities and tastes of great diversity, nothing any longer prevents men from avowing them openly. The leading opinions of men become similar in proportion as their conditions assimilate; such appears to me to be the general and permanent law,—the rest is casual and transient.

I believe that it will rarely happen to any man amongst a democratic community, suddenly to frame a system of notions very remote from that which his contemporaries have adopted; and if some such innovator appeared, I apprehend that he would have great difficulty in finding listeners, still more in finding believers. When the conditions of men are almost equal, they do not easily allow themselves to be persuaded by each other. As they all live in close intercourse, as they have learned the same things together, and as they lead the same life, they are not naturally disposed to take one of themselves for a guide, and to follow him implicitly. Men seldom take the opinion of their equal, or of a man like themselves, upon trust. . . .

Men who live in democratic societies are not connected with each other by any tie, and so each of them must be convinced individually; whilst in aristocratic society it is enough to convince a few,—the rest follow. If Luther had lived in an age of equality, and had not had princes and potentates for his audience, he would perhaps have found it more difficult to change the aspect of Europe.

The Tendency towards
Political Centralization

As the men who inhabit democratic countries have no superiors, no inferiors, and no habitual or necessary partners in their undertakings, they readily fall back upon themselves and consider themselves as beings apart. I had occasion to point this out at considerable length in discussing individualism. Hence such men can never, without an effort, tear themselves from their private affairs to engage in public business; their natural bias leads them to abandon the latter to the sole visible and permanent representative of the interests of the community, that is to say, to the State. Not only are they naturally wanting in a taste for public business, but they have frequently no time to attend to it. Private life is so busy in democratic periods, so excited, so full of wishes and of work, that hardly any energy or leisure remains to each individual for public life. I am the last man to contend that these propensities are unconquerable, since my chief object in writing this book has been to combat them. I only maintain that at the present day a secret power is fostering them in the human heart, and that if they are not checked they will wholly overgrow it.

I have also had occasion to show how the increasing love of well-being, and the fluctuating character of property, cause democratic nations to dread all violent disturbance. The love of public tranquillity is frequently the only passion which these nations retain, and it becomes more active and powerful amongst them in proportion as all other passions droop and die. This naturally disposes the members of the community constantly to give or to surrender additional rights to the central power, which alone seems to be interested in defending them by the same means that it uses to defend itself.

In ages of equality no man is compelled to lend his assistance to his fellow-men, and none has any right to expect much support from them, so every one is at once independent and powerless. These two conditions, which must never be either separately considered or confounded together, inspire the citizen of a democratic country with very contrary propensities. His independence

From *Democracy in America*, pt. 2, bk. 4, chaps. 3, 4, and 5.

fills him with self-reliance and pride amongst his equals; his debility makes him feel from time to time the want of some outward assistance, which he cannot expect from any of them, because they are all impotent and unsympathizing. In this predicament he naturally turns his eyes to that imposing power which alone rises above the level of universal depression. Of that power his wants and especially his desires continually remind him, until he ultimately views it as the sole and necessary support of his own weakness. . . . The sovereign, being necessarily and incontestably above all the citizens, excites not their envy, and each of them thinks that he strips his equals of the prerogative which he concedes to the crown. . . .

In democratic communities nothing but the central power has any stability in its position or any permanence in its undertakings. All the members of society are in ceaseless stir and transformation. Now it is in the nature of all governments to seek constantly to enlarge their sphere of action; hence it is almost impossible that such a government should not ultimately succeed, because it acts with a fixed principle and a constant will, upon men, whose position, whose notions, and whose desires are in continual vacillation.

It frequently happens that the members of the community promote the influence of the central power without intending it. Democratic ages are periods of experiment, innovation, and adventure. At such times there are always a multitude of men engaged in difficult or novel undertakings, which they follow alone, without caring for their fellow-men. Such persons may be ready to admit, as a general principle, that the public authority ought not to interfere in private concerns; but, by an exception to that rule, each of them craves for its assistance in the particular concern on which he is engaged, and seeks to draw upon the influence of the government for his own benefit, though he would restrict it on all other occasions. If a large number of men apply this particular exception to a great variety of different purposes, the sphere of the central power extends insensibly in all directions, although each of them wishes it to be circumscribed.

Thus a democratic government increases its power simply by

the fact of its permanence. Time is on its side; every incident befriends it; the passions of individuals unconsciously promote it; and it may be asserted, that the older a democratic community is, the more centralized will its government become. . . .

If all democratic nations are instinctively led to the centralization of government, they tend to this result in an unequal manner. This depends on the particular circumstances which may promote or prevent the natural consequences of that state of society,—circumstances which are exceedingly numerous; but I shall only advert to a few of them.

Amongst men who have lived free long before they became equal, the tendencies derived from free institutions combat, to a certain extent, the propensities superinduced by the principle of equality; and although the central power may increase its privileges amongst such a people, the private members of such a community will never entirely forfeit their independence. But when the equality of conditions grows up amongst a people which has never known, or has long ceased to know, what freedom is (and such is the case upon the continent of Europe), as the former habits of the nation are suddenly combined, by some sort of natural attraction, with the novel habits and principles engendered by the state of society, all powers seem spontaneously to rush to the centre. These powers accumulate there with astonishing rapidity, and the state instantly attains the utmost limits of its strength, whilst private persons allow themselves to sink as suddenly to the lowest degree of weakness.

The English who emigrated three hundred years ago to found a democratic commonwealth on the shores of the New World, had all learned to take a part in public affairs in their mother country; they were conversant with trial by jury; they were accustomed to liberty of speech and of the press,—to personal freedom, to the notion of rights and the practice of asserting them. They carried with them to America these free institutions and manly customs, and these institutions preserved them against the encroachments of the State. Thus amongst the Americans it is freedom which is old,—equality is of comparatively modern date. The reverse is occurring in Europe, where equality, introduced by absolute power and under the rule of kings, was already infused into the habits of nations long before freedom had entered into their conceptions.

I have said that amongst democratic nations the notion of government naturally presents itself to the mind under the form of a sole and central power, and that the notion of intermediate powers is not familiar to them. This is peculiarly applicable to the democratic nations which have witnessed the triumph of the principle of equality by means of a violent revolution. As the classes which managed local affairs have been suddenly swept away by the storm, and as the confused mass which remains has as yet neither the organization nor the habits which fit it to assume the administration of these same affairs, the State alone seems capable of taking upon itself all the details of government, and centralization becomes, as it were, the unavoidable state of the country.

Napoleon deserves neither praise nor censure for having centred in his own hands almost all the administrative power of France; for, after the abrupt disappearance of the nobility and the higher rank of the middle classes, these powers devolved on him of course: it would have been almost as difficult for him to reject as to assume them. But no necessity of this kind has even been felt by the Americans, who, having passed through no revolution, and having governed themselves from the first, never had to call upon the State to act for a time as their guardian. Thus the progress of centralization amongst a democratic people depends not only on the progress of equality, but on the manner in which this equality has been established.

At the commencement of a great democratic revolution, when hostilities have but just broken out between the different classes of society, the people endeavours to centralize the public administration in the hands of the government, in order to wrest the management of local affairs from the aristocracy. Towards the close of such a revolution, on the contrary, it is usually the conquered aristocracy that endeavours to make over the management of all affairs to the State, because such an aristocracy dreads the tyranny of a people which has become its equal, and not infrequently its master. Thus it is not always the same class of the community which strives to increase the prerogative of the government; but as long as the democratic revolution lasts, there is always one class in the nation, powerful in numbers or in wealth, which is induced, by peculiar passions or interests, to centralize the public administration, independently of that hatred of being governed by one's neighbour, which is a general and permanent feeling amongst democratic nations.

It may be remarked, that at the present day the lower orders in England are striving with all their might to destroy local independence, and to transfer the administration from all the points of the circumference to the centre; whereas the higher classes are endeavouring to retain this administration within its ancient boundaries. I venture to predict that a time will come when the very reverse will happen.

These observations explain why the supreme power is always stronger, and private individuals weaker, amongst a democratic people which has passed through a long and arduous struggle to reach a state of equality, than amongst a democratic community in which the citizens have been equal from the first. The example of the Americans completely demonstrates the fact. The inhabitants of the United States were never divided by any privileges; they have never known the mutual relation of master and inferior, and as they neither dread nor hate each other, they have never known the necessity of calling in the supreme power to manage their affairs. The lot of the Americans is singular: they have derived from the aristocracy of England the notion of private rights and the taste for local freedom; and they have been able to retain both the one and the other, because they have had no aristocracy to combat. . . .

The democratic nations of Europe have all the general and permanent tendencies which urge the Americans to the centralization of government, and they are moreover exposed to a number of secondary and incidental causes with which the Americans are unacquainted. It would seem as if every step they make towards equality brings them nearer to despotism. . . .

. . . During the aristocratic ages which preceded the present time, the sovereigns of Europe had been deprived of, or had relinquished, many of the rights inherent in their power. Not a hundred years ago, amongst the greater part of European nations, numerous private persons and corporations were sufficiently independent to administer justice, to raise and maintain troops, to levy taxes, and frequently even to make or interpret the law. The State has everywhere resumed to itself alone these natural attributes of sovereign power; in all matters of government the State tolerates no intermediate agent between itself and the people, and in general business it directs the people by its own immediate influence. I am far from blaming this concentration of power, I simply point it out.

At the same period a great number of secondary powers existed in Europe, which represented local interests and administered local affairs. Most of these local authorities have already disappeared; all are speedily tending to disappear, or to fall into the most complete dependence. From one end of Europe to the other the privileges of the nobility, the liberties of cities, and the powers of provincial bodies, are either destroyed or upon the verge of destruction.

Europe has endured, in the course of the last half-century, many revolutions and counter-revolutions which have agitated it in opposite directions: but all these perturbations resemble each other in one respect,—they have all shaken or destroyed the secondary powers of government. The local privileges which the French did not abolish in the countries they conquered, have finally succumbed to the policy of the princes who conquered the French. Those princes rejected all the innovations of the French revolution except centralization: that is the only principle they consented to receive from such a source.

All these various rights, which have been successively wrested, in our time, from classes, corporations, and individuals, have not served to raise new secondary powers on a more democratic basis, but have uniformly been concentrated in the hands of the sovereign. Everywhere the State acquires more and more direct control over the humblest members of the community, and a more exclusive power of governing each of them in his smallest concerns.

Almost all the charitable establishments of Europe were formerly in the hands of private persons or of corporations; they are now almost all dependent on the supreme government, and in many countries are actually administered by that power. The State almost exclusively undertakes to supply bread to the hungry, assistance and shelter to the sick, work to the idle, and to act as the sole reliever of all kinds of misery.

Education, as well as charity, has become in most countries at the present day a national concern. The State receives, and often takes, the child from the arms of the mother, to hand it over to official agents: the State undertakes to train the heart and to instruct the mind of each generation. Uniformity prevails in the courses of public instruction as in everything else; diversity, as well as freedom, are disappearing day by day....

In proportion as the duties of the central power are augmented, the number of public officers by whom that power is represented must increase also. They form a nation in each nation; and as they share the stability of the government, they more and more fill up the place of an aristocracy. In almost every part of Europe the government rules in two ways; it rules one portion of the community by the fear they entertain of its agents, and the other by the hope they have of becoming its agents.

But this is as yet only one side of the picture. The authority of government has not only spread, as we have just seen, throughout the sphere of all existing powers, till that sphere can no longer contain it, but it goes further, and invades the domain heretofore reserved to private independence. A multitude of actions, which were formerly entirely beyond the control of the public administration, have been subjected to that control in our time, and the number of them is constantly increasing.

Amongst aristocratic nations the supreme government usually contented itself with managing and superintending the community in whatever directly and ostensibly concerned the national honour; but in all other respects the people were left to work out their own free will. Amongst these nations the government often seemed to forget that there is a point at which the faults and the sufferings of private persons involve the general prosperity, and that to prevent the ruin of a private individual must sometimes be a matter of public importance.

The democratic nations of our time lean to the opposite ex-

treme. It is evident that most of our rulers will not content themselves with governing the people collectively; it would seem as if
they thought themselves responsible for the actions and private
condition of their subjects,—as if they had undertaken to guide
and to instruct each of them in the various incidents of life, and to
secure their happiness quite independently of their own consent.
On the other hand private individuals grow more and more apt to
look upon the supreme power in the same light; they invoke its
assistance in all their necessities, and they fix their eyes upon the
administration as their mentor or their guide.

I assert that there is no country in Europe in which the public
administration has not become, not only more centralized, but
more inquisitive and more minute: it everywhere interferes in
private concerns more than it did; it regulates more undertakings,
and undertakings of a lesser kind; and it gains a firmer footing
every day about, above, and around all private persons, to assist,
to advise, and to coerce them.

Growing Economic Role of the State

Formerly a sovereign lived upon the income of his lands, or the
revenue of his taxes; this is no longer the case now that his wants
have increased as well as his power. Under the same circumstances which formerly compelled a prince to put on a new tax, he
now has recourse to a loan. Thus the State gradually becomes the
debtor of most of the wealthier members of the community, and
centralizes the largest amounts of capital in its own hands.

Small capital is drawn into its keeping by another method. As
men are intermingled and conditions become more equal, the
poor have more resources, more education, and more desires;
they conceive the notion of bettering their condition, and this
teaches them to save. These savings are daily producing an infinite number of small capitals, the slow and gradual produce of
labour, which are always increasing. But the greater part of this
money would be unproductive if it remained scattered in the
hands of its owners. This circumstance has given rise to a
philanthropic institution, which will soon become, if I am not
mistaken, one of our most important political institutions. Some
charitable persons conceived the notion of collecting the savings

of the poor and placing them out at interest. In some countries these benevolent associations are still completely distinct from the State; but in almost all they manifestly tend to identify themselves with the government; and in some of them the government has superseded them, taking upon itself the enormous task of centralizing in one place, and putting out at interest on its own responsibility, the daily savings of many millions of the working classes.

Thus the State draws to itself the wealth of the rich by loans, and has the poor man's mite at its disposal in the savings-bank. The wealth of the country is perpetually flowing around the government and passing through its hands; the accumulation increases in the same proportion as the equality of conditions; for in a democratic country the State alone inspires private individuals with confidence, because the State alone appears to be endowed with strength and durability.

Thus the sovereign does not confine himself to the management of the public treasury; he interferes in private money-matters; he is the superior, and often the master, of all the members of the community; and, in addition to this, he assumes the part of their steward and paymaster.

The Growth of Bureaucracy

The central power not only fulfils of itself the whole of the duties formerly discharged by various authorities—extending those duties, and surpassing those authorities—but it performs them with more alertness, strength, and independence than it displayed before. All the governments of Europe have in our time singularly improved the science of administration: they do more things, and they do everything with more order, more celerity, and at less expense; they seem to be constantly enriched by all the experience of which they have stripped private persons. From day to day the princes of Europe hold their subordinate officers under stricter control, and they invent new methods for guiding them more closely, and inspecting them with less trouble. Not content with managing everything by their agents, they undertake to manage the conduct of their agents in everything: so that the public administration not only depends upon one and the same power, but it is more and more confined to one spot and concentrated in the same hands. The government centralizes its agency whilst it increases its prerogative,—hence a twofold increase of strength. . . .

The Growth of Industrial Capital

There exists amongst the modern nations of Europe one great cause, independent of all those which have already been pointed out, which perpetually contributes to extend the agency or to strengthen the prerogative of the supreme power, though it has not been sufficiently attended to: I mean the growth of manufactures, which is fostered by the progress of social equality. Manufactures generally collect a multitude of men on the same spot, amongst whom new and complex relations spring up. These men are exposed by their calling to great and sudden alternations of plenty and want, during which public tranquillity is endangered. It may also happen that these employments sacrifice the health, and even the life, of those who gain by them, or of those who live by them. Thus the manufacturing classes require more regulation, superintendence, and restraint than the other classes of society, and it is natural that the powers of government should increase in the same proportion as those classes.

This is a truth of general application; what follows more especially concerns the nations of Europe. In the centuries which preceded that in which we live, the aristocracy was in possession of the soil, and was competent to defend it: landed property was therefore surrounded by ample securities, and its possessors enjoyed great independence. . . . Personal property was of small importance, and those who possessed it were despised and weak: the manufacturing class formed an exception in the midst of those aristocratic communities; as it had no certain patronage, it was not outwardly protected, and was often unable to protect itself. Hence a habit sprang up of considering manufacturing property as something of a peculiar nature, not entitled to the same deference, and not worthy of the same securities as property in general; and manufacturers were looked upon as a small class in the bulk of the people, whose independence was of small importance, and who might with propriety be abandoned to the disciplinary passions of princes. On glancing over the codes of the middle ages, one is surprised to see, in those periods of personal independence, with what incessant royal regulations manufactures were hampered, even in their smallest details: on this point centralization was as active and as minute as it can ever be.

Since that time a great revolution has taken place in the world; manufacturing property, which was then only in the germ, has spread till it covers Europe: the manufacturing class has been multiplied and enriched by the remnants of all other ranks: it has grown and is still perpetually growing in number, in importance, in wealth. Almost all those who do not belong to it are connected with it at least on some one point: after having been an exception in society, it threatens to become the chief, if not the only, class; nevertheless the notions and political precedents engendered by it of old still cling about it. These notions and these precedents remain unchanged, because they are old, and also because they happen to be in perfect accordance with the new notions and general habits of our contemporaries.

Manufacturing property then does not extend its rights in the same ratio as its importance. The manufacturing classes do not become less dependent, whilst they become more numerous; but, on the contrary, it would seem as if despotism lurked within them, and naturally grew with their growth.

As a nation becomes more engaged in manufactures, the want of roads, canals, harbours, and other works of a semi-public nature, which facilitate the acquisition of wealth, is more strongly felt; and as a nation becomes more democratic, private individuals are less able, and the State more able, to execute works of such magnitude. I do not hesitate to assert that the manifest tendency of all governments at the present time is to take upon themselves alone the execution of these undertakings; by which means they daily hold in closer dependence the population which they govern.

On the other hand, in proportion as the power of a state increases, and its necessities are augmented, the state consumption of manufactured produce is always growing larger, and these commodities are generally made in the arsenals or establishments of the government. Thus, in every kingdom, the ruler becomes the principal manufacturer: he collects and retains in his service a vast number of engineers, architects, mechanics, and handicraftsmen.

Industrial Corporations

Not only is he the principal manufacturer, but he tends more and more to become the chief, or rather the master of all other manufacturers. As private persons become more powerless by becoming more equal, they can effect nothing in manufactures without combination; but the government naturally seeks to place these combinations under its own control.

It must be admitted that these collective beings, which are called combinations, are stronger and more formidable than a private individual can ever be, and that they have less of the responsibility of their own actions; whence it seems reasonable that they should not be allowed to retain so great an independence of the supreme government as might be conceded to a private individual.

Rulers are the more apt to follow this line of policy, as their own inclinations invite them to it. Amongst democratic nations it is only by association that the resistance of the people to the government can ever display itself: hence the latter always looks with ill-favour on those associations which are not in its own power; and it is well worthy of remark, that amongst democratic nations, the people themselves often entertain a secret feeling of fear and jealousy against these very associations, which prevents the citizens from defending the institutions of which they stand so much in need. The power and the duration of these small private bodies, in the midst of the weakness and instability of the whole community, astonish and alarm the people; and the free use which each association makes of its natural powers is almost regarded as a dangerous privilege. All the associations which spring up in our age are, moreover, new corporate powers, whose rights have not been sanctioned by time; they come into existence at a time when the notion of private rights is weak, and when the power of government is unbounded; hence it is not surprising that they lose their freedom at their birth.

Amongst all European nations there are some kinds of associations which cannot be formed until the State has examined their bye-laws, and authorized their existence. In several others, attempts are made to extend this rule to all associations; the consequences of such a policy, if it were successful, may easily be foreseen.

If once the sovereign had a general right of authorizing associations of all kinds upon certain conditions, he would not be long without claiming the right of superintending and managing them, in order to prevent them from departing from the rules laid down by himself. In this manner, the State, after having reduced all who are desirous of forming associations into dependence, would proceed to reduce into the same condition all who belong to associations already formed,—that is to say almost all the men who are now in existence.

Governments thus appropriate to themselves, and convert to their own purposes, the greater part of this new power which manufacturing interests have in our time brought into the world. Manufactures govern us,—they govern manufactures.

DEMOCRATIC DESPOTISM

I had remarked during my stay in the United States, that a democratic state of society, similar to that of the Americans, might offer singular facilities for the establishment of despotism; and I perceived, upon my return to Europe, how much use had already been made by most of our rulers, of the notions, the sentiments, and the wants engendered by this same social condition, for the purpose of extending the circle of their power. This led me to think that the nations of Christendom would perhaps eventually undergo some sort of oppression like that which hung over several of the nations of the ancient world.

No sovereign ever lived in former ages so absolute or so powerful as to undertake to administer by his own agency, and without the assistance of intermediate powers, all the parts of a great empire: none ever attempted to subject all his subjects in-

From *Democracy in America,* pt. 2, bk. 4, chap. 6.

discriminately to strict uniformity of regulation, and personally to tutor and direct every member of the community. The notion of such an undertaking never occurred to the human mind; and if any man had conceived it, the want of information, the imperfection of the administrative system, and above all, the natural obstacles caused by the inequality of conditions, would speedily have checked the execution of so vast a design.

When the Roman emperors were at the height of their power, the different nations of the empire still preserved manners and customs of great diversity; although they were subject to the same monarch, most of the provinces were separately administered; they abounded in powerful and active municipalities; and although the whole government of the empire was centred in the hands of the emperor alone, and he always remained, upon occasions, the supreme arbiter in all matters, yet the details of social life and private occupations lay for the most part beyond his control. The emperors possessed, it is true, an immense and unchecked power, which allowed them to gratify all their whimsical tastes, and to employ for that purpose the whole strength of the State. They frequently abused that power arbitrarily to deprive their subjects of property or of life: their tyranny was extremely onerous to the few, but it did not reach the greater number; it was fixed to some few main objects, and neglected the rest; it was violent, but its range was limited.

But it would seem that if despotism were to be established amongst the democratic nations of our days, it might assume a different character; it would be more extensive and more mild; it would degrade men without tormenting them.... Democratic governments may become violent and even cruel at certain periods of extreme effervescence or of great danger; but these crises will be rare and brief. When I consider the petty passions of our contemporaries, the mildness of their manners, the extent of their education, the purity of their religion, the gentleness of their morality, their regular and industrious habits, and the restraint which they almost all observe in their vices no less than in their virtues, I have no fear that they will meet with tyrants in their rulers, but rather guardians.

I think then that the species of oppression by which democratic nations are menaced is unlike anything which ever before existed in the world: our contemporaries will find no prototype of it in their memories. I am trying myself to choose an expression which will accurately convey the whole of the idea I have formed of it, but in vain; the old words despotism and tyranny are inappropriate: the thing itself is new; and since I cannot name it, I must attempt to define it.

I seek to trace the novel features under which despotism may appear in the world. The first thing that strikes the observation is an innumerable multitude of men all equal and alike, incessantly endeavouring to procure the petty and paltry pleasures with which they glut their lives. Each of them, living apart, is as a stranger to the fate of all the rest,—his children and his private friends constitute to him the whole of mankind; as for the rest of his fellow-citizens, he is close to them, but he sees them not;—he touches them, but he feels them not; he exists but in himself and for himself alone; and if his kindred still remain to him, he may be said at any rate to have lost his country.

Above this race of men stands an immense and tutelary power, which takes upon itself alone to secure their gratifications, and to watch over their fate. That power is absolute, minute, regular, provident, and mild. It would be like the authority of a parent, if, like that authority, its object was to prepare men for manhood; but it seeks on the contrary to keep them in perpetual childhood: it is well content that the people should rejoice, provided they think of nothing but rejoicing. For their happiness such a government willingly labours, but it chooses to be the sole agent and the only arbiter of that happiness: it provides for their security, foresees and supplies their necessities, facilitates their pleasures, manages their principal concerns, directs their industry, regulates the descent of property, and subdivides their inheritances—what remains, but to spare them all the care of thinking and all the trouble of living?

Thus it every day renders the exercise of the free agency of man less useful and less frequent; it circumscribes the will within a narrower range, and gradually robs a man of all the uses of himself. The principle of equality has prepared men for these things: it has predisposed men to endure them, and oftentimes to look on them as benefits.

After having thus successively taken each member of the community in its powerful grasp, and fashioned them at will, the supreme power then extends its arm over the whole community. It covers the surface of society with a network of small complicated rules, minute and uniform, through which the most original minds and the most energetic characters cannot penetrate, to rise above the crowd. The will of man is not shattered, but softened, bent, and guided: men are seldom forced by it to act, but they are constantly restrained from acting: such a power does not destroy, but it prevents existence; it does not tyrannize, but it compresses, enervates, extinguishes, and stupefies a people, till each nation is reduced to be nothing better than a flock of timid and industrious animals, of which the government is the shepherd.

I have always thought that servitude of the regular, quiet, and gentle kind which I have just described, might be combined more easily than is commonly believed with some of the outward forms of freedom; and that it might even establish itself under the wing of the sovereignty of the people.

Our contemporaries are constantly excited by two conflicting passions; they want to be led, and they wish to remain free: as they cannot destroy either one or the other of these contrary propensities, they strive to satisfy them both at once. They devise a sole, tutelary, and all-powerful form of government, but elected by the people. They combine the principle of centralization and that of popular sovereignty; this gives them a respite: they console themselves for being in tutelage by the reflection that they have chosen their own guardians. Every man allows himself to be put in leading-strings, because he sees that it is not a person or a class of persons, but the people at large that holds the end of his chain.

Freedom: A Statement of Faith

Though there can be no certainty about the future, three facts are plain to see in the light of past experience. First, that all our contemporaries are driven on by a force that we may hope to regulate or curb, but cannot overcome, and it is a force impelling them, sometimes gently, sometimes at headlong speed, to the destruction of aristocracy. Secondly, that those peoples who are so constituted as to have the utmost difficulty in getting rid of despotic government for any considerable period are the ones in which aristocracy has ceased to exist and can no longer exist. Thirdly, that nowhere is despotism calculated to produce such evil effects as in social groups of this order; since, more than any other kind of régime, it fosters the growth of all the vices to which they are congenitally prone and, indeed, incites them to go still farther on the way to which their natural bent inclines them.

For in a community in which the ties of family, of caste, of class, and craft fraternities no longer exist people are far too much disposed to think exclusively of their own interests, to become self-seekers practicing a narrow individualism and caring nothing for the public good. Far from trying to counteract such tendencies despotism encourages them, depriving the governed of any sense of solidarity and interdependence; of good-neighborly feelings and a desire to further the welfare of the community at large. It immures them, so to speak, each in his private life and, taking advantage of the tendency they already have to keep apart, it estranges them still more. Their feelings toward each other were already growing cold; despotism freezes them.

Since in such communities nothing is stable, each man is haunted by a fear of sinking to a lower social level and by a restless urge to better his condition. And since money has not only become the sole criterion of a man's social status but has also acquired an extreme mobility—that is to say it changes hands incessantly, raising or lowering the prestige of individuals and families—everybody is feverishly intent on making money or, if

From the Foreword to *The Old Régime*.

already rich, on keeping his wealth intact. Love of gain, a fondness for business careers, the desire to get rich at all costs, a craving for material comfort and easy living quickly become ruling passions under a despotic government. They affect all classes, even those who hitherto have seemed allergic to them, and tend to lower the moral standards of the nation as a whole if no effort be made to check their growth. It is in the nature of despotism that it should foster such desires and propagate their havoc. Lowering as they do the national morale, they are despotism's safeguard, since they divert men's attention from public affairs and make them shudder at the mere thought of a revolution. Despotism alone can provide that atmosphere of secrecy which favors crooked dealings and enables the freebooters of finance to make illicit fortunes. Under other forms of government such propensities exist, undoubtedly; under a despotism they are given free rein.

Freedom and freedom alone can extirpate these vices, which, indeed, are innate in communities of this order; it alone can call a halt to their pernicious influence. For only freedom can deliver the members of a community from that isolation which is the lot of the individual left to his own devices and, compelling them to get in touch with each other, promote an active sense of fellowship. In a community of free citizens every man is daily reminded of the need of meeting his fellow men, of hearing what they have to say, of exchanging ideas, and coming to an agreement as to the conduct of their common interests. Freedom alone is capable of lifting men's minds above mere mammon worship and the petty personal worries which crop up in the course of everyday life, and of making them aware at every moment that they belong each and all to a vaster entity, above and around them—their native land. It alone replaces at certain critical moments their natural love of material welfare by a loftier, more virile ideal; offers other objectives than that of getting rich; and sheds a light enabling all to see and appraise men's vices and their virtues as they truly are.

True, democratic societies which are not free may well be prosperous, cultured, pleasing to the eye, and even magnificent, such is the sense of power implicit in their massive uniformity; in them may flourish many private virtues, good fathers, honest

merchants, exemplary landowners, and good Christians, too—
since the patrimony of the Christian is not of this world and one of
the glories of the Christian faith is that it has produced such men
under the worst governments and in eras of the utmost depravity.
There were many such in the Roman Empire in its decline. But, I
make bold to say, never shall we find under such conditions a
great citizen, still less a great nation; indeed, I would go so far as
to maintain that where equality and tyranny coexist, a steady
deterioration of the mental and moral standards of a nation is
inevitable.

Such were my views and thus I wrote twenty years ago, and
nothing that has taken place in the world since then has led me to
change my mind. And, having proclaimed my love of freedom at a
time when it was made much of, I can hardly be blamed for
championing it today, when it is out of fashion.

Moreover, as regards my love of freedom, I differ less from
those who disagree with me than they may imagine. Can there
exist a man so mean-spirited that he would rather be at the mercy
of a tyrant's whim than obedient to laws which he himself has
helped to enact—provided of course that he believes his nation to
have the qualities enabling it to make a proper use of freedom?
Even despots do not deny the merits of freedom; only they wish
to keep it for themselves, claiming that no one else is worthy of it.
Thus our quarrel is not about the value of freedom *per se*, but
stems from our opinion of our fellow men, high or low as the case
may be; indeed, it is no exaggeration to say that a man's admiration of absolute government is proportionate to the contempt
he feels for those around him. I trust I may be allowed to wait
a little longer before being converted to such a view of my fellow
countrymen.

Bibliography

THE WRITINGS OF ALEXIS DE TOCQUEVILLE

Collected Works

Oeuvres complètes. Edited by Gustave de Beaumont. 9 vols. Paris: Michel-Lévy Frères, 1860–66.

Vols. 1–3   *De la démocratie en Amérique*
Vol. 4   *L'Ancien Régime et la Révolution*
Vols. 5–6   *Oeuvres et correspondance inédites*
Vol. 7   *Nouvelle correspondance entièrement inédite*
Vol. 8   *Mélanges, fragments historiques et notes sur l'Ancien Régime, la Révolution et l'Empire, voyages, pensées entièrement inédits*
Vol. 9   *Etudes économiques, politiques et littéraires*

Oeuvres complètes. Edited by J. P. Mayer. Paris: Gallimard, 1951–.

Tome 1   *De la démocratie en Amérique.* 2 vols. Introduction by Harold J. Laski. 1951.
Tome 2   Vol. 1, *L'Ancien Régime et la Révolution.* Vol. 2, *Fragments et notes inédites sur la Révolution.* Introduction by Georges Lefèbvre. 1953.
Tome 3   *Ecrits et discours politiques.* Vol. 1, Introduction by J. J. Chevallier and André Jardin. 1962.
Tome 5   Vol. 1, *Voyages en Sicile et aux Etats-Unis.* 1957. Vol. 2, *Voyages en Angleterre, Irlande, Suisse et Algérie.* 1958. Introduction by J. P. Mayer.

Tome 6   *Correspondance anglaise.* Vol. 1, *Correspondance entre Alexis de Tocqueville et Henry Reeve et John Stuart Mill.* Introduction by J. P. Mayer. 1954.

Tome 8   *Correspondance d'Alexis de Tocqueville et de Gustave de Beaumont.* 3 vols. Introduction by André Jardin. 1967.

Tome 9   *Correspondance d'Alexis de Tocqueville et d'Arthur de Gobineau.* Introduction by J. J. Chevallier. 1959.

Tome 11   *Correspondance d'Alexis de Tocqueville avec P.-P. Royer-Collard et avec J. J. Ampère.* Introduction by André Jardin. 1970.

Tome 12   *Souvenirs.* Introduction by Luc Monnier. 1964.

The following volumes of this edition have yet to appear: Tome 3, vol. 2; Tome 4, *Ecrits sur les systèmes pénitentiaires en France et à l'étranger;* Tome 6, vols. 2–3; Tome 7, *Correspondance familiale;* Tome 10, *Correspondance locale;* Tome 11, vols. 2–3, *Correspondance générale;* Tome 13, *Mélanges littéraires et économiques.*

Major English Translations

Democracy in America. The Henry Reeve text as revised by Francis Bowen, further corrected and edited by Phillips Bradley. New York: Vintage Books, 1954.

Democracy in America. Translated by George Lawrence, edited by J. P. Mayer and Max Lerner. London: Fontana, 1968, and Garden City, N.Y.: Doubleday, 1969.

The Old Régime and the French Revolution. Translated by Stuart Gilbert. Garden City, N.Y.: Doubleday, 1955.

On the State of Society in France before the Revolution of 1789, and on the Causes which led to that Event. Translation of *L'Ancien Régime et la Révolution* by Henry Reeve. London: John Murray, 1856.

Recollections. Translated by George Lawrence, edited by J. P. Mayer and A. P. Kerr. Garden City, N.Y.: Doubleday, 1970.

The Recollections of Alexis de Tocqueville. Translated by

Alexander Teixeira de Mattos. London: Henry & Co., 1896.
Journey to America. Translated by George Lawrence, edited by
J. P. Mayer. Revised and augmented edition in collaboration
with A. P. Kerr. Garden City, N.Y.: Doubleday, 1971.
Journeys to England and Ireland. Translated by George Law-
rence and K. P. Mayer. New Haven: Yale University Press, and
London: Faber and Faber, 1958. New, augmented edition,
New York: Arno Press, 1979.
The European Revolution and Correspondence with Gobineau.
The sketches for the continuation of *L'Ancien Régime*, to-
gether with the Gobineau correspondence, translated and
edited by John Lukacs. Garden City, N.Y.: Doubleday, 1959.
*Correspondence and Conversations of Alexis de Tocqueville with
Nassau William Senior from 1834 to 1859.* 2 vols. Edited by
M. C. M. Simpson. London: H. S. King, 1872.
Memoir, Letters and Remains. 2 vols. London, Macmillan, 1861.
*On the Penitentiary System in the United States and Its Applica-
tion to France.* With Gustave de Beaumont. Translated by
Francis Lieber, introduced by Thorsten Sellin. Carbondale and
Edwardsville: Southern Illinois University Press, 1964.
*Report Made to the Chamber of Deputies on the Abolition of
Slavery in the French Colonies.* Boston: J. Munroe & Co.,
1840. Reprinted Westport, Conn.: Negro Universities Press,
1970.

SELECTED WORKS ON TOCQUEVILLE

Aron, Raymond. *Main Currents in Sociological Thought.* Vol. 1.
New York: Basic Books, and London: Weidenfeld and Nicol-
son, 1965.
Brogan, Hugh. *Tocqueville.* London: Fontana, 1973.
Brunius, Teddy. *Alexis de Tocqueville: The Sociological Aes-
thetician.* Uppsala: Acta Universitatis Uppsaliensis, 1960.
C.N.R.S. *Alexis de Tocqueville: Livre du centenaire, 1859–1959.*
Paris: Editions du Centre National de la Recherche Scienti-
fique, 1960.

Drescher, Seymour. *Tocqueville and England.* Cambridge, Mass.: Harvard University Press, 1964.

Gargan, Edward T. *Alexis de Tocqueville: The Critical Years, 1848-51.* Washington, D.C.: Catholic University of America Press, 1955.

———. *De Tocqueville.* London: Bowes and Bowes, 1965.

Goldstein, Doris S. *Trial of Faith: Religion and Politics in Tocqueville's Thought.* New York: Elsevier, 1975.

Herr, Richard. *Tocqueville and the Old Régime.* Princeton, N.J.: Princeton University Press, 1962.

King, Preston. *Fear of Power: An Analysis of Anti-Statism in Three French Writers.* London: Frank Cass, 1967.

Laski, Harold J. "Alexis de Tocqueville and Democracy." In F. J. C. Hearnshaw, ed., *The Social and Political Ideas of Some Representative Thinkers of the Victorian Age.* London: G. G. Harrap, 1933.

Lawlor, Mary. *Alexis de Tocqueville in the Chamber of Deputies: His Views on Foreign and Colonial Policy.* Washington, D.C.: Catholic University of America Press, 1959.

Lively, Jack. *The Social and Political Thought of Alexis de Tocqueville.* Oxford: The Clarendon Press, 1962.

Mayer, Jakob P. *Prophet of the Mass Age: A Study of Alexis de Tocqueville.* London: J. M. Dent & Sons, 1939.

———. *Alexis de Tocqueville: A Biographical Study in Political Science.* New York: Harper & Row, and London: Hamish Hamilton, 1960.

Nantet, Jacques. *Tocqueville.* Paris: Seghers, 1971.

Pierson, George W. *Tocqueville and Beaumont in America.* New York and London: Oxford University Press, 1938.

Poggi, Gianfranco. *Images of Society: Essays on the Sociological Theories of Tocqueville, Marx, and Durkheim.* Stanford, Ca.: Stanford University Press, 1972.

Smelser, Neil J. "Alexis de Tocqueville as Comparative Analyst." In *Comparative Methods in the Social Sciences.* Englewood Cliffs, N.J.: Prentice-Hall, 1976.

Stinchcombe, Arthur L. *Theoretical Methods in Social History.* New York: Academic Press, 1978.

Zeitlin, Irving M. *Liberty, Equality, and Revolution in Alexis de Tocqueville.* Boston: Little, Brown, 1971.

Zetterbaum, Marvin. *Tocqueville and the Problem of Democracy.* Stanford, Ca.: Stanford University Press, 1967.

Index

Adorno, Theodor W., 43n, 46n
Algeria, 4, 11, 37, 276, 345–47
Alienation, 33, 301–2
Old Régime and the French Revolution, The, 9–10, 16–17, 18, 19, 23, 24, 25, 26, 27, 32, 33, 163–242, 280–82, 290–300, 377–79
Anomie, 35, 290–93
Argenson, Marquis d', 184
Aristocracy, 3, 14, 20, 26, 38, 47, 65, 100, 102, 111–14, 141, 145, 150, 156, 159–61, 171, 196–99, 201–5, 212–13, 219, 293–95, 301–4, 307–9, 322–25
Armies, 120, 127–29, 172, 247
Assembly, Constituent (1789), 194, 224, 252
Assembly, Constituent (1848), 13–15
Assembly, National (Second Republic), 275–78
Associations, 23–24, 35, 37, 64, 81–84, 110–15, 372–73

Barrot, Odilon, 13, 15, 261
Beaumarchais, P.-A. C. de, 230
Beaumont, Gustave de, 2, 4, 5, 6, 7, 8, 15, 18, 26–27, 41n, 42n, 311
Bendix, Reinhard, 43n
Berlin, Sir Isaiah, 21, 43n

Bernadotte, Marshal, 249
Biddiss, Michael D., 42n
Blacks, American, 35, 106, 325–27, 333–41
Blanqui, Auguste, 22
Bonaparte, Louis Napoleon. *See* Napoleon III
Bourgeoisie, French, 4, 12, 33, 198–99, 201–2, 205–9, 220, 250–51, 267
Burke, Edmund, 171, 194, 197, 204, 237

Caesar, Julius, 321
Cahiers of 1789, 196, 219, 220
Canada, French, 25, 74–5, 348
Castes, 156–57, 199–200
Centralization, 2–3, 14, 23–24, 59–66, 181, 211, 361–73
Chamber of Deputies (under July Monarchy), 10, 11, 13, 30, 252
Charles I, King of England (1625–49), 264–65
Charles VII, King of France (1403–61), 202
Charles X, King of France (1824–30), 3, 259, 265
Chartism, 12
China, 144
Church, in France, 14, 166–70, 236, 248